AMERICA'S AMBASSADORS TO ENGLAND
(1785—1928)

JOHN ADAMS.

AMERICA'S AMBASSADORS TO ENGLAND
(1785—1928)

A NARRATIVE OF ANGLO-AMERICAN DIPLOMATIC RELATIONS

BY BECKLES WILLSON
AUTHOR OF "AMERICA'S AMBASSADORS TO FRANCE,"
"THE BRITISH EMBASSY IN PARIS," ETC.

LONDON
JOHN MURRAY, ALBEMARLE STREET, W.

TO

NORMAN W. GRIEVE

IN TOKEN OF FRIENDSHIP

FIRST EDITION 1928

PREFACE

In the present work I have essayed the portraiture of some forty successive official representatives of the American nation, since the political schism with the Mother Country was acknowledged in 1783. My aim, however, has been something more than a series of historical presentments of eminent Americans who happened to fill a certain office, and whatever interest may attach to these studies I shall have failed if the idea which has inspired me is not apprehended by the reader. It is to present, in all its significant fluctuations, the life of a relationship, racial, political, intellectual, moral and social, altogether without parallel in history.

The forty personages who figure in this gallery were, we say, diplomatists and their technical function was diplomacy. But there was that, from the first, in their attitude, their contacts and experiences, which set them wholly apart from their colleagues of the Diplomatic Corps. In their personalities, their public and private utterances and behaviour, they reveal, though so remotely bred, the unmistakable *ethos* of our English race. Alien antecedents, national prejudices, exerted their full effect ; yet always, in crucial moments, these men have thought, felt and acted towards current phenomena precisely as Englishmen of their temperament, education and station would have done and not at all as aliens would do.

Thus, at a stroke, we enrich the political and social annals of this country with a new line of authentic English statesmen, who may be described as extra-official attendants upon every Government since Shelburne's time, and whose popularity and moral and intellectual example is generally equivalent to that enjoyed by any English Cabinet Minister.

Also, what this narrative illustrates is not merely the moral solidarity of the English race—which we might take for granted—but the reaction upon English history, public opinion, thought and manners, as well as upon diplomatic machinery, of American history, opinions and customs, as expressed by the American representatives in England.

That the English nation could not remain impervious to the new ideas and new habits of thought which derived from the new experiences, new conditions and broader horizons of America, was inevitable. If the American Revolution freed the colonists from the British political system, it also helped to free the English from the worst defects of Toryism, that heavy formalism and official procrastination which such spirits as Gouverneur Morris and Rufus King noted and deplored. The process would have been far swifter but for the reaction of the French Revolution and the common belief that America sympathized with that convulsion. We know now that no hide-bound Tory squire, hot for prerogative and shuddering at the name of liberty, ever held the tenets and practices of the Jacobins in greater horror and detestation than did Washington, Hamilton, Adams, Morris, Pinckney and Jay.

Nurtured in the school of necessity, the American envoys, five of whom became Presidents and ten Secretaries of State, were practical men. They were generally lawyers. Such men could hardly fail to make themselves heard and felt in Downing Street, and in dealing with them, Shelburne, Pitt, Grenville, Canning, Castlereagh and their successors are observed to discard pomp and ceremony and, as if conscious that the eye of a new and critical constituency on the other side of the Atlantic was upon them, took surprising pains at propitiation.

In discussing international issues with Morris, Jay and King, the new *ad hominem* note is first discernible in British diplomacy, a note plainly absent in its dealings with the envoys of other Powers. The impatience, often the irritation, shown by Monroe, William Pinkney and John Quincy Adams, over delays in redressing grievances was only the same as that of the English Opposition leaders, by reformers like Wilberforce, Burdett, Brougham and Sydney Smith. Common sense, candour and aversion to cant, characteristic of the American representatives, were qualities which the

Whigs had already made familiar. Yet it is certain that long before the Whigs and Liberals came into power the effect of a visit to Downing Street of the American Minister was to open the windows and to dust the parchments; while as for the bulk of the nation, the masses, they came to consider these men as representing a wholesome frame of mind, a political, moral and intellectual emancipation, as well as representing America.

Then, just before the mid-century, with a shock came the realization that freedom, fair play, justice and lofty ideals were not, as had been supposed, more general in America than in England, and that amongst the people of the far-flung United States and even in their central Government, intolerance, political corruption and self-aggrandizement flourished much as it did elsewhere, and this in spite of all the high-flown moral sentiments of the Declaration of Independence and the virtuous treatises of Priestley, Paine and Barlow. It was about this time that Minister Stevenson was engaged in defending negro slavery and apologizing for the slave trade and his successor was endeavouring to explain away the unhappy repudiation of American State bonds. Texas was annexed, Mexico invaded, and Cuba and Canada were threatened by filibusters. It was then that Sydney Smith began his rhetorical denunciations of American public morality and Charles Dickens, Mrs. Trollope and others laid bare the crudities of American society.

While the English intelligentsia experienced a reaction and a resentment against America, the American intelligentsia, for their part, began to be assailed by doubts, both of the possibility of continued national unity and of the ultimate success of their national experiment, and so were first moved to a social and literary *rapprochement* towards the Mother Country, which, it may be said, has continued down to our own day. In this connexion I recall Mr. Whitelaw Reid once saying to me, when the subject of Court presentations of his countrymen and countrywomen was mentioned: "I wonder what would have happened if Jefferson's idea, lately revived by Henry Watterson, had been adopted, and we had never had any resident Minister at this Court." This eminent Ambassador wholly assented to my suggestion that the practical tribute to feudal institutions involved had acted as a valuable social safety-valve, furnishing a vent for the natural aspirations of a restless and wealthy young democracy.

Whatever the political conditions and tendencies happened to be, the two countries exchanged supplementary qualities; albeit while *Americanism* as a moral and political gospel spent itself, taking on a commercial and economic complexion, *Englishism*, being inherent in both peoples, has persisted, and often seems to be a more active and pervasive principle amongst the American wealthy element than it is with the rising classes in England itself. When Lord Palmerston from a lofty English moral plane tried to rebuke Charles Francis Adams, he found himself, to his mortification, rebuked from a still loftier plane. Certes, in the correspondence we see which was the completer Englishman of the two. If it is a question of dignity or propriety or simple justice, the American envoys, for all that they represent a welter of races and undisciplined forces, could always be trusted to emulate Hampden and Chatham rather than Jackson and Cleveland. To-day, as Professor Fletcher Johnson says, the American nation is the most composite in the world, but the foundations are English, the framework remains English and the spirit and expression are English. Whatever there is of novelty, is chiefly novelty of interpretation and application. There is manifest less and less insistence upon differences in civilization and more upon common possessions. Every American Minister to London pays his tribute to Shakespeare, Milton, Burke, Burns and Dickens, if one does not yet see the British envoy to Washington commemorating Emerson, Parkman and Longfellow before American audiences. Not that American writers, as well as American statesmen, have not had their influence on English life and thought, yet there is less that is alien to the English nature in their literary classics than in Sheridan, Disraeli, Rossetti, Pater, Wilde, Conrad, Mr. Bernard Shaw and other acknowledged glories of modern English literature.

What we do not all yet apprehend is that England is as composite as America, although the process has been spread over centuries instead of merely decades. Nor, even yet,

have Latin, Celt, Teuton and Oriental been merged into a
single racial type. What has happened here, as on the other
side of the Atlantic, is that the English *ethos* informs and
governs. London is the true capital of both peoples.
National policies, like political parties, may diverge, economic
interests may occasionally clash, but there are fundamental
things, permanent values, which, though threatened, are
still valid.

There has been, from the first, much talk about Anglo-
Saxon "misunderstanding," and Walter Page was only
echoing his predecessor, John Adams, when he wrote : "The
longer I live here the more astonished I become at the fundamental ignorance of the British about us and at our fundamental ignorance about them." But, it may be asked, in
what human society or department of knowledge is there not
"misunderstanding"? Does one social stratum understand
the other? Do the Socialists understand the Tories or the
Tories the Socialists? Does Essex understand Forfarshire
or Cornwall? America, like the movement of the planets
or the principles of biology, will never be understood by more
than a fraction of the English population, nor is it at all
essential to peace and good-will that we should scrutinize
habits and customs and the mere apparatus of life too closely.
The great desideratum is faith in one another, a belief in
the common mission of the English-thinking race to ame-
liorate human conditions which might otherwise never be
ameliorated.

"As the world stands," wrote Ambassador Page, "the
United States and Great Britain must work together and
stand together. . . . This is the only job now in the world
worth the whole zeal and energy of all first-class thorough-
bred English-speaking men."

In the preparation of these diplomatic studies I have
availed myself of a large number of State Papers and published works, most of which are indicated in the footnotes.
The bulk of the official correspondence I myself have transcribed from the archives of the London Embassy, courteously placed at my disposal by his Excellency the present
Ambassador. To those interested in Anglo-American relations it may prove a convenience to be able to gauge the

international political temperature at various periods and to compare at a glance the opinions of successive Ambassadors upon the issues of their day. Amongst the figures which emerge from an undeserved obscurity I may mention that of Aaron Vail (1832–6), who, although only acting-Minister, was a competent and attractive diplomatist. The mid-century combative types who did little to promote cordial relations were Stevenson, Bancroft and Dallas. I have been able to shed a little further light upon the causes of the recall of John Lothrop Motley and his successor, General Schenck, as well as upon the forgotten part which the latter played in the *Alabama* negotiations.

On the whole, it will be seen that, perhaps because they were mostly successful lawyers, journalists and men of letters, the American envoys were primarily masters of expression, and their diplomacy consisted rather in making their causes acceptable to public opinion than merely to the transient chief of the Foreign Office. Often they seem to be advocates addressing a vaster jury and studious to create a favourable personal impression. Of them all, one is inclined to give Whitelaw Reid the highest place. In his own person, in tact, in sympathy and in munificence, he was an ideal representative of his country. Although of Scottish origin, he took all the finer English qualities, adapted them and magnified them, so that he looked, acted, spoke and spent like an English aristocrat, who is usually the simplest of men, while yet retaining his local loyalties and that precious humorous mental detachment which more than any other single quality proclaims the American.

The world is watching intently the issue of the opposing ethnic forces in America. Thus far the English leaven has continued to work, but there may come a time when the composite ingredients may cease to react. What these studies demonstrate is that no matter from what race the representative American springs, his culture is English, and that although, like John Jay, Van Buren and Roosevelt, he disavow one drop of English blood, when he lands on English soil he is, in the larger sense, at home.

August 17, 1928.

B. W.

CONTENTS

CHAPTER I

CHAPTER XII

LIST OF ILLUSTRATIONS

NOTE.—*These portraits are reproduced by courtesy of his Excellency the American Ambassador, from the collection on the walls of the London Embassy.*

AMERICA'S AMBASSADORS
TO ENGLAND

CHAPTER I

JOHN ADAMS (1785–1788)

On the morning of May 31, 1785, King George III arose from his couch in St. James's Palace conscious that he had that morning to perform, in the adjoining chamber, a ceremonial duty which might prove intensely disagreeable. Only tact and complete candour could carry it off successfully, and in the exercise of these virtues the King would have to be met half-way.

The situation the monarch had to face was the culmination of a long constitutional and personal struggle. Ten years before what might be described as a dynamic minority of his subjects, dwelling in the thirteen British colonies in America, had precipitated a revolt against British laws and the British political connexion. The revolt, although its issue was for some time precarious, had succeeded, the King's forces, including the Loyalists, had been beaten, and eventually the Peace of Versailles had been signed, conceding to the united colonies their independence and status as a nation.

From first to last in this struggle the King had occupied a peculiar position which, such is the tardiness of final historical judgments, is only now, after a century and a half, being correctly understood. For, whatever the views of his ministers and critics, George III had early conceived that his prime duty was to that part of the American population which maintained its allegiance, which looked to him as its sovereign, and besought him in a thousand memorials,

1

couched in the most vehement and supplicatory terms, not to desert those who were faithful to the British connexion. These Loyalists, even after the Declaration of Independence, fluctuated in numbers between one-half and one-third of the American population, and in point of view of wealth, station and intelligence, were not the least estimable element.

Deputations of these Loyalists had flocked to England and filled the royal ears with their protestations.[1] They represented that the American revolt had been conceived and was being conducted by Whigs, radicals and demagogues impelled by vanity, greed and a contempt for authority, and they described in some detail the personal character and motives of some of the Revolutionary leaders. George was no psychologist; he did not trouble about nice distinctions of political intransigence. He had no difficulty in recognizing the breed. They seemed to him to be precisely the same kind of mischievous doctrinaires and hot-heads who had long been giving him trouble at home. When they pictured Samuel and John Adams, Thomas Jefferson and Patrick Henry, and narrated their rhetorical demands for liberty, freedom from taxation, freedom from military service, the rights of man and the wrongs of governments, the royal mind flew at once to John Wilkes, Beckford and Sawbridge. When it was said that such respectable persons as Washington and Franklin and Jay had joined the disaffected party in America, he pointed to the adhesion of Burke and Fox and Priestley to the disaffected party in England. In short, Massachusetts was the same as Middlesex, and Boston in America was on the same footing as Boston in Lincolnshire. Against such men and such secessionist doctrine he felt it his duty to hold out to the last, and he held out to the last.

[1] The American Tories claimed to be Englishmen and asserted that " the non-English strains of the back-country lent great propulsive force to the movement for independence and republican government." Joseph Galloway estimated that in the patriot army there were scarcely one-fourth who were natives of America, about one-half Irish, the other fourth were English and Scotch. Commenting on this, Schlesinger says : " This statement fails to do justice to the other foreign-born soldiers who fought in the War of Independence." " There is reason to believe," states J. T. Adams (*New England in the Republic*), " that more Americans actually served as Loyalists with the British than with the Revolutionary armies."

It was now all over—had been over these two years. The formal schism had been accomplished. That united empire for which he had striven was rent in twain. The revolted colonies were now States ; it only remained to be seen what the United States were going to do with their new political independence.

The ink on the Treaty of Peace had been dry for over two years, yet so far little or nothing had been done towards carrying out its provisions. England had indeed made a move, but it was not one calculated to placate or endear. The commercial policy which was to be adopted towards the Americans was discussed in the Parliament of 1783. The youthful Pitt, in the first flush of high office in Shelburne's brief ministry, had shown " an inclination to follow alike the impulses of his heart and the dictates of his education " by proposing a measure placing the ships of the United States on the same footing as other nations, and laying no higher duties upon their products than were levied upon British producers. Moreover, it generously threw open to America the commerce with the West Indies and the other British colonies. A notable political gesture this, and one naturally agreeable to the New England merchants and shipowners. But it was, on the face of it, rather one-sided. It hardly sufficiently considered the national interests of the Mother Country. It was one thing to be magnanimous, but charity, it was argued, should begin at home. British commerce, British navigating interests, badly needed support. Moreover, as Lord Sheffield pointed out in a speech which much offended the Bostonians, was it good Imperial policy ? Adopting the views of certain American loyalists now at Court, such as Deane, Galloway and Oliver, this nobleman painted in vivid colours " the ruin and confusion in which the colonists were involved by the state of anarchy consequent upon their independence. He even ventured to predict that out of this chaos New England at least would in the end solicit to come back as a repentant child to the maternal embrace."

Such an attractive prospect was irresistible and in the following July the Ministry decreed the exclusive system, first by Orders in Council and later by Acts of Parliament.

2

The former colonies were to be treated as foreigners, as they had, indeed, elected to be, and shut out from all trade with the British oversea dominions.

This measure, provocative of so much resentment in New England, had, however, nothing to do with the Treaty previously made between the two countries, which still awaited fulfilment. From the British standpoint the Americans did not and could not act because they were not yet a nation. They might never be a nation. Pitt and his Foreign Minister, Lord Carmarthen, had to deal with simply a Congress whose authority was doubtful and disputed. Congress, for instance, had promised to urge the individual States to restore to the Loyalists their confiscated rights and properties. Yet these continued without redress and the American courts of law were still closed to British creditors. In consequence, the British Government persisted in occupying certain frontier posts which should, under the Treaty, have been surrendered to the United States.[1]

Impelled by angry public opinion at home, Congress now took the first step : it appointed a Minister Plenipotentiary to the British Court. The Minister thus appointed was John Adams.

King George knew all about John Adams. He knew that together with his cousin, Samuel Adams, he had been one of the earliest and most intractable of the insurgents.[2] He had, indeed, been expressly omitted from the list of those whom, in 1777, his Majesty had been ready to pardon. Nevertheless, there was a saving mercy in the appointment : the King was grateful that it was not Thomas Jefferson who was to be sent —the Virginian atheist and demagogue who had gratuitously held him up to the world in his celebrated piece of rhetoric as a " tyrant." It was at least in Adams's favour that he had objected to those passages in the Declaration of Independence, although he had not gone the length of expunging them.

[1] The forts still garrisoned by the British were Ogdensburg, Oswego, Niagara, Erie, Sandusky and Mackinaw. The neighbouring Indians favoured the British and continued to make trouble for the Americans.

[2] Mr. Fletcher Johnson speaks of Adams as " a singularly unfortunate choice. Able and patriotic as he was, he had little capacity for diplomatic negotiation ; he was impetuous, irascible, pugnacious ; and he was strongly prejudiced against England."—*America's Foreign Relations*.

Adams had now arrived in London, by way of Paris, where his friend Jefferson had been appointed American Minister in succession to Dr. Franklin. As his country's representative at the English Court, Adams had three objects to pursue. One was to persuade the British Government to recall its forces from the frontier posts; secondly, to secure an indemnity for the three thousand negro slaves who had followed the British after the war; and thirdly, to negotiate a commercial agreement between the two countries. The King having consented to receive privately, at St. James's Palace, the first American Minister to his Court, the whole town knew of the impending meeting and the diplomatic circle was agog from an early hour. The Master of the Ceremonies appeared and led the new envoy into the royal closet. The King, standing at the far end of the room, with only his Minister, Lord Carmarthen, at his side, saw approaching him, with the usual genuflexions, a middle-sized man, plump and florid. He had a masterful blue eye, a strong, firm mouth and his court wig suggested, as much as it concealed, the polished baldness of his cranium. To King George this person appeared at first glance not only a familiar type of Englishman, but the most familiar of all, the very prototype of England—John Bull himself. And, in truth, this resemblance extended to moral and mental character as well, although Adams had recently expressly repudiated the idea.

" Narrow and illiberal prejudices, peculiar to John Bull, with which I might perhaps have been in some degree infected when I was John Bull, have now no influence over me." [1]

Now, however, he boasted he was " John Yankee and as such I shall live and die." And it must be admitted that to

---

[1] To a Foreign Ambassador in Paris, Adams had vehemently rejected the suggestion that, after all, he was " English " : " Neither my father or mother, grandfather or grandmother, great-grandfather or great-grandmother, nor any other relation that I know of, or care a farthing for, has been in England these one hundred and fifty years; so that you see that I have not one drop of blood in my veins but what is American." Now, inasmuch as New England was really an extension of Old England, in race, laws, customs and manners, so with equal truth could a Cornishman or Manxman proclaim that he was not " English " and had never been in England.

Adams's original qualities of vanity, stubbornness and arrogance, there was a far greater admixture of shrewdness, not to
say, slyness, than Fielding's Squire Western possessed.

Great-grandson of a Devonshire yeoman who had settled
in New England, Adams was now fifty—King George's senior
in age by three years.[1]   As his ablest biographer says of him,
" his youth had been provincial, but he was no backwoods-
man."   He did not belong, however, to the aristocratic New
England set, yet had studied at Harvard, and after hesitating
between the church and the law had decided on becoming
a lawyer.   In 1765, when he was thirty, he had been actively
drawn into the movement of protest against the British
Government's taxation measures, which the costly war just
ended with France rendered so necessary.   He was one of
the first to divine how the dispute would end.   But like
Washington and others, he was always ready to show his
contempt for mob prejudice.   When the British officer
commanding the badgered King's troops ordered them to
fire on the Boston mob and so was indicted for manslaughter,
Adams promptly undertook his defence.   Courage, as well
as vanity, was a dominant trait in his character.   Later,
Adams was chosen one of Massachusetts's representatives
to the Continental Congress, and he himself proposed the
selection of Colonel Washington of Virginia to command the
American volunteer army besieging Boston in 1775.   He was
one of the committee for framing the Declaration of
Independence, and in the following year was sent to assist
Dr. Franklin in Paris.   There could hardly, however, fail
to be an imperfect sympathy between the aged, easy-going
philosopher and the active, impatient, critical Adams.   Nor
had he ever any liking for the French.   Adams was appointed
first American Minister to Holland, and in 1782 became one
of the Peace Commissioners, taking such a high tone as
completely to overbear the British commissioners and even
his colleague Franklin, so that quite unexpected concessions
resulted.   It was not bluff, it was not sheer arrogance ; it

[1] As an illustration of the perverse attitude of nearly all nineteenth-century
American historians towards George III, the enlightened biographer of
Adams, J. T. Morse, refers to " the poor, old King in his desperation "
struggling to avoid peace with America. The period is 1782. The King
was then forty-four, six years George Washington's junior !

was rather Adams's intense conviction of the rectitude of his own cause and the rectitude of every cause which he championed.[1] From such moral heights even the greatest figures amongst his compatriots were naturally dwarfed. Franklin was a worldly old trifler. Washington was a personable but mediocre officer whom Adams had dragged out of obscurity in order to propitiate the Virginians.[2] For Dickinson, Pinckney and, later, even Jefferson, he entertained an Olympian contempt ; while as for the great Federalist, Alexander Hamilton, Adams came to loathe his very name.

Arriving in London, Adams had borne himself proudly as befitted a conqueror—for was not the American Revolution and American Independence largely his own work ?—convinced that he and not another was the authentic " Father of his Country," and that to his own exertions, eloquence, courage and astuteness was due the triumph of the American cause.[3]

To do John Adams justice, he was really an able man, much abler, perhaps, than many of his countrymen (apart from his numerous able descendants) are yet disposed to concede. But who, to-day, knowing the true story of the American separation, the extent to which the cause of the colonists had been championed by the most distinguished Englishmen and supported by vast numbers of the English people, knowing, too, the half-hearted way Imperial unity had been promoted in the field and the fact of the Loyalists and their sacrifices and sufferings, can repress an amused wonder at a man who, on his first arrival in the English capital, could achieve such a pitch of arrogance as to write :

" *This people cannot look me in the face ; there is conscious guilt and shame in their countenances when they look at me. They feel that they have behaved ill and that I am sensible of it.*" [4]

[1] " The fervour of his manner, which in moments of excitement was always impressive, lent an air of earnest and intense conviction to his words."—Morse : *John Adams*.

[2] " Adams," remarks Mr. Rupert Hughes, " was in a very real sense Washington's creator."—*George Washington*.

[3] It is curious that Mr. Philip Guedalla should omit John Adams altogether from his very entertaining *Independence Day*. But, then, Mr. Guedalla's reading of history must appear, even to his admirers, a little perverse.

[4] *The Works of John Adams*.

What, if the truth be told, the English people really felt was that their ministers and generals had between them made a shameful mess of things in America, involving them in increased taxation. But in general they felt no particular ill-will towards the Americans, save in so far as they resented the treatment of the Loyalists. Chiefly, their feeling was one of curiosity as to what the colonists would do with their new gift of independence and whether they would not eventually weary of being kept outside the Imperial fold.

One diverting and illuminating episode connected with Adams's first arrival in London ought not to be omitted. He relates it himself :

" The post-boy (who, upon asking where I would be carried, was answered ' to the best inn in London, for all are alike unknown to me ') carried us to the Adelphi buildings in the Strand. Whether it was the boy's cunning, or whether it was mere chance, I know not, but I found myself in a street which was marked JOHN's Street. The postilion turned a corner, and I was in ADAMS Street. He turned another corner, and I was in JOHN ADAMS Street ! I thought—surely, we are arrived in Fairyland. How can all this be ? " [1]

Fairyland, indeed ! Paradise, where even the very streets were named after the great man who had rent asunder the British Empire. John and Adams and John Adams Streets ! If only others had been named Abigail and Quincy and Samuel ! It is characteristic that in his explanation of the phenomenon Adams retains, not very ingenuously, the final " s " in the patronymic of the brothers Adam, although he must have known that it was inaccurate :

" I was informed that the Adelphi Hotel and all the streets and buildings about it had been planned and executed by two architects of the name of Adams . . . that the elder brother, John Adams, had been permitted by Lord Mansfield, to give his own name to all the streets he had erected and the name of the Adelphi (the Brothers) to the hotel."

But it is time to return to the Palace, less than a mile away, where on this May morning King George, in mingled

[1] C. F. Adams : *The Works of John Adams.*

curiosity and apprehension, is observing the ceremonial approach of the sturdy, red-faced gentleman from America. At a signal from the King, Lord Carmarthen, the only other occupant of the royal closet, quietly effaces himself in the shadows by the window, and the interview—not the least significant and memorable in British history—runs its course.

" I made," reported Minister Adams that evening to Secretary Jay, " the three reverences, according to the usage established at this and all the northern Courts of Europe, and then addressed myself to his Majesty in the following words :

" Sir, the United States of America have appointed me their Minister Plenipotentiary to your Majesty and have directed me to deliver to your Majesty this letter which contains the evidence of it. . . . I think myself more fortunate than all my fellow-citizens in having the distinguished honour to be the first to stand in your Majesty's royal presence in a diplomatic character ; and I shall esteem myself the happiest of men if I can be instrumental in recommending my country more and more to your Majesty's royal benevolence and of restoring an entire esteem, confidence and affection, or, in better words, the old good-nature and the old good-humour between people who, though separated by an ocean and under different governments, have the same language, a similar religion and kindred blood."

This was an excellent beginning. For the first time, the ancestor of a lengthy line of American diplomatic representatives at the Court of St. James, enunciated those familiar yet always affecting sentiments of racial unity and filial good-will destined to be uttered not only on similar occasions, but whenever Englishmen and Americans formally and convivially assemble on either side of the Atlantic down to our own day. Such a note, so flattering, so unexpected, could not fail to relieve and gratify the King. Adams concluded :

" I beg your Majesty's permission to add that, although I have some time before been entrusted by my country, it was never in my whole life in a manner so agreeable to myself."

" The King [he reported] listened to every word I said, with dignity but an apparent emotion. Whether it was the nature of the interview or whether it was my visible agitation that touched him, I cannot say. But he was much affected and answered me with more tremor than I had spoken with."

Adams thus renders the King's answering speech :

" Sir, the circumstances of this audience are so extraordinary, the language you have now held is so extremely proper and the feelings you have discovered so justly adapted to the occasion that I must say that I not only receive with pleasure the assurance of the friendly dispositions of the United States, but that I am very glad the choice has fallen upon you to be their Minister."

Could anything have been more magnanimous ?

" I wish you, Sir, to believe, and that it may be understood in America, that I have done nothing in the late contest but what I thought myself indispensably bound to do by the duty which I owed my people. I will be very frank with you. I was the last man in the kingdom to consent to the separation ; but the separation having been made and having become inevitable, I have always said, as I say now, that I would be the first to meet the friendship of the United States as an independent Power." [1]

Here was a frank and generous avowal and should at once and for ever have dissipated the legend that George was " bigoted " and " vindictive." But the interview was not over yet. The sovereign had heard something of Adams's attitude towards the French, and was doubtless curious to know if it coincided with his own.

" The King then asked me whether I came last from France, and upon my answering in the affirmative, he put on an air of familiarity, and smiling, or rather laughing, said, ' There is an opinion among some people that you are not the *most attached* of all your countrymen to the manners of the French ? '

" I was surprised at this, because I thought it an in-

[1] " I dare not say," explains Adams, " that these were the King's precise words," although " his Majesty's pronunciation was as distinct as I ever heard " ; yet such was his own recollection of them.

discretion and a departure from the dignity. I was a little embarrassed, but determined not to deny the truth on one hand, nor leave him to infer from it any attachment to England on the other. I threw off as much gravity as I could and assumed an air of gaiety and a tone of decision, as far as was decent, and said, ' That opinion, Sir, is not mistaken : I must avow to your Majesty that I have no attachment but to my own country.'

" The King replied, as quick as lightning, ' An honest man will have no other.'

" The King then said a word or two to the Secretary of State, which being between them I did not hear, and then turned round and bowed to me, as is customary with all kings and princes when they give the signal to retire. I retreated, stepping backward, as is the etiquette, and making my last reverence at the door of the chamber, I went my way. The Master of the Ceremonies joined me the moment of my coming out of the King's closet and accompanied me through the apartments down to my carriage, several stages of servants, gentlemen-porters, and under-porters roaring out like thunder, ' Mr. Adams's servants,' ' Mr. Adams's carriage,' etc. I have been thus minute, as it may be useful hereafter for others to know." [1]

It is a good picture and Adams's enjoyment of his experience was natural enough.[2] He thought it best, however, to warn his Government not to expect too much.

" The conversation with the King, Congress will form their own judgment of. I may expect from it a residence less painful than I once expected, as so marked an attention from the King will silence many grumblers ; but we can infer nothing from all this concerning the success of my mission."

In this warning he was only prudent. Nevertheless, he may well have felt elated as he drove back to his lodgings. For the moment the prospect of improved Anglo-American relations seemed brighter than it had been for years. He had acquitted himself with credit. He had seen and spoken

[1] Adams to Jay, June 2, 1785.
[2] Adams anticipates the criticism that he is indulging in too much ceremony. It was impossible to avoid it. " The essence of things is lost in ceremony in every country in Europe. We must submit to what we cannot alter. Patience is the only remedy."

familiarly with his former sovereign, the King of England. He had delivered his message : the interview had been an unqualified success.

What, one wonders, were the King's own reflections after the interview ? Did he, in consequence of the agreeable language and behaviour of Adams, cherish the illusion that the Americans might, after all, not prove incurably recalcitrant, that they might yet, after a period of political confusion and commercial distress, " solicit," as Lord Sheffield imagined, " to come back as a repentant child to the maternal embrace " ?

Meanwhile, closer relations need not be forced. There was no necessity for immediate action. The troublesome business was over, the American envoy had been received, and received cordially : the political issue depended entirely on the temper and conduct of the States whom he represented.

Adams, on his part, lost no time in announcing formally to Lord Carmarthen the threefold object of his mission. Then came disillusion. He had five months to wait before any answer came. Meanwhile, news of domestic political dissension was coming from America and public opinion in England was hardening itself. Adams could not fail to note the growing unfriendly attitude of the British Ministry and people. As he wrote Secretary Jay :

" I have the honour to agree fully with you in your opinion that ' it is manifestly as much in the interest of this country to be well with us as for us to be well with them ' ; but this is not the judgment of the English nation, it is not the judgment of Lord North and his party, it is not the judgment of the Duke of Portland and his friends, and it does not appear to be the judgment of Mr. Pitt and the present set."

He found, indeed, the general opinion to be that America was helpless to raise a revenue, to exclude foreign shipping, to build a fleet or even to agree among themselves.[1]

---

[1] The individual States were left free, in defiance of all treaties, to establish their own separate tariff systems. Thus, if the Congress made a treaty of commerce with a foreign nation providing for free trade between it and America, any State could at will annul that treaty by prescribing a tariff or even by prohibiting all commerce with the nation in question. Moreover, each State had its own code of laws dealing with religious liberty, personal

In his memoir of his grandfather, Charles Francis Adams (himself, like his father before him, long afterwards Minister to the Court of St. James) exposes clearly the state of things current in 1785 :

" The situation of an envoy from one nation to another is likely to be made imposing as well as agreeable in direct proportion to the impression that prevails in the world of the power and energy of the Government by which he is sent.

" For a short time after the close of the struggle, the different sovereigns of Europe awaited with curiosity the results that were to follow the successful establishment of American independence. But, as the accounts came, symptomatic of nothing but anarchy and confusion, the inference grew general that the experiment of self-government had failed and that the new nation would prove of little account in the affairs of the globe. To an indifferent observer looking from the English point of view, Mr. Adams soon ceased to appear as representing anything but disorder. . . . The causes for this state of things were too far off to be analysed. It was enough that the attempt to re-establish the ordinary course of justice had been met with resistance, to convince a European that an aversion to paying debts honestly contracted had much more to do with American notions of liberty than principle.   Hence he held up his hands in amazement at the profligacy of a community which refused to execute its recognized contracts and determined to waste no more sympathy upon a people thus proving itself beneath his contempt.   In Great Britain, especially, this spectacle was witnessed with a mixed feeling of disgust and exultation. No disposition existed to palliate faults or to overlook errors. The observation of them served rather as a relief to wounded pride."

Consequently, the answer to Adams's note took the form of an emphatic refusal on all points. The King's Government, he was informed, would not relinquish the frontier forts nor pay any indemnity for the slaves until the long outstanding debts due to British merchants were paid.

and property rights, and many other matters directly affecting the status of citizens or subjects of other lands ; and in this diversity there was danger of immeasurable embarrassment and trouble.—Johnson : *America's Foreign Relations.*

Adams might raise an angry protest that the Treaty contained no such stipulation, which was true, but it did provide that the creditors of either country should not be legally impeded in the recovery of their debts, and America " was notoriously putting legal obstacles in the way of British creditors." As for his proposal of a commercial agreement with America, what advantage could it bring England ? By enforcing the existing navigation laws, foreign trade was all but closed to the erstwhile colonies. As a recent writer observes, England " was getting all the trade she wanted with America without having to concede any reciprocal advantages." [1]

Thus, it is evident, it required a vast amount of assurance and the command of much rhetorical sophistry, to confront the Court and public opinion in London. Adams was well supplied with both these commodities, and for nearly three years he endeavoured, but with diminishing confidence, to brazen out a very awkward situation. His grandson tells us that—

" the monarch, never well reconciled to the triumph of his subjects, became less and less disposed to put restraint on his feelings.

" He was cold. Of course, his family were cold. Of course, the courtiers followed the example. What is not in vogue with the quality in England is sure to be slighted by the commons. There was no cordiality anywhere excepting among the dissenters and the very few who leaned to republican doctrines ; no better association than this to prove how unfashionable was everything American. Of civility, cold and formal, such as only the English know how in perfection to make offensive, there was enough. No marked offence, but supercilious indifference. Official representations lay long unheeded. The courtesy of sending out a minister to America was left unregarded."

But what could be expected ? There was another side and a cause for all this. The States had done little to promote good feeling. Their treatment of the Loyalists after the Peace was outrageous, while in utter disregard of the Treaty they placed, in one form or another, impediments in the way

---

[1] Mowat : *The Diplomatic Relations of Great Britain and the United States.*

of the collection of British debts.[1] Secretary Jay himself declared that there " had not been a single day since the ratification of the Treaty on which it had not been violated by one or other of the States."

Fortunate was it, therefore, for Adams that during his lengthy and fruitless sojourn in London he could find relaxation in the infinite variety of the London scene, in the friendship of several of his diplomatic colleagues, such as the French Ambassador and the Dutch and Swedish Ministers, and the good-will and hospitality of several Whigs. And, after all, he had the companionship and support of that lively and engaging lady, the wife of his bosom. Abigail Adams, indeed, would have been a notable character anywhere. Her letters to her husband have been published, and they reveal her affection, her talent for observation, her judgment and her prejudices in the most attractive style. The daughter of a New England parson, Mrs. Adams found herself at the age of forty " suddenly transplanted to Europe from a small and quiet country town to be the first representative of her sex from the United States at Court." Mrs. Adams was delighted with England, which she had been brought up to regard as " home." London especially enchanted her ; at first she was ready to admire and enjoy everything. She was beginning to make friends, but soon, alas ! was made aware of a blight in London society upon everything American—a blight which intensified as time went on. The Loyalist ladies, her own countrywomen, were there before her, and they continued to come, penetrating into all circles with their tales of ill-treatment and oppression, and especially did they make their influence felt at Court.[2] By Queen Charlotte, the American Minister's wife was received civilly enough, but any friendliness she showed could only be intermittent in such an atmosphere, and once or twice

[1] Johnson : *America's Foreign Relations.*

[2] " Our scandalous spoliation, persecution and expulsion of all who were even suspected of having been British sympathizers during the Revolution ; a crime compared with which the British expulsion of the Acadians was a trifling and negligible episode. The result was the loss to this country of thousands of its most valuable citizens and the engendering of resentment and estrangement in Canada instead of cordial and helpful friendship."—Johnson : *America's Foreign Relations.*

her Majesty's " coldness " was so marked that everyone noticed it. And when Minister Thomas Jefferson came over from Paris and was presented at Court, even the King behaved rudely ; it is said he actually turned his back upon that gentleman, as well as upon Adams, his presenter. If so, George was only human and may have found it hard to forgive those uncomplimentary periods in the Declaration which had gibbeted him before the world and posterity.

And Mrs. Adams also was human and feminine, and so could not forgive the Queen for her coldness towards her. Years afterwards, when she heard that the English throne was in danger from French revolutionary doctrines, she could find it in her heart to write to her daughter :

" Humiliation for Charlotte is no sorrow for me. She really deserves her full portion for the contempt and scorn which she took pains to discover."

More than sixty years later her grandson wrote :

" Of course, the courtiers followed the lead thus given to them, and the impression made against America at the very outset of its national career has hardly been effaced down to this day."

Which is surely an exaggeration, if not really absurd. But even had it been true, the fault lay, as John Adams himself was later to confess, with his own countrymen. His grandson, while deploring the royal " coldness," admits that Mrs. Adams, despite all drawbacks, " enjoyed much her residence in the Mother Country." As for the Minister himself—

" it is not to be inferred that he did not derive much enjoyment from many of the events which were taking place in the world around him. The indifference of the Court and Ministers could not prevent him from enjoying the oppor- tunities presented of witnessing the contests of eloquence almost daily occurring in the two Houses of Parliament. Mr. Adams heard Burke and Pitt and Fox and Sheridan and Camden, and was present at the opening of the solemn proceedings against Warren Hastings. It was the age of strong intellect in England. Nothing like it had occurred since the reign of Queen Anne and nothing like it has been seen since. For the mind of the human race seems to be, in this respect, like the surface of the earth it inhabits, which must lie fallow at intervals between periods of excessive productiveness, in order to recruit from its exhaustion." [1]

While in London, the domestic happiness of the Adamses was further increased by the marriage of their daughter to Colonel Smith, the Secretary of Legation.[2] Besides frequent attendance at balls and parties, especially those given at the French Embassy, and visits to the theatre, Adams made an occasional tour of the English countryside. At Stratford-on-Avon, in April 1786, he committed, it is painful to record, one act of vandalism which would have sent a shiver through the frame of his diplomatic successors. True, he pleads he was only doing what others had always done ; but subsequent American representatives have had to consider the force of their example.

Visiting Shakespeare's birthplace, " they showed us," records Adams, " an old wooden chair in the chimney corner where he sat. *We cut off a chip, according to custom.*"

It is alleged that to this shocking practice of his countrymen is due the total extinction of a relic for which to-day more than one American collector would be prepared to pay a larger sum than Congress could probably then have raised on the security of all the Colonies !

At last the first American Minister realized the stark and painful truth. He was in an impossible position. He represented no real power. There was no real national Government at home—no army, no navy, no money. His own official salary was so reduced that it was impossible for him " to keep a style of living like the other foreign Ministers," which was " humiliating."

" Some years hence [wrote his wife] it may be a pleasure to reside here in the character of American Minister, but

---

[1] Charles Francis Adams : *The Works of John Adams* (*Life*, 1856).

[2] Unhappily this son-in-law's future conduct, long after their return to America, was hardly calculated to reflect credit on himself or the Adams family.

with the present salary and the present temper of the English
no one need envy the Embassy." [1]

About the shortcomings of his countrymen Adams now felt
bitter and made no effort to conceal his bitterness.   It was
high time he returned home.   He was not one to favour—

" that species of logic, not infrequent among political leaders
of all nations, whereby a different standard of right can be
assumed at home from that which is proclaimed abroad,
another rule acted upon individually from that which is
presented in official station."

This hopeless abatement of logical perfection in Adams
is to his lasting credit as a citizen and an honest man.   He
wrote to Jay asking leave to return home to private life.
He had, it seems, taken too high a ground throughout in his
behaviour to the British Government.   He had hardly been
as humble, as conciliatory to opinions and prejudices as the
circumstances called for.

But even had Adams lingered another year or two for
American Confederation to be established and the French
Revolution to burst forth, it is doubtful if he would have
succeeded in his English mission.   Such success was to be
obtained only by a diplomat of different origin, character
and temper, one who was less uncompromising and less
vain.

And so Adams, first in the line of American Ministers
Plenipotentiary to London, presented in February 1788
his letter of recall.   On this occasion the King was again
courteous and affable, only Adams was now in no mood for
royal compliments.   He had failed in his mission and felt
his failure would damage his political prospects at home.
A Convention was in session in New York, formulating a
national Constitution under which a ruler for America would
be chosen.   The form of government had not yet been
settled nor the name by which the chief executive was to be
called.   Many expected it to be King—an elected king.

---

[1] Both her son and grandson came to reside in England in that character.
But the later times also were " out of joint," and both Adamses came in for
less pleasure than work and anxiety.

Adams had no doubt as to his own claims, yet he feared the
first place would now go to Washington—to a soldier, not,
as was just and prudent, to a statesman—Washington, the
man he had made. Ingratitude, however, could not go so
far as to deny him the second place—whether of Prince or
High Chancellor or Great Elector or Vice-President. Nor,
in the issue, did it do so.

When he landed on his native shores, Adams had been
absent altogether in France, Holland and England nearly
ten years. A resolution came to be, though tardily, passed
by Congress thanking " for the patriotism, perseverance,
integrity and diligence with which he hath ably and faithfully served his country."

BIOGRAPHICAL NOTE

Adams succeeded Washington in the Presidency in 1797.
But his triumph was embittered by his enemies and the
narrowness of his election. He served only a single term,
and lived on afterwards into extreme old age, dying, like
Jefferson, on July 4, 1826, the official, though not the actual,
anniversary of the Declaration of Independence. Half a
century later his biographer, J. T. Morse, could pen this
epitaph :

" Mr. Adams's high appreciation of his own pre-eminent
merits and distinguished services remained with him to
comfort and console him to the end. His vanity and supreme
self-satisfaction passed away only with his passing breath."

CHAPTER II

MORRIS (1790–1792)

IN 1789 General Washington was inaugurated President of the United States, but still the British Government held aloof. No envoy had yet been sent to Philadelphia. It was high time that this unsatisfactory state of affairs should cease. Events were passing in France which might profoundly affect American relations with that country, and also those between England and America. Yet after Adams's failure, overtures were difficult. The President, mindful of the dignity of the new nation, bethought him of sending a personal envoy, one whom he could trust and who would not fail to be received, for his own sake, in the highest British circles.

Such an American was at that moment in Paris, a brilliant young lawyer, named Gouverneur Morris. With him Washington had for some years been in close personal relations. Born in 1752, Morris belonged to the Colonial aristocracy, a fine, stalwart figure of a man, despite the loss of a leg occasioned by a carriage accident. He had been a member of the Constitutional Convention ; its labours over, Morris suddenly abandoned politics for commerce.

He set out for France, arriving in January 1789, and remaining there for the remainder of the year in constant correspondence with Washington on the affairs of the Revolution. To him, in October, the President addressed a letter asking him to undertake a mission to England—

"to converse with His Britannick Majesty's Minister on these points, viz. whether there be any, and what objections to performing those articles in the Treaty which remain to be performed on their part and whether they incline to a Treaty of Commerce with the United States on any and what terms."

It was not, however, before the following March that Morris was able to enter upon his special presidential embassy. He carried his credentials in Washington's own hand, the office of Secretary of State being just then vacant. On the 27th day that month he reached London, where his brother, General Staats Long Morris, who had married the Duchess of Gordon, then resided.

From the Diary kept by Morris we may derive a pretty exact account of his movements.

" Arrive at five o'clock at Froome's Hotel, Covent Garden. Go to bed at ten o'clock, and am but just fairly nestled there, when my brother, General Morris, arrives. My sister is also at the door, but does not come in."

On the following day he wrote :

" This morning (March 28th) at ten, I go to General Morris's. A very sisterly reception from his lady. Stay and chat till near twelve, then visit the Marquis de la Luzerne, Ambassador from France. He tells me the news from Paris, and in reply to my question of who is to replace Necker, he says that the story of his going away is all fabricated by Calonne. I tell him that I am persuaded that he will quit, and that I do not consider it as a misfortune. I find, however, that he is much an advocate of M. Necker and his measures. This is extraordinary, for he has, I think, good sense enough to see the faults which have been committed. Call on the Duke of Leeds,[1] who is not at home ; leave a card and tell the porter I will write a note. Go to the Duke of Luxembourg's ; admitted with difficulty ; his son receives the letter with which I am charged by his brother, the Duke being in bed. Return home ; write a note to the Duke of Leeds, asking to know the time when it will be most convenient for his Grace to receive certain communications which Mr. Morris is desired to make in a semi-official capacity to his Britannic Majesty's Ministers by the President of the United States of America. Go to the French Ambassador's to dinner. The Vicomtesse says she has a great deal to say about the affairs of France when she sees me with less company. Return home, and find a note from the Duke of Leeds, giving me a rendez-vous for to-morrow at half past two. I told the

---

[1] Foreign Secretary in the Pitt Ministry, the Lord Carmarthen of p. 4.

Marquis de la Luzerne this morning that I was directed to call on the Ministry here for a performance of the Treaty, and enjoined him to secrecy. (He told it everywhere.) I think it prudent to be in a situation to say always to the French Court that every step taken by us has been with their privity."

Two days after his arrival Morris communicated Washington's letter to the Duke of Leeds. The latter expressed himself " with some warmth of approbation," saying :

" I am very happy, Mr. Morris, to see this letter, in the President's own hand. I assure you it is very much my wish to cultivate a friendly and commercial intercourse between the two countries, and more, and I can answer for the rest of his Majesty's servants that they are of the same opinion."

Morris replied :

" I am very happy, my Lord, to find that such sentiments prevail, for we are too near neighbours not to be either very good friends or very dangerous enemies."

The confidential envoy then proceeded to mention the points of the Treaty which remained to be performed, observing that, by the Constitution of the United States, all obstacles to the recovery of British debts had been removed, any doubt on that head being obviated by the organization of a Federal court which had cognizance of all causes arising under the Treaty. The Duke was very happy to receive this information. Morris then went on to mention the two points remaining to be fulfilled on their part—i.e. the posts and compensation for exported negroes. The Duke " hemmed and hawed " : he had " long wished that something had been done, but something or another had always interfered." He changes the conversation, Morris brings it back, and then he changes again. It is evident that his Grace is confining himself to general assurances. Morris told him that there was a little circumstance which operated very disagreeably in America. " I know what you are going to speak about," interrupted the Duke, " our not sending out a Minister. I wished to send you one, but then I wished to have a man every way equal to the task, a man of abilities, and one agreeable to the people of America,

GOUVERNEUR MORRIS.

but it was difficult; it is a great way off." "My Lord," observed Morris, "you cannot want men well qualified, and I am certain that there are many who will be glad to accept it."

Meanwhile, as the Duke did not appear too well informed, the American suggested that he might like to examine the American Constitution, the Treaty of Peace, and other vital documents, which the nobleman thought was a happy inspiration. In the course of the conversation he mentioned a letter he had written to John Adams, in which he expressed the opinion that the performance of the Treaty should be article by article, as they stood in order. But the envoy thought it would be " proper for us to execute the Treaty fully on our part, and then call for execution by them, for that if each were to delay until the other should act, all treaties would be illusory." Morris left Washington's letter with the Duke of Leeds to be copied and returned.

Morris's shrewd policy was to be " intimate at the French Ambassador's, to a certain point." So after dining with the Marquis de la Luzerne he entered into a long conversation on the state of French politics.

" He tells me that he thinks Lafayette and Necker ought to coalesce, as the only means of saving France. I tell him that his idea may be good, but I am sure it will not take effect. He asks if Mr. Jefferson was not much consulted in the beginning of the Revolution. I tell him that I believe he was, and fear that his ideas were in many respects too democratical. He speaks of Jefferson with much contempt as a statesman and as one who is better formed for the interior of Virginia than to influence the operations of a great people. I own that I am rather surprised at this sentiment, because Mr. Jefferson has in general excited favourable ideas of his intellectual faculties."

Yet Morris could himself be a pretty summary critic of Jefferson on occasion.

Once at a dinner at Sir John Sinclair's he heard a gentleman of anti-American views hold forth.

" He is, if an enemy, a dangerous one, because he can always produce just as much matter as he pleases. I foolishly enter into an argument with him . . . 'twould have been better to let him enjoy his opinions, and to inculcate them.''

One of the company told Morris that he thought it probable he would be appointed Minister to the English Court. Morris thought that a Minister should not yet be appointed. This sentiment produced surprise, but Morris justified it on the ground that the Ministry did not really wish to form a connexion with America.

One evening was memorable. He dined in company with Charles James Fox, and he enters a description in his Diary :

" I observe that Mr. Fox scrutinizes me closely to see what I am. I give him all opportunity for that purpose. His manners are simple. He speaks lightly of Chatham, who, says he, was a fortunate man, and that the successes in the war were to be ascribed to a measure of his father's, which was the capture of the French ships and seamen before the Declaration ; I observe that it was also to be attributed to the great force sent out to America by Lord Chatham. In the course of conversation I ask him what system the present administration have with respect to America. He says that he thinks they have not as yet adopted any ; that he does not imagine Mr. Pitt will take any trouble about the matter, but will leave it to Lord Hawkesbury and Mr. Grenville, who are both of them indisposed to us, whereas Pitt himself is rather friendly than otherwise.

" I ask him the character of the Duke of Leeds. He speaks of him contemptuously, but says he takes upon himself a little lately. He says that he and Burke are now almost alone in their opinion that we should be permitted to trade in our own bottoms to their islands, the West Indies ; that this opinion loses ground daily, though for his part he persists in it. I tell him that it is a solid principle of policy, for that our position renders the islands so materially dependent on us that they should make it our interest to keep them in possession ; that further, if we choose to lay them under disadvantages in our ports, we can materially injure their navigation, whereas the admission of our vessels into their islands can do them no harm in that respect. All this is true, but I suspect that we shall be obliged in America to give them the conviction of their senses.''

Attending the trial of Warren Hastings, Morris heard Burke and Fox in argument.

" The former [hc wrote] has quickness and genius, but he is vague, loose, desultory, and confused. Mr. Fox has not the needful self-possession to make a great speaker. He is obliged to abstract himself so much in pursuit of the matter that he is extremely deficient in manner. He is a slovenly speaker, but he is acute and discerns well. He does not sufficiently convey to others the distinctions which he feels ; his mind appears like a clouded sun, and this I believe results from the life he leads. Temperance, application, and the possession of competence with moderation to enjoy it, would render him very great, if unhappily his faculties be not at that point when a continuation of former habits becomes necessary to keep them alive."

All this was well said and gave a very good picture of Fox at this time.

April was drawing to a close, the Duke of Leeds continued silent, and the President's letter remained in his hands. "I am still waiting," Morris wrote to Washington on the 28th, "for intelligence from the Ministers, who (to judge by appearances) slumber profoundly upon the application made to them." But the very next day the Duke acknowledged all Morris's notes, pleading indisposition for his long delay and expressing the sincere wish of England to fulfil her engagements with the United States.

All the same, the outlook for a treaty was not rosy and Morris wanted to know why. He assured the Duke of the determination of America to perform in the fullest manner every stipulation she had made. He expressed a—

" sincere hope that he might be mistaken in supposing that his Grace showed a disinclination to securing an amiable intercourse by the force of a treaty, and assured him how unhappy he should be to convey a false impression on this subject, which might be prejudicial to both countries. He begged therefore that he might be set right." [1]

Few men could be more florid and deferential than Morris in his official communications.

[1] Anne Cary Morris : *Gouverneur Morris.*

" I thought it best [he told Washington] to heap coals of fire on their heads, and thereby either bring them into our views or put them most eminently in the wrong. . . . I have some reason to believe that the present administration intends to keep the posts and withhold payment for the negroes. If so, they will cover their breach of faith by the best pretexts in their power. I incline to think also that they consider a treaty of commerce with America as being absolutely unnecessary and that they are persuaded they shall derive all benefit from our trade without treaty.

" In the matter of treaties, very much will, I think, depend upon the situation of France. From the conduct of the aristocratic hierarchy in the Low Countries, who are instigated and supported by Prussia, I have long been thoroughly convinced that the alternative of war or the most ignominious terms of peace would be proposed to the Imperial Courts. Counting upon the absolute nullity of France, and supposing that their country can at any moment intimidate that into abject submission, Prussia and Poland will, I think, join themselves to Turkey and Sweden against Russia and Austria, which are both exhausted and one of them dismembered. Probably the war will be commenced before the letter reaches your hands, and then Britain and Holland are to be the umpires or, rather, dictators of peace. Perhaps there never was a moment in which this country found herself greater, and consequently it is the most unfavourable moment to obtain advantageous terms from her in any bargain. It appears clearly that the favourable moment for us to treat is not yet come. It is indeed the moment for this country, and they seem determined to let it pass away." [1]

We now come across the beginning of that long dispute about Impressment.

Morris had been urged to protest against American seamen being forced into the British service, and he drew up a memorial to the Lords of the Admiralty. At a personal interview with the Duke of Leeds, he told the latter that their press-gangs have entered American vessels with as little ceremony as those belonging to Britain. He added with irony, " I believe, my Lord, this is the only instance in which we are not treated as aliens."

[1] Morris to Washington, May 2, 1790.

The Duke winced at this, acknowledged the practice to be wrong, and promised to speak to Lord Chatham on the subject.

" You know, my Lord, that when a wound is recently healed it is very easy to rub off the skin." Morris added his wish that " some plan may be adopted, founded on good faith, which may prevent the concealment of British seamen, while it secures those of America from insult."

He suggested the idea of certificates of citizenship from the British Admiralty courts overseas to American seamen, an idea which rather pleased the Duke, who said he would consult his colleagues. The next day Morris called in Downing Street and found young Mr. Pitt and the Duke sitting together. Morris was presented, and the trio entered into conversation. Pitt approved Morris's idea of a certificate from the Admiralty in American waters.

Pitt went on to say that—

" the delay of compliance on our part had rendered that compliance now less effectual, and that cases must certainly exist where injury had been sustained by the delay. I observe generally that delay is always a kind of breach, being, as long as it lasts, the non-performance of stipulations. But, descending a little more into particulars, I endeavour to show that the injury is complained of by the Americans for the non-payment of money due by this Government to the owners of slaves taken away. On the whole, I observe that inquiries of this sort may be very useful if the parties naturally seek to keep asunder, but that, if they mean to come together, it would be best to keep them entirely out of sight, and not to perform on both sides as well as the actual situation of things will permit."

The Prime Minister said he wanted to cultivate a good understanding with America : it might be well to reconsider the whole subject, and on general grounds to see whether some mutual compensation could not be made.

" If I understand you, Mr. Pitt," broke in Morris, " you wish to make a new treaty instead of complying with the old one."

The Prime Minister admitted this to be *in some sort* his

idea. Morris observed that even on that ground he did not see what better could be done than to fulfil the existing treaty.

MORRIS : " As to the compensation for negroes taken away, it is too trifling an object for you to dispute, so that nothing remains but the posts. I suppose, therefore, that you wish to retain the posts ! "

PITT : " Why, perhaps we may."

MORRIS : " They are not worth the keeping, for it must cost you a great deal of money, and produces no benefit. The only reason you can desire them is to secure the fur-trade, and that will centre in this country, let who will carry it on in America. . . . I only state the retaining them as *useless to you* ; but this matter is to be considered in a different point of light. Those who made the peace acted wisely in separating the possessions of the two countries by so wide a water. It is essential to preserve the boundary if you wish to live in amity with us. Near neighbours are seldom good ones, for the quarrels among borderers frequently bring on wars. It is therefore essential for both parties that you should give them up, and to us it is of particular importance, because our national honour is interested. You hold them with the avowed intention of forcing us to comply with such conditions as you may impose."

PITT : " Why, sir, as to the considerations of national honour, we can retort the observation and say our honour is concerned in your delay of performance of the treaty."

MORRIS : " No, sir ; your natural and proper course was to comply fully on your part, and if then we had refused a compliance you might rightfully have issued letters of marque and reprisal to such of your subjects as were injured by our refusal. But the conduct you have pursued naturally excites resentment in every American bosom. We do not think it worth while to go to war with you for these posts, but *we know our rights, and will avail ourselves of them when time and circumstances may suit*."

Plain speaking such as this could not fail to impress Pitt, who asked Morris if he had power to treat.

" I told him I had not, and that we would not appoint any person as Minister, they had so much neglected the former appointment. He asked me whether we would appoint a

Minister if they did.   I told him that I could almost promise that we should, but was not authorized to give any positive assurance.   We then conversed loosely upon the manner of communicating on the subject.   In the course of it I tell him that we cannot take notice of their consuls, or anything which they may say, because they are not characters known or acknowledged by us."

It is hardly surprising that Pitt's pride was "a little touched at this."

" I suppose, Mr. Morris, that attention might as well be paid to what they say as that the Duke of Leeds and I should hold the present conversation with you."
" By no means, sir," answered Morris.   " I should never have thought of asking a conference with his Grace if I had not possessed a letter from the President of the United States."

Whereupon Pitt said they would in like manner write a letter to one of their consuls in America, to which Morris replied :

" Yes, sir, and the *letter* would be attended to and not the consul, who is in no respect different from any other British subject."

Pitt's comment was that " etiquette ought not to be pushed as far as to injure business, and keep the countries asunder."

It was certainly a spirited, interesting and candid interview.

All that spring and summer the American emissary, known to be President Washington's intimate friend and spokesman, was made a good deal of in London, attending dinners and receptions and mixing with various exalted persons in British politics and society.   One is reminded of Colonel E. M. House and his confidential mission a century and a quarter later ; he too was provided with a Presidential letter.

As an enterprising bachelor and very much the ladies' man, even though his dancing days were over, Morris always had an eye open for the fair sex. His Diary hints at numerous gallantries, and there are many satiric and often malicious references to the ladies. Thus he records :

"To Mrs. Low's rout; a number of Americans there. Among the guests is Mrs. Mallet, who still looks toward triumph, and has a less unnatural manner than she had about fifteen years ago. She seems *not unwilling to extend her dominion ;* but this will not do for *me*."

On another occasion :

"Visit Lady Tancred. She seems more indebted for her beauties to art than I had imagined at the first view. I learn that she is sister to my old friend General Montgomery."

Sometimes he drops into rhyme, as :

"To-night, when I come in, I find on my table an invitation from Mrs. Church to breakfast to-morrow at twelve. I write the following answer :

> Dear Madame, believe me, 'tis not without sorrow
> I do not partake of your breakfast to-morrow ;
> So kind a request it is hard to refuse,
> But an envious Demon my pleasure pursues,
> Resolved, with the blasts of cold duty, to blight
> The blossoms of joy and the buds of delight."

Morris's belief in female fidelity is hardly deep-rooted.

"I visit the Duchess of Gordon. Colonel Lenox and his lady are here. She is a finer woman than is imagined— quick feelings, I think, and tenderness, which will by and by meet some object more likely to command the heart than the Colonel, who seems to be a good-tempered fellow."

There are many references to the Revolution just then in progress on the other side of the Channel. At dinner at the Marquis of Lansdowne's that nobleman professed—

"sentiments respecting the Constitution of France to the French who are here, which I believe to be foreign to his heart. Dr. Price is one of the guests, who is one of the Liberty-mad people. After dinner, being together in the drawing-room a few minutes, the noble marquis advances sentiments to me far less friendly to France, but full of love and kindness for America. I am, however, at liberty to believe just as much as I please."

"To-day (June 24), at dinner at the French Ambassador's [continues the Diary], there are a number of the Corps Diplomatique, and what suits me better, a fine turtle. Advices from France announce the total abolition of the French nobility, down to the very arms and livery; this upon motion of some of the Whig nobles. There is also a strange address to the Assembly from a junto of all nations. It seems as if the Revolutionists were studying how best to excite a strong opposition to their measures. Heaven knows how this will end, but I fear badly, unless they are saved by a foreign war. Go from hence to General Morris's, and sit some time with them. He says there will be no war, and from his manner of speaking I think he has been told so by some person who is in the secret."

"The Marquis de la Luzerne tells me to-day (July 2) at dinner that the Duke of Orleans has taken leave of the King with the intention to return.

"He cannot go into any country well, nor remain here, when the war breaks out. He asks me why I suppose always that there will be war? I tell him that I have long been convinced of it, for many reasons.

"*Vous dites toujours des choses extraordinaires qui ne se réalisent.*"

But this time Morris was right.

Happening to mention William Short, the Chargé in Paris, Luzerne spoke of him as being *fou*, and rendered so by Jefferson.

"I tell him that he will probably be appointed Minister in France. He seems not well pleased, but says he is probably a very suitable person. He is vexed at Lafayette's conduct respecting the noblesse, and says that, although he has a good deal of management (*conduite*) in his affairs, he has done much evil from the want of genius (*esprit*), in which idea he is not entirely wrong."

In writing, himself, to Short in Paris, Morris reveals his own political temper, which was that of Hamilton, Jay and all the Federalists of that day.

"Those who court the people have a capricious mistress; a mistress which may be gained by sacrifices, but she cannot be so held, for she is insatiable. The people will never continue attached to any man who will sacrifice duty to their caprice. In modern days we have, I believe, more virtue than the ancients ; certainly we are more decent. But the principles of human nature are the same, and so shall we find the pursuits of man to be, if we can but penetrate that veil of decency by which young ambition is decorated."

Morris was in the happy position of being able to mix diplomacy with business. One of his undertakings for certain friends in America was to negotiate in London and Paris for the sale of estates in various parts of the country. There was, of course, a general feeling of distrust of a country so far away and so uncultivated, but some considerable properties were disposed of.

In a letter to Washington, dated August 30, he hopes that in a day or two he may—

" learn something of their intentions here respecting us. And if I do not hear from them, shall make a final address to his Grace of Leeds. It is very flattering to me, Sir, that you are so kind as to approve of my communications with the ministers of this country, so far as they had gone in the beginning of May. I earnestly hope that my subsequent conduct may meet the same favourable interpretation. This you may rely on, that if in any case I go wrong, it will be from an error of judgment."

Impatient at the long delay on the part of Leeds in replying to his letter of April 30, he now again wrote :

" I have patiently waited in this city to the present hour, though called by many affairs to the Continent. But my departure cannot be much longer delayed, and therefore it becomes necessary to intrude once more on your Grace's attention."

The Duke would gladly have put off the whole business, but Morris was importunate and another interview took place.

" I see at once by his countenance, when I arrive at his office, that he feels himself obliged to cut an awkward part. He says that he is still earnestly desirous of a real *bona-fide* connexion, not merely by the words of a treaty but in reality. He says that as to the two points of the Treaty, there are still difficulties. He wishes they could be got out of the way, and then hesitates and drops the conversation. Finding from this that he is to hold a conference with me which is to amount to just nothing at all, I determine to learn as much as I can from his looks. I, therefore, begin by observing that I am extremely sorry for it, but that the affair of the posts seems to present an unsurmountable barrier to any treaty, because it will serve as a pretext to ill-disposed persons.

" In case of Britain and France going to war, ' which, if it does not happen this year or the next, will probably happen within twenty years—which is but a moment in the age of empires—we can give the West Indian islands to whom we please without engaging in the war at all, and that we shall certainly in such case consider whether it is our interest that they should be subject to England or France, and act accordingly.' "

The Duke's face fell and his manner changed. He asked Morris what the United States thought of the undefined claim of Spain to the New World. Morris was—

" very willing to be pumped, and therefore I tell him carelessly that I don't think it will make any impression upon our minds, for that the Spaniards are in fact so apprehensive of us that they are disposed to sacrifice a great deal for our friendship ; that the only reason they had for withholding the navigation of the Mississippi River was from the apprehension of a contraband trade, which was the reason why, in my opinion, they must stake the last man and the last shilling upon the present affair of Nootka Sound, rather than admit the right of selling there by British subjects. He owns that the danger of contraband ought to be considered in dealing on this subject, for that nations, like individuals, ought to treat with candour and honesty."

On the whole, it was Morris's conjecture that the British Ministry—

" will rather concede a little than go to war with Spain, if France is in force to join her ally ; but they want to be in a position to deal advantageously with us in case they should find it necessary. I believe the debates in Council on this subject have been pretty high, and that the American party has been outvoted, or else that in feeling the ground they have found themselves too weak to bring forward the question."

At any rate, Morris had to be content for the present and so re-crossed the Channel. But early in December he was again back in London, with several pressing business affairs on his hands. For a fortnight he gave himself up to dull daily conferences with City men. He continued to go out a good deal in the evening; but the stiffness of London society manners never quite suited his tastes, and he invariably found the rout and the evening entertainment tiresome.

"There was no pleasant intercourse between the men and the women. I go one evening to the Duchess of Gordon's. Here in one room the young are dancing, and in another the old are gambling at a faro-table. I stay but a little while, for the party is to me vastly dull. The male dancers are very indifferent."

On December 18 he again presented himself at the Foreign Office, hoping to find his business had advanced, but he did not see the Duke. He told the Under-Secretary, Burges:

"I have presented myself to let them know that I am alive; that I shall write from hence to America that I leave town next week; that I will wait on the Duke at such time as he may indicate; that if I learn nothing more than that things are just as I left them I shall merely say so; that it may be worth their while to consider whether the measures proposed last session in Congress respecting the commerce with this country may not be adopted, and what the consequence would be."

This was decisive enough—to the point of brusqueness. But Morris was now growing angry at the treatment his country was receiving from the British Government. One evening, dining with Lord Lansdowne, he was goaded into giving the company "my honest sentiments respecting Britain and America, which are not pleasing, but I do not mean to please."

Towards the close of June the startling news came from Paris that the King and Queen of France had made their escape from the Tuileries and had got six or seven hours' start of their keepers. " This," notes Morris, " will produce some considerable consequences. If they get off safe, a war is inevitable; and if retaken, it will probably suspend for some time all monarchical government in France."

He was anxious to get back to Paris, because " I think the confusion will work favourably to the sale of American lands."

In a postscript he writes the words : " Eleven at night. Intelligence is received that the royal fugitives are intercepted near Metz."

On receipt of this news Morris crossed the channel and was much implicated in French affairs for months.[1] When he returned to London, Morris at last prevailed upon the new Foreign Secretary, Lord Grenville, to name a British Minister Plenipotentiary to " the Court of President Washington " at Philadelphia.

It was perhaps not a great deal, after all his efforts, to have accomplished. But it was a beginning; it marked the inception of regular and mutual diplomatic relations ; for in return for Great Britain's appointment of George Hammond, the President sent a Minister Plenipotentiary to London.

For this post Morris himself might have been chosen, but affairs in France were fast reaching a tragic crisis, and Washington felt that in Gouverneur Morris he had just the masterful, intrepid spirit needed to urge and safeguard American interests there.

On February 6, 1792, Morris wrote in his Diary :

" Mr. Constable calls on me this morning and tells me I am appointed Minister Plenipotentiary to the Court of France. Mr. Penn, where I dine, congratulates me on my appointment, but expresses his regret that it is not to this country."

BIOGRAPHICAL NOTE

Gouverneur Morris was elected to the Senate in 1800. He became Chairman of the New York Canal Commission, and was otherwise interested in public works. He died in 1816.

[1] See : *America's Ambassadors to France.*

4

CHAPTER III

PINCKNEY AND JAY (1792–1796)

THE sending by the British Government of George Hammond to America removed all objections to the appointment of a regular Minister to the Court of St. James, and Thomas Pinckney accordingly received his credentials.[1] It was a good choice had it not been for the disastrous and unexpected events produced by the French Revolution. Pinckney was a tall, handsome man of forty-one, bearing a certain physical resemblance to General Washington. His great-grandfather emigrated to South Carolina in 1692, and his father had been agent for that colony in London about the middle of the following century. Thus it came about that Thomas Pinckney and his elder brother Charles were educated in England at Westminster School, Christ Church, Oxford, and at the Middle Temple, where they were duly called to the Bar. Both returned to America, fought during the Revolution, and were rewarded with political honours by their native State.

The English Whigs at least gave Pinckney a cordial reception. Under-Secretary Burges wrote to his chief, Lord Auckland :

" We have a new American Minister, Mr. Pinckney, an old friend and brother Westminster of mine, whose manners and temper exactly qualify him for the place he has taken. I have known him about thirty years and I do not know a more worthy and excellent man."

If the King and Court were not exactly cordial, they were at least civil. Unfortunately the impression prevailed, not

---

[1] The name was originally spelt Pincheni. Pinqueny, Pinckney, Pinkini and Pinkney are variations of that original. The last-named spelling was adopted by another American family, of which William Pinkney was an illustrious member.

only in England but throughout Europe, that America sympathized with the French Revolution, and this made Pinckney's position awkward from the first. It needed more than Minister Morris's dangerous Royalist exploits in Paris to counteract the general belief in American approval of the revolutionaries.

To Thomas Jefferson, now Secretary of State, Pinckney wrote (December 12, 1792) :

" In my first communication I mentioned the civility with which I was received at St. James and at the office of Foreign Affairs. The only circumstance worth mentioning in my conference with the King was that Lord North's rope of sand appeared not to have been entirely effaced from his Majesty's memory ; so I infer from his mentioning the different circumstances between the Northern and Southern parts of our country tending to produce disunion. I declined entering on any discussion, observing only that we agreed very well at present and hoped a continuance of the same disposition.

" I have been constant in every attendance at the King's levées since the return of the Court to St. James, and placing myself in the circle of foreign ministers, his Majesty never fails to have a few moments' conversation with me on the weather, or other topic equally important, but the great variety of incidents that has lately occurred in European politics he never touches upon with me.

" Indeed not only the King but most of his courtiers and (except the Pole) all the foreign ministers, seem to consider the Americans as united in principles with the French, and as having, by example at least, assisted in exciting the commotion with which a great part of Europe is convulsed, and consequently are not very agreeable associates. Some of the foreign ministers with whom I am most intimate have told me that this idea prevails ; at the same time they have been polite enough to make, themselves, a proper distinction between the modes of conducting the Revolutions in the two different countries.

" Although I consider this an honourable testimony of the great conduct of my country, it serves to keep me at a greater distance from those to whom it is my business to have most intercourse than would otherwise be the case. The Queen received me with great affability at my audience ; but at the drawing-rooms, though she condescends to say a few words to me, yet she gives a marked priority to any person near. It is, in short, very evident that I am by no means in favour in any of the apartments of St. James.

" You may be sure that I avoid everything that tends to widen the distance, by keeping as clear as possible of all European politics, by forbearing all mention of the cold civility that I experience, and in general by aiming at a conciliatory conduct. Of the Diplomatic Corps the Minister from Poland converses freely with me, and we are on good terms ; the rest consider me as one who, with respect to the present European politics, neither rejoices in their joy nor is afflicted with their sorrow. They have all, however, paid me the compliment of the first visit, except the Russian Minister, and with whom I have no acquaintance.

" P.S.—Since writing the above the Russian Minister has sent me his card."

The Minister had established his Legation at No. 1 Great Cumberland Place. Mrs. Pinckney, very shy and in delicate health, could be of little assistance socially to her husband. One of her friends had complained even before she had sailed for England :

"Mrs. Pinckney has too great fondness for retirement. She has been in tears ever since her husband's appointment."

The English climate only increased her frailty, and in less than two years the poor lady breathed her last.

Soon after Pinckney's arrival, the stream of refugees from France began pouring into England. The American Legation in London, as in Paris, became the goal and sanctuary of large numbers of these. France—particularly the French aristocracy—had helped America, they argued ; reasonably enough, it was now America's turn to help them.

Minister Pinckney they regarded " as a species of electric battery so highly charged with national gratitude that the slightest touch would elicit a response." [1]

But Pinckney could do little for them, and for a long time his intercession, even for the most illustrious amongst the *émigrés*, was worse than useless.

---

[1] Rev. C. C. Pinckney : *Thomas Pinckney*.

THOMAS PINCKNEY.

The fate which had overtaken Lafayette, although not so tragic as that of countless other French nobles, could hardly leave Americans unmoved. While Lafayette lay in an Austrian dungeon, his brother-in-law the Vicomte de Noailles escaped to London on his way to America. There Pinckney gave him the following letter to Washington :

"LONDON, *March* 12, 1793.

" M. de Noailles, who is the bearer of this letter, requires no introduction to you. His situation and services during the late war you witnessed ; and you are well acquainted with the subsequent events which placed him in his present predicament. You will find him warmly participating in the anxiety we all feel for the welfare of our friend M. de Lafayette. On this subject I have only to say that I have done whatever I thought consistent with propriety in an unauthorized official manner to alleviate his misfortunes ; and that I shall esteem myself peculiarly happy if I can be instrumental in testifying the gratitude of my country to one who has rendered her such eminent services, in any way that may be deemed expedient."

Washington, as we know, did his utmost, but several years were to pass before Lafayette obtained his freedom.

In February 1793 the French threw down the gauntlet to Great Britain. It was quickly seen that the war thus declared would react on the relations of both countries with America. To begin with, it opened up the prospect of a brisk contraband trade with both combatants, but especially France, and the enterprising New England merchants and shipowners got busy at once.

But Britain had no intention that the enemy should receive supplies from America if her fleet could stop such traffic, and similarly France took instant measures to prevent American commerce with Britain. Orders were issued for the capture of all American ships found carrying contraband goods. Naturally, the British navy was far the more effective of the two Powers, and managed to blockade the operations of the New England skippers, to their corresponding discontent. Just then, too, a large party in America had got what was called the " Bastille fever." They were animated by a sort of " love-frenzy " for France and the revolutionary doctrines.[1] Jefferson, Monroe and his friends approved as far as they dared with all the revolutionary excesses in Paris which were so shocking Washington, Hamilton and the Federalists.

When the President issued his Proclamation of Neutrality in April, America found herself between the devil and the deep sea. If her eager merchants tried to land cargoes in France, their ships were promptly captured or sunk by the British; if they attempted trade with Britain, they got scant mercy from the French navy and privateers. But this was a minor matter and could be condoned; their anger was chiefly directed against the Mother Country, as mistress of the seas. Besides, there was another cause of lively resentment. England was making trouble for them within their own territory. For the frontier posts continued to be held, with the accompanying monopoly of the fur trade and the restlessness and hostility of the border Indians. Congress was urged to take extreme measures, even to a declaration of war. On March 26, 1794, an embargo was proclaimed against British shipping which lasted two months. In the following month it was proposed to suspend all commercial intercourse with Britain. War really seemed likely, but, in spite of the fiery New England skippers, the western speculators and the fur traders, war was the last thing Washington wanted.[2]

"Peace [he wrote, in one of his stately periods] ought to be pursued with unremitted zeal before the last resource, which has so often been the scourge of nations, and cannot fail to check the advancing prosperity of the United States, is contemplated."

[1] " French fashions for the first time invaded our country; and civic feasts, liberty caps, and the salutation of ' citizen ' and ' citizeness ' became common in our streets."—C. R. Fish : *American Diplomacy.* Elsewhere this writer observes that that sympathy with France was at least partly due to the general prosperity which resulted from the outbreak of hostilities.

[2] "I am led by several little circumstances, not easily detailed or explained, to believe that the late administration looked upon a war with us as inevitable, and I am of opinion that the instructions of November 6 were influenced by that idea. I do also believe that Lord Dorchester was instructed to act conformably to that idea, and that Simcoe was governed by it."— Jay to Washington, July 21, 1794.

There was another way out. He and Hamilton agreed that it was imperative to renew negotiations with London to get the Treaty of 1783 fulfilled or a new one to take its place. But who was the man to undertake such a task ? Minister Pinckney could not be expected to succeed. He was already, Morris reported, looked at rather askance in British Court circles. Respectable and amiable, he lacked driving power. Besides, Pinckney was, from Hamilton's standpoint, an outsider ; he did not belong to the inner Federalist clique and could not know what was in the mind of the administration.[1]

The President would like to have sent Hamilton himself, but such an appointment was hopeless—the great Federalist had too many enemies and the Senate would have vetoed it. It was then that Hamilton suggested the Chief Justice, John Jay, " the only man in whose qualifications for success there would be perfect confidence."

True, there was opposition even to Jay. It was urged that he had monarchical principles, that he was indifferent about the great question of Mississippi navigation, that he was attached to England and disliked France, and moreover, that the Chief Justice of the United States should not be sent on such a mission. But the real objection of the mob arose from the fear that war might be averted.

" You have no idea [wrote John Adams] what horror some persons are in, lest peace should continue. The prospect of peace throws them into distress."

Another thing that the opposition feared was that if Jay succeeded in making a good treaty, his success would weaken, if not destroy, Jefferson's chances for the Presidency.

But Jay himself held another opinion. He said, before he had heard of his selection :

" Such were the prejudices of the American people that no man could form a treaty with Great Britain, however advantageous it might be to the country, who would not by his agency render himself so unpopular and odious as to blast all hope of political preferment."

[1] Pinckney, according to John Adams, was " a man of prejudices and strongly pro-Gallican," but this is not based on anything we now know of Pinckney's character.

At least in embarking upon his adventure he realized what was in store for him.

" If Washington shall think fit to call me to perform this service, I will go and perform it to the best of my abilities, foreseeing, as I do, the consequences to my personal popularity."

On May 12, 1794, Jay embarked for England. He was accompanied by his son Peter Augustus, and his secretary, Colonel John Trumbull, a remarkably able man, who had also become famous as a portrait painter.

Jay was then in his fiftieth year, tall, hook-nosed, with a pair of flashing blue eyes. He was descended from Pierre Jay, a French Huguenot, who after the Revocation of the Edict of Nantes had emigrated to America. He had no drop of English blood in his veins, which was a diplomatic advantage at the moment. " Not being of British descent, I cannot be influenced by that delicacy towards their national character, nor that partiality for it, which might otherwise be supposed not to be unnatural."

Nevertheless, he had imbibed all the English traits of mind, morals and manner, so that the English themselves found him indistinguishable from any of their own ruling class. He had received his education at King's College, New York (endowed from funds raised in England by his brother, who was knighted in consequence), and had early distinguished himself as a lawyer. During the War of Independence he had been sent by Congress as Minister to Spain, and afterwards he had taken a leading part in Paris, along with Adams and Franklin, over the Peace negotiations. We have seen him as Secretary of State in correspondence with Adams in London.

Washington's Instructions to Jay (written by Hamilton) were as follows :

" The mission upon which you are about to enter, as Envoy Extraordinary to the Court of London, has been dictated by considerations of an interesting and pressing nature.

" You will doubtless avail yourself of these to convince Mr. Pinckney, our Minister in Ordinary there, of the necessity of this measure, and will thus prevent any wound to his sensibility. He may be assured that it is the impression, which will naturally accompany this demonstration of the public sentiment, and not the smallest abatement of confidence in him, which has recommended a special appointment; nor will any of his usual functions be suspended, except so far as they may be embraced in the present commission. It would be unnecessary to add, but for the sake of manifesting this fact, and removing difficulties which may arise in your own breast, that you will communicate with him without reserve.

" A full persuasion is entertained that, throughout the whole negotiation, you will make the following its general objects : To keep alive in the mind of the British Minister that opinion which the solemnity of a special mission must naturally inspire, of the strong agitations excited in the people of the United States, by the disturbed condition of things between them and Great Britain ; to repel war, for which we are not disposed, and into which the necessity of vindicating our honour and our property may, but can alone, drive us ; to prevent the British Ministry, should they be resolved on war, from carrying with them the nation ; and, at the same time, to assert, with dignity and firmness, our rights, and our title to reparation for past injustice."

Jay's chief objects were thus enumerated : The execution by Britain of the Treaty ; compensation for the seizure of American ships ; a treaty of commerce and, in case the British Government were unfavourable, to effect co-operation with other European Powers in armed neutrality for the protection of neutral trade. International extradition was also desirable.

As to the commercial treaty, Jay was to obtain reciprocity of trade, especially with regard to the West Indies, and the limitation of the right of search, recognition of the doctrine that free ships make free goods, assent to the American contention concerning blockade, and also, if possible, fishing privileges in the North-East. The duration of the proposed treaty was to be fifteen years only. If Britain declined to agree, Jay was instructed to communicate with his Government and await further orders. He was to take no step which would infringe on America's treaty with France. But Jay had already discussed the whole subject freely with

Hamilton, King and the other Federalists, and he knew just how far he would be supported if he judged any deviation from his instructions necessary.

There was one pregnant passage in the President's letter:

"If the British Ministry should hint at any supposed predilection in the United States for the French nation, as warranting the whole or any part of these instructions, you will stop the progress of this subject, as being irrelative to the question in hand. It is a circumstance which the British nation have no right to object to us; because we are free in our affections and independent in our government. But it may be safely answered, upon the authority of the correspondence between the Secretary of State and Mr. Hammond, that our neutrality has been scrupulously observed." [1]

"The passage across the Atlantic was pleasant [records Trumbull in his *Autobiography*], and on the 1st of June we must have been near, almost within hearing, of the decisive naval battle which was fought on that day, between the British and the French fleet."

Such a moment was not the most propitious for exacting concessions from the British Government, especially on the part of a country without a navy or an army. Fortunately, the British Foreign Office was in the hands at that moment of a Minister who genuinely desired peace rather than war with America.

On his arrival in London, Jay put up at the Royal Hotel, Pall Mall, and at once got into touch with the resident American Minister, Pinckney. The latter had already written his brother:

"As to Jay's mission, if I should say that I had no unpleasant feelings on the occasion I should not be sincere; but . . . convinced of the expediency of adopting any honourable measure which may tend to avert the calamities of war, I consider Mr. Jay's appointment, from the solemnity of the mission, supported by his established reputation, diplomatic experience and general talents, as the most probable method of effecting this purpose."

It was well said and Pinckney lent a generous support

[1] Instructions to Jay dated Philadelphia, May 6, 1794.

to Jay, who never encroached on the ordinary functions of the Legation. Pinckney, however, was immensely relieved when he was ordered by the President to go on a special mission to Madrid. In his absence the Secretary of Legation, William Allen Deas, discharged his duties.

Jay called upon Lord Grenville at the Foreign Office, and had not been five minutes with that nobleman before perceiving his benevolent character and intentions.

William Wyndham, Lord Grenville, was Pitt's cousin, the son of George Grenville, the Prime Minister (1763–5) who was responsible for the Stamp Act, and the brother of Earl Temple. He was scholarly, amiable and high-minded, and he and Jay were destined to become warm personal friends.

With both sides reasonably inclined, it seemed a pity to befog the issue with laborious correspondence. At the first interview, therefore, the American suggested the plan of a *viva-voce* intercourse, at least " until there should appear a probability of coming to some amicable mutual understanding." Grenville agreed. They would employ no secretaries or copyists, and so escape the influence of public opinion and national feeling outside. The negotiation was not to be, observed Jay—

" a trial of diplomatic fencing, but a solemn question of peace or war between two peoples, in whose veins flowed the blood of a common ancestry, and on whose continued good understanding might perhaps depend the future freedom and happiness of the human race."

The talks, not less earnest because informal, went on weekly, sometimes daily, in Downing Street.

Meanwhile, other diplomatic events in which an American Minister figures were occurring on the other side of the Channel.

Robespierre's agent in America, Gênet, had made himself so objectionable by his high-handed conduct that Washington had insisted on his recall ; this naturally involved the recall also of Morris, the American Minister in Paris. He had been succeeded by James Monroe, one of Jefferson's pro-Gallican friends and adherents. Between Jay and Monroe there was a gulf fixed.

It is not surprising that Monroe and his friends should have looked askance at the objects of Jay's mission or that Jay was anxious to conclude his business before Monroe reached Paris, where he would be obliged " to quiet the apprehensions of France and prevent her from taking umbrage " at his treaty.

On June 23 Jay reported to Washington :

" The observations I have hitherto made induce me to believe that the war with France is popular, and that a war with us would be unpopular. The word *Jacobin* is here a term of reproach, and used as such among the common people. They who wish the reform of this Government do, I apprehend, wish a certain degree of success to the present French cause, not because they like it, but because they think such success would promote their favourite objects. I often hear gentlemen converse on these subjects, but I think it prudent to be reserved ; as to their internal parties and divisions, I make it a rule to remain silent."

While he was thus engaged with Grenville at the Foreign Office, Jay was going about London with his eyes open, making friends and acquaintances, and studying the conditions of the day. In one of his letters to Washington he wrote :

" Ideas of the rights of man, and the inferences deducible from them, are spreading among people. Veneration for royalty, abstractedly considered, has abated ; and although the King is popular, yet it is said that the Prince of Wales and the Duke of York are not. The prosperity of Britain results from and depends on many causes ; complicated machines are most liable to derangement. Should there be a scarcity of corn, want of employment to the manufacturers, or signal convulsions or disasters in the East or West Indies, or in Ireland, or on the sea, the Government would find their task very arduous. Alarm and distress will abate pride and obstinacy ; and when the multitude begin to feel severely their passions frequently take a new and dangerous direction."

He was specially interested in King George III, who had received him cordially, and his character-sketch of the monarch deserves quoting :

" Before I came here, I had no idea that the King was so popular as he is ; his reign having been marked by national calamities produced by reprehensible measures. But his popularity is owing to his private rather than his official character. As a man, there is much in him to commend ; and I have not heard any vice imputed to him. As a domestic man, affectionate and attentive to his queen and children and affable to all about him, he is universally esteemed. Few men are so punctual in all things. He patronizes the arts and sciences. He pays uncommon attention to agriculture, and delights in his farms. He lays out about ten thousand pounds a year in improving and embellishing the royal estates. He is industrious, sober and temperate, and has acquired much various knowledge and information. He converses with ease, and often with adroitness, and has an uncommon memory. They who ought to know him concur in these accounts. That he is a great and a wise king, I have not heard asserted. That he does (to use a vulgar expression) as well as he knows how, seems not to be doubted ; but yet some say that he occasionally is cunning instead of being wise. I have heard him described as being a great man in little things, and as being generally well-intentioned, pertinacious and persevering."

The American Minister soon had occasion to know that the King was conciliatory. Jay launched a protest against a particularly flagrant capture of American ships. Grenville wrote at once, after consultation with the King—

" to assure Mr. Jay that it is his Majesty's wish that the most *complete and impartial justice* should be done to all the citizens of America, who may, in fact, have been injured by any of the proceedings above mentioned. All experience shows that a naval war, extending over the four quarters of the globe, must unavoidably be productive of some inconveniences to the commerce of neutral nations, and that no care can prevent some irregularities in the course of those proceedings, which are universally recognized as resulting from the just rights incident to all belligerent Powers. But the King will always be desirous that these inconveniences and irregularities should be as much limited as the nature of the case will admit, and that the fullest opportunity should be given to all to prefer their complaints, and to obtain redress and compensation where they are due."

On August 5 Jay reported to the President :

" Our prospects become more and more promising as we advance in the business. . . . A treaty of commerce is on the carpet. . . . The King observed to me the other day, ' Well, sir, I imagine you begin to see that your mission will probably be successful.' ' I am happy, may it please your Majesty, to find that you entertain that idea.' ' Well, but don't you perceive that it is like to be so ? ' ' There are some recent circumstances ' (the answer to my representation, etc.) ' which induce me to flatter myself that it will be so.' He nodded with a smile, signifying that it was to those circumstances that he alluded."

Towards the middle of September Jay wrote Hamilton that he intended to conclude the business on admissible terms : " I shall do it and risk consequences, rather than by the delay of waiting for opinions and instructions, hazard a change in the disposition of this Court."

Monroe had ere this arrived in Paris and was making himself conspicuous by his zeal, even though Robespierre had gone to the guillotine and his own credentials were thereby invalidated. Monroe's oration to the Convention was printed in London, and has, wrote Jay, " caused a disagreeable sensation in the public mind here."

But the Treaty was now ready, every precaution being taken that no detail should leak out and upset Monroe's precarious position in Paris.

Jay had been instructed to obtain the surrender of the frontier, compensation for spoliations, and compensation for the negro slaves. As to the latter the American contention (framed by Jay himself when he was Secretary of State) was that three thousand negroes were within the British lines at the time of the Evacuation, that these slaves, relying on proclamations that offered freedom, had retired with the army, in spite of the clause in the Treaty of Peace which provided that the troops should be withdrawn without " carrying away any negroes or other property." To this contention Grenville replied that once within the British lines, slaves became free and could not be regarded as property, and therefore refused to consider compensation. Secretly Jay, as an anti-slavery man, sympathized with this reasoning.

At any rate, he waived the claim, although in doing so he must have shocked his Southern friend and colleague, Pinckney.

It was agreed that the western posts should be surrendered by June 12, 1796. Jay demanded compensation for such detention, but Grenville reminded him that it was wholly owing to Congress having allowed the States to prevent the recovery of British debts.

The British Government agreed to make full and complete compensation to American citizens for losses sustained " by reason of irregular or illegal captures or condemnations under colour of authority or commissions from his Majesty " wherever adequate compensation could not be had by law, such damages to be ascertained by a board of five commissioners to sit in London. The claims were to be decided " according to the merits of the several cases and to justice, equity and the law of nations." These commissioners were also to hear the claims of British subjects for losses by captures within American waters and to award the compensation payable by the United States.

As to the British pre-revolutionary debts in America, in all cases where the collection had been barred or their value impaired by " legal impediment " since the peace, full compensation should be made by America, following the judgment of a board of five commissioners which was to meet in Philadelphia.

Disputes concerning boundaries were referred to joint commissioners. British and American citizens holding lands in the United States or in any British possession were confirmed in their rights, a clause which was much objected to in America.

Finally, war between the two countries should never be made the pretext for confiscation of debts or annulment of contracts between individuals. This latter constituted a novel principle in international diplomacy.

But it was the commercial clauses in the Treaty which came to arouse the chief hostility in America, although, for the first time, reciprocal freedom of commerce was established between the two countries. American vessels were admitted to trade between their own ports and the East Indies, and

American vessels of not over seventy tons burden were permitted to carry merchandise of American growth or manufacture to the British West Indies and export to their ports West Indian products, on condition that the United States prohibited and restrained the carrying away of molasses, sugar, coffee, cocoa or cotton, in American vessels, either from the British islands or the United States to any part of the world except the United States, reasonable sea stores excepted.

That cotton was destined to be one of the great staples of American export never occurred to Jay. He only thought of it as a peculiarly West Indian product.[1]

Contraband was defined and privateers were required to give security not to injure the commerce of the neutral. Throughout, however, the Treaty implied that the flag does not cover the enemy's goods and that provisions might become contraband—all of which was a part of current international law.

Jay, of course, failed to obtain an article against Impressment, although he urged it on Grenville repeatedly. He was glad to be quit of his labour, and at last, with a thankful heart, he could write home to his friend Hamilton (November 19, 1794) :

" My task is done ; whether *finis coronat opus*, the President, Senate, and public will decide.

" This letter goes by the packet, and the Treaty with it ; some parts of it require elucidation to common readers. I have not time for comments ; Lord Grenville is anxious to dismiss the packet ; I therefore write in haste. If this Treaty fails, I despair of another. If satisfactory, care should be taken that the public opinion be not misled respecting it, for this reason the sooner it is ratified and published the better. I really think the good disposition of this country should be cherished. I came here in the moment of exultation and triumph on account of Lord Howe's victory. From that day to this I have experienced no change in sentiments or conduct relative to the negotiation. I must, though not without

---

[1] It is entertaining to read that in 1794, when an American ship entered Liverpool with eight bags of cotton fibre as part of her cargo, it was confiscated as an unlawful importation " on the assumption that so large a quantity could not have been the produce of the United States."

JOHN JAY.

reluctance, conclude ; not being fit for a winter voyage, I shall stay here till spring. Indeed, I shall want repairs before I am quite fit for any voyage. God bless you."

To this he added handsomely :

" I ought not to omit mentioning the acknowledgments due from me to Mr. Pinckney, with whom I have every reason to be satisfied, and from whose advice and opinions I have derived light and advantage in the course of the negotiation. His approbation of the Treaty gives me pleasure, not merely because his opinion corresponds with my own, but also from sentiments I entertain of his judgment and candour."

On the same day Jay penned the following to Oliver Ellsworth :

" The negotiation is terminated by a Treaty. It will with this letter go by the packet, which, in expectation of this event, has been detained above a week.

" In my opinion, we have reason to be satisfied. It is expedient that the ratification should not be unnecessarily delayed. The best disposition towards us prevails in the Cabinet, and I hope they will have reason to be content with the delicacy and propriety of our conduct towards them and the nation. Further concessions on the part of Great Britain cannot, in my opinion, be attained. The Minister flatters himself that this Treaty will be very acceptable to our country, and that some of the articles in it will be received as unequivocal proofs of good-will. We have industriously united our efforts to remove difficulties, and few men would have persevered in such a dry, perplexing business, with so much patience and temper as he has done."

" These [writes in our own day John Spencer Bassett of the Treaty] were hard terms from an unforgiving mother. In return for complete freedom and trade we got the right to send our ships to the East Indies and our insignificant vessels to the West Indies. We might not carry the island products to Europe, and we bound ourselves not to carry cotton across the Atlantic. The mention of the cotton-gin in the same year was probably not known to Jay. Had this feature of the agreement gone into force, it would have wrought a great injury to the southern States. . . .

5

" Jay's treaty was a home-thrust at our French alliance.
. . . If left, as was probable, to Federalist hands for execution,
it would be a serious blow to French influence in the United
States." [1]

Other leading American writers, such as Russell Fish,
concede the distinct advantages accruing to America from
the Treaty, and the unsoundness of the contemporary
public view. A few objections were, however, well founded.

" Jay himself realized very keenly the unsatisfactory
nature of some of its provisions. He did not attempt in his
letter to Randolph to justify them, *per se*. His chief defence
. . . was that it was the best that could be made at that
time and that it would be much better than none at all ;
both of which propositions were entirely true. Moreover,
the objectionable clause about West Indian trade was to
last for only two years, the clause about contraband did not
abandon the position thitherto taken by the United States,
and the prevailing clauses were identical with those in treaties
thitherto made between England, France and Holland. It
may be added that Jay had endeavoured to secure the
insertion of a clause abolishing privateering altogether, but
Grenville was not prepared for so radical a step." [2]

" To unprejudiced eyes [comments Pellew], after the
lapse of a hundred years, considering the mutual exasperation
of the two peoples, the pride of England in the successes in
the war with France, the weakness and division of the
United States, the Treaty seems a very fair one." [3]

" Jay's treaty [in W. G. Sumner's opinion] was a master-
piece of diplomacy, considering the time and the circumstances of this country." [4]

But perhaps the most convincing tribute to the real
advantages America derived under the Treaty came from
the uncompromising Lord Sheffield, who in 1812 welcomed
the opportunity of a war which would give Great Britain
the chance of annulling the Treaty of 1795, in which Lord
Grenville had been " duped by Jay the American."

[1] J. S. Bassett : *The Federalist System.*
[2] Willis Fletcher Johnson : *America's Foreign Relations.*
[3] *Life of Andrew Jackson.*
[4] *Life of John Jay.*

" I, on my part [wrote Grenville to Jay in 1796], should have thought that I very ill consulted the interests of my country, if I had been desirous of terminating the points in discussion between us on any other footing than that of mutual justice and reciprocal advantage ; nor do I conceive that any just objection can be stated to the great work which we jointly accomplished, except on the part of those who believe the interests of Great Britain and the United States to be in contradiction with each other or who wish to make them so."

The Treaty was signed and dispatched in duplicate by separate ships. Jay stayed on in London for some months longer, hoping to get word from America of the manner of the Treaty's reception before his departure. He well knew how it would be loathed in France.

Jay made many friends in England—the Bishop of London (whose parents were American born), Henry Dundas, Sir William Scott, Sir Henry Newenham, Edmund Burke (to whom he afterwards sent cuttings of apple trees), Lord Chancellor Loughborough (who invited him to attend the trial of the Pyx and sent him a brace of grouse), Sir John Sinclair (who invited him to his country seat), Lord and Lady Mornington, Jeremy Bentham and Dugald Stewart. William Wilberforce wrote in his Diary :

" Dined at Hampstead to meet Jay (the American envoy), his son, etc.—quite American—sensible. I fear there is little spirit of religion in America ; something of French, tinctured with more than English simplicity of manners ; very pleasing, well-informed men." [1]

Months passed, and still all that Jay could hear from America was that it was believed that a Treaty with England had been signed. By March 1795 the Treaty itself had not arrived. It afterwards appeared that the British postal authorities, by a " strange negligence," managed to put both packets aboard the same ship, the *Tankerville*, which went to the bottom. Meantime, all sorts of gossip was afloat in America concerning the Treaty and the friends of France were filled with angry suspicions. Jay resolved to

[1] *Life of Wilberforce.*

wait no longer.   He took leave of Grenville, making to the Minister the final friendly observation that " if America was set right as to the affair of the Indians and relieved from West India judges and privateers not better than Indians, ill-humour having nothing to feed upon, would die away."

On Jay's return the Treaty was published, and a wave of popular indignation swept through the country.   Jay was burned in effigy, and his friends who attempted to defend the Treaty were howled down and even stoned.   But President Washington never flinched at all this clamour.   He knew it was either the Treaty or war with England.   Congress eventually assented, and on April 30, 1796, the Treaty went into operation.

It was found to work better than had been expected by its detractors.   Grenville had promised Jay some concessions not formally included, and he kept his promise.   The Admiralty Courts in the West Indies were overhauled.   The Senate had rejected the East Indian article, but trade with the islands was, with certain restrictions, thrown open to the Americans.

" The Maritime New Englanders [says Professor Mowat], who had begun by an unreflecting hatred of the Treaty, soon came to see its solid advantages for them—a share in the British East India trade, and indeed the avoidance of war itself with Great Britain."[1]

Jay, then, had succeeded ; but on his political fortunes the Treaty exerted a most baleful effect.   It cost him his popularity and his chances for the Presidency.

Meanwhile, Minister Thomas Pinckney continued in London.   In Spain he had displayed real ability as a diplomat by negotiating the once-famous Treaty of San Ildefonso.

" It is surprising now [remarks his descendant][2] to read of the enthusiastic reception of this Treaty and of the vast importance attached to it in the public mind.   The successful negotiation was hailed with a bursting of applause which established the reputation of the negotiator as a skilful diplomatist and very nearly seated him in the Vice-President's chair."

The Treaty concerned the western boundary of the

[1] Mowat : *Diplomatic Relations.*   [2] Rev. C. C. Pinckney : *Thomas Pinckney.*

Mississippi and the Florida boundary, together with navigation privileges—all of which, although valuable at the time,
were soon to be superseded by the purchase both of Louisiana
and Florida by the United States.

A century later Senator Lodge uttered this tribute :

" Thomas Pinckney, who really did something, who did
work worth doing and without many words, has been
forgotten, while many of his contemporaries, who simply
made a noise, are freshly remembered in the pages of
history." [1]

In view of Pinckney's Spanish performance it is rather
interesting to speculate whether he would have been able to
have done what Jay did in London. Had his merits been
underrated ? One inclines to the belief that Pinckney was
too heavily handicapped at the English Court by his English
education, his American combatant record and his former
pro-French sentiments, to have produced the right impression,
have created the right atmosphere in English Court circles.

As to Pinckney's pro-Gallicanism, if he ever had any, it
must have perished with Louis XVI. He organized the
Americans in London into a Committee of Relief, and met
demands of the French *émigrés* as far as he was able. But
his best efforts could not content them : some were openly
insolent ; others went sorrowfully from the Legation murmur-
ing against the ingratitude of republics.

Up to the close of his mission the Minister was deluged
with letters from English prisons and from prison-ships along
the coast, complaining of the illegal detention of American
seamen accused of being deserters from the British navy and
imprisoned until they had agreed to serve. Here is one
of these letters from the Legation records :

" FALMOUTH, *May* 18, 1795.
" On board H.M. ship *Galatea.*

" HONOURED SIR,—
" I write wishing to let you know that I was taken in a
French ship by the *Galatea* frigate, that I was forced to stay
on board the *Galatea*, for I was not willing to enter the

---

[1] H. C. Lodge : *Life of Washington.*

service. But I was obliged to and was threatened to be sent to the East Indies if I would not enter—and so I would let you know that I am an American. I would wish to have my clearance if possible for I am in much distress. I can prove I am an American by Thomas Bell and James Isaacs, they was taken on board the same ship. I would be glad if you would let me have my clearance if possible. I have not taken any Bounty yet. We are going out soon so direct your letter to Plymouth or Portsmouth. Witness my hand,

"MELZAR HATCH.

P.S.—Mark Nelson and Richard Smith remain on board in like condition."

The worthy Melzar's hopes of instant release were not fulfilled. All that the American Minister could do was to address a letter to the Foreign Secretary.

"Mr. Pinckney, Minister Plenipotentiary of the United States of America, presents his compliments to Lord Grenville and begs leave to call his attention to the case of Melzar Hatch and three other seamen, detained on board H.M.S. *Galatea* in British waters. They claim to be American sailors and offer proof in support of their claim.

"Mr. Pinckney requests Lord Grenville to endeavour to obtain an order for their release as soon as possible."

There were a good many such requests made, and the grievances were doubtless just.

Lord Castlereagh avowed at a later period that no fewer than "three thousand five hundred seamen in the British Navy claimed their discharge as American citizens, of whom one thousand seven hundred were probably entitled to it."

A sailor named John Pridy wrote (August 9, 1795) that—

"the treatment on board an English man-of-war is so different from what we might expect as American subjects, as being at such a distance from our families and uncertainty of their situation, makes us very uneasy. . . . Consider, Sir, after an absence of two years and upward from a wife and five helpless children what my situation must be, and what theirs is, to lose a husband and a father and be in the service of another country against inclination, unable to afford them any relief or comfort—such is the situation of me . . .

"JOHN PRIDY."

Minister Pinckney was insistent, and in six weeks Pridy went home to his family on an American ship.

Pinckney's mission drew to a close. Rufus King had written to Alexander Hamilton :

" Mr. Pinckney has asked leave to return home : he will now add the goodwill of those who have been so gratified with the Spanish Treaty."

To this Hamilton replied (May 4, 1796) :

" In the event of Pinckney's return to this country, I am of opinion, all things considered, it is expedient you should replace him."

Two months later the Minister took his leave of the King and sailed for America towards the close of the year. It is a curious fact that while on his homeward voyage his elder brother, Charles Cotesworth Pinckney, was on his way as American Minister to France. The vessels which bore them passed in mid-ocean.

BIOGRAPHICAL NOTES

Pinckney became Federalist candidate for President in an unsuccessful attempt to frustrate Adams. He was subsequently member of Congress. In the War of 1812 he commanded a district as Major-General. He spent the last years of his life in retirement at Charleston, and died in 1818.

Jay was elected Governor of New York State on his return and re-elected in 1798. Refusing the Chief Justiceship he retired to his estate, dying in 1829.

CHAPTER IV

RUFUS KING (1796–1802)

RUFUS KING was one of Hamilton's close friends and satellites. Although only forty-one, he had already served eight years in the American Senate. Born in Maine and educated at Harvard, he had done a little soldiering and some rather more successful lawyering when he met and married an heiress, the beautiful Miss Alsop of New York. After his marriage he settled down to a political career. With Hamilton he became especially intimate, was one of his most ardent supporters, and when the Jay Treaty was attacked, collaborated with him in the famous letters signed "Camillus," which made a deep impression on the thinking community.

King is described by a contemporary as being "an uncommonly handsome man in face and form, he had a powerful mind, well cultivated, and was a dignified and graceful speaker. He had the appearance of one who was a gentleman by nature and had well improved all her gifts." [1]

"The mission to England," King wrote nearly a generation later, "I was desirous to have. I had reason to know that General Washington had thought of giving it to me when Mr. P[inckney] was appointed. I unhesitatingly accepted it." The new Minister arrived in London July 23, 1796, with his wife and family of four small boys, together with his brother Cyrus, who acted as the Minister's secretary for a year or so.

A week after his arrival he was presented to King George III, who expressed his satisfaction with the prospect of a lasting friendship and harmony between the two countries. He declared, reported the Minister, "that he sincerely desired to live in friendship with the United States and

---

[1] W. Sullivan : *Public Men of the Revolution.*

58

he would execute with the most scrupulous good faith the Treaty lately concluded with them."

In the Treaty negotiated by Jay two of the articles provided for the adjustment of claims preferred by private individuals against the two Governments. The claims were to be adjusted by five commissioners under each article, two of each set to be chosen by the respective Governments and the fifth by lot cast by the four. One board was to sit in London, while another sat in Philadelphia. Amongst the members of the former were Christopher Gore, William Pinkney (afterwards Minister) and John Trumbull, the soldier-painter who had been secretary to Jay.

With this commission Rufus King was both personally and *ex-officio* in very close relations. " I think you must feel yourself," wrote his predecessor Pinckney from America, " much supported in the social line by all the public agents of the United States in London."

By this time it did not seem as if war between France and America could be far distant. Minister Monroe had carried things with such a high hand in Paris as to compromise his country, and Washington had recalled him. The office of Secretary of State, from which Jefferson had retired, was now filled by Timothy Pickering, who wrote King that " the dissatisfaction and uneasiness produced by Mr. Monroe's letters . . . had determined the President to recall him." It was far from certain, however, that his successor, General C. C. Pinckney, who arrived in December 1796, would be able to ride the storm.

Meanwhile, in his relations with the British Government, Minister King was bent on a conciliatory course. He showed a capacity to see two sides to a question. In spite of all the gratuitous advice he received " to stand up for America's rights," he was not to be goaded into impatience or ill-temper. American seamen were suffering from occasional impressment and Lord Grenville was certainly very slow in tackling this abuse.

" But," King wrote the Secretary of State (October 16, 1796), " as they [the British] believe that their national safety depends essentially upon their marine, they feel unusual caution relative to a stipulation that by mere possibility can deprive their navy of a single seaman, who is a real British subject, or that may even diminish the chance of obtaining the services of those who are not British subjects, but who by various pretences are detained in service as such. Hence . . . they desire to postpone a convention with us on this subject till the return of peace. In the meantime their officers may show more caution in impressing our seamen and more justice in discharging them when claimed.

" I have no reason to doubt the sincere desire of this Government to cultivate our esteem. I believe that the administration, together with the nation throughout, desire to live with us in friendship, and I do not think they would for a slight cause disagree with us. But their colony trade and marine are topics intimately and exclusively connected with their prosperity and security and more deeply with their prejudices. If we cannot agree, we may still remain friends."

After the debates, the impassioned philippics, the violent threats in and out of Congress on this question of Impressment, King's calm and reasonable words must have come as a relief to Washington, now on the eve of retiring from the Presidency.

Similarly, King was ready to admit that if the British marine captured American vessels, they were occasionally justified.

" Allured by the hope of high freights, some of our people have lent their names to cover enemy goods. One or two such cases having been detected, have cast a suspicion upon all our vessels employed in a similar trade." [1]

And two months later we find him reporting to Pickering :

" Very few American vessels have for some time past been taken by the British cruisers in these seas. Three or four American ships bound with rich cargoes from Surinam to Amsterdam have been sent in and are in the course of an Admiralty trial. *Some discoveries unfavourable to the American claims have in one or two of these cases been made and operate against others in the same trade.*" [2]

Of English good-will the Minister found abundant evidence, especially in the esteem felt for Washington.

[1] King to J. Q. Adams, November 10, 1796.
[2] This sentence was significantly sent in cypher.

" Nothing [he wrote, February 6, 1797] can exceed the applause that is given here to our Government, and no American who has not been in England can have a just idea of the admiration expressed among all parties of General Washington.   It is a common observation that he is not only the most illustrious, but also the most meritorious character that has hitherto appeared.   The King is without doubt a very popular character among the people of this nation ; it would be saying very much to affirm that, next to him, General Washington is the most popular character among them, and yet I verily believe this to be the fact."

Hardly was John Adams inaugurated as Washington's successor than the trouble with France reached an acute stage.

In revenge for the affront put upon France by Jay's Treaty, the Directory declined to receive Pinckney as a Minister.   Whereupon, the President nominated three commissioners to treat with the Foreign Minister, Talleyrand, whose demand for bribes gave rise to the notorious X.Y.Z. scandal.   With these American commissioners Minister King corresponded from the moment of their arrival in France. He told them to stand out firmly against Talleyrand, who had already tried to obtain a bribe from the British Government. " He has offered to make peace for a million pounds," King reported, " but the Cabinet last night gave a decided negative to such a proposal."

The American Minister took great pains to ascertain English public opinion.   On November 12, 1797, he wrote to Pickering :

" I employed a few weeks of the autumn in travelling through the interior, including some of the manufacturing towns of the country. . . . I endeavoured to form an estimate of the public opinion on the subject of the war, which for a long time past I have thought could not soon be concluded.   The result of my observations is that an opinion exists, which is nearly if not quite general, that this Government has sought peace with sincerity and that France has not been willing to make it on terms consistent with the safety and independence of England ; hence I infer that the nation, but without zeal or enthusiasm (for they show neither), will support the Government in carrying on the war, and that they will give this support in the belief that, without it, the nation must sink beneath the blows of their enemy."

A few weeks later he wrote :

" France perseveres in the capture and condemnation of our ships, she continues to decline to treat with us and even to receive our envoys, while she employs all the influence left her to discredit our Government and to divide our people. " If [argued King] we are denied the right of Embassy, if we cannot navigate the ocean in security, are not free to choose our own governors unless they are agreeable to France —then peace had no value and must be sacrificed." [1]

The faint remaining hope of amicable settlement with France seemed extinguished early in 1798.

The Directory passed a resolution aimed at all neutral shipping, and proceeded from words to acts.

" The French [remarked King, grimly] have a new theory for the future quiet and happiness of Europe, which is to be completely so, when France has nothing to ask, and the rest of Europe nothing to give."

About this time there came a communication from the American Minister in London regarding South America which deserves to be read in the light of events happening a quarter of a century later.

" Two points [he reports, February 26, 1798] have within a fortnight been settled in the English Cabinet respecting South America. If Spain is able to prevent the overthrow of her present Government and to escape being brought under the entire control of France, England (between whom and Spain, notwithstanding the war, a certain understanding appears to exist) will at present engage in no scheme to deprive Spain of the possession of South America. But if, as appears probable, the army destined against Portugal and which will march through Spain, or any other means which may be employed by France, shall overthrow the Spanish Government, and thereby place the resources of Spain and of her colonies at the disposal of France, *England will immediately commence the execution of a plan long since digested and prepared for the complete independence of South America.*

[1] To Pickering, December 23, 1797.

" If England engages in this plan she will at Philadelphia propose to the United States to co-operate in its execution. Miranda [1] will be detained here under one pretence or another until events shall decide the conduct of England.

" The revolution of Spain is decreed ; the attempt will be made, and the success is scarcely doubtful.   The President may therefore expect the overture of England, and will, I am persuaded, act upon it, under the influence of that wise and comprehensive policy which, looking forward to the destinies of the New World, shall in the beginning by great and generous deeds lay deep and firm the foundations of lasting accord between its rising Empires."

In America President Adams was facing not only the belligerent attitude of France, but a domestic political crisis. He dared not make any closer *rapprochement* with England, because the Jeffersonian party regarded that country as an enemy. As for joining hands with her in liberating the Spanish colonies, the prospect of further republics in the New World excited scant enthusiasm in the breast of John Adams.   France grew daily more overbearing and the British Government magnanimously offered, if so requested, to lend a convoy to American ships. To this proposal Pickering replied (April 2) :

" Threatening as is the aspect of our affairs with France, the President does not deem it expedient at this time to make any advances to Great Britain. The interests of her own commerce will on some occasions lead her to afford convoys to ours. . . .

" All this is very convenient in our present defenceless condition, but how disgraceful to the United States if we continue to depend on the protection of the British Navy without any reasonable exertion on our part to protect ourselves."

On the same day that Pickering was writing this in Philadelphia, Rufus King was penning in London a further message to the Secretary of State about South America.

" It should be known to you that South America is on the eve of revolution. England has prepared, and waits only for the events that the march of the French army into

[1] The Spanish Ambassador.

Spain will effect, to send an expedition to commence the revolution which shall make South America independent. If it is not assured to become independent by England, the work will be done by France, who will introduce there her detestable principles, divide it into small republics, put bad men at their head, and by these means facilitate her meditated enterprises against us. We have an immense interest in that event, as well as in the manner in which it shall be accomplished. England will at Philadelphia ask the co-operation of the United States. France has formed and will not be diverted from her plan respecting the United States. . . . Your mission must therefore fail, and if so, the sooner the better. . . . The French system once established in South America and the West Indies, we shall be in perpetual risque; on the other hand, the independence of South America on wise principles, will put an end to the old colony and commercial system to the United States and a new balance among nations. This communication is most strictly confidential."

Yet a few days later (April 6) he wrote that :

" England, since the arrival of Miranda here, but without his knowledge, has informed Spain that she will not countenance or assist the Spanish colonies in becoming independent, but that she will join her in resisting the endeavours of others to accomplish it."

Although King had nothing to complain of in his personal treatment, he was occasionally out of patience with British diplomatic methods.

" The indifference, the procrastination, and in short the exclusive principles by which they consider almost every question that is brought before them, should admonish us, as it has done every other nation, to depend on ourselves as much and upon others as little as possible." [1]

But when news came that America also was preparing for war with France, all indifference vanished. British Ministers and public opinion became galvanized.

" Men of all parties and every country [King writes, July 28] agree in applauding the moderation, the justice and the

[1] June 7th, 1798.

RUFUS KING.

wisdom of our Government. The publication of the French negotiations has given reputation to our country and besides been advantageous by closing the mouth of the apologists of France."

If war came, the Minister urged the Adams administration to take advantage of the great opportunity offered by the revolutionary movement in South America.

" The destiny of the New World is in our hands. We have a right and it is our duty to deliberate and act, not as secondaries, but as principals. The object and the occasion are such as we ought not on respect to ourselves and others to suffer to pass unimproved."

He reported (August 16) that he had had a lengthy talk with Grenville on the probability of a revolution in South America.

" He was fuller and more explicit than he had been on any former occasion, . . . treated of the practicability and of the means of effecting the measure, tended to show to me that they have at times considered and combined with their views of a future connexion with the United States the independence of the Spanish continental colonies. I did not perceive that they have any recent information about the present temper, disposition or plans of these colonies, a knowledge more easily procured from the United States than from Europe and which is indispensably requisite to the success of an enterprise to accomplish the Revolution. He spoke of the Government to be established in these as a revolution. He thought our system would attract and receive their approbation, and made some remarks upon the apprehensions to be entertained on account of their genius and character . . . and concluded by observing he was more and more confirmed in the opinion, that none but Englishmen and their descendants knew how to make a revolution."

It is odd to read that at the same time Vans Murray, the American Minister at the Hague, was suggesting to Rufus King England's help to expel the French from Holland during Bonaparte's absence in Egypt.

" Mr. Murray has on several occasions informed me that dispositions and views existed among certain influential persons in power, in the country where he is, to throw off the odious dominion of France; the object of these communications has been to procure from England assurances of support on certain points and relaxation in the rigour with which the war is carried on, particularly against the Dutch fisheries.

" These communications have always been so loose, informal and imperfect that I have, on his account as well as others, felt considerable embarrassment in permitting myself to be drawn into an affair, the real character whereof I was so little able to appreciate. So far as I could give precision to the principal wishes of these persons, they desire an assurance from England that she would discard the Prince of Orange, co-operate with them to extricate themselves from France and assist them in establishing a Government which should exclude the Stadtholderate."

So King saw Grenville, and went into the business freely and frankly. He was given assurance that should Holland again abolish the Stadtholderate, an arrangement ought certainly to be concluded with England. But farther than this Grenville would not go. The American Minister also did a good turn for Holland by suggesting a relaxation of the British blockade, which was causing much distress to the population dependent upon the Dutch fisheries.

No Englishman could have written with greater satisfaction of the victories of the British fleet than King when, on October 3, 1798, he reported to Secretary Pickering :

" Nelson's victory off the Nile has been more glorious and decisive than any recorded in the annals of naval Powers ; of thirteen ships of the line and four frigates which composed the French force, eleven ships and two frigates remained on the scene of action."

It is surprising to find how well informed the American envoy was of the course of French military policy and Napoleon's designs. In the same dispatch he writes :

" Buonaparte arrived at Alexandria three days after the English fleet had left it. Alexandria was immediately taken possession of : a corps of five thousand troops were left there. Buonaparte with about eighteen thousand men proceeded to Cairo, which he entered on the twenty-second July. The landing and progress of the French were resisted by the Mamelukes and Arabs; and tho' the contests were always unequal, there is reason to believe that the French suffered considerable loss.

" The ultimate object of Buonaparte is India; but his complete establishment in Egypt was first to be accomplished. A letter from the Commissary-General complains of this want of provisions and particularly of wine or of some substitute, without which the waters and climate of Egypt will, in his opinion, destroy the army. Buonaparte himself is disappointed and dejected; in a private letter to a friend at Paris he writes his despondency, expresses his intention to return to Paris this winter and gives orders that his house should be prepared to receive him."

But, of course, all this intelligence King received from Grenville, with whom he was now on the most intimate terms, as fast as the dispatches came in either at Cleveland Row or Dropmore. It was in 1798 as if the two countries were in close political alliance.

Grenville had a useful scheme concerning sugar duties to propose to the American Government—in order that both might raise supplies. He wrote to King (October 4):

" It is by mutual agreement we should retain so much of our drawback on sugars and *you* charge the export of that article for foreign consumption with such duties as would supply both of us a considerable revenue from foreign countries on an article in which our two nations have no competitors nor are likely to have any."

But the scheme was not espoused in America, although in the autumn of 1798 King is found urging on the President and Hamilton the seizure of the French sugar colonies, Louisiana and the French West Indies. The American War Department were sadly short of cannons and muskets, and King assured them that " in the event of an actual rupture with France, we shall instantly receive a part of what they [the British Ordnance Department] possess and that the supply shall be continued."

So the Minister saw General Rose, Lord Cornwallis's deputy, who said that if the need became very urgent, he

6

would take it upon himself to supply the Americans with five thousand muskets from the Tower of London.[1]

Here, indeed, was a surprising turn of Fortune's wheel!

The State of New York voted two hundred thousand dollars for arms and wrote over to King to purchase muskets and munitions. The Minister was set scouring Europe for weapons to slay their late allies, the French. He managed to procure several thousand German weapons in Hamburg, " an imitation of the English model, but not as good." England had been forced, however, to buy sixty thousand German muskets. There was now no other source of supply, and meanwhile King reported that he had ordered three thousand new weapons to be ready in the spring of 1799.

But it was one thing to be closeted with Lord Grenville and exchange confidential military plans and friendly sentiments, and quite another thing when the prospective Allies met in the person of their maritime commanders on the high seas. There it was to be feared the American sailor too often found himself the under-dog, who if he escaped the malevolence of the French frigates would encounter indignities from the British. From Philadelphia, Secretary Pickering renewed his indignation over British naval impressment and the continued insults to the American flag, although he acknowledged the—

" generally friendly and polite behaviour of the British naval officers towards ours and of their readiness to protect our merchant vessels against the plunderers of the world and to afford them relief when in distress. An instance has very lately occurred in the *Chesapeake*. A British vessel of war seeing an American vessel aground on a dangerous shoal sent down cables, anchors and thirty seamen who got her off, and this saved a valuable ship and cargo which in the next four and twenty hours would have been dashed to pieces and lost."

Such friendly passages made good reading in London.

" Now," pleaded the Secretary of State, " we wish for perfect harmony between our two countries. Why then go on wounding us ? " King made the plea known to Grenville, but it was clear that until the principle of Impressment was

[1] King to Pickering, October 5, 1798.

formally given up untoward incidents were bound to occur. The Stars and Stripes might not resemble the Union Jack, but it was hard to distinguish the features and speech of a Yankee sailor, especially when he had served in English ships from early boyhood, from those of an English one. And in any case it was better to serve such a country as England than any other in Europe. As King wrote the President, " weakness, corruption and indecision " characterized all Europe, outside England.

" The firmness, the courage and the resources of England, joined to the docility of the people and the wonderful ease with which the laws are adapted to the new and dangerous condition of surrounding circumstances, are the highest eulogium of its Constitution."

While America's entry into the war hung in the balance, thousands of the new eagles, half-eagles, dollars, quarters and dimes were emerging too slowly from the American mint to satisfy the popular demand. It therefore occurred to some ingenious and nefarious American in London to produce a brand-new American paper currency for foreign consumption. A London printer took the order in good faith and had already worked off some twenty thousand sheets of notes when word came to the American Legation. The Minister visited the establishment, detected the counterfeit and put the affair in the hands of the police. The issue was confiscated, but the culprit was never discovered.

King reported that—

" the commercial condition of England is extremely prosperous, and notwithstanding the hazardous and really dreadful situation of Ireland, this country is united in an uncommon degree, and appears resolved to persevere in the war. The Minister, at the opening of his budget, estimates the total income of all the people of Great Britain at a hundred million per annum ; and it is confidently expected that the taxes of this year will considerably exceed one-third of this sum."

While the Minister penned that letter, expressing his opinion that America would do well to take her stand by

England's side in the struggle against France, that it would be humiliating if the American people were again deceived by French artifices, President Adams had made his decision against war. Putting aside all counsellors and acting on his own judgment, he staked his country's interests on France's honour and desire for peace. After all the indignities American envoys had suffered and French envoys had inflicted, Adams was ready to sponge the slate clean. He therefore nominated Vans Murray, then at the Hague, to be Minister at Paris. Talleyrand, now repentant, agreed to receive him, and all chance of America entering the war against France was over.

Such a decision could hardly fail to bring disappointment to the country to which Rufus King was accredited.

" For some time past [he reported, October 11] and ever since the news of another mission to France, I have observed here a coldness towards the United States—an indifference to their affairs, a disposition to give unfavourable interpretations to their conduct, and in my ordinary intercourse with the Government I have met with more difficulties than I had before been accustomed to experience."

He therefore felt it due to his country to display a like reserve and keep away from Grenville and the Court. But on October 1 the Foreign Minister sent for him, and a very lengthy, animated and occasionally heated conversation took place. Grenville complained of the temper and disposition of the American Government shown by the breakdown of the Claims Commission in Philadelphia to adjudicate upon American debts, and the passage of a law by Congress for the protection of American seamen. " They [the British] had given up the pledge they held for the fulfilment of the Treaty of Peace [i.e. the frontier posts], and they must consider the non-performance of the last Treaty on [America's] part as a breach of faith."

King denied any intention of repudiation or unfriendliness. He said that the law complained of " had not been passed until we had without success endeavoured to conclude some agreement with England for the security of our seamen ; and then but with the sole and just view of exempting our citizens from an injury and oppression practised upon the people of no other country." The Claims Commission had interrupted its sessions, not because the claims of British creditors were proving too large, but because the American commissioners claimed the right of adjudication in the matter of claims recoverable by common law, which was contrary to the Treaty.

" I added that I knew the integrity of the Government I served. I had been the witness of its sincere disposition and earnest efforts to live in harmony and friendship with England. . . . But if the sentiments that I had been controverting were really entertained by the English Government I could not expect to see much good-will or good-humour between the two countries."

It was certainly a relationship full of vicissitudes. The wise course in a Minister was to make the best of it.

At the beginning of this summer King had acquired a pleasant country retreat at Mill Hill. Three of his boys were now at English schools, and in 1799 he found himself—

" in a position of great and growing influence in behalf of his country, with whose Government he was in hearty accord in its policy towards England ; and of pleasant relations with English Ministers who recognized his intelligence, firmness in maintaining his country's cause, and courteous and dignified demeanour. . . . His own home, where everything contributed to his happiness and where a charming wife presided . . . attracted all who came within its hospitable and quiet influence." [1]

King had formerly been a great smoker, " so much so that the room in which he worked was always full of the fumes and smell of tobacco." But one of the first discoveries the Envoy made in England was that the gentlemen of that day did not smoke. Difficulties placed in the way of smokers were so great that he gave up the habit and never resumed it.

News came early in 1800 of Washington's death, and the American Minister put himself and his family into mourning. The English newspaper comments (save the official *Gazette*)

---

[1] C. W. King : *Life and Letters of Rufus King.*

were respectful, but King could not help noticing that at the next levée the event passed unnoticed by the Sovereign, nor was it mentioned by the Queen at the drawing-room, although other topics were broached to the Minister.

" This disrespectful omission and want of magnanimity was," he reported, " a concerted neglect."

It is all very sad, of course, but George III was only human : he could never forgive his former subject, Colonel Washington, or the language and the measures he had used against the Loyalists.

The year 1800 was full of difficulties, but Minister King never relaxed in advancing the interests and the claims of his country, and in endeavouring to maintain Anglo-American harmony, in spite of the loud resentment against England which prevailed at home. Liston, the British Minister in Washington, got himself into trouble by writing a satirical letter concerning the President and members of his Cabinet —which was really intended only as a confidential *jeu d'esprit*. Nevertheless, he was recalled. A more grievous loss to King was the President's sudden dismissal of his Secretary of State, Pickering, who was found guilty of plotting with Hamilton against Adams's re-election.

" It all demonstrated," wrote Pickering to King, " the President's unbounded vanity, ambition, selfishness, revenge and a heart cankered with envy." King sympathized. He himself was nervous how the British Government would take Adams's new Treaty with France ; but Grenville, although stating dryly that one or two points had " somewhat of a less friendly appearance than could be wished," thought it not inconsistent with the Anglo-American Treaty.

There was another Treaty which was to involve King in a great deal of petty trouble and anxiety, and incidentally to provide enormous entertainment for his friends and family. It was with a very small potentate—the Bey of Tunis. For his consent to this Treaty the Bey had stipulated, not a cash bribe, but a set of costly gifts. These gifts the American Minister was requested to purchase in London, but after going from jeweller to jeweller and from one dealer to another, he found that the whole would have to be specially fabricated. The articles were not completed for a year, and when finally delivered at Tunis in an American warship caused a considerable local sensation.[1]

Before President Adams had yielded his place to Jefferson, Pitt was out of office in England. He resigned February 9, 1801, and overtures for peace with France followed.

Rufus King wrote to Grenville his condolences, with an expression of his personal regard.

" I have too clearly seen the Danger to which the Principles which are the foundation of all social Happiness have been exposed not to have conceived the most favourable sentiments for the Persons who have displayed so much firmness and perseverance in their Defence. . . .
" The Duty of Governing is never more arduous than when circumstances, such as at present exist, place the Ill-disciplined and the Ignorant in the power of the un-principled or the Ambitious."

Never were aristocratic sentiments more uncompromisingly expressed. There was still hope for a republic whose repre-sentative could be so orthodox.

Grenville opined, however, that there was no occasion for alarm. Good and able statesmen would be forthcoming from the Opposition. Only the crisis was too much for the unhappy monarch, who became seriously ill. Addington took the seals of office as Premier and Lord Hawkesbury became Foreign Secretary.

The American Envoy now began to see more of the Whig leaders, and on April 3, 1801, we find him dining with Lord Lansdowne (formerly Shelburne). In the course of the evening the subject of the Peace negotiations of 1783 came up, and his host confided to Minister King that in his opinion the American, Henry Laurens, was a rascal !

---

[1] The gifts expressly stipulated for were as follows :
  1 fusee, 6 feet long, mounted with gold, set with diamonds.
  4 fusees with gold mounting, ordinary length.
  1 pair of pistols mounted with gold, set with diamonds.
  4 pairs of pistols mounted with gold.
  1 pair of pistols set with diamonds.
  1 diamond ring.
  1 gold repeating watch, with diamonds.
  1 gold snuff-box, set with diamonds.
  6 pieces brocade of gold.
  £1,000 worth of silver trinkets.

" Franklin wanted to do everything by cunning, which was the bottom of his character : that the American Peace was a stock-jobbing one, and that d'Aranda and the French Minister gambled in the English funds."

Which is an entertaining sidelight on a famous transaction in diplomacy.

When it came to the matter of Impressment, King found Addington's Ministry just as difficult as Pitt's had been.

" The pretence upon which our seamen are taken [he complained to Erskine, March 11] is that the King has a right to the service of his subjects, and all who speak English are, in the practice of the Navy, considered so unless they can prove the contrary, a fact not easily established by a seaman, on account of the habitual carelessness of his character, even before an impartial tribunal."

Erskine was sympathetic, but in view of the national feeling on the subject was as helpless as the Tories.

With Jefferson as President, Rufus King could hardly hope for a continuance in London as Minister.

" When I left [he wrote to a friend just after Jefferson's inauguration], we expected that the war would be at an end in two or three years ; and that an opportunity would then present itself for a reversion concluded by Mr. Jay ; which would be advantageous to the United States and favourable to our reputation. The war still goes on and the change of men in America will probably be followed by corresponding changes in Europe. I therefore expect a successor."

In this event he intended to pass the winter on the Continent and return home in the summer of 1802.

Monroe, who hated King, addressed a letter to Jefferson (April 30, 1801) :

The opinion was " that our present Envoy in London should be withdrawn. They think nothing is done unless that is done : that as every calamity, foreign and domestic, we have experienced from Great Britain is due to a person known to be friendly to her interests, acquainted with our interior, able to influence her councils and plan her measures against us, he ought not to be left there under the present administration."

It is alleged by Monroe's defenders that this letter, although existing in Monroe's hand, was never sent. It may be so. At all events, Jefferson stayed his hand and Rufus King remained at his post for another two years. In 1802 he went on a visit to Paris at the same time that C. J. Fox was staying in the French capital. The Whig leader offered to present the American to Bonaparte. But as an Anglo-American Treaty was then in process of negotiation and King knew that Bonaparte, the great Corsican, was an object of detestation to George III, he declined the interview. Later, on his return to London, the British monarch went up to the American Minister at a levée and said to him : " Mr. King, I am very much obliged to you. You have treated me like a gentleman, which is more than I can say of all my subjects." [1]

The Minister resigned his post August 5, 1802, writing to the Secretary of State : " It is now six years that I have resided in this country. When I left America it was not in my expectation to be absent more than four years." So long as the war continued, he had felt it his duty to remain ; but now that peace had been signed and his own negotiation completed, he begged to be allowed to return home the following April.

Rufus King had a due sense of his own importance and expected a grateful country—even though a republic—to behave handsomely towards him.

" As I am, moreover, desirous to carry home with me my library, furniture, carriages, and other bulky articles, it would be a great accommodation to me if the President would allow me a passage in a frigate or other national vessel, which at the same time would relieve my family from any concern in respect to the cruisers of Morocco or any other piratical State and save me from the heavy charges which I must otherwise incur, returning home after seven years' residence in the most expensive country of Europe."

He begged also to be allowed to carry home on the warship a few horses and sheep for breeding purposes !

The Department of State, not then so niggardly in these matters as it afterwards became, graciously acceded to these

---

[1] *Letters of Dr. Charles Lieber.*

modest requests, so that when in the summer in 1803 the Minister returned to American shores it was with a proper degree of éclat.   Of his mission Rufus King afterwards wrote :

" I lived more intimately with the public men of England, as well with those of the Opposition as of the Government, than any foreigner of my time.   I frequented the society of literary men and have been in correspondence with several of the most distinguished civilians of the Old World."

Before he left England a Convention with Great Britain respecting boundaries, negotiated between himself and Lord Hawkesbury, had been signed.   Three days later came word from Paris of a somewhat vaster diplomatic transaction. Minister Livingston, assisted by James Monroe, had signed the Treaty with Napoleon for the purchase of Louisiana.

BIOGRAPHICAL NOTE

Rufus King continued to play a part in public affairs in America for the next twenty years.   He was elected to the Senate, and in 1825 was again sent as Minister to England.

CHAPTER V

MONROE (1803–1807)

SOME seven years before, James Monroe, a stalwart Virginian lawyer and the close friend of Jefferson and Thomas Paine, had been American Minister to France, where he had consorted rather too freely with the doctrinaires and demagogues to give much pleasure to his Government.

Since then he had been again sent, rather superfluously, to Paris, to assist Livingston in negotiating the Louisiana Treaty. Having long coveted the English mission, he was now instructed to relieve Rufus King in London. King and Monroe were, we know, not on the best of terms. Amongst the late Minister's friends in London was Christopher Gore, a member of the American Claims Commission, which was still in session, and from his letters we are able to gain a good deal of inner knowledge of the life of the Monroes in the British capital.

The new Minister arrived on July 18, 1803, and was shortly afterwards received by King George and the Foreign Secretary, Lord Hawkesbury, later to become Lord Liverpool. Monroe's first impression was that the great majority of people in England misunderstood the people of the United States. On the other hand, Charles Gore was convinced that Monroe misunderstood the English.

"Monroe knows little that passes in London [Gore wrote, August 24]. He has seen Hawkesbury twice; once on his arrival and once on his introduction to the King. He has also seen Hammond once. . . . He appears to have a sort of creed that it is improper to know what is passing in relation to European Powers, unless the United States are directly interested. He will therefore have a quiet time in England, for you know they do not press their knowledge, no more than their civility, on any man."

At the first official dinner to which he was asked, Monroe found himself seated, quite properly, according to the then order of precedence, at the foot of the table between two representatives from German principalities. He was furious at what he considered an indignity.

"'James Monroe doesn't care where he eats his dinner,' he said, 'but to find the American Minister put at the bottom of the table between two little principalities no bigger than my farm in Albemarle made me mad.' So angry was he that when the first toast, 'The King,' was given and all rose to drink it, Mr. Monroe in reseating himself put his wine-glass down in the finger-bowl, splashing the water. This made his German neighbours exchange sarcastic smiles, and he was rapidly getting too angry when the Russian Minister, who was at the right hand of the presiding Minister of State, rose and offered his toast, 'A health and welcome to our latest-comer, and the President of the United States.' 'Then I saw clear again,' said Monroe." [1]

Soon after Monroe's entrance into the Legation there occurred an amusing illustration of the want of confidence and cordiality towards the American Government ever since the French advances. Robert Fulton, of steamboat fame, wrote to the firm of Boulton & Watt for two steam engines to be shipped to New York, the engines to be constructed according to the designs of the notorious pro-Gallican and future Minister, Joel Barlow. Downing Street heard of it and took it into their heads to believe the engines " were intended for Fulton's diving machines that are to blow up the British Navy, the dockyard, etc., at Portsmouth, of which they have some apprehension." [2]

Accordingly, having scented this terrible plot, the Government ordered Boulton & Watt not to ship nor to fill the orders. The destination of New York might be only a ruse and " so soon as the vessel carrying them should be in the Channel they might be transhipped for France and affixed to those terrible instruments of destruction."

Monroe protested, and his countryman Gore, who was on good terms with George Hammond, now Under-Secretary at

[1] Jessie Benton Fremont : *Souvenirs of my Time.*
[2] C. Gore to Rufus King, August 20, 1803.

JAMES MONROE.

the Foreign Office, explained that the engines were destined only for Fulton's new steamboat, in which he was being financed by Livingston; but the Ministry thought there was something very suspicious in the whole business, and the order was not rescinded.

Several years were to pass before Fulton's steamboat, equipped with Boulton & Watt's engines, was to ply the Hudson River.

It was perhaps this prevalent atmosphere of suspicion which drove Monroe into relative seclusion. He frequented the society of the American Consul, Erving, who was Gore's enemy, and carried republican simplicity so far as even to dispense with a Secretary of Legation. Once Washington Allston, the painter, called on him for a passport, to be informed that the Minister was far too busy for such trifles as passports. Allston was referred to the Consul, although at that time a passport from the Minister was necessary to safety on the Continent, consular certificates being collected at the British Alien Office before embarking.

There came many other complaints at the Legation, but they went unheeded.

Towards the close of the year President Jefferson's impolite behaviour towards the new British Minister, Anthony Merry, became known in London. Partly in retaliation for this, the Monroes found themselves snubbed socially. In a long letter to Secretary Madison (March 3, 1804) the Minister tells of his experiences with the aristocratic members of the diplomatic circle with whom he and his wife dined. When Mrs. Monroe called, her calls were not returned. There seemed to be a studied attempt to humiliate the republican Monroes, and, sad to relate, their compatriots, Gore and King, appear to have been rather pleased.[1]

Monroe was now so clearly out of his element in London that his friend and patron, Jefferson, offered him the Governor-

---

[1] George Morgan: *James Monroe.* Of the Merry episode, Morgan observes: " It is hardly too much to say that the episode served to reawaken in England the feeling of hostility toward America, and perhaps has something to do with the war that broke out a few years later." When Gore dined at Hawkesbury's : " His Lordship took me aside," he wrote to King, " and mentioned the unpleasant accounts they had received from Washington. . . . In this silly business, they probably see here a disposition to affront England, and it will, with others, increase a growing discontent with us."

ship of Louisiana. Meanwhile, it was arranged that he would go to Spain, to relieve Minister Pinckney. Secretary Madison also wrote, requesting Monroe to bring before the British Government the plan of a Convention covering the subjects of Impressment, Blockade and Search.

Monroe replied to the President that the proposed office in Louisiana was insufficient recompense for his great services. At the same time, he hoped to extricate himself speedily from his disagreeable English situation. How disagreeable it was, how uncivil the British could be, he would give a shocking instance :

" At Ld. Holland's table, when speaking with his lady, who appears to me to be an amiable woman, on the subject of our climate, of its variety, etc., I mentioned that while the northern parts were perhaps in snow, the southern enjoyed the bloom of spring ; that in February at Charlestown they had the *course* ; and from want of other topics of conversation, I added that on such occasions there was always a great concourse of people with gay equipages, etc. Ld. Castlereagh asked me what kind of equipages had they ? I co'd not be but surprised at the enquiry, nevertheless replied, such as I saw here. Sir Wm. Scott then remarked that he had had lately read an account of a grand fête at the Cape of Good Hope which concluded with that all ' the beauty, taste and fashion of Africa were assembled there.' This occasion'd some mirth, as you will suppose, at our expense, in which I could not partake."

To compare Charleston, South Carolina, with Cape Town —it was positively indecent, and the insult rankled. Yet had Minister Monroe but known it, Cape Town, even in 1804, had its racecourse, whose titled frequenters dressed in the latest modes from Paris.

To the Secretary of State Monroe reported (June 3, 1804) :

" While the late Ministry was on the decline it seemed useless to press it on any concerns of ours. I remained tranquil in the hope of availing myself with effect of the moment when it should either recover its strength, or, retiring, give place to another, with which I might treat on the important concerns entrusted to me. As soon as Lord Harrowby came into office, he notified it to the Foreign

Ministers, and invited them to an interview at his office on the concerns of their respective countries. As each was introduced separately, I took occasion to mention to him the subjects which were depending with his predecessor, more especially the project of a treaty concerning impressments and other topics, and the interest of the State of Maryland in some bank stock, which I hoped might soon be concluded. I mentioned to him, also, that I had lately received from you the ratification of the treaty respecting boundaries, by the President, with the advice of the Senate, with the exception of the fifth article, which I wished to submit to his consideration. He replied, that he was glad I had turned his attention in those subjects, since he would make them the particular object of his research, but hoped that I would not press any of them, as he had so lately come into office, and had so many concerns before him of the first importance to his country, and of a nature very urgent."

Later, the American Envoy had an interview with the Foreign Secretary, of which he writes :

" The conduct of Lord Harrowby through the whole of this conference was calculated to wound and to irritate. Not a friendly sentiment towards the United States or their Government escaped him. In proposing a postponement of the interests in which we were a party, he did not seem to desire my sanction but to assume a tone which supposed his will had settled the point. By his manner he put it out of my power, in assenting to the delay, to mingle with it any expressions declaratory of the pleasure with which I acceded to an arrangement which accommodated his Government or himself. Such expressions can never be used with propriety, except where they are voluntary, and acknowledged to be founded in generous motives. But no sentiment of that kind seemed to animate him on this occasion. Everything that he said was uttered in an unfriendly tone, and much more was apparently meant than was said. I was surprised at a deportment of which I had seen no example before since I came into the country, and which was certainly provoked by no act of mine ; yet I am persuaded it did not produce an improper effect on my conduct. I did not reciprocate the irritation by anything that escaped me. I am equally well persuaded that I made no improper concession, and let it be clearly seen that I felt that I represented a respectable and independent nation, whose Government could not be intimidated, or compelled to lose sight of its dignity by an abandonment of its just claims in its transactions with any other."

It was futile for Monroe to attempt to do business with Pitt or Harrowby. It were better to wait for a Whig administration. Meanwhile, the Minister agreed to visit Madrid to try to settle matters with Spain. The Spaniards were still extremely sore about the way they had been treated over their late colony of Louisiana, reluctantly relinquished by them to France and promptly sold by Napoleon to America. Accordingly, early in October 1804 Monroe left England and was absent on the Continent until the following July.

" Monroe [says his most painstaking biographer] never worked harder or with more ability than when in Spain seeking the acquisition of the Floridas or in England endeavouring to insure future peace. He was clear and forceful in logic and language. He let nothing drag. He preserved the amenities, so that no don of Castille could question his courtesy. In a word, Monroe was at his best ; but conditions were against him. Only by the lavish use of bribes could the Floridas have been acquired at that time, and Monroe was both clean-minded and clean-handed." [1]

The Minister returned from his Spanish mission, having accomplished nothing.

" During a century of American diplomatic history [says Henry Adams, caustically] a Minister of the United States has seldom if ever within six months suffered at two great Courts such contemptuous treatment as had fallen to Monroe's lot. That he should have been mortified and anxious for escape was natural. He returned to England, meaning to sail as quickly as possible."

Meanwhile the war between France and England was being waged with increasing intensity, and it was not likely that the latter country would neglect any weapons which her control of the sea gave her. The fact that she might thereby injure her former American colonies, who had lately made a fresh

---

[1] George Morgan : *James Monroe.*

treaty with her enemy and whose Chief Executive was a notorious Francophile and an atheist to boot, would hardly restrain her hand. Of course, the New England merchants were violently angry at the disposition of the British Ministry to shackle their sea-commerce. As one of them wrote :

" Our merchants are anxious for their property and irritated at a conduct in the British which they think not only unjust, but perfidious. They thought that it was Monroe's fault—he could not get on with the English."

" If *you* had been in London, a different state of things would have existed," wrote Gore to Rufus King, and suggested that Jefferson should promptly request his friend to return to his former post.

Primarily, the British had no wish to injure America. Even the well-disposed Wilberforce thought the naval laws " indispensable and necessary not only to our interest, but to our very existence."

As he wrote to Rufus King in America (November 7, 1805), less than three weeks after Trafalgar :

" You know us Englishmen, such as we are, our good qualities and our bad ones, and I would venture to affirm that your residence in this country may have produced impressions concerning the personal character of my countrymen which books alone never would supply and thereby enable you to account for instances of conduct otherwise inexplicable."

The argument used by Sir Francis Baring in a letter to Rufus King recalls that frequently heard before America's entry into the Great War (1914–18), the application of the final clause being to Germany :

" My opinion is, as it always has been, that Britain was the bulwark to America and that the downfall of one would be followed by the destruction of the other. Indeed, I cannot discover in what manner universal empire is to be prevented if the power of France remains intact, for its impulse is irresistible."

Monroe protested to Madison (October 18, 1805) that he thought the present prospect hopeless.

7

" No disposition has been shown to prescribe, by treaty, any restraint on the impressment of our seamen whenever the Government may be so disposed, or even when any of its officers in the West Indies or elsewhere may think fit. On the subject of boundary nothing has been lately said, nor does there appear to be any inclination to enter on it. I have also reason to think that this Government is equally disposed to postpone an arrangement of our commerce in general, by treaty, for any number of years. On this point, however, I cannot speak with so much confidence as on the others, having never made any proposition that was calculated to obtain an explicit declaration of its sentiments. The conversations which I had with Lords Hawkesbury and Harrowby before I went to Spain on other subjects, naturally brought this into view ; but being incidentally, it was only slightly touched. The proposition which was made by the latter, to consider the Treaty of 1794 in force, was as a temporary expedient, not a permanent regulation. From that circumstance, and the manner in which they both spoke of that Treaty, I concluded that their Government would be willing to revive it for an equal term. It might, however, have been made only to obtain delay. You will observe that in my note of the 23rd ultimo I have taken the liberty to mention the subject in a manner to show that it is not one to which the United States are indifferent, or which the President wishes to postpone. Although I have no power to form a treaty of so comprehensive a nature, yet I thought I might with propriety open the subject, so far at least as to ascertain the views of this Government on it for your information.

" On a review of the conduct of this Government towards the United States, from the commencement of the war, I am inclined to think that the delay which has been so studiously sought, in all these concerns, is the part of a system, and that it is intended, as circumstances favour, to subject our commerce at present and hereafter to every restraint in their power. It is certain that the greatest jealousy is entertained of our present and increasing prosperity, and I am satisfied that nothing which is likely to succeed will be left untried to impair it."

All this was purely Monroe's imagination. But soon an event happened which seemed to change the face of affairs. Pitt died of old age at forty-six, and Charles Fox came into office, as Foreign Secretary under Grenville. The American Minister was again filled with hope.

" As soon as Mr. Fox took possession of his office [reported Monroe, February 12, 1806], he requested an interview with the foreign Ministers, which took place yesterday. We were introduced separately. As soon as the ceremony of the interview had passed, I observed that I presumed he had been too short a term in office to have made himself acquainted with what had occurred between his predecessors and myself, more especially the last one. He said he had not had time to read the papers, though he presumed he had a general idea on some of the topics. In respect to the immediate question, he asked whether I had made to them, or they to me, any proposition ? I gave a short sketch of the part which our respective Governments had acted since the commencement of the present war towards each other.

" He heard me with much attention and apparent interest ; intimated that he had been accused of being too friendly to America, and when I spoke of the treaty with Russia, he observed that he had thought that the arrangement made by it was a good one, though I did not understand him as pledging himself by the remark to its conditions. I requested that he would make himself master, as soon as in his power, of the correspondence between Lord Mulgrave and myself, and give me an interview, which he promised. I am happy to add, on a view of all circumstances, that I think the prospect of arranging our affairs with this Government, especially that one which respects our trade with the colonies of its enemies, on satisfactory terms, a very favourable one. It is certain that nothing more favourable was, or could reasonably have been expected from the first interview with the present Minister."

No wonder Monroe, after all the disappointments he had undergone, was optimistic. After this first interview he wrote of Fox as one " who in half an hour put me more at my ease than I ever felt with any person in office since I have been in England."

Two months passed. It was apparent, alas ! that Fox's health was precarious. Only with difficulty could he attend to business. On April 18 Monroe reported :

" I received yesterday a note from Mr. Fox appointing

to-morrow (Saturday, 19) for an interview, with which I shall of course comply. I met him afterwards and had a conversation with him in the Queen's drawing-room, which, being of an interesting nature, I hasten to communicate to you. He took me aside, and observed that we must now soon settle our business. I replied, that I hoped he was ready to do it. He intimated that he was so essentially ; that we would begin it on Saturday and pursue it without delay until it was concluded. Some remarks of his having led the conversation to the merits of the principal topic, I told him that he must leave us in enjoyment of the trade question, and pay us for the property taken. To this first proposition he immediately assented. To the second he said there would be no objections. He added that he had taken steps to prohibit the further condemnation of our vessels and cargoes, as I had desired, of which he intended to have informed me by note, but had been prevented by other business ; he had no objection, however, still to do it."

All seemed now in train. But ten days later Monroe reported :

" Having waited a week after my interview with Mr. Fox, without receiving either of the communications which he then promised me, I called on him on the 25th, to know the cause, and to confer freely again on our affairs, if he should be so disposed."

But Fox was not disposed. By this time both Jefferson and Madison had lost patience. The Minister in London was muddling matters. It was decided to send a Joint Commissioner to work with Monroe in negotiating a new treaty. At the end of May the Minister learnt that William Pinkney, lately a member of the Claims Commission, was to be sent. It was a shock to Monroe ; nevertheless, as he himself had previously been sent to aid Livingston in Paris and Charles Pinckney in Madrid, he could hardly resent being in turn yoked to another. Nevertheless, " the blow to Monroe's pride was great, and shook his faith in the friendship of Jefferson and Madison." [1]

Monroe wished to return home in the following autumn. He confessed that but for the recent seizure of American

[1] Morgan : *James Monroe.*

ships, he would have gone at once. One of his daughters was ill; and by the advice of a physician, he took her to Cheltenham. Mrs. Monroe was ailing, too. She had suffered from rheumatism ever since the fête of Napoleon's coronation at Paris. " I leave Mr. Purviance in town," he added, " and shall keep an apartment to which I shall repair occasionally." Purviance, whom the State Department had appointed his Secretary of Legation, would notify him whenever he should be needed. Following came a letter from Madison (May 15, 1806) :

" This will be put into the hands of Mr. Pinkney, whose appointment jointly with you, by a commission extraordinary, has been already communicated, and who proceeds to London with the powers and instructions for carrying the Joint Commission into effect. This you will find embraces a larger field of negotiation and convention than fell within the instructions heretofore given you in your capacity of Minister Plenipotentiary alone. The commission extraordinary, therefore, will not be without important objects, even if those previously committed to yourself should fortunately have been obtained. Mr. Pinkney carries with him also a commission and letter of credence as your successor, in case you should persist in your intention of returning after the occasion which suspended it shall be over. A letter of farewell also for yourself goes by him, of the same provisional character."

The Secretary of State, it will be seen, was taking no risks : he had planned for every contingency.

An American Quaker, William Dillwyn, who was at this time living at Leyton with his family, recorded in his letters to his friends his meetings with the Minister. These are of considerable interest. Under date of March 10, 1806, he wrote :

" Monroe, the American Ambassador, having taken a good house at Leyton adjoining this parish for his temporary accommodation, I paid him a visit this morning and was much pleased with his friendly republican, unassuming manners. He seemed quite pleased with my freedom in calling on him and readily engaged to dine here with his wife and two daughters this day se'night. In conversation

he rather increased my Hope that the present existing uneasiness between our country and this Government will be
dissipated by a more conciliatory disposition in the present
Ministry than appeared in their predecessors. Be it so—
for a war would unavoidably add to the irksomeness of our
separation in many respects ; and of selfish opponents this
nation already has an ample share. Buonaparte is repeating
his threats of Invasion and the preparations to repel it are
no less active on every point deemed accessible. Happy
for the nation as for Individuals would it be had we solid
grounds for Reliance on a better Protection than human
effort can afford. Some seem to think the Corsican too
wicked to be employed even as an Instrument of Punishment,
but altho' I have never felt much alarmed by any Ideas of
his succeeding in his ambitious Designs on these Kingdoms I
cannot easily appreciate the strength of an argument of that
kind."

On the day appointed (March 10, 1806) Dillwyn writes :

" Our four girls, etc., etc., are as busy in their Preparations
to entertain them [the Monroes] as if they thought Republican
and Spartan Manners were not necessarily synonymous, and
Lydia deprecates my censure by hinting that she means the
compliment as much to her father as to the Minister. . . .
I have often had occasion to remark that the lower orders
of people here are more ignorant than the same class in my
native country. I find a notion prevails among poor neighbours that the Greatest Man in America, by them y'clept
a King, is expected as our guest."

" 19th.—Our expected Guests came, accompanied by a
Purviance of Baltimore (of the Philadelphia family of that
name), probably attached to the Embassy. Monroe married
a Cartwright [Kortright] of New York. She knows a good
deal of our friends there, and is herself of a friendly, social
disposition. Several hours passed in as much Freedom and
Ease as if we were assembled on the banks of the Hudson,
the Delaware, or Potomack. Monroe's general information
and particular knowledge of American affairs render his
conversation very interesting, and I believe we parted
mutually pleased with the opportunity of such a joint excur-
sion to our native shores. Our young folks were highly
delighted with it, the elder Daughter, about 18, much
resembling Lydia in the artless Frankness of her Manners."

Two months later (May 12) he records :

" The day before yesterday, with my three younger daughters (Judy being not then well enough), I dined with Monroe, the American Ambassador, and could collect nothing from him discovering the hope that the Ministers were disposed to settle matters in dispute by amicable negotiation. It was an agreeable afternoon." [1]

But agreeable afternoons were rare now with Monroe. Fox, from whom he had expected so much, was a dying man.

In April Congress had passed a Non-Importation Act against British goods, and in the following month the British Ministry issued an Order-in-Council blockading the whole coast of Europe, from Brest to the Elbe. This action, six months later, provoked Napoleon's Berlin Decree, placing an embargo on all trade with Britain. Monroe thought to discuss these matters fully with the Foreign Secretary in June, when Fox seemed a little better.

" The interview was at his own house, on the anniversary of the King's birth, in a general rendezvous of the Diplomatic Corps. In that we touched on some interesting subjects, particularly the outrages committed at New York by the British cruisers, our Non-Importation Act, and the affair of General Miranda. But as we could not treat those subjects with advantage in a crowd, it was agreed to postpone the consideration of them to the 6th, when I promised to attend him at his office for the purpose of entering more fully into them."

Pinkney now arrived and found that Fox had been obliged to turn over the negotiations to his relative Lord Holland, and to Lord Auckland. Now ensued what was probably Minister Monroe's worst time. He knew that Madison was jealous of him. He had imposed on Monroe the task of negotiating a treaty under impossible conditions.

" If the treaty should fail, the blame would fall upon Monroe ; if it should succeed, the credit would be with Pinkney. No one would suppose that Madison would make any great effort to secure the success of a negotiation when

[1] MS. *Letter-book of William Dillwyn*: Letter to Samuel Emlen. Philadelphia Public Library.

success might make the negotiator the next President of the
United States. . . . Monroe could not doubt the President's
coldness toward the treaty ; he could not fail to see that the
Secretary's personal wishes were rather against than for it ;
and when he studied the instructions he could not but admit
that they were framed, if not with the intention, at all events
with the effect, of making a treaty impossible. No harder
task could well have been imposed than was laid upon
Monroe." [1]

In his *Memoirs* Lord Holland has indited his recollections
of Monroe and the negotiations :

" We found the two American commissioners fair, explicit,
frank and intelligent. Mr. Monroe (afterwards President)
was a sincere Republican, who during the Revolution in
France had imbibed a strong predilection for that country,
and no slight aversion to this. But, he had candour and
principle. A nearer view of the consular and imperial
Government of France, and of our Constitution in England,
converted him from both these opinions. . . . He was plain
in his manners and somewhat slow in his apprehension ;
but he was a diligent, earnest, sensible, and even profound
man.

" His colleague, who had been partly educated in England
and was a lawyer by profession, had more forms and readiness
of business, and greater knowledge and cultivation of mind ;
but perhaps his opinions were neither so firmly rooted nor so
deeply considered as those of Mr. Monroe. Throughout our
negotiation, they were conciliatory, both in form and in
substance."

Fox died of dropsy on September 13. Ten weeks later
Monroe and Pinkney, disregarding their instructions, put
their names to a treaty which, comments Henry Adams, is—

" remarkable for combining in one instrument every quality
to which Jefferson held most strenuous objection. Impressments were set aside ; no indemnities were obtained for
American losses in 1805 ; and, in regard to the colonial trade,
a compromise was invented which no self-respecting Government would admit." [2]

News of the treaty which had thus been made by Monroe
and Pinkney reached Washington on March 3, 1807. David

---

[1] Morgan.   [2] Adams : *History of the United States.*

Montague Erskine, who had succeeded Anthony Merry as British Minister, went at once to Madison, who asked him " what had been determined on the point of impressment of seamen." When Madison learned that nothing had been done, he "expressed the greatest astonishment and disappointment."

That same evening a joint Committee of Congress waited on the President and asked him whether the Senate would be called upon to consider the treaty. " Certainly not," said Jefferson emphatically.

So the treaty sought by the Minister to England with so much pains and involving so many delays and discouragements, was already dead. Afterwards Monroe defended himself to Congress and his fellow-countrymen in ten folio pages of the State Papers :

" The failure of our business with Spain and the knowledge of the renewal of the negotiation and the manner of it, which were known to everyone, were sensibly felt in our concerns with England. She was not willing to yield any portion of what she called her maritime rights, under the light pressure of the Non-Importation Law, to a Power which had no maritime force, nor even sufficient to protect any one of its ports against a small squadron, and which had so recently submitted to great injuries and indignities from Powers that had not a single ship at sea.

" Under such circumstances it seemed to me highly for the interest of our country and to the credit of our Government to get out of the general scrape on the best terms we could, and with that view to accommodate our differences with the great maritime Power on what might be called fair and reasonable conditions, if such could be obtained. I had been slighted, as I thought, by the Administration in getting no answers to my letters for an unusual term, and in being subjected to a special mission, notwithstanding my remonstrance against it on thorough conviction of its inutility, and by other acts which I could not but feel, yet believing that my service in England would be useful there, and by means thereof give aid to the Administration and to the Republican cause at home, I resolved to stay, and did stay for those purposes. The treaty was an honourable and advantageous adjustment with England. I adopted it

in the firm belief that it was so, and nothing has since occurred
to change that opinion."

Monroe's action in Paris had been repudiated in 1796
by Washington ; that in London was now repudiated by his
successor. Henry Adams sums up :

" In many respects Monroe's career was unparalleled, but
he was singular above all in the experience of being disowned
by two Presidents as strongly opposed to each other as
Washington and Jefferson, and of being sacrificed by two
Secretaries as widely different as Timothy Pickering and
James Madison. . . . Doubtless only personal friendship and
the fear of strengthening Federalist influence prevented
President Jefferson from denouncing Monroe's conduct as
forcibly as President Washington had denounced it ten
years before ; and Jefferson's grounds of complaint were
more serious than Washington's. Monroe expected and even
courted martyrdom, and never quite forgot the treatment
he received. In private, George Hay, Monroe's son-in-law,
who knew all the secrets of his career, spoke afterwards of
Jefferson as ' one of the most insincere men in the world ;
. . . his enmity to Mr. Monroe was inveterate, though
disguised, as he was at the bottom of all the opposition to
Mr. Monroe in Virginia.' "

The discredited envoy remained in London until October
29, 1807, and then sailed for home, leaving Mrs. Monroe and
his daughters behind for the present.

Monroe's character and achievement and their apparent
incompatibility with his future renown, is still something
of a mystery. He had been absent five years altogether and
in that period had been " insulted by every Foreign Secretary
in France, Spain and England." [1] This is not strictly true :
Charles James Fox had been Foreign Secretary and he had
not " insulted " Monroe ; he was a sick man, and he had
merely temporized with him.

Pinkney was in London awaiting orders. Between the
failure of the treaty and the Minister's departure for America
a stirring event had happened on the high seas which for a
time profoundly affected Anglo-American relations, bringing,

[1] Adams : *History of the United States.*

indeed, both countries to the verge of war. A British warship, the *Leopard*, sent in search of British deserters known to be on board, fatally fired on the American frigate the *Chesapeake*.

But Jefferson had no desire for war any more than Adams had eight years before. A proclamation was issued allaying the popular excitement and instructions to demand an apology and redress were instantly dispatched to London. There Monroe was on the point of yielding his office to William Pinkney.

BIOGRAPHICAL NOTE

Monroe was elected for the second time Governor of Virginia in 1811. From thence he was called to the Secretary-ship of State. He was President 1817–25. He died in 1831.

CHAPTER VI

WILLIAM PINKNEY (1807–1811)

WILLIAM PINKNEY, a young Baltimore lawyer of thirty-two, had been appointed by President Washington one of the members of the American Claims Commission in London. Pinkney, who was only very remotely related to the aristocratic Pinckneys, was a self-made man, the son of a sturdy Northumbrian who had emigrated to America and remained loyal to the British connexion throughout the revolutionary war. His son, child though he was, took the side of the Maryland insurgents ; entered a law office, was duly called to the Bar and distinguished himself in Maryland State politics. For eight years Pinkney remained in England after his appointment, in daily companionship with men of superior parts and breeding ; his duties exacted a high degree of judicial talent. Amidst such surroundings Pinkney's powers were ripened and his manners polished.

Pinkney returned home reluctantly enough, when the commission broke up in 1804. In Maryland his vigorous attitude to the question of British search and seizure, as well as his valuable experience abroad, pointed him out to President Jefferson as a valuable coadjutor to Monroe and eventually as that unlucky Minister's successor.

" It would [wrote Pinkney to Madison, October 10, 1807] have been much more agreeable to me that a Chargé d'affaires should be left and that I should remain in my character of Commissioner Extraordinary until the Government of the United States should have an opportunity of taking its own course. . . . In awaiting here the orders of the President, I am ready to return or to remain, as he shall think the interest of our country requires."

This was at the height of the *Leopard* and *Chesapeake*

94

affair, when it seemed as if war with America was certain. Canning, now Foreign Secretary, had already admitted to Monroe that the King of England " neither does nor has at any time mentioned the pretension of a right to scarch ships of war, in the national service of any State, for deserters."

Admiral Berkeley, therefore, had clearly exceeded his powers. He was recalled, and steps were begun towards the compensation eventually paid by the British Government.

Meanwhile, Congress had been goaded into passing the President's Embargo Act, which virtually cut off America from the rest of the world, prohibiting her own vessels from quitting American ports and suspending all foreign commerce. For this heroic remedy seemed to Jefferson the only way to deal with the situation and prevent war with either England or France, or both.

On January 7, 1808, Pinkney reported to Secretary Madison :

" I sent you some days ago a newspaper containing the French retaliatory decree, dated at Milan, the 25th of December. . . . You will find by the papers of this morning that it has been followed up by another. This country has ventured upon an extraordinary struggle with France, by which she has everything to lose and nothing to gain. The gross impolicy of the later Orders-in-Council (to say nothing of their insulting tone and their injustice to neutral States) begins to develop itself and will soon be manifest to all. I am greatly deceived if it will not in a few weeks be matter of surprise among all descriptions of people here that a manufacturing and commercial nation like Great Britain could have expected anything but disaster and ruin from such a measure.

" Hopes are entertained in England, that our Non-Importation Act will have been repealed upon the arrival of an intended extraordinary mission from this country ! That law was passed upon unquestionable grounds of policy and justice, and although it has been heretofore properly *suspended*, I do not see how our honour could fail to become a mere shadow, if it should now be abandoned even for a time. The mission of Mr. Rose would not seem to justify even the suspension of it, until the nature and extent of his powers were known, and after they were known it could justify nothing. He has no powers to arrange on the topic of impressment, the great foundation of the Non-Importation Act ; and his Government has not only reasserted its obnoxious pretension on that subject in a public proclamation, but has even gone the length of declaring that it cannot consent to impair it."

Pinkney, like most Americans of that day, held the Orders-in-Council in particular aversion :

" The time when they were issued—the arrogant claims of Maritime dominion which they support and execute—and the contempt which they manifest, in the face of the world, for the rights and powers of our country, make them altogether the most offensive act that can be laid to the charge of any Government. The least appearance of a disposition to submit to such an attempt will encourage to further aggressions, until our national spirit will be lost in an habitual sense of humiliation, our character known only to be despised and our rights considered, like those of the petty States of Europe, the sport and prey of the strongest. There is an opinion here that we are likely to become a divided people when a rupture with Great Britain is in question, but this opinion . . . will undoubtedly be gloriously falsified if there should be occasion, by the patriotism of our people in every quarter of the Union."

Pinkney's optimism was, as we shall see, only partially justified when the clash finally came.

On the 24th of the same month he wrote :

" The anxiety which has been for some time past rapidly increasing relative to the United States is now very great and very general. The belief is everywhere entertained that we shall be found to have taken a strong attitude. A hope is, however, indulged that it will be short of war. . . . A dignified, firm and temperate course on our part must soon produce its proper effect on Great Britain and I should hope on France also.

" The most friendly dispositions are constantly professed by Ministers and I am quite sure that they are averse from a war with us ; yet the King's Speech will satisfy you that there is no present intention of yielding anything to our claims."

Personally, the American Minister admitted that he was

treated on all hands with great kindness and respect. He went to receptions and dinner parties and was frequently in the company of such people as the Duke of Norfolk, Erskine, Canning, Holland, Grenville, Lauderdale and Grey.

At the same time, he was not surprised to be told that Mr. Perceval had observed that if America was bent on having a war, it was perhaps as well, " as a check to our maritime growth was becoming indispensable."

And there were just then a good many American ships in British ports for whose safety Pinkney was anxious. He thought it " too strong a step to urge their departure," but they would be better at home.

All this time the President's credentials and instructions had not arrived. " My situation," wrote Pinkney (February 6), " will, I fear, become a little embarrassing if you forswear much longer to send my credentials or some precise instructions." He got them at last (April 25), and at once wrote :

" I feel very sensibly the delicacy and kindness of the assurances which you are so good as to give me, that the purpose of nominating me to the permanent Legation here was never for a moment suspended in the mind of the President."

Just before he was presented to the King, Pinkney had his first experience of that species of embarrassment which awaits an envoy whose confidential dispatches become public property in the country of their origin—a proceeding which later became of too frequent occurrence.

In this case it was his dispatch of January 7 which was read out in the Senate and so got into the newspapers. Pinkney hoped it would produce no bad effect, but if it had done any good he did not ask to be spared. A year later, when another of his confidential letters was printed in the English Press, Pinkney cheerfully reassured Madison :

" I do not believe that it will injure my standing here ; but if it did, it can only lead to my recall, and would not imply the disapprobation of my own Government. . . . Send me back to my profession with your good wishes, whenever it shall be thought expedient."

Of his audience of the King, Pinkney wrote :

" My reception was particularly kind and gracious ; with every evidence of a desire of the King to continue in friendship with us.

" But if we continue at peace with France they will recede here, on certain points with infinite difficulty and reluctance, if they recede at all.   They will not go to war if they can help it ; but it is to be doubted whether they are prepared to do what may be indispensable to the re-establishment of interrupted friendship."

May 10, 1808, Pinkney reported to Madison :

" They [the British] will not go to war if they can help it . . . they will be content to have things as they are, and to trust to the influence of events, and a hope will perhaps be indulged that we cannot persevere in the Embargo—that weary of our system of self-denial, pressed by French aggression and alarmed by the widespread domination and restless ambition of France, we shall at length be induced to acquiesce in the principles and practices of Great Britain (which must necessarily produce a contest with her enemy) or at once to make common cause with her against that enemy.   What is to be the system of France with regard to us I know not ; but it is sufficiently obvious that in the angry struggles of these rival Powers, our rights are forgotten by both, and that it requires all the tried wisdom and firmness of our Government and all the virtue of our people to conduct us in safety and with honour through the tempests that agitate this part of the world."

All this was very lofty and very patriotic ; but America had still to learn that she was not quite independent of Europe and that her existence as a nation imposed obligations and concessions.

On June 5 Pinkney wrote of his projected interview with George Canning :

" I intend to press by every argument in my power the propriety of their abandoning immediately their Orders-in-Council and of proposing reparation for the outrage on the *Chesapeake*.   I shall, for obvious reasons, do this informally as my own act."

WILLIAM PINKNEY.

Pinkney had his interview with Canning on June 28. At their very first meeting, remarks a contemporary American writer—

" the duplicity of our Cabinet and its agents gave a crooked bent to the negotiation, from which there was not enough of the elasticity of truth and sincerity in the man to recover it. They had a long conference, and in that conference Mr. Pinkney urged the expectation of his Government that the British would rescind their Orders-in-Council. To this Mr. Canning replied that the Orders-in-Council were not levelled at the United States as an act of hostility to them, but at France as an act of retaliation for the ' Berlin Decree.' Canning hinted that America ought to apply to France for satisfaction rather than to Britain." [1]

Pinkney then intimated that the Embargo would be repealed if the British withdrew the Orders—it was a suggestion of his own, quite without official authority, but he put it forward as his own belief.

As he afterwards stated to the Foreign Minister :

" I told you explicitly that the substance of what I suggested was from my Government ; but that the manner of conducting and illustrating it was all my own. I even repeated to you the words of my instructions, as they were upon my memory."

But was Pinkney's so-confident assertion borne out by the facts ? When his instructions are inspected they are found to contain not one single word of that import, but, on the contrary, directions the very reverse.

Madison had referred Pinkney to his own answer to the British Minister, Erskine, which was :

" The United States are well warranted in looking for a speedy revocation to a system which is every day augmenting the mass of injury for which the United States have the best claims to redress."

He had expressly told Pinkney :

" Still it is to be understood that while the insult offered in the attack on the *Chesapeake* remains unexpiated, you are

[1] *The Memoirs of Thomas Jefferson.*

8

not to pledge or commit your Government to consider a
recall of the Orders-in-Council as a ground on which a
removal of the existing restrictions on the commerce of the
United States with Great Britain may be justly expected."

This would, in truth, seem to be a positive order not to
give the British Government reason to expect that the
Embargo should be repealed, even though the Orders-in-
Council were.

Pinkney seems to have been well aware of this, for on
June 5 he had written to Madison mentioning his approaching
interview with the British Foreign Minister, when he would
press the subject of repeal.

" But I shall, for obvious reasons, do this informally, as
my own act," adding, " You may be assured that I will
not commit our Government by anything I may do or say."

No wonder he was afterwards charged with an attempt to
" cajole " Canning. But to succeed in such an attempt was
beyond even Pinkney's considerable powers.

" If [wrote Canning] the Embargo is considered as a
measure of hostility, his Majesty cannot consent to buy it
off. If, as has been more generally represented by the
Government of the United States, it is only to be considered
as an innocent municipal regulation, which affects none but
the United States themselves, and in which no foreign
States have any concern, his Majesty does not conceive that
he has the right or the pretensions to make any complaint
of it : and he has made none. But in this light there appears
not only no necessity, but no assignable relation, between
the repeal by the United States of a voluntary self-restriction
and the surrender by his Majesty of his right of retaliation
against his enemies."

As the author of the *Memoirs of Jefferson* already quoted
shrewdly observed, the American Government were not so—

" grossly ignorant of the character of the British Ministers
as to expect them to be the dupes of such contemptible
cajolery. They could not really imagine that the British
nation, which maintains a lofty pre-eminence over the
nations of Europe, would be intimidated into a surrender
of its rights of attacking her murderous enemy with his own
weapons, would consent to be bullied and plundered, under

the name of tribute, and made to fetch and carry like a dog
by Buonaparte. Would such a Government as that of
Great Britain suffer the world to believe that it could be
coerced by our Embargo or subdued by our miserable timid
system and suicidal policy ? "

So imminent did war seem in the early summer of 1808
that Pinkney began to arrange for his departure. The
removal of his eldest son from school troubled him : his
eminent Whig friend, Lord Holland, thought he should
not be removed and handsomely offered to stand *in loco
parentis* to the youngster. He wrote (June 1, 1808) :

" From fear that you might have thought what I said to
you about your boy a mere matter of form, I write again
to say I have talked it over with Lady Holland, and that
if we are to encounter the misfortune of a war with America,
and upon leaving this country you should wish your son to
pursue his education *here*, Lady Holland and myself beg to
assure you that without the least inconvenience to us, we can
take care of him during the holidays ; and between them
ascertain that he is going on properly and give you all the
information you would require upon the progress of his
studies, of the state of his health."

All through that summer Pinkney strove to induce Canning
to abandon the Orders of 1807, even, as we have seen, promising a suspension of the Embargo Act. At first the British
Foreign Minister was struck favourably by the idea, but at
subsequent interviews he grew chillier. He asked Pinkney
to put his proposal in writing ; but the American objected to
a written correspondence, and especially to any formal offer
until he knew that it would be acceptable. But Canning
was wary : Pinkney's suggestion " implied that the Embargo
was produced by the British Orders-in-Council—that this
could not be admitted." He hinted that there were other
causes. American historians of the war of 1812 have
clearly demonstrated that there were other causes. The discussions were frequent and warm, but never " in any degree
unfriendly," in language or manner.

So at last Pinkney was moved to compose a note, which,
at first very lengthy, he afterwards reduced, and delivered
to Canning on August 26. The Minister promptly rejected

the American's argument and a heated correspondence ensued. Pinkney spoke out his mind on the whole issue as he had done from the first.

" I am not able [he reported on October 11, 1808] to judge whether my reply to Canning's letter will be approved by the President. I need not say that I hope it will. At any rate, it can do no harm, as it is simply my act. If ill received, as perhaps it may be, it can only affect myself."

Canning had pretty broadly hinted that the American Embargo was concerted with France. It had always been alleged in England that the President knew nothing about the British Orders-in-Council when he recommended the Embargo in his Message. Consequently, the only reason for including Great Britain in that instrument was approval of the French plan of a Continental blockade.

Madison wrote to Pinkney (November 9, 1808) :

" The conduct of the British Cabinet in rejecting the fair offer made to it and even sneering at the course pursued by the United States proves . . . a confidence that events were taking place here which would relieve it from the necessity of repealing the Orders-in-Council. But Canning might be disappointed in his estimate of American opinion."

"The disposition," the Secretary wrote a month later, " to prefer war to the course hitherto pursued, is rather gaining than losing ground.

". . . I cannot believe that there is so much depravity or stupidity in the Eastern States as to countenance the reports that they will separate from their brethren rather than submit any longer to the suspense of their commerce."

Nevertheless, it was a risk for the Federal Government, as events were to prove.

On January 23, 1809, Pinkney wrote :

" I dined at Mr. Canning's with the *Corps Diplomatique,* on the 18th, the day appointed for the celebration of the Queen's birthday. Before dinner he came up to me and, entering into conversation, adverted to a report which he said had reached him that the American Ministers (here and in France) were about to be recalled."

Pinkney denied any knowledge of this. Canning then took him aside and—

" observed that according to his view of the late proceedings of Congress, the resolutions in committee of the whole appeared to be calculated, if passed into law, to remove the impediments to an arrangement with the United States upon the two subjects of the Orders-in-Council and the *Chesapeake*."

Consequently—

" they were willing to consider the law to which the resolutions were preparatory as putting an end to the difficulties which prevented satisfactory adjustments with us."

As all this occurred rather unexpectedly (although his reception at Court and other circumstances of much more consequence had seemed to give notice of some change, Pinkney asked for a day or two to consider. But, he intimated to Canning, his own opinion of the resolutions in Congress was the same he had previously stated.

A formal meeting took place on January 22, when the matter was fully discussed. From Madison (who had just been elected to the Presidency) the Minister heard, in a letter dated February 11, 1809 :

" If the Non-Intercourse as proposed should be adopted, it will leave open a trade to all the Continent of Europe, except France."

On April 26 a fresh British Order-in-Council was issued by which the blockade declared by the previous Orders was restricted to the ports of France and Holland. In forwarding a copy, Pinkney wrote :

" I venture to hope that this measure will open the way to reconcilement, without detriment to our interests or our honour. . . . The change does undoubtedly produce a great effect in a commercial view, and removes many of the most disgusting features of that system of violence and monopoly against which our efforts have been justly directed. The Orders of November were in execution of a sordid scheme of commercial and fiscal advantage in which America was to be sacrificed. They were not more atrocious because through British ports and obliged to pay British imposts. As a

belligerent system the Orders were nothing. They were a
trick of trade—a huckstering contrivance to enrich Great
Britain and drive other nations from the seas. The new
system has a better air. Commerce is no longer to be forced
through this country. We may go direct to Russia and to
all other countries, except to France and Holland, and the
Kingdom of Italy and their colonies. . . . There can be no
question that this change gives us all the immediate benefits
which could have arisen out of the acceptance of our overture
of last year."

And the best of it was the Americans would

" pay no price. We give no pledge of any sort. The
Embargo is already repealed after the end of the approaching
session of Congress. The Non-Intercourse law will expire at
the same time."

And again :

" I am not sure that we have not got rid of the most
obnoxious portion of the British Orders *in the most acceptable
way.*"

On March 4, 1809, Madison had succeeded Jefferson as
President. Almost his first step was to conclude an arrangement with Erskine, the British Minister in Washington, who
definitely promised that the Orders-in-Council would be
repealed and satisfaction given for the attack on the *Chesapeake.* Anglo-American trade was forthwith to be renewed.
No sooner, however, was this arrangement known to Downing
Street than it was disavowed and the temerarious Erskine
recalled. In his place F. J. Jackson was sent out to
Washington as special envoy ; but he brought no olive
branch. On the contrary, he entered at once upon an
acrimonious correspondence with Smith, the new Secretary
of State, imputing to the American Government a knowledge
of the fact that, in concluding an arrangement with them,
Erskine was acting entirely without instructions.

" Jackson's course [wrote Pinkney when he heard of it,
December 10] is an extraordinary one and his manner is
little better. The British Government has acted for some
time upon an opinion that its partisans in America were too
numerous and strong to admit of our persevering in any

system of repulsion to British injustice. . . . Yet [the added] the people of England are rather better disposed than heretofore to accommodate with us."

He had been asked why, since the treatment American shipping received from France was the same or worse than that they received from England, did his Government not seek war with France ?
Pinkney undertook to explain. The gist of his explanation was that there was absolutely nothing to be got out of France.

" Upon France, I fear, we have no means of acting with effect. Her ruler sets our ordinary means at defiance. We cannot alarm him for his colonies, his trade, his manufactures, or his revenue. . . . A war with France would not help our case. It would aggravate embarrassments in all respects. For our honour it could do nothing. The territory of this mighty Power is absolutely invulnerable ; and there is no mode in which we could make her feel either physical or moral coercion. We might as well declare war against the inhabitants of the Moon or the Georgium Sidus." [1]

But, with England—who was then struggling for her life against Napoleon—a bloody war could be safely threatened !
Minister Pinkney had heard that George Rose was to have been sent to Washington as special envoy, if Erskine's arrangement had not been disavowed, and he felt—

" bound to say that a worse choice could not have been made. Since his return to England he has, I know, misrepresented and traduced us with an industry that is absolutely astonishing, notwithstanding the cant of friendship and respect with which he overwhelms the few Americans who see him."

Canning was now out of the Ministry, being succeeded by Lord Bathurst. By March 1810 Pinkney could write " with certainty that a more friendly disposition towards the United States exists in this country at present than for a long time past."
It was hardly to be expected that all the fire-eaters at home would be pleased at the efforts of their country's representative in London to prevent war. Pinkney's notes and dis-

[1] Pinkney to Secretary Smith, December 10, 1809.

patches seemed to many too tame—too pacific and conciliatory. There began therefore a campaign of abuse against him, and clamours for his recall.

"I am told [he wrote Secretary Monroe, August 13, 1810], and have indeed seen, that I am assailed with great acrimony and perseverance in some of the American newspapers. It is possible that increasing clamour, though it can give me no concern, may make it convenient that I should be recalled. . . . I have really no wish to continue for any purpose looking to my own advantage. . . . The disproportion between my unavoidable expenses and my salary has ruined me in a pecuniary sense."

As a matter of fact Pinkney had spent all his hoarded earnings during his occupancy of the Legation on necessary social entertainment and the education of his children, and it was growing imperative that he should return to the practice of his profession in America. To be honest, he said, he must hasten home.

"The compensation (as it is oddly called) allotted by the Government to the maintenance of its representatives abroad, is a pittance which no economy, however rigid, or even mean, can render adequate. I have in fact been a constant and progressive loser, and at length am incapable of supplying the deficiencies of the public allowance."

In the same dispatch from which quotation has just been made, Pinkney reported that a new Foreign Secretary, Lord Wellesley, had answered his letter about the Embargo. Wellesley's reply was—

"the production of an indolent man—making a great effort to reconcile things almost incongruous and just showing his wish without executing it. Lord Wellesley wished to be extremely civil to the American Government ; but he wished, at the same time, to be very stately—to manage Jackson's situation—and to intimate disapprobation of the suspension of his functions. He was stately, not so much from design as because he cannot do otherwise. . . . For Jackson, personally, Lord Wellesley cares nothing. In his several conferences with me, he never vindicated him, and he certainly did not mean in his letter to undertake his defence.

It is impossible that he should not have (I am indeed sure that he has) a mean opinion of that most clumsy and ill-conditioned Minister."

To Wellesley himself he wrote (November 3, 1810) that he had heard from Minister Armstrong in Paris that he " had received from the French Government a written and official notice that it had revoked the decrees of Berlin and Milan, and that after November 1 those decrees would cease to have any effect."

After such a welcome announcement he confidently expected to hear that the British Government had at last revoked their objectionable Orders-in-Council. Lord Wellesley had himself told him of the King's earnest desire to see the commerce of the world restored to that freedom which is necessary for its prosperity and his readiness to abandon the system which had been forced upon him, whenever the enemy should retract the principles which had rendered it necessary.

But, to his surprise and chagrin, the " indolent " Wellesley still expressed doubt on the cardinal point. Napoleon had not revoked the Decrees. Whereupon Pinkney proceeded in a lengthy note (December 10, 1810) to bring conviction to the doubting head of the British Foreign Office.

Wellesley would have liked to share the American Minister's confidence, but his Government, he said, remained without " authentic intelligence " of the revocation of the French Decrees. Pinkney now nearly lost his temper, and after adroitly begging the question for several foolscap pages, concluded thus :

" I should only fatigue your lordship by pursuing further a point so plain and simple. I will therefore merely add to what I have already said, on this branch of the subject, that the strong and unqualified communication from General Armstrong to me may perhaps, without any great effort of courtesy, be allowed to contain that ' authentic intelligence ' which your lordship is in search of. He could scarcely have been free from doubt if the occasion was calculated to suggest it, and if he had really doubted, would hardly have spoken to me with the confidence of conviction."

Unsuspecting Napoleon's carefully planned duplicity, he sought to prove, by an array of sophistical arguments, that the Decrees of the Emperor were not in force because of the absence of such facts as would appear if they were in force.

" Every motive which can be conjectured to have led to the repeal of the edicts invites to the full execution of that repeal, and no motive can be imagined for a different course. . . . These conclusions [he announced] are alone conclusive."

Pinkney's credulity did not stop there.

" It is known that American vessels bound confessedly to England have, before the 1st of November, been visited by French privateers and suffered to pass upon the foundation of the prospective repeal of the Decree of Berlin and the proximity of the day when it would become an actual one. . . . If there are not even stronger facts to show that the Decree of Milan is also withdrawn, your lordship can be at no loss for the reason. It cannot be proved that any American vessel is practically held by France." [1]

If he had chosen to press his American colleague in Paris, Minister Crawford could have told him a different story, for the authorities at Brest, Havre and Lorient had received no Imperial order on the subject about detaining American shipping.

To sum up : It was one thing for the French Minister, the Duc de Cadore, to declare the Decrees had been repealed ; it was quite another formally to repeal them. And so, England —ever rightly sceptical of Napoleonic good faith—refused to give up for nothing her Orders-in-Council and her blockades.

Yet Pinkney continued to the end to stick to his contention. On January 14 he wrote again to Lord Wellesley :

" I am not in possession of any document which you are likely to consider as *authentic*, showing that the French Decrees are absolutely revoked upon the single condition of the revocation of the British Orders-in-Council ; but that the information, which I have lately received from the American Legation at Paris, confirms what I have already stated, and I think proved to your lordship, that those Decrees are repealed, and have ceased to have any effect. I will now

[1] Pinkney's letter must now be pronounced a disingenuous example of special pleading based on no real evidence whatever.

trespass on you no further than to suggest that it would have given me sincere pleasure to be enabled to say as much of the British Orders-in-Council, and of the blockades, from which it is impossible to distinguish them."

On the same day he formally advised the Foreign Secretary that as there was now no British Minister at Washington, the American Government desired to recall him.

" After a lapse of many months since I had the honour to receive and convey to my Government your lordship's repeated assurances, written as well as verbal (which you declined, however, to put into an official form) that it was your intention *immediately* to recommend the appointment of a minister plenipotentiary from the King to the United States, and the British Government continues to be represented at Washington by a Chargé d'affaires, and no steps whatever appear to have been taken to fulfil the expectation which the above-mentioned assurances produced and justified, it has become my duty to inform your lordship, in compliance with my instructions, that the Government of the United States cannot continue to be represented here by a Minister Plenipotentiary.

" As soon, therefore, as the situation of the King's Government will permit, I shall wish to take my leave and return to America in the United States frigate *Essex*, now at Plymouth, having first named, as I am specially authorized to do, a fit person to take charge of the affairs of the American Legation to this country."

On February 28, 1811, Pinkney had his audience of leave at Carlton House and stated to the Prince Regent the ground upon which it had become his duty to retire, expressing his regret that his efforts to re-establish the relations between the two countries had failed. He added that he saw no reason to expect that the great work of reconciliation was likely to be accomplished by any other peaceful agency.

In truth the two countries were drifting daily closer to that war which many had long seen to be inevitable.

In Professor Mowat's opinion, indeed—

"an Anglo-American war might have occurred without surprising anyone, at almost any time after 1793. The Jay Treaty, which the Americans considered to be a very one-sided affair, had averted war for a time; after that the diplomacy of Rufus King at London and of Robert Liston at Washington had tided over many difficulties. The Monroe Treaty of 1806 (although it was never completed) and the Erskine Treaty of 1809 (although it was still-born) had eased the tension. But the tension always reappeared. Great Britain, being engaged in a life-and-death struggle with France, could not afford to compromise much on the question of the neutral carrying trade and the question of impressing British subjects from American merchant ships." [1]

BIOGRAPHICAL NOTE

On arrival home in June 1811 Pinkney resumed his law practice. In September he was elected to the Maryland State Senate, and in December was chosen by Madison Attorney-General of the United States, a post which he held until the beginning of 1814, when the great increase in his practice caused him to resign it. In 1816 he was appointed Minister to Russia, where he remained two years. Later he took his seat in the American Senate, and died February 25, 1822.

[1] Mowat : *Diplomatic Relations.*

CHAPTER VII

JOHN QUINCY ADAMS (1815–1817)

In Paris when General Armstrong was American Minister, the Secretary of Legation was one of the earliest of America's professional diplomats, forty years of age—Jonathan Russell. When Armstrong quitted his post, the Secretary carried on the business of the Legation until a successor arrived.

On July 27, 1811, James Monroe wrote to Russell :

" This letter will be delivered to you by Mr. Barlow, who is appointed to represent the United States at Paris as their Minister Plenipotentiary. You will deliver to him the papers in your possession, and give him all the information in your power, relative to our affairs with the French Government.

" The President has instructed me to communicate to you his approbation of your conduct in the discharge of the duties which developed on you, as Chargé d'affaires at Paris, after the departure of General Armstrong, which I execute with pleasure. As an evidence of his confidence and favourable disposition, he has appointed you to the same trust in London, for which I enclose you a commission. . . .

" Your services in France will have given you such knowledge of your duties at London, that I shall not go into detail in this communication respecting them. It is wished and expected that you and Mr. Barlow will communicate fully on the subject of your respective duties, and co-operate together in the measures which are deemed necessary."

Russell accordingly went to London and exerted himself energetically to prevent the two countries drifting into the war which he saw it was Napoleon's policy to bring about. But the British Declaration and Order-in-Council of the following April lessened the chances of peace. We have already seen that both Lord Wellesley and his successor

111

Castlereagh refused to believe in the revocation of the Berlin and Milan Decrees. Russell pleaded with Castlereagh (April 26, 1812) :

" I will seek still to confide in the spirit which your lordship, in your note and in the conversation of this morning, has been pleased to say actuates the councils of his Royal Highness in relation to America, and still to cherish a hope that this spirit will lead, upon a review of the whole ground, to measures of a nature better calculated to attain its object ; and that this object will no longer be made to depend on the conduct of a third Power, or upon contingencies over which the United States have no control, but alone upon the rights of the United States, the justice of Great Britain, and the common interests of both."

A fortnight after this letter was written, Spencer Perceval, the British Prime Minister, was assassinated in the lobby of the House of Commons by a demented Liverpool broker, and the Ministry promptly disintegrated. In June the Liverpool administration was formed, and on the 23rd of that month an Ordinance was issued suspending the Orders-in-Council. A copy of the Ordinance was sent to the American Chargé d'affaires, who wrote to Castlereagh three days later :

" In communicating this document to my Government, I shall with much satisfaction accompany it with the hopes which you state to be entertained by his Royal Highness the Prince Regent that it may accelerate a good understanding on all points of difference between the two States. I am the more encouraged to believe that these hopes will not be disappointed, from the conversation of this morning, that, in the opinion of your lordship, the blockade of the 16th May, 1806, had been merged in the Orders-in-Council, now revoked, and extinguished with them ; and that no condition contained in the Order of the 23rd instant is to be interpreted to restrain the Government of the United States from the exercise of its rights to exclude British armed vessels from the harbours and waters of the United States, whenever such exclusions shall, from a general policy, be extended to the armed vessels of the enemies of Great Britain. This assurance I am happy to consider as evidence of a conciliatory spirit, which will afford, on every other point of difference, an explanation equally frank and satisfactory."

Yet even before Russell had penned these words the long-meditated hostilities were actually declared by his own Government. On June 1 President Madison had recommended a Declaration of War, and on the 18th the measure was approved by Congress.

The news took several weeks to reach London, where it was received by the Government with surprise and chagrin, emotions which were shared to the full by Russell, who had been in hopes of effecting a final reconciliation. But in order fully to satisfy America, and in particular Monroe, who was out to " fight to a finish," the British Government would have to give up the right of Impressment. But would they ? Russell lost no time in urging Castlereagh to declare the Ministry's intentions on this head, and on August 29 had the mortification to learn that Great Britain could not possibly consent " to desist from its ancient and accustomed practice of impressing British seamen from the merchant ships of a foreign State."

It was virtually only this subject which separated the two countries, for on every other issue their interest was mutual for peace and co-operation. And after all the pother made about it for twenty years, Impressment was really no great and oppressive grievance, as the leading New England ship-owners, who were generally opposed throughout to the war, made haste to show. Since 1793, it appeared, fewer than five thousand British seamen had been impressed from American merchant ships, which were the only ships concerned. Three important shipmasters testified that of all their crews they could only recall five men who had been impressed. But popular feeling had been stirred : the Southerners and Westerners wanted war, and they got it. It may, however, be mentioned here that they did not get freedom from impressment as a result of this war. Before it began and in its early stages they had other hopes. They conceived that Canada and the British North American possessions would be easily conquered and added to the Union. In this hope, too, they were destined to bitter disappointment.

For England the war could not have come at a more unwelcome, a more critical moment. When it broke out, Napoleon was on his way to Moscow at the head of an enormous army. He had uttered the boast, " In five years' time I shall be master of the world."

To prevent this calamity, England was straining her sinews to the utmost. It seemed a cruel hardship that at such a time the forces of America should be launched against her—America, the daughter State, whose national ideals and aims were so totally opposed to those of Napoleon and which had suffered equal indignity and loss at the hands of France.

" At the moment of the declaration of war [wrote Monroe to Russell in London, August 21] the President, regretting the necessity which produced it, looked for its termination and provided for it."

He stipulated for a repeal of the Orders-in-Council and the cessation of Impressment.[1]

" If [Lord Castlereagh observed] the American Government was so anxious to get rid of the war, it would have an opportunity of so doing on learning of the revocation of the Orders-in-Council."

In October Monroe told the French Minister, Serrurier, at Washington :

" The English wish for peace with America ; they wish it at any cost ; they offer all that America demands, and negotiations are going to open, or rather are continuing, and henceforth openly."

This was rather a strong way of putting it, but it is a curiosity of the international situation that diplomatic contact was never interrupted during those thirty months of war. Russell and Castlereagh continued their exchange of notes in London.

In the autumn of 1813 the Americans had been beaten in the field at Chateauguay and Chrysler's Farm, and again in the following year at Lundy's Lane. Canada was now safe. Washington, on one side of the Atlantic, was captured ; the French were well beaten on the other. The Peninsular War

---

[1] Admiral Mahan sees a threat in Monroe's reminder of " the injuries which cannot fail to result from a prosecution of the war." " In transcribing his instructions," comments Mahan, " Russell discreetly omitted the latter phrase ; but the omission, like the words themselves, betrays consciousness that the administration was faithful to the tradition of its party, dealing in threats rather than deeds."—A. T. Mahan : *The War of* 1812.

was ended, Napoleon had abdicated, and on May 30, 1814, peace between the Allies and France was proclaimed at Paris.

Yet Castlereagh and Russell were still exchanging notes, and the war went on. At last, through the mediation of the Emperor Alexander of Russia, commissioners were appointed on both sides, and in August they met in Ghent. The Americans sent Albert Gallatin, an able statesman of Swiss birth and actually Secretary of the Treasury; John Quincy Adams, late Minister to Russia; Henry Clay, Speaker of the House; and James Assheton Bayard, a distinguished lawyer. To these was naturally added the name of the London Chargé d'affaires, Russell himself, who had incontestably proved his ability.

As to the British commissioners, Lord Gambier was a naval officer, if not of "discreditable repute," at least of no very high standing; Henry Goulburn, "a mere tyro in diplomacy"; and William Adams, who is characterized as "an academic jurist." The trio "had apparently been selected because they were mediocrities and could therefore be trusted to take no initiative, but mechanically reflect the mind of the British Ministry." [1]

The story of the negotiations which led to the Treaty of Ghent does not properly belong to these pages. They lasted five months, and were hardly notable for good temper and an absence of friction. Indeed—

"never in the history of diplomacy [says an American historian] has concord been produced from such discordant elements as had been brought together at Ghent. . . . Dissension seemed to have become the mother of amity and, . . . in diplomacy as in marriage, it had worked well to begin with a little aversion."

We know now that Castlereagh at Vienna had been converted to the idea of peace, and wrote to his chief, Lord Liverpool, to finish the business with America.

"With the Peace of Ghent [says Professor Mowat] there was an end also of the period of bad feeling between the British and American Governments. From the signing of the Treaties of Independence in 1782–3 to the signing of the

[1] Adams: *History of the United States.*

Treaty of Ghent there was mutual suspicion and irritation. But in the War of 1812–14 both Powers found themselves ; they had each proved a good match for the other in the fight ; and in the final settlement neither had to suffer the mortification of defeat.   There were no rankling sores left." [1]

When it was all over, it was announced that President Madison had appointed one of the commissioners, Gallatin, to represent the United States at Paris ; Jonathan Russell was rewarded with the mission to Norway and Sweden ; while John Quincy Adams became Minister to England.

The new Minister had passed a large part of his life in diplomacy : at a tender age he had assisted his father, John Adams, and Dr. Franklin in Paris.   Yet at forty-eight he was still far from being the perfect diplomatist.

" His manners," in John Fiske's judgment, " were stiff and disagreeable ; he told the truth bluntly, whether it hurt or not ; and he never took pains to conciliate anyone.   The best of men in his domestic circle, outside of it he had few warm friends, but he seemed to have a talent for making enemies."

Perhaps an apology is due for quoting the impertinence of young James Gallatin, who records in his *Diary* :

" Mr. Adams is really a thorn : he is absolutely ' Yankee ' and of a common type.   Why he is a Minister here I cannot understand.   He is totally unfitted for the post."

" I cannot," Adams himself avows, " always restrain the irritability of my temper " ; and on another occasion during the negotiations at Ghent : " I must not forget to keep a constant guard upon my temper," which shows that he was conscious of this defect.   The guard was there, but, alas ! it was perpetually being overpowered.

After leaving Ghent, Adams in February 1815 visited Paris, where he remained during the Hundred Days, and on May 25—three weeks before Waterloo—arrived in London. Four days later he met the Foreign Secretary and handed him his credentials as Minister Plenipotentiary from the United States.

[1] Mowat : *The Diplomatic Relations of Great Britain and the United States.*

JOHN QUINCY ADAMS.

" Lord Castlereagh had appointed eleven o'clock this morning for me to see him at his house in St. James's Square. After waiting nearly an hour beyond that time for my carriage, I took a hackney-coach and went there."

Such lack of punctuality would not have been very agreeable to Castlereagh, but this morning he was preoccupied by another distinguished visitor.

" The Duke of Orleans was with him and I waited about another half-hour before he received me. I gave him a copy of my credence to the Prince Regent, upon which he said he would take the orders of his Royal Highness as to the time when he would receive it. There was some general conversation upon the subject of the concerns mutually interesting to the two nations. I assured him of the disposition on the part of the American Government to perform with the utmost fidelity all their engagements contracted in the late Treaty of Peace and to adopt every other measure calculated to consolidate the friendship and promote the harmony between the two countries, as a token of which an Act of Congress had passed previous to the close of their late session tendering on the part of the United States a reciprocal abolition of all discriminating duties of tonnage and upon merchandise imported in our own or British vessels. . . . I mentioned also, the message of the President recommending the exclusion of foreign seamen, not already naturalized, from the naval and merchant service of the United States in a measure which Congress, owing to the shortness of time, had not acted upon, but which would probably hereafter be adopted."

Castlereagh observed that while he was glad to hear that, there—

" was an opinion abroad that the American Government encouraged and invited foreign seamen. As to the principle involved, he was afraid there was little prospect of coming to an agreement as . . . no British Government could possibly abandon the right to the allegiance of British subjects."

" I said [reported Adams] that I saw no better prospect than he did of an agreement upon the principle. But it was not the disposition of the American Government or nation

to apply the force of arms to the maintenance of any abstract
principle. The number of British seamen naturalized in
America was so small that it could be no object of concern
to this Government. If British subjects were excluded for
the future, there could be no motive for taking men from
American vessels. If the practice totally ceased, we should
never call upon the British Government for any sacrifice
of their principle. When the evil ceased to be felt, we should
readily deem it to have ceased to exist.

" He said that there would be every disposition to guard
against the possibility of abuse, and the Admiralty was now
occupied in prescribing regulations for the naval officers,
which he hoped would prevent all cause of complaint on the
part of the United States."

The conversation then drifted on the appointment of
commissioners under the Treaty of Ghent to negotiate a
treaty of commerce. Castlereagh had only waited for
Adams's arrival as American Minister to name a British
Minister to Washington, and he now named Sir Charles
Bagot.

On June 8 the Minister was presented to the Prince Regent
at Carlton House. As he approached, the Prince said, " Mr.
Adams, I am happy to see you." He then took the President's letter and, without opening it, delivered it immediately
to Lord Castlereagh, and said, in answer to Adams, that
" the United States might rely, with the fullest assurance,
upon his determination to fulfil on the part of Great Britain
all the engagements with the United States."

" He then [reported the Minister] asked me if I was
related to Mr. Adams who had formerly been the Minister
from the United States here. I said I was his son. He
inquired whether I had ever been before in England. I had.
With a public mission ? Once, with a special mission,
during the absence of the Minister then accredited here.
He said he had known two of the former Ministers of the
United States here, who were Mr. Pinckney and Mr. Rufus
King—very gentlemanly men. Mr. King was very much
of a gentleman. Where was Mr. Pinckney now ? I said
there had been two Mr. Pinckneys here as Ministers from the
United States. ' Ah ! ' said he, ' but I mean the Mr.
Pinckney who was here before Mr. King.' I said he was

now a general in the army. ' In the army ? ' said he. ' I did not know that. Had he ever been in the army before ? ' I said he had. ' And where is Mr. King ? ' I said he was now a member of the Senate of the United States. ' And how did you like living there at Brussels ? ' said the Prince. ' Your Royal Highness probably means Ghent ? ' said I. ' Ay ! Ghent ! So it was,' said he ; ' and how did you like Ghent ? ' I said we liked it very much, for the result of what was done there. ' Oh, yes ! ' said he ; ' but I mean, did you find any society there ? ' I said we had found society ; that Ghent was a very ancient and venerable city, with proud recollections ; that its inhabitants thought and talked of it, as the residence where a great sovereign holds his Court. ' Ay ! ' said the Prince, ' there are a number of those great old cities there.' "

After a few further colloquial interchanges on the same intellectual level, Adams took his leave. He may be pardoned for not being impressed : this was perhaps one of the Prince Regent's bad mornings ; he acquitted himself better with Adams's successor, Richard Rush.

The following day Adams had to undergo an ordeal which further disgusted him with the pomp and pageantry of Courts. He was, incredibly, asked to pay for it, and his frugal New England soul revolted.

" I was scarcely risen this morning, when the marshals, grooms, porters, and attendants at the palace came to present their humble duty, bringing their books to show what had been paid them by all the foreign Ministers, and other persons presented at Court. Mr. Lawrence and Mr. Moore soon afterwards came for their passports, which I gave them. Mr. Campbell came, and I made a settlement with him for our passage in the *Olga*, for which I gave him an order upon Mr. Williams. Mr. Brown, the tailor whom I have employed, came, with great terror and many apologies asked me if I could pay him twenty-five pounds upon his bill. I paid him his whole bill, at which he expressed much surprise. He told me that if he should do the same to any of his customers here, they would never have employed him again."

On the other hand, as partial compensation for all this expense the British Government at this period made a gift of money to all retiring ambassadors and ministers. Pinckney, King and Monroe had apparently not been above taking a little tip of £500 on their departure from the English Court.

Yet it must not be supposed that Adams really was not fond of society or unpopular in society. Night after night, as he records in his diary, he attended receptions and routs, danced, played cards, talked and ingratiated himself with the people about him.[1]

But Adams doubtless did all this from conscientious motives. It is hardly likely that he really enjoyed the intenser social life.

His first official business was, of course, to assist in the negotiation of an Anglo-American treaty of commerce. His fellow-commissioners, Clay and Gallatin, had already arrived and were impatient to get the job finished and return to America. The British commissioners, on their part, evinced no signs of hurry. It was different, said one of them, when we were at Ghent, for " there we had nothing else to do." Clay was pessimistic from the first. He told Adams he did not expect the negotiation would come to anything, and that if Gallatin had been of his mind they would have persisted in going away immediately.

He seemed, however, inclined to sign the article for the direct trade, as formulated in the rejected Treaty of 1806. Adams told him he—

" did not think it worth the trouble of signing our names for that. The trade was so much more valuable and important to them than to us, that we had in their interest a much more certain pledge for its continuance than any treaty could be, and I thought we might risk more than we could gain by showing an anxious desire for treaty stipulations, to secure what we knew we should have without them. It would encourage them to demand substantial advantages from us in return from them. He said they had no reason to suppose from anything that had passed that we were desirous of a commercial treaty."

On June 19 the plenipotentiaries met at the Board of Trade, and there ensued a discussion, in which there was much

---

[1] *Memoirs of John Quincy Adams,* Vol. II. Schuyler : *American Diplomacy.*

misunderstanding and wrangling. Adams himself refrained from taking an active part. He reported :—

" The whole business is conducted with so much precipitation ; and the reference is so continual to the conferences which had taken place before my arrival, upon the substance of which the ideas of the two parties are so widely different, that I have not felt it safe or prudent to enter into the debates, and have been entirely silent. It became perfectly clear to me this day that upon no one of the three points for which the negotiation was commenced is there any likelihood of our coming to an agreement with the British plenipotentiaries. Their counter-project presents the article relating to the intercourse with Canada so drawn that it would indirectly give them the trade with Indians within our territories, and it does not admit us to navigate the river St. Lawrence, even down to Montreal. They disavowed the intention of obtaining thus indirectly the Indian trade, but they inflexibly resisted the allowance of our navigating the waters under their exclusive jurisdiction, even for rafts, to carry lumber and flour to Montreal."

The next day Clay again threatened to break off the negotiation.

On June 21 Adams told Gallatin that if the British plenipotentiaries should continue inflexible on the East Indian and Canadian articles, he thought it would be best to sign a convention in a single article equalizing the duties without pretending to make it a treaty of commerce—

" that our countrymen would think it worse than ridiculous if we should give them for a treaty of commerce an instrument filled with articles of mere form, about admitting consuls and the like, which, with or without treaty, would stand on precisely the same footing, and without containing a single article to settle any of the points, commercial or political, which really belong to treaties of commerce—that for equalizing the duties being such that it might safely rest on the legislative acts of the two countries without a treaty."

Gallatin differed from this opinion and said that as to the political articles, they did not properly belong to treaties of commerce, and he did not know why they were ever put into them. He thought they seldom were.

" I said they were in all the modern treaties of commerce,
and instanced that of 1786 between France and England, in
which Great Britain had admitted the principle of free ships
making free goods.   He said he never knew that, and he
believed I was mistaken.

" I afterwards appealed to Mr. Clay, who remembered
as I did, but Mr. Gallatin persisted in his unbelief.   He said
he had thought of two proposals to make relative to the
East Indian article.   One was, to offer a reciprocal admission
of British ships from the East Indies into the United States.
The other was, to shorten the whole convention to a middle
term between the eight years originally proposed and the two
years to which the British plenipotentiaries wish to reduce
the East Indian article."

While all this was happening in a dismal public office in
Whitehall, the fate of Europe and perhaps the world, trembling
in the balance, had been decided across the Channel.   It took
nearly four days for the news of the battle of Waterloo to
reach London.   On June 22 Adams records in his diary :

" Shortly after rising this morning I received a note from
Lord Castlereagh's office, announcing the splendid and
complete victory of the Duke of Wellington and Marshal
Blucher over the French army, commanded by Bonaparte
in person, on Sunday last, the 18th.   In the course of the day
I received from the same office two copies of the *Gazette
Extraordinary*, containing the Duke of Wellington's dispatch
of the 19th.

" 23rd.—In the evening we all rode round the streets to see
the illuminations for the great victory of the 18th.   They
were not general, nor very magnificent.   The whole range
of their variety was, ' Wellington and Blucher,' ' Victory,'
' G.P.R.' and ' G.R.'   The transparencies were very few,
and very bad.   We came home at about midnight."

A week later Adams records that—

" between one and two o'clock Messrs. Clay and Gallatin
came to my lodgings, to consult with me upon the note
which we received last evening from the British plenipotentiaries.   Mr. Clay thought no reply from us was
necessary.   I thought one indispensable.   Of two alternatives
which we offered them in our last note they accept one, but,
with pretensions of generosity, as if they were granting a

favour, which I thought it essential to repel. I insisted on this, until Mr. Gallatin took from his pocket the draft of a note which he had prepared and with the substance of which I was satisfied. Mr. Clay ultimately consented to sign it, and immediately transcribed it from the draft. We took it with us, and delivered it ourselves to the British plenipotentiaries. We were now agreed upon the substance of the Convention, which is to be for four years from the signature, and consists of five articles. From the drafts made of the second article on both sides, its ultimate form was agreed upon. Mr. Gallatin had inserted the exception relative to the West Indies in the body of the article. Mr. Robinson had proposed to make a separate article of it. The conclusion was to put it in a paragraph at the close of the article.

" There was in the East Indian article a proviso that American vessels might touch for refreshment, but not for commerce, at British places in the African or Indian Seas, in their voyages to or from the British possessions in India.

" Mr. Gallatin observed to the British plenipotentiaries that this did not allow the same privileges to American vessels going to or from China. The limitation was a novelty ; it had not been in the former treaties ; and he mentioned it now, not that we intended to make a point of it, but for the British plenipotentiaries to consider whether it was worth adhering to—particularly as it would not prevent a single American voyage to China."

Even when they had agreed, the squabbling over the material part of the treaty went on ; over the preamble, over a question of form and precedence in signing, and long and wearisome arguments ensued. The Americans were always professing to be in a hurry and eager to be off, forgetful of the fact that their British colleagues were also members of Parliament with important debates to attend and political and social duties to perform. Even amongst themselves Adams and Clay could not agree, and at the last moment Gallatin refused his assent to Adams's somewhat pedantic changes in the textual formula. Adams obstinately held out, and to gain his end had the whole draft copied out in conformity with his own ideas. This procedure angered Gallatin, ordinarily the mildest of mortals, and he said in a " peremptory and somewhat petulant " manner :

" ' Oh, that is entirely wrong ; it will throw the whole
business into confusion. Why, you yourself said yesterday
it was not necessary in the body of the treaty.' I said I had
observed that *it was not so material* in the body of the treaty,
but if the British plenipotentiaries gave up the point in the
preamble and ratifying clause, it was impossible that they
should object to the admission of the same principle in the
body of the treaty. I then showed him the copy of the
Treaty of Paris which I have, printed in France, and in which
the King of France is first named in the first article, as well
as in the preamble. He was yet, however, not satisfied,
and asked me if I had told Mr. Clay of the directions I had
given for making out our fair copy, and what Mr. Clay said
to it. I told him that I had ; that Mr. Clay disapproved the
directions that I had given as he did, and thought the whole
point of no importance.

" Mr. Gallatin then said that I must give the transcriber
orders to make out the copy without any alteration in the
body of the treaty ; which I peremptorily refused, and added,
in a heated and angry manner, ' Mr. Gallatin, you and Mr.
Clay may do as you please, but I will not sign the treaty
without the alternative observed throughout.' ' Now, don't
fly off in this manner,' said Mr. Gallatin. ' Indeed, sir,'
said I, " I will not sign the treaty in any other form. I am
so far from thinking with Mr. Clay that it is of no importance,
that I think it by much the most important thing that we
shall obtain by this treaty. The treaty itself I very much
dislike, and it is only out of deference to Mr. Clay that I
consent to sign it at all.' "

Adams's objections to-day read to us as distinctly petty,
and much time and trouble were expended in gaining his
point. As to precedence in the treaty (now re-entitled a
convention), the American plenipotentiaries solved it by
naming the United States first in their copy while the British
plenipotentiaries put *Great Britain* first in theirs. Then on
July 3—which they might easily and patriotically have made
the 4th—the copies were brought by the plenipotentiaries
to the Board of Trade to be signed and sealed. Suddenly
Adams discovered that he had forgotten his official seal.

There was nothing for it : he must go back himself to the
Legation, in Gallatin's carriage, for the dignified Swiss-
American statesman was the only one who boasted a vehicle

of his own. When at length he returned, the copies were collated and several errors found : the copyists had to be called in and the corrections then and there made. At last all was in order and the instrument was signed. But no—the title had been omitted by the engrosser. Whereupon Adams wrote it on a separate piece of paper to be inserted at the head of the American copy, *naming the United States first*, " Mr. Goulburn copied from mine the title for *their* copy, transposing the order of the parties," as was done throughout the instrument in deference to Adams's susceptibilities.

The six negotiators raised their heads from the foolscap, and Goulburn, who had been one of the Ghent commissioners, observed to Adams, " Well, this is the second good job we have done together." " Yes," was the answer ; " and I only hope we may do a third, going on from better to better."

The next day—the anniversary of the Declaration of Independence—Clay left London, and Gallatin soon after followed, to take up his post as Minister to France. Adams, now alone, became an object of congratulations. Amongst those who called upon him was William Wilberforce, who expressed his high satisfaction at the restoration of peace between the two countries.

" He spoke about an abusive article in the *Quarterly Review* against America, concerning which he had received from America letters from two gentlemen, one of them enclosing an answer to it, which he had not had time to read. He found the article was ascribed to Mr. Canning, he thought erroneously, and he should write to Canning about it.

" I said the *Review* was represented as being under the patronage of Mr. Canning, but the *article*, in two pamphlets answering it which I had received from America, was ascribed to Mr. Southey, who had, however, denied being the author of it, in a letter published in a late *Courier*. I explained to Mr. Wilberforce the manner in which the friends of Great Britain in America were affected by such publications as that article in the *Quarterly Review*. He said that he lamented it, but that those were not the general sentiments of this nation, and that the *Quarterly Review* itself was a work of limited circulation, much more limited than that of the *Edinburgh Review*."

It would be interesting to have Adams's opinion of

Sydney Smith's subsequent remarks on America in the *Edinburgh.*

Soon Adams was busy composing a long note to Castlereagh, which he found hard work. The draft occupied nearly an entire day. Then he began a fair copy, and—

" continued writing it in the evening until near eleven o'clock. The experience of the last summer has made me distrustful and diffident of my own drafts. My own colleagues were then so dissatisfied with everything that I wrote, and adopted so little either of my reasoning or my style, that it has, or ought to have, taken away all my self-sufficiency, and abated all confidence in my faculty either to convince an antagonist or to satisfy those whose cause I would support. But I am now alone, and must perform my duty in my own way. Whatever error there may be in the performance of it, let there be none of neglect, and no deficiency of earnest zeal. I hope this communication may not have been too long delayed."

Castlereagh was, in fact, off for Paris, leaving Adams to the care of Lord Liverpool, who in his first interview with the American Minister went over at length the terms of the late treaty and convention and took exception to Adams's contention that all private property was to be restored, " including slaves." He thought they could—

" not be considered precisely under the general denomination of private property. A table or a chair, for instance, might be taken and restored without changing its condition ; but a living and a human being was entitled to other considerations. " I said that the treaty had made no such distinction. The words implicitly recognized slaves as private property. They were in the article alluded to—' slaves or *other* private property.' I did, however, readily admit the distinction, and still more a human being, was to be regarded in a different light from the inanimate matter of which other private property might consist, and if on the ground of that difference the British plenipotentiaries had objected to restore the one, while they agreed to restore the other, we should have readily discussed the subject."

At the same time, Great Britain having enticed away American negroes with promises of freedom, ought to restore them or their money value to their owners. Adams argued the case at great length, citing numerous authorities and precedents.

" Lord Liverpool is a man of remarkable mildness and amenity of manner. I perceived that he was under some embarrassment how to take what I was saying ; that in referring him to the ample and obvious sources of evidence through which they may ascertain the facts, without recurring to the medium of the American Government, he thought I was shrinking from the production of any evidence on our part."

About this time the Minister took a private house in the London suburb of Ealing.

" One of the strongest reasons for my remaining out of town is to escape the frequency of invitations at late hours, which consume so much precious time, and with the perpetually mortifying consciousness of inability to return the civility in the same manner. Social life is intolerably trying."

Here, one thinks, spoke the real John Quincy Adams.

At the beginning of 1816 he had an interesting talk with Alexander Baring,[1] the banker, touching the troops which the English Government had just sent over to Canada.

" I said that the disposition upon both sides seemed at present so pacific that I hoped we should have a long and quiet peace. I was sorry, however, to hear that they were increasing their armaments on the lakes of Canada, because arming on one side would make it of course necessary to arm on the other and we had been disposed, on the contrary, to disarm there.

" He said their arming was the foolishest thing in the world, ' for,' said he, ' we are " the lamb " in Canada ; it is in vain for us to think of growing strong there in the same proportion as America. But surely our Ministers will consent to disarm there on both sides.'

" I said they had always a sufficient security against a sudden attack upon Canada, by the exposed state of our commerce.

---

[1] Baring had represented the famous banking firm in America for some years, and in 1798 had married the daughter of Senator Bingham, of Pennsylvania. He was not made a peer until 1835.

" He replied that *he wished the British Government would give us Canada at once.* It was not worth Sir James Yeo's hundred-gun ship, and was fit for nothing but to breed quarrels."

These sentiments were those of the future Lord Ashburton, who went out in 1843 to negotiate a treaty in settlement of the American-Canadian boundary !

Adams had a long interview with Castlereagh on the latter's return (January 25) about Canada, armed vessels on the Great Lakes, the Indians and a variety of other subjects, which the Minister recorded verbatim in his diary—twenty closely printed pages of questions and answers : a notable feat of memory.

During the next month he attended a banquet at the Mansion House given by the Lord Mayor to two Austrian Archdukes, at which the Duke of Kent, the future father of Queen Victoria, was present. We learn that after the ladies had retired and the principal toasts had been drunk, the Duke gave " The United States of America, and perpetuity of the friendship between Great Britain and them." Whereupon Adams rose and, addressing the Lord Mayor, said that—

" sensibly affected as I was by the honour done by his Royal Highness to my country in the toast he had given, it was impossible for me to do more than to echo the sentiment he had expressed. I would ask leave therefore to offer, in a twofold manner, the earnest wish I entertained that between the ancient and the new hemisphere there may henceforth be no division other than that of the ocean, and that the harmony between Great Britain and the United States may be as lasting as the language and the principles common to both."

At a subsequent dinner in the same place the toast of—

". . . ' The American Minister ' was given next after the Dukes of Kent and Sussex, and his own toast at the former dinner was repeated by the Duke of Kent. In thanking the Lord Mayor for the honour done him by the toast, Adams reminded him of the observation made by a distinguished and ingenious traveller in the United States, a foreigner. He had remarked that from the moment when an Englishman landed in the United States he still found himself at home, while a foreigner of every other nation, whatever length of time he resided in America, still felt himself a stranger. ' It was my earnest wish that the first part of this observation might ever prove to be true, and I would add the hope that it might also prove reciprocal. I would say, therefore, " May every Briton who sets his foot in America, and every American who visits England, still find himself at home ! " ' "

To this generous sentiment Adams expected a fervid response ; but the Englishman at a City dinner is strongly addicted to postprandial precedents—and the American Minister had, it appeared, been entrusted with the toast " The Lord Mayor and the City of London." His having by a generous impulse side-tracked himself made the sticklers for etiquette most uncomfortable, and although they cheered a little, they blushed—for Adams.

Not a second time was the Minister to be caught napping, and on the next occasion—it was the great Easter Monday banquet—he ended his brief oration properly. This speech is admirable in itself and not only shows Quincy Adams at his best, but might well serve as a model for all similar responses delivered and still to be delivered on the same subject and on a kindred occasion by American envoys, official and unofficial. The toast was " The President of the United States of America," and Adams said :

" My Lord, I pray your Lordship to accept my hearty thanks for the honour which you have done my country in drinking the health of its Chief Magistrate. I receive it as an earnest of peace, harmony and friendship between the two countries. To promote peace, harmony and friendship between Great Britain and the United States is the first duty of my station. It is the first wish of my heart. It is my first prayer to God. I hope it will not be deemed unsuitable on this occasion to recur to considerations of a religious nature. In ordinary cases and at ordinary times it may be proper and sufficient for Britons and for Americans to say to themselves, ' It is our interest on both sides to live in peace, harmony and friendship together.' But, my Lord, the event which was yesterday commemorated by religious solemnities, and which is the day commemorated at this table in the convivial and loving cups of your Lordship and Ladyship, is the most important event that ever occurred upon this globe. It is an event in which we are all interested —a pledge to us all of immortality. It is the warrant to us all of another state of existence, where all is peace, harmony and friendship. May it ever have the proper influence on the minds of your Lordship's countrymen and of mine! May it ever remind them of a higher motive than any possible temporal interest to peace, harmony and friendship! In return for your Lordship's obliging toast, I beg leave to drink ' All religious blessings and all temporal prosperity to the Metropolis of the British Empire and its Chief Magistrate.' "

Adams's frequent flights of oratory were nearly always well received, but there were times when he was called upon to speak with no or insufficient preparation, which was a great trial to him.

" The truth is [he confesses to his diary], I was not gifted by nature with the talent of extemporaneous speaking, and have got through without discredit only by revolving during dinner-time what to say : a process not remarkably favourable to the enjoyment of the conviviality of the table."

Once when he thought he had got through a speech successfully he was—

" aggravated by an observation of a gentleman who sat opposite to me at the table, that he had heard at one of these same dinners, some years ago, a speech from Mr. Pinkney, which he should never forget, and of which he spoke in an ecstasy of admiration. I confess the eulogy might have come at a more acceptable moment ; but this tablecloth oratory is one of the duties of an American Minister in this country which I had not anticipated."

Besides, comparison with an official predecessor still living is doubly odious.

It was not until March 21, after a residence in England of nearly eleven months, that Adams and his wife were presented at a Queen's drawing-room at Buckingham House.

" Mr. Chester accompanied and conducted me to the Queen's cabinet. The Earl of Morton, her Majesty's Lord Chamberlain, introduced me. The Queen was standing about the middle of the chamber. Just behind her, at her right hand, stood the Princess Augusta ; at her left, the

Princess Mary ; further back, several ladies-in-waiting, and the Duke of Kent in military uniform.   I had been repeatedly told, and particularly by Mr. Chester this morning, that the Queen always expected on these occasions to be addressed in a set speech.

" I said thus : ' Madam, the President of the United States having accredited me to his Royal Highness the Prince Regent, I have been ambitious of the honour of being admitted to your Majesty's presence, to assure you of the respect entertained by the Government of the United States for your Majesty's person, and the veneration uniformly felt for your Majesty's character.' "

Some thirty years before this same Queen Charlotte had turned her back coldly upon John Quincy Adams's father and mother, and the latter had written bitterly :

" Humiliation for Charlotte is no sorrow for me.   She really deserves her full portion for the contempt and scorn which she took pains to discover."

But such feelings could hardly survive in her son's breast as he gazed upon this venerable and afflicted lady whose royal husband, George III, was at that moment in confinement at Windsor, a pathetic, broken, white-bearded figure, bereft of his reason.

" ' The political relations [Adams went on to tell the Queen] between the two countries have been subject to the versatility which attends all human affairs.   Causes of dissension, and even of enmity, have sometimes unfortunately risen between them.   These are now removed.   It is hoped, and most earnestly desired by my country, that they may be permanently removed.   But the reverence commanded by your Majesty's virtues is subject to no such change.   It has been invariably entertained by my Government under every variety of circumstances, and I can express no wish more propitious to the happiness of both countries than that the friendship and harmony between them may hereafter be equally lasting and unalterable.' "

The aged Queen answered that she was much obliged to the American Government for the sentiments the Minister had expressed in their name and spoke feelingly concerning an illness from which Adams himself had recently suffered.

10

" She inquired also concerning the climate of my own
country, and I told her how much milder and more pleasant
I found that of England than the one from which I had last
come, which was Russia. She asked me whether I was
related to the Mr. Adams who had been formerly the
Minister to this country, and appeared surprised when I
answered that I was his son. She forgot that I had given her
the same answer to the same question twenty years ago,
and had apparently no recollection that I had ever been
presented to her before. She now dismissed me, and I
withdrew with Mr. Chester."

It was a curious meeting, and old John Adams must have
read his son's account of it with mixed feelings.

After several months of public and private dinners, Court
parties and receptions, at which it sometimes happened
that Adams was almost the only gentleman in the company
in full Court dress (amusing enough, this, in view of a later
dispensation !), the American envoy began again to think
seriously of business. He went to dine with Lord Castlereagh,
where the dinner, he says, was " very light, served upon
plate and porcelain of many different kinds, looking as if
they had been collected from a pawnbroker's shop. The
servants were all out of livery." He told the Foreign Secretary that the American Government was desirous of negotiating an additional treaty or convention. " What about ? "
Castlereagh asked in surprise. In the first place, responded
Adams, the old subject—seamen : President Madison thought
the time was peculiarly favourable for arranging for the
mutual exclusion of each other's sailors in their respective
navies and merchant marine. Then there was another
matter. The commerce between the United States and the
British colonies was wholly carried on in British vessels.
Was this just and proper ? Castlereagh agreed to a discussion which began in Downing Street on July 18. In the
course of a lengthy talk the old difficulty about Search was
again disclosed. " The people of this country," said Castlereagh, " consider the remedy which we have always used
hitherto (i.e. the Rule of 1756) as the best and only effectual
one. If we give up this Right of Search, how will it be
possible to devise any regulation as efficacious ? "

Adams proceeded to argue the point ; when he had talked for an hour Castlereagh grew restless. After a further twenty minutes, he tells us in his diary, Castlereagh—

" drew up his feet as if he was about to rise from his chair. The servants had told me that he was to attend a Cabinet Council ordered at two o'clock, and it was now near three. One of the red morocco dispatch-boxes had been brought to him by a servant a few minutes before, which he had opened, and taken a paper from it, at which he had frequently cast his eyes while we were talking. I saw his impatience, and, rising from my chair, said,
" ' I have received a letter from Liverpool, complaining that there is still levied upon merchandise sold at auction, when imported in American vessels, a duty of five per cent., which is not levied when the goods are imported in British vessels.' "

Adams then harangued his lordship for a further quarter of an hour, and on taking his leave observed with satisfaction " on passing through the entry of the office that it was by the clock just upon the stroke of three." If Adams ever carried a watch at these interviews, he was apparently careless about consulting it.

The American Minister frequently saw the Duke of Wellington, but the first time when he reminded him that they had met before in Paris, the Duke had forgotten him and Adams was duly chagrined.

" This is one of the many incidents from which I can perceive how very small a space my person or my station occupies in the notice of these persons and at these places."

A mortifying reflection to a vain man !

Another source of chagrin was that the British Government declined to enter into any arrangement about the West Indian trade, and on the question of seamen Castlereagh thought they had better leave things as they were for the present, although he would listen to any American proposal.

Adams makes a shrewd observation concerning William Cobbett, who had recently gone to America :

" Earl Bathurst asked me whether I was acquainted with Mr. Cobbett, and whether I thought the American Govern-

ment would give him any encouragement. I said I had
never seen him, and did not suppose there would be any
intercourse between him and the American Government.
I knew not what his projects or intentions were in going to
America, but if he should interest himself much in the
politics of that country, I should, from the character of his
mind, expect very soon to see him writing against that
Government."

Not long after this Adams met George Canning at dinner
at the French Ambassador's. He had just been given a post
in the Cabinet.

" Mr. Canning came late, after the company had sat down
to table. He made acquaintance with me by asking me to
help him to a dish that was before me, and to take a glass of
wine with him. After dinner, at his request, the Earl of
Liverpool formally introduced him to me. This gentleman,
whose celebrity is great, and whose talents are perhaps
invariably so, is noted for the bitterness of his inveteracy
against the United States, and I suppose considers it as a
rule of personal courtesy to make up by an excess of civility
for the rancour which he has so constantly manifested against
us. Mr. Russell more than once mentioned to me that
such had been his conduct toward him. He and Lord Liverpool both talked about the great and rapid increase of the
population of the United States. They inquired when the
next Presidential election would take place, and who would
probably be elected. I told them Mr. Monroe. Lord
Liverpool said he had heard Mr. Monroe's election might be
opposed on account of his being a Virginian. I said that had
been made a ground of objection to him, but would not avail."

At the close of the year Adams and Castlereagh had a talk
about the African trade, which Castlereagh said was attaining
such shocking proportions that the British Government was
thinking of proposing an international force to be stationed
off the African coast to capture the slave-trading vessels and
rather hinted at America's being asked to co-operate. Adams
quickly changed the subject. He had no desire to stir up a
hornets' nest in America—especially as his friend and predecessor, Monroe, had just been elected President and there
was already talk that he was to name him, Adams, for the
high office of Secretary of State.

On March 20, 1817, Adams wrote to his Government :

" The day before yesterday I had an interview with Lord Castlereagh, when he informed me that the British Government had come to a determination respecting the commercial part of the proposals for the negotiation of a further treaty, which I had made last September, that they were still not prepared to abandon their ancient colonial system, but they were willing to extend to the United States the benefits of the Free Port Act to the same extent that they were now enjoyed by the vessels of European nations and to give a partial admission of our vessels to the island of Bermuda and to Turk's Island. And, with regard to the intercourse between the United States and the adjoining British provinces, they would renew a proposal heretofore made, founded altogether upon the principle of reciprocity ; which proposal he read to me from a paper which he said was not quite finished, but which would be sent to me in the course of the next day. Last evening I received a note from Mr. Hamilton, the Under-Secretary of State in the Foreign Department, with a draft of four articles."

This paper he sent on to Washington. A month later (April 17, 1817) he accepted the post of Secretary of State, and duly apprised Castlereagh of this and of his intention to return as soon as possible to America.

Before his departure Adams attended a debate in Parliament and heard the youthful Robert Peel.

" The most eloquent speech of the evening, and one of the most eloquent that I ever heard, was that of Mr. Peel, Chief Secretary to the Lord Lieutenant of Ireland, a subordinate office in the Ministry, of which Peel is the ablest member. He is quite a young man, but already in high repute, and likely to become the most distinguished personage in the kingdom. His speech was against the Catholics, and had the effect to make the worse appear the better reason. It far more than outweighed all the speeches in their favour. It was heard with the most undivided attention, and at its close was long and loudly cheered from every part of the House. Its style and manner were altogether temperate, but persuasive, energetic, but without vehemence ; the language elegant and plain, but moderately ornamented ; the sentiments so liberal that they almost disguised the illiberality of the cause. Its effect upon the House was evident, and I perceived it no less by the anguish of two or three Roman Catholic clergymen who were sitting beside me under the gallery."

Adams took his leave of the Prince Regent on May 14. Before the interview, Chester, the Assistant Master of the Ceremonies, took the American Minister aside and asked him—

" in what manner I should choose to receive the usual present given to foreign Ministers on the termination of their missions, which, he said, was for Ambassadors one thousand pounds, and for Ministers of the second order, five hundred. I told him that by the Constitution of the United States no person in their service was permitted to accept a present from any foreign sovereign, and I must therefore decline any one that might be offered me here. He said that, having had some idea of the existence of such a regulation in America, he has made inquiries at the office how the fact had been in the cases of former American Ministers, and had found the present had been in some instances accepted, and in others declined. I told him I supposed the cases of acceptance were prior to the Constitutional prohibition ; that I must for my part decline it and would explain to Lord Castlereagh my motives for so doing. He acquiesced in this with apparent cheerfulness, though probably not without reluctance."

Chester's reluctance was due to the fact that, according to custom, ten per cent. of such gifts went into his own pocket, so that he was a substantial sufferer through Adams's scruples.[1]

At his final interview with the Prince who was shortly to become George IV, Adams was impressed unfavourably.

" The character of this person [he wrote] is a composition of obtundity and of frivolity. He is a Falstaff without the wit, and a Prince Henry without the compunctions. His only talent is that of mimicry, which he exercises without

[1] " Lord Castlereagh, in the course of his negotiations at the Vienna Congress, and at Paris, received twenty-four snuff-boxes, each worth one thousand pounds sterling, besides other articles equally costly ; but even there they at least found it necessary to put a check upon this market of snuff-boxes, and dispensed with the presents in concluding some of the treaties. The practice here is to give money—which has not even the palliation of sentimentality to plead in its favour."—Adams : *Diary*.

regard to dignity or decorum, to the fitness of his own character, or to the feelings of others. His supreme delight is to expose persons dependent upon him to ridicule, and to enjoy their mortification. He seemed not to comprehend how it was possible to manage a Government where the members of the executive Government could not sit as members of the Legislature, and he thought the mode of communication between the Legislative and Executive Departments, by the means of Committees, was a sucking of brains on both sides, which must encumber all public business and increase all its difficulties. He spoke, however, in perfect good humour, and dismissed me as graciously as he has received me."

On Sunday, June 1, the American Minister had his last talk with Lord Castlereagh. It was chiefly about Spain, then at loggerheads with the United States, and he threw out a hint that Great Britain might be inclined to offer mediation. He asked Adams if the United States were not very desirous of obtaining a cession of the Floridas.

"I told him [says Adams] that we contended that the cession of the West Florida was included in that of Louisiana, because it had formed a part of the original French colony, the whole of which had been retroceded by Spain to France, and then by France to the United States."

At least, the Foreign Secretary knew the policy of the American Administration at first hand.

Adams bade a final adieu to London on June 10, 1817, when he set out on his voyage home, to assume the duties of Secretary of State.

BIOGRAPHICAL NOTE

J. Q. Adams became President in 1825. Four years later, instead of going into retirement he re-entered Congress, and there served actively until his death in 1848.

CHAPTER VIII

RICHARD RUSH (1817–1825)

DESCENDED from a captain of horse in Cromwell's army, the son of perhaps the most eminent physician in America, Richard Rush began life with unusual advantages, and at thirty-four was Attorney-General of the United States. He had handsome features, a graceful person and a quiet manner ; he possessed, moreover, a certain key to official favour in that he enjoyed the intimacy and the confidence of John Quincy Adams and the whole Adams family.

It was Minister Adams who urged his name upon President Monroe as his successor in London, and while Adams was on his way to Washington as Secretary of State, Rush temporarily fulfilled the duties of that important office.

Rush arrived in England in the middle of December 1817, accompanied by his wife, four small children, a youthful secretary and three servants. Despite the inclemency of the season and the uncertainty of his diplomatic prospects, Rush felt his spirits rise as he approached the Mother Country. He was, he avowed, one of those Americans whom the idea of England stirs from their earliest years.

" Her fame is constantly before him. He hears of her statesmen, her orators, her scholars, her philosophers, her divines, her patriots. In the nursery he learns her ballads. Her poets train his imagination. Her language is his, with its whole intellectual riches, past and for ever newly flowing ; a tie, to use Burke's figure, light as air and unseen, but stronger than links of iron.

" ' Is it not fit,' he reflected, ' that two such nations should be friends ? Let us hope so. It is the hope which every Minister from the United States should carry with him to England. It is the hope in which every Minister of State should meet him. If, nevertheless, rivalry is in the nature of things, at least let it be on fair principles. Let it be generous, never paltry, never malignant.' "

On December 23 Rush had his first interview with Lord Castlereagh, who was much more cordial than he had been with Adams. Yet he did not neglect to ask after the health both of Rush's predecessor and of President Monroe, as well as to comment amiably on the prosperity of the United States, observing that the prosperity of one commercial nation contributed to that of the others. " There was a simplicity in his manner," commented Rush, " the best and most attractive characteristic of a first interview."

Rush proceeded to take a furnished house in " the quiet Ambassadors' quarter," north of Oxford Street near Portman Place. He attended many official dinners, where, in spite of long wars with that country, French clothes and French cooking still ruled. Even the conversation was in French.

The Minister's impression from the first was that he was " amongst gentlemen who would not try to over-reach him."

With the Prime Minister, Rush appears to have been most favourably impressed.

" If Lord Liverpool was not the ablest man of the body, he was essentially its head. With a sound judgment improved by public affairs, he was fitted for the business of a nation. What he did not take in by promptitude, he mastered by perseverance ; not that he was deficient of the former, but that he paused upon his first conclusions. Systematic and grave, educated in maxims which he conscientiously approved, however others may have dissented from them ; courteous, yet inflexible ; with a personal character eminently pure, and a high reputation for official probity, his influence, as it rested upon practical qualities, went on to increase ; so that during the whole term of my residence, I never heard that a change of ministry was for one moment seriously in contemplation. Such was the Premier whom I found and left in power." [1]

Even the Prince Regent, whom all did not esteem, received no disparagement from Rush. At his receptions at Carlton House usually great numbers of generals and admirals

[1] Rush : *Memoranda of the Court of London.*

attended, forty or fifty at a time. Nearly all were wounded—lacking a leg, an arm or an eye. They had " done their duty," they told Rush simply. One scarred and battered veteran had fought at Saratoga, 1777. There were also maimed heroes from India, Canada and Spain. " Other nations," is Rush's comment, " chiefly fight on or near their own territory ; the English everywhere."

On January 3 the new Minister opened up his business with Castlereagh—the British confiscation of slaves in the late war and the duties to be levied under the Commercial Convention of 1815. These were small matters, but Castlereagh had a larger one to discuss—America's share in the West India trade. President Monroe wished for full reciprocity : the British Government offered only limited privileges. Rush said that what his people wanted was a measure " that would open the trade fully, and above all give to British vessels no privileges of any kind whatever, direct or incidental, over the vessels of the United States." Otherwise, the latter would be reluctantly obliged to close their ports to British ships from the West Indies. At present these could sail from Liverpool to New York, unload and load again, thence to the West Indies and back again to England, with a threefold profit. American vessels were confined to the direct route from New York to Liverpool—not three sides, but a single side of the triangle.

" Very well [said Castlereagh], we cannot complain, although we shall be sorry, if you carry out your threat. I offer you a set of four modifications of our Navigation Laws—you are at liberty to reject them. But England has so long maintained her Colonial system she cannot easily change it now."

At a subsequent interview the Foreign Secretary raised the question of the North-west Boundary line, which had been omitted from the Treaty of Ghent, i.e. the line contemplated in the previous Treaty of 1783 from the most north-western point of the Lake of the Woods to the Mississippi.

Rush replied he had no instructions on that head. Geographical knowledge had much improved since 1783. Now they knew that the only line that could be run in such a direction would never strike the Mississippi at all ; to run it lower down would be to invade the territory of the United States. The President and Congress would hardly consent to have this question considered by a Joint Commission, bound up with those of Slaves and Oregon.

On February 25, the day before her birthday, Rush was presented to Queen Charlotte, of whom he leaves a pleasanter sketch than Adams's.

" The Queen was then seventy-six. Her birthday was on the day following. As I entered the room and during the whole interview, there was a benignity in her manner which in union with her age and rank was both attractive and touching. The tones of her voice had a gentleness, the result in part of years ; but full as much of a desire to place a stranger at ease. The scene as it first broke upon me, its novelty, its tranquil yet impressive stateliness, became almost immediately, by her manner, one of naturalness and ease. . . . Throughout a long life she had been uniformly distinguished by her private virtues and her efforts to imprint them upon the times. I saw her sinking below the horizon ; as the splendours of her day were setting, she had a consciousness that it was not for those alone she had lived."

The following day at the drawing-room Rush fairly had his breath taken away by the magnificence of the scene. The moving multitude on the grand staircase, the robed royalty in the presence-chamber—these partly prepared him. Then the doors were all opened.

" You saw a thousand ladies richly dressed. All the colours of nature were mingling their rays together. . . . No lady was without her plume. The whole was a waving field of feathers. . . . The diamonds encircling them, caught the sun through the windows and threw dazzling beams around. Then the hoops ! I cannot describe these. They should be seen. To see one is nothing. But to see a thousand —and their thousand wearers ! Each lady seemed to rise out of a gilded little barricade, or one of silvery texture. It was brilliant and joyous. Those to whom it was not new, stood at gaze, as I did—Canning for one. His fine eye took it all in. You saw admiration in the gravest statesmen : Lord Liverpool, Huskisson, the Lord Chancellor, everybody.

I had already seen in England signs enough of opulence and power. Now I saw, radiating on all sides, British beauty."

On June 20, 1818, Rush had another interview with Castlereagh, in which the latter read him a draft of a note inviting America to co-operate with Great Britain in putting down the Slave Trade ; but Rush, realizing the delicate state of public opinion in America on this subject, remained—as Adams had done—silent.

On the topic of Impressment Rush himself submitted a proposal " to exclude from their naval as well as merchant service all British seamen, native as well as naturalized, on condition that Britain did the same and would agree not to impress men out of American vessels thereafter."

As the Convention of 1815 was for three years only and was about to expire, Castlereagh offered no obstacles to the proposal of a general Treaty of Commerce. President Monroe thought it would strengthen Rush's hand if Gallatin came over from Paris to assist him in the negotiations which were timed to take place in the course of the summer.

When, however, Rush saw Castlereagh again, news of a certain tragic episode in Florida had reached England and was creating great excitement. During the late war a British force had landed in Florida, captured Pensacola, and stirred up the Spaniards and Indians against the United States. When they left, an Englishman named Ambrister, a lieutenant-colonel of Marines, remained behind, and soon became associated with a trader named Arbuthnot, who had great influence with the Seminole tribe.

General Andrew Jackson, ordered by Monroe to punish the Seminoles, invaded East Florida, and made prisoners of both Englishmen. Being convicted by court-martial for aiding the Indians and making war against the United States, Jackson made short work of the offenders. He shot one and hanged the other. Secretary Adams vigorously maintained that they were dealt with according to the law of nations, but the affair naturally produced a wave of fierce indignation in England.

When Rush was questioned by Castlereagh, he told him that the two men had properly paid the penalty of their misdeeds.

" Our Indian wars [he explained] generally begin with massacres on the frontier and originate in one and the same cause. They had been produced by British traders intruding themselves with evil intentions among the Indians. The Government of the United States were in possession of documents to show that if not all the Indian wars which President Washington had been compelled to wage, the most formidable of them, were instigated and sustained on the side of the Indians by British traders. *It was to these two individuals that the war with the Seminoles was to be ascribed.* Without their instigation it would never have taken place. . . . Ambrister had been taken in arms and his guilt called for the last punishment."

All this might be true, but it did not prevent popular excitement in London becoming intense over the affair. The newspapers kept up their fire ; they fiercely denounced the American Government and " tyrant," " ruffian " and " murderer " were among the epithets freely applied to Jackson. Later, Castlereagh told Rush that war might easily have been produced on this occasion " if the Ministry had but held up a finger."

Such an incident was particularly awkward for the success of the proposed international negotiations, but, luckily, Castlereagh and his colleagues were not the sort of statesmen to pay much attention to popular clamour. Later, when Rush was dining in company with the Neapolitan Minister, the latter—

" seemed anxious to learn if England had taken any serious exception to the proceedings of our army in Florida, and the execution of the two British subjects. I said that she had not. 'Then,' said he, 'the newspapers *may go on to bark* ; they bark dreadfully in England, but the Ministers don't mind them.' "

At this period European diplomacy was much exercised over the question of Spain and her revolted colonies in the New World. The allied sovereigns were due to meet at Aix-la-Chapelle and formulate the policy of the Holy Alliance. This conference Castlereagh himself was attending on behalf of the Prince Regent, and meanwhile the attitude of England was being carefully studied. Naturally the Government wished to have the support of America, but not yet was it prepared to recognize the independence of the new republics. In America, on the other hand, public opinion, led by Henry Clay, was insistent on complete independence.

On July 31, 1818, Rush saw Castlereagh at the French Embassy, and, after reading all the British notes relative to the South American colonies, informed him that the desire of the American Government was that these colonies should be completely emancipated from the parent State, that the United States would never take part in any scheme of pacification except on that basis.

Castlereagh looked grave and said he was sorry to hear it. But Rush insisted that any other policy was impossible.

" They owed it to the actual position of the colonies : to their future destinies—to the cause of human liberty in the new hemisphere. . . . It was a noble spectacle to see the United States stretch out their powerful hand to these infant communities, anticipating the freest Government of Europe in announcing the decree of their independence."

Rush in his *Memoirs* pays tribute to Clay for his championship of the South American Republics.

" Mr. Canning, at a subsequent day, earned a brilliant portion of his fame by throwing the mighty ægis of Britain over their freedom : which but enhances the fame of their American champion, who was foremost in the competition."

In the middle of August Gallatin arrived from Paris, and he and Rush accepted Lord Castlereagh's invitation to spend a week-end at his country-seat, North Cray, in Kent, and meet the two British delegates who had been appointed to confer with them on the treaty. The weather, the house and lawns and the hospitality were equally perfect. In the midst of informal talks with Castlereagh, Robinson and Goulburn, the two American envoys strolled about the lawns and admired the flowers and sweetbrier hedges.

At dinner every topic was discussed save that of the negotiations.

" My colleague and myself found ourselves at home. Invited for the purpose of fulfilling public duties to the house of an English Minister of State, entrenched in confidence and power, we found ourselves members of his domestic circle, the partakers of a hospitality as easy as delightful."

Next day was Sunday, and they took their leave " just as Lord and Lady Castlereagh were starting off for the village church, walking, followed by their servants "—a pleasing feudal procession.

The topics which were to be treated of by Rush and Gallatin were, according to the former's memorandum, these :

1. Slave question under Treaty of Ghent.
2. Fisheries.
3. North-western boundary line.
4. Columbia River question.
5. Intercourse between the United States and British West Indian islands.
6. Intercourse by sea between the United States and British North American colonies.
7. Inland intercourse.
8. Impressment.
9. Blockades.
10. Colonial trade in war time.
11. List of contraband.

This list indicates compendiously all the outstanding Anglo-American problems of the second decade of the century.

At the beginning of September, while the new convention was being hammered out at the Board of Trade, Castlereagh set out for Aix-la-Chapelle. Before his departure he made a momentous announcement to Rush that the Cabinet, after careful and anxious consideration, had decided to yield to America's wishes and " *give up Impressment.*" Rush was naturally overjoyed at the declaration. It would probably, pursued Castlereagh, shock the public feeling in England when they heard of it, " but they were prepared " to meet the consequences. Impressment would cease, on America's engaging not to employ British seamen. The formal proposals would be ready as soon as the Americans were ready with those relating to the fisheries and the West Indian trade.

But although a new Commercial Convention was concluded

and on October 20 was signed, nothing more was heard of the subject of Impressment. It was perhaps prudently decided to let " sleeping dogs lie."

On Castlereagh's return Rush called upon him at his house in St. James's Square to talk to him about the South American Republics, a theme which was becoming more and more absorbing. He had received a dispatch from Washington which seemed to infer that Britain was prepared for recognition.

Castlereagh said he was surprised that the American Government should think England shared its opinion about the recognition of the colonies. Such a thing he never contemplated. For himself he held to the supremacy of Spain. He thought the colonies should be brought back, not, however, by force, but by moral suasion. He went on to express regret—

" that the United States viewed the question of Independence in the colonies differently from England ; giving as a reason the probable weight of their counsels with the colonies ; so that, although my Government was no formal party to the mediation, if nevertheless, it had harmonized Independence, the hope would have been increased of seeing the dispute healed the sooner through the influence which, from local and political causes, the United States might naturally be supposed to have with the colonies.

" How far it was practicable to settle it, giving back to Spain her supremacy, and granting to the colonies a just Government under her sway, was not for him to say ; but it was the hope to which the European Alliance still clung.[1]

" He admitted that Buenos Ayres had given better proofs of capacity to exist as an independent community than any of the other Colonies ; and he fully admitted, also, the present and prospective value of our commerce in that quarter, when I mentioned to him that it consisted, on our side, of such articles as naval stores, ready-built vessels, furniture, timber, and fish—without enumerating others. The whole tone of his conversation was conciliatory, and he said, in conclusion, that the frank disclosure I had made to him of the President's

[1] Yet Castlereagh before his death came to realize the situation. In his instructions to the Duke of Wellington at the Congress of Verona in 1822 he wrote : " It is evident from the course which events have taken that their recognition [i.e. the revolted Colonies] has become merely a question of time."

views and intentions, would be received by His Majesty's Government in the friendly spirit in which it had been made."[1]

At the beginning of the New Year the bells of the British kingdom tolled for the death of George III (January 29, 1820), the monarch who had striven so long, so courageously and so vainly against the secession of America. Two years before Queen Charlotte had passed away, and this very month witnessed also the death of the Duke of Kent, father of the future Queen Victoria.

Accordingly, the Diplomatic Corps met at the Saxon Minister's, and agreed that their servants, more especially their coachmen and footmen, should be put in black for the late King. The venerable Saxon Minister remarked that as it would be " an extra expense, of course our *Courts* will make a suitable allowance for it ! " " The American Minister, who was at the meeting, made no objection to the step and put his servants in black accordingly ; but as to *his* ' Court ' at Washington, it is certain that he never troubled it with any such item of expense."[2]

Rush refers in his dispatches to the King's funeral, which took place (February 16) at Windsor. " The shops in London were all shut, the streets deserted, and the tolling of the great bell of St. Paul's was heard."

A week later he protested verbally to Castlereagh against British interference in Canada with the Indians living across the American border—a sore subject. Documents on the subject had just reached him from Washington. He was surprised to find his lordship not risen, although it was eleven o'clock.

" The servant immediately requested me to walk into the reception-room, while he went upstairs with my card. He returned with a request from his Lordship that I would go up to his chamber, on which I said that I should be most unwilling to disturb him if unwell. The servant repeated his Lordship's request and desire to see me, and accordingly I went up. There I found him sitting before the fire on a sofa, in his flannel gown. With his wonted courtesy, he apologized for giving me the trouble of coming upstairs ;

---

[1] Rush to Adams, February 12, 1819.   [2] Rush : *Memoranda.*

11

to which I answered how happy I was to do so, unless I found him unwell, in which case I would not say a word on business, but have the honour of calling some other time. He said no, he was quite well, but fatigued from being kept up until nearly daylight through a cause he would mention; but requested I would first proceed to the object of our interview, which he had not forgotten, and desired to hear from me the disclosures I had to lay before him."

When Rush had finished, the Foreign Secretary then divulged that " he and his colleagues of the Administration had been kept up all night and almost until dawn by the affair of Thistlewood's conspiracy." Liverpool and his whole Cabinet had narrowly escaped assassination.

Rush notes on March 25, 1820: " News arrives of the cession of the Floridas by Spain to the United States."

America having planted herself firmly in Florida, was not likely to be dispossessed. The Spaniards had no alternative but to treat for cession, and on February 19 Spain gave up the territory for the sum of five and a half million dollars.

" The English papers raise a clamour, charging ambition and rapacity upon the United States. They say nothing of the acquisitions which England has been making in all parts of the globe, by her arms or policy, since the days of Elizabeth and Cromwell. Even if we were to show some tincture of this quality, still, as her own children, disposed to act in her own spirit, her journalists might make allowances; but, in fact, we acquire Florida by fair treaty; we give Spain the *quid pro quo* to the uttermost farthing; and the last thing that I anticipate is complaint from a mind like that of Lord Castlereagh."

Five years had passed since the defeat of Napoleon and affairs in Europe on the surface seemed tranquil enough. Castlereagh, sitting at his own dinner-table surrounded by the Diplomatic Corps, said openly to Rush:

" May the happy tranquillity long continue! Europe requires repose. Each State has had enough of war, and enough of glory, and ought to be content."

Here he paused an instant, but, resuming, he proceeded: " And you too, YOU of America, Mr. Rush, ought also to be satisfied ; you left off very well, and ought to wish for nothing but a continuance of peace."

" I felt [comments the American complacently] this delicately-conveyed compliment to my country. He knew that our war with Britain had terminated in victory on our side, by sea and land."

One can only say that if such opinion was really entertained by Rush's distinguished host, it was not one shared by the more enlightened of the Minister's compatriots and contemporaries, nor, it must be added, by historians.

Castlereagh was ever friendly and repeatedly assured Rush of the value he attached to American friendship.

" ' Let me deal candidly,' he once said. ' It can little be supposed, were it an open question, that we would not prefer that Spain should own the Floridas to their falling into your hands. She is weak—you are strong ; but the treaty has been made, and we prefer its ratification to the possibility of any serious disturbance to the pacific relations between the United States and Spain. These we are sincerely desirous to see maintained, from the propitious influence that it will continue to shed upon the general repose of the world.' I said that I was sure my Government would hear with great satisfaction the expression of such sentiments."

Rush was the first American Minister who had to deal to any extent with British emigration on any considerable scale to America. Yet he was a fair man who could see that the subject had two sides. He used to say :

" The bad subjects of Britain we do not want ; the good, it is no part of my provision to be instrumental in drawing away."

During the summer of 1820 Rush saw the new King, George IV, at somewhat closer quarters and under less favourable conditions than at first.

" The day was hot—excessively so for England. The King seemed to suffer ; he remarked upon the heat to me and others. It is possible that other heat may have aggravated, in him, that of the weather. Before he came into the entrée-rooms from his closet, X, of the Diplomatic Corps, taking me

gently by the arm, led me a few steps with him, which brought
us into the recess of a window. ' Look,' said he. I looked,
and saw nothing but the velvet lawn, shaded by trees, in the
Palace gardens. ' Look again,' said he. I did, and still my eye
took in only another part of the same scene. ' *Try once more,*'
said he, cautiously raising a finger in the right direction.
X had a vein of drollery in him. I now, for the first time,
beheld a peacock displaying his plumage. At one moment
he was in full pride, and displayed it gloriously ; at another,
he would halt, letting it droop, as if dejected. In his wake,
a smaller bird, of glossy feathers (the female), followed,
teasing and annoying the peacock at every turn. ' Of what
does that remind you ? ' said X. ' Of nothing,' said I ;
' *Honi soit qui mal y pense,*' for I adopted the King's motto
for him ; and then added, that *I* was a republican, *he* a
monarchist ; and that if he dreamed of unholy comparisons
where royalty was concerned, I should have to tell upon him,
that it might be reported to his Court ! He quietly drew off
from me, smiling, and I afterwards saw him slyly take another
member of the Corps to the same spot, to show him the
same sight."

This is the typical Rush touch—suave, polished, sprightly.
His public bearing was always correct, yet he missed nothing.

To the King's brother, the Duke of Sussex, the American
Minister was definitely attracted. The account he gives of
this Duke's sturdy character, robust common sense and
political enlightenment, shows him to great advantage.
Thus, on one occasion :

" The Duke of Sussex sat at the head of his table, in true
old English style, and was full of cordiality and conversation.
I cannot resist the satisfaction of putting down a small part
of what fell from him. General principles of government
coming to be spoken of, he expatiated on the benefits of free
government ; declaring, that ' *as all men, kings as well as
others, were perpetually prone to abuse power when they got to
the possession of it, the only safe course was, to limit its exercise
by the strictest constitutional rules.*' In the palace of Kings,
and from the son and brother of a king, I should not have
been quite prepared for this declaration, but that it was not
for the first time I had heard him converse in the same way.
The sentiments which it embodied even with new strength
and precision, I now listened to with renewed pleasure. If

such sentiments flourished so near the British Throne, what may we not be allowed to think of the race of sturdy and spirited Englishmen who settled the United States in the days of Elizabeth, Cromwell and the Stuarts ? "

If Rush was guarded and uncritical respecting George IV, it was otherwise with some of his British friends. One, Lord Erskine, frequently expressed himself with extreme frankness. Once on the way to a dinner-party, Erskine took a seat in the American Minister's carriage.

" On the way out he was full of sprightliness. Always straightforward and powerful at the Bar and in Parliament, this distinguished peer indulges in eccentricities in conversation. ' England,' said he, ' *is a blackguard country.*' ' A great country,' I rejoined. ' *Yes,*' said he, ' *a great blackguard country ; a boxing, fighting country, and don't you call that blackguard ? '* I said that he jumped to his conclusions faster than I could follow. ' *Aye,*' said he, ' *you are* accredited to the King ; *but for all that, the King has been constantly fighting with Providence ; Providence gave him high endowments, with a fine person, and had been trying to make him the head of a great and glorious people ; but the King had been for ever battling it with Him, and at the end of about the thirteenth round, with the advantage of good bottle-holders, he had now fairly beaten Providence off the ground !* ' "

All this fantastic wealth of metaphor had reference to George IV's conduct towards Queen Caroline, whose legal case was just then in Erskine's hands.

While the new Argentine nation was in its birth-throes the design was imputed to France of erecting a throne at Buenos Ayres, and placing a Prince of the Bourbon line upon it. Rush saw Castlereagh and told him that if the accounts were well founded, he knew his Government and country " would deplore such a course on the part of France."

Castlereagh replied that it was a total surprise to England ; that the Cabinet had only very recently heard of it and hoped it might not prove true to the extent stated, otherwise it showed a spirit of intrigue, which he had hoped had gone out of fashion among nations. " It was the more strange in the eyes of England," commented Rush, " as it has been going on, if true, at the very time when the Foreign Enlistment Bill was brought before Parliament." Rush remarked upon the difference between the course of the United States and France ; for " whilst we had expressly disclaimed all intention of accepting any special advantages over other nations, from the South American communities, it appeared, if the accounts were true, that France was for appropriating every advantage to herself." [1]

Four years passed. In America Monroe had been re-elected President and showed no inclination to change his envoy in London. Rush had gone for some months without meeting Castlereagh, and then they met at a dinner-party. The Foreign Secretary was effusively cordial, exclaiming :

" ' Why I have not seen you these hundred years ! ' ' My misfortune, my Lord,' Rush replied. ' It is proof,' said he, ' how smooth the waters are between our two countries.' ' But,' the Minister rejoined quickly, ' we must contrive to ruffle them a little, if their smoothness is to be followed by our separation ! ' ' No, no,' cried Castlereagh, ' that won't do.' More passed in the same strain, the bystanders of the Diplomatic Corps seeming to relish this friendly international and personal tone between us."

At the Coronation, which took place July 19, 1821, Rush was an attentive and even enthusiastic spectator. After it was all over the Master of Ceremonies, Sir Robert Chester, waited upon Rush with a Coronation medal, of which he asked his acceptance. " It was of gold, with a bust of the King on one side, and on the other several emblematical representations, including Britannia with Neptune's trident. One of these medals, he said, was due by ancient custom to every Minister Plenipotentiary at the English Court when the King was crowned ; he was distributing them and was happy to hand me mine."

But, to Chester's surprise, Rush, with expressions of

---

[1] The Minister's son, Benjamin Rush, remarks : " If the rumour of the design here imputed to France in 1820 were really founded, it would seem that the ill-starred attempt of Napoleon III to establish an Empire in Mexico forty years afterwards was not the first instance of a *spirit of intrigue*, as Lord Castlereagh, and afterwards the Duke of Wellington, well called it, on the part of France, in matters in which the United States were so nearly concerned." —Preface to *A Residence at the Court of St. James.*

respect towards his Majesty proper to be used, and under every sensibility to the honour of being invited to his Coronation, alleged that the constitution of the United States prohibited the gift.

"Sir Robert, with his usual courtesy, then tendered it to Mrs. Rush, saying that our Constitution surely did not mention the ladies ! But here I was driven to quote the old common law upon him, which was part of our inheritance in the United States, a good inheritance we thought it, though it did, ungallantly, make the wife's gold the husband's ; so that it ended in our losing the medal both ways."

Had the incident occurred in our own day, the Married Woman's Property Act might have ensured to the lady the possession of the coveted medal, and even the Minister might have asked and received Congress's permission to accept it, or have begged the postponement of its presentation until he was once more a private citizen. But Rush's becoming Secretary of the Treasury immediately on his return to America would perhaps have made acceptance of " British gold " politically inconvenient.

After Castlereagh's tragic death by his own hand, in August 1822, Rush referred to his own dispatches to attest the " candid and liberal spirit " in which Castlereagh had ever been disposed to deal with American affairs.

" Let those who would doubt it, consult the archives of the two nations since the end of our revolutionary war and point out the British statesman, of any class or party, who, up to the period of his death, made more advances or did more, in fact, towards placing their relations upon an amicable footing."

Rush repeated his opinion that had Castlereagh not left England to attend the Congress, he would have settled with the United States, in the negotiation then pending, the question of Impressment.

Castlereagh was succeeded by Canning, who had long entertained strong and clear views on the subject of Brazil, Argentina, Bolivia, Chile, Peru and the rest, and meant now to act upon them.

On August 16, 1823, Rush had a memorable interview with Canning about Spain and her late colonies. The British

Government had already clearly intimated that it did not intend to tolerate any French meddling with the process of South American independence. " What," asked Canning, " would your Government say to going hand in hand with England in such a policy ? "

" He did not [reported Rush] think that concert of *action* would become necessary, fully believing that the simple fact of our two countries being known to hold the same opinions would, in its moral effect, put down the intention of France, if she entertained it. This belief was founded, he said, upon the large share of the maritime power of the world which Great Britain and the United States shared between them, and the consequent influence which the knowledge of their common policy on a question involving such important maritime interests, present and future, could not fail to produce on the rest of the world."

When Rush questioned Canning, the latter stated that Great Britain never contemplated making up the quarrel between Spain and her colonies, but she would never interfere to prevent it, although he admitted such a thing was highly improbable. At present, however, no step had been taken towards recognition of the new republics.

" Reverting to his first idea, he again said, that he hoped France would not, even should events be favourable to her arms in the Peninsula, extend her views to Spanish America, for the purpose of reducing the colonies, nominally indeed for Spain, but in reality to subserve ends of her own ; but that if, unhappily, she did meditate such a course, he was satisfied that the knowledge that the United States would be opposed to it as well as England, could not fail to have its decisive influence in checking it. In this way good might be done, and peaceful prospects made more sure all round."

Canning had long since divined the secret intention of the Holy Alliance ; it was to aid Spain in bringing back the revolted South American colonies. Personally, he would have liked to recognize their independence forthwith, but Great Britain's continental engagements at present tied his hands. Action might be brought about with the aid of America, and on September 18, 1823, Canning proposed to Rush that the time had come for a mutual understanding.

Why should America hold aloof ? Why not join England in the proposed European Congress on South American affairs and throw her weight against the policy of the Holy Alliance ?

" As to the proposals he had submitted to me [Rush reported to Washington] I said that I was sure he would himself appreciate the delicacy and novelty of the ground upon which I stood. The United States, it was true, would view any attempt on the part of France, and the continental Alliance, to resubjugate those new States, as a transcendent act of national injustice, and indicative of progressive and alarming ambition ; yet, to join Great Britain in a declaration to this effect, might lay them open in some respects to consequences, upon the character and extent of which it became my duty to reflect, with great caution, before making up my mind to meet the responsibilities of them. The value of my declaration, it was agreed, would depend upon its being formally made known to Europe. Would not such a step wear the appearance of the United States implicating themselves in the political connexions of Europe ? Would it not be acceding, in this instance, at least, to the policy of one of the Great European Powers, in opposition to the projects avowed by others of the first rank ? This, hitherto, had been no part of the system of the United States ; the very reverse of it had been acted upon. Their foreign policy had been essentially bottomed on the great maxim of preserving peace and harmony with all nations, without offending any, or forming entangling alliances with any. Upon the institutions, as upon the dissensions, of the European Powers, the Government and people of the United States might form, and even express, their speculative opinions ; but it had been no part of their past conduct to interfere with the one, or, being unmolested themselves, to become parties to the other. In this broad principle laid one of my difficulties under his proposals.

" He replied, that however just such a policy might have been formerly, or might continue to be as a general policy, he apprehended that powerful and controlling circumstances made it inapplicable upon the present occasion. The question was a new and complicated one in modern affairs. It was also full as much American as European, to say no more. It concerned the United States under aspects and interests as immediate and commanding, as it did or could any of the States of Europe. They were the first Power established

on that continent, and now confessedly the leading Power.
They were connected with Spanish America by their position,
as with Europe by their relations; and they also stood
connected with these new States by political relations. Was
it possible that they could see with indifference their fate
decided upon by Europe? Could Europe expect this
indifference? Had not a new epoch arrived in the relative
position of the United States towards Europe, which Europe
must acknowledge? Were the great political and commercial
interests which hung upon the destinies of the new continent,
to be canvassed and adjusted in this hemisphere, without
the co-operation or even knowledge of the United States?
Were they to be canvassed and adjusted, he would even add,
without some proper understanding between the United
States and Great Britain, as the two chief commercial and
maritime States of both worlds? He hoped not, he would wish
to persuade himself not. Such was the tenor of his remarks."

But Rush could only answer :

" My country has acknowledged the independence of these
South American Republics, and wishes to see them received
into the family of nations. . . . I must procure instructions
from home before entering into any joint understanding. . . .
Immediate recognition offers, however, the true basis of our
concert."

Canning, however, was not yet prepared to recognize the
republics.

When Monroe got Rush's dispatch he replied :

" You could not have met Canning's proposals better if you
had had the whole American Cabinet at your right hand."

There was a Cabinet meeting and Monroe produced the
draft of his famous Message of December 1823, protesting
against future colonization by any European Power and
against the extension of the system of the Holy Alliance to
the Western Hemisphere.

The Monroe policy (or Doctrine) was contained in two
separate declarations :

1. That it was impossible for the Allied Powers to extend
their political system to any part of America, without
endangering our peace and happiness; and " equally

impossible, therefore, that we should behold such interposition, in any form, with indifference."

2. Alluding to discussions between the United States and Russia, then commenced with a view to arranging the respective claims of the two nations on the north-west coast of America, the President also declared that " *the occasion has been judged proper for asserting, as a principle in which the rights and interests of the United States are involved, that the American continents, by the free and independent condition which they have assumed and maintain, are henceforth not to be considered as subjects for future colonization by any European Powers.*"

The first of these declarations was probably expected by England, and was well received. It was recognized at once that it referred to the hostile plan of the Allied Powers against the late Spanish colonies. But it was otherwise with the second declaration, which was not, and never has been, formally acquiesced in by Britain or by any European Power.

While President Monroe was, at the instigation of George Canning, incubating his celebrated Doctrine, the American envoy in London was busy negotiating a new general Anglo-American treaty. It embraced the Slave Trade, North-west Boundaries and the Navigation of the St. Lawrence. The negotiations, although laborious, were occasionally animated. Good temper prevailed on both sides throughout. But all was to no purpose. The treaty was concluded, signed and dispatched to America. There, although approved by Monroe and Adams, it failed to please the Senate. Great surprise and even bewilderment was expressed in London, but, as Rush explained :

" England had no solid foundation for complaint at the refusal of the Senate to ratify the Convention as signed in London. She knew it to be a fundamental provision of our Constitution that no treaty was finally valid until it received the sanction of that body. . . . Yet it is not to be disguised that she was disappointed at the result."

For months the Minister occupied his time in compiling a lengthy report of the treaty negotiations, which, in August 1824, he sent to the Secretary of State. Little further now remained for him to do. Personally he was welcome everywhere in London society. His graceful face and figure and bland smile were known to all, and, although a good talker, Rush was even a better listener. He himself felt that his talents were being wasted abroad, and so, when his friend Quincy Adams came to the Presidency, Rush was offered and accepted a place in the Cabinet at home. He notes in his diary (April 20, 1825):

"Attended the levée. Gave Mr. Canning information of my recall, having been invited home by President Adams, to preside over the Treasury Department at Washington."

A week later Rush had his farewell audience of the King, and he and Mrs. Rush with their family bade farewell to the scene of so much practical diplomacy and social activity and much personal happiness in England.

BIOGRAPHICAL NOTE

Rush filled for a short time the post of Secretary of the Treasury. He was sent to France as Minister 1847–51, and died in 1859.

CHAPTER IX

KING AND GALLATIN (1825–1827)

SINCE the long and successful mission of Rufus King over twenty years had passed. Those two decades had left an indelible mark on the world's history. They had also enfeebled the ex-Minister's once-robust frame and blanched his remaining locks. But his intellect was still acute—he was one of those few men in America who possessed what was called the " European mind "—and he enjoyed the respect of all cultivated men.

When John Quincy Adams was elected President in 1825, King was a Senator whose term would expire in the following March. Adams was anxious to conclude a new treaty with England, and he believed that Rufus King, despite his years, would best compass that end.

" There was [says Schouler] something touching in the return of this illustrious statesman to the crowd of London that he might serve the son abroad as he had served the father." [1]

Adams told him that the success of his administration would depend upon the treaty " concerning which a negotiation had been commenced, had reached a given stage without coming to an agreement, and which, at the request of England, was to be again resumed." The cardinal points of this negotiation were English colonial trade with the United States, the navigation of the River St. Lawrence and the settlement of the boundaries. The President paid a high tribute to King's past diplomatic record and sent him forth with his blessing.[2]

[1] *History of the United States.*

[2] King's old friend, Gore, wrote him : " Mr. Adams certainly says no more than can be justified in speaking of the high character you have sustained in the Old Country and which has doubtless not been diminished by the contrast displayed in the weakness, caprice and queer temper of some who have represented the United States there since your return."

The aged Minister's ill-fortune began on the voyage, which was very rough ; he was constantly sick and became much debilitated.   When he reached Liverpool (June 26) he had to be carried to his hotel and remained there several days in an effort to recover his health.   A doctor advised his going to Cheltenham, and although his arrival in London was being awaited, he stayed in that watering-place for over six weeks. It was all rather unfortunate, as Parliament had risen and the Court and Cabinet scattered.   All the more gratifying was it therefore to receive a letter from Canning himself proposing to come to see him.

" My dear old friend [wrote the British Foreign Secretary, July 28, 1825], the pleasure of renewing our very old acquaintance, which authorizes me, I hope, so to address you, induces me to take Cheltenham in my way to the north of England.   I hope to arrive there on Monday and to pay my respects to you that evening or early the following day, as may best suit your convenience."

On August 2 King records in his diary :

" Mr. Canning arrived last evening and came to my house at 9 o'clock this morning.   After the ordinary salutations I expressed my thanks for his making me this visit and my satisfaction that the United States and Great Britain thought alike on the subject of Cuba and the new States. . . . I alluded in general terms to the employment of the influence of the United States to engage Russia, France and Great Britain to influence Spain to make peace with the new States by acknowledging their independence.

" Mr. Canning replied that such a hope was desperate ; that Russia was unchangeable on this point . . . that Alexander now avows the doctrine that crowns and succession can lawfully be regulated by Kings and Emperors only. . . . I asked whether Austria, Russia or France would be likely to admit of change in this theory ?   He answered that France had one foot in the water and one foot on the land, and as respects the water foot she seemed inclined to agree or rather not to disagree with England ; that while England despaired of the favourable interposition of Russia and of the temper of Spain to make peace with the new States by acknowledging their independence, they felt themselves so greatly reinforced and sustained by the views of the United States and the agreement which existed between the United States and England in these views, that they had directed all their efforts to prevail on Spain to conclude an armistice with the new States, which would in the end lead to peace."

Canning suggested a triple note to Spain, as he thought France would join the United States.

King sent off a long dispatch to Secretary Henry Clay a week later asking for instructions on this British proposal, but by the time a reply arrived other events had caused postponement of its consideration by Canning and his colleagues, and so nothing resulted.

In political circles much was expected of King and the welcome accorded to him by old friends was very comforting. Lord Grenville wrote from Dropmore (August 25) :

" It was with great pleasure that I heard of your return to this country in a public character. It is to us a very flattering testimony of the impressions which you received from your former residence among us, and it is on public grounds very gratifying to think that this part of the intercourse between our two countries will pass through the hands of a person as sincerely desirous of promoting goodwill and friendship between them as I well know you to be."

The Minister was at length well enough to come up to London and there took up quarters at 20 Baker Street. On his arrival he found himself confronted by a peculiar case which for a time caused much heart-burning. The aged ex-President Jefferson, chief promoter of the University of Virginia, had induced a certain Woolwich instructor, Bonnycastle by name, to come out to America as professor. But Bonnycastle had previously signed a bond for £500 " not to enter into any foreign service without the consent of his Government." This consent he had never applied for and consequently the bond was forfeit. King with confidence applied to Canning in Bonnycastle's behalf. But this request turned out to be no trifle. The Admiralty was shocked at the request.

" If [they wrote the Foreign Secretary] the application had come originally from the Government of the United States for the discharge of Mr. Bonnycastle for the purpose mentioned in your letter, their Lordships would probably

have viewed the matter in a different light ; but in consequence of the mode and the circumstances under which
Mr. Bonnycastle quitted His Majesty's Service they cannot
help entertaining considerable apprehension that a compliance
with your request would be attended with injurious consequences."

Bonnycastle had in fact been educated gratuitously at
Woolwich as an American might have been educated at West
Point or Annapolis and then proceeded, despite his solemn
undertaking, to enter the service of another State without
notification or permission. It was then that Jefferson
intervened with a petition, backed by the American Minister.
Canning continued to regard the matter as one in which
a principle was at stake. Besides, why this silence on the
part of the peccant professor himself ? Why should he
" throw upon a foreign Government the pleading of his
cause ? " It was—

" not so much the unwillingness to let Mr. Bonnycastle go free
as the probable effect of taking no notice of the contumacious
and ungrateful manner in which he has *taken* that liberty
without asking it. If such conduct passes unreproved, is
it not clear that establishments hitherto national will be
henceforth nurseries for the rest of the world ? "

Nevertheless King had set his heart on pleasing Jefferson
in this case of Bonnycastle—Jefferson, his old political
opponent, who had now scarce a year to live. And so he
made it a personal matter between George Canning and himself and thereby gained his point. The case is a curious
one, and has few diplomatic precedents. Canning wrote :

" As between Government and Government the decision
must have been otherwise. . . . But what *could not* be
conceded officially is yielded to *Mr. King's personal desire ;*
and I rejoice that in so yielding it, we enable Mr. King to
gratify an old political antagonist, which is the *next* thing to
the gratifying of an old political friend."

The legal proceedings against the offender, whose conduct
" is considered by the British Government as most discreditable," were forthwith relinquished. It is worth adding
that Bonnycastle, who was the son of the mathematical

master at Woolwich and the younger brother of the soldier, Sir Richard Bonnycastle, had gone out to Virginia to teach "moral philosophy." Two years later this pretence was abandoned and he assumed the chair of mathematics at the new University.

King was soon plunged into an active correspondence with Canning on affairs of greater moment and saw him frequently, although he did not present his letter of credence to King George IV until November 11. A mixed commission was just then sitting in Washington to fix the amount of indemnity for the slaves carried away by England after the war of 1812. It was moving so slowly and unsatisfactorily that the American Government wished to terminate it and proposed that a fixed sum be named by way of compromise. King saw Secretary Addington at Canning's request and named two million dollars. Canning was shocked.

"But your total claims only come to £380,000. And now you suggest that we pay you £450,000. Do you call this a ' compromise ' ? If so, it is at once declined." [1]

Whereupon King proceeded to show that the Foreign Secretary had overlooked the at least ten years' detention of the slaves, bringing the total to $2,693,120. But Canning said his Government declined to consider interest. Letters, more or less heated, passed to and fro, and on January 28 Canning wrote :

"The undersigned begs leave (he trusts without offence) distinctly and finally to decline entering with Mr. King into an examination *here* of the *merits* of the questions which the commissioners are appointed to decide ; the very object of the appointment of such a commission by treaty being to exonerate two Governments from the necessity of a direct diplomatic discussion thereupon."

King protested against the suggestion of such a thing, and hoped that instructions would be given to the commission to go on with its work. He wrote home to Clay that he had been disappointed with Canning and that temper was playing too great a part. Moreover, other disappointments were in store. It was a bad time to make any commercial

[1] Canning to King, January 19, 1826.

12

arrangement. " A spirit of intoxicating satisfaction and self-gratification on the subject of what is here called Free Trade has spread itself through the country." A few weeks later Canning ended all negotiation and transferred the whole business to Washington. King wrote Clay, March 3, that " this left your Envoy to infer that confidence in him no longer existed . . . which he feels to be wholly unmerited."

There were other matters besides the slaves indemnity, but King did not push these because of the employment of Ministers in other and more engrossing matters. In truth, besides his state of health, a sense of injustice began to prey on his mind, and he decided that his time of usefulness was over. " The condition of my health requires that I resign the mission " was the way he first put it to the President (March 20), but a week later he stated the reason more definitely :

" The transfer to Washington of matters entrusted to me at this post is an indignity to my feelings and evinces a defect of confidence in me as the representative of the United States which I feel cannot but impair my influence in the future discharge of that trust. A treatment so wholly undeserved I am not willing to do."

Canning indeed made another and propitiatory move, but without success. He wrote King (April 20, 1826) :

" The undersigned, his Majesty's Principal Secretary of State for Foreign Affairs, has the honour to request Mr. Rufus King, Envoy Extraordinary and Minister Plenipotentiary of the United States, to have the goodness to inform the undersigned whether Mr. King is provided with the instructions for the resumption of the negotiations of last year, with respect to a settlement of boundaries upon the north-west coast of America ? The undersigned is particularly induced to make this inquiry by having received from Mr. Vaughan a copy of the communication, lately addressed by the President of the United States to the House of Representatives, of that part of Mr. Rush's correspondence of last year which relates to this important subject.
" The undersigned has to add that the British Plenipotentiaries, Mr. Huskisson and Mr. Addington, are perfectly

prepared to enter into conferences with Mr. King thereupon ; and either to renew the proposal brought forward by Mr. Huskisson and Mr. Stratford Canning in their conference of the 13th of July, 1824, and unanswered, or to bring forward another ; or to discuss any new proposal on the same subject which may be suggested on the part of the Plenipotentiary of the United States. The undersigned has the honour to renew to Mr. Rufus King the assurance of his high consideration."

A careful perusal of all the correspondence conducted after King's inauspicious beginning of his mission leads to one inevitable conclusion. King was not the man he had been : he was proud, touchy and prejudiced ; and he had gone about business in quite the wrong way with Canning, who had at the outset, as we have seen, endeavoured to please him.

When he had gone, all difficulty seemed to disappear, and his successor closed with the British offer of $1,200,000 in full settlement of the Slaves Claims.

King persisted in demanding his recall, and sailed for home on July 3, 1826, after being only a single year in England.

One aged and trusted veteran having thus failed them, Adams and Clay resolved to try another. Albert Gallatin had been one of the chief negotiators with themselves of the Treaty of Ghent in 1814 and had since been Minister to France. He was of aristocratic French lineage, a thin, dark-skinned man with a prominent nose, lofty forehead and long lank locks, now grown white. His knowledge of European politics was profound and his even temper and courtly manners had saved many an awkward negotiation and too animated debate. At the Legation in Paris he had been accustomed to rely on the secretarial assistance of his lively son James, from whose diary posterity may learn many diverting details of his father's personal and official history. Thus in May 1826 the son writes :

" I cannot realize what has happened. We are actually going to England. Mr. Rufus King (our Minister in London)'s health has broken down. Most important matters have to be negotiated. The President has begged father to take his place. He has accepted, but on the condition that he goes on a special mission and not as a resident Minister, that he is at liberty to return in a year ; that an ample sum is to be put at his disposal, as he knows that outward show has a great effect on the English people. This has all been agreed to privately. These are the most important negotiations and can only be placed in the hands of a very strong man. The whole of the commercial questions to be finally settled. The most important are the North-eastern and North-western Boundary questions. Also, the Commercial Convention which father negotiated in 1815 in London and again in 1818 to last ten years."

Gallatin *père* himself wrote to a friend :

" You will have seen by the newspapers that I am appointed Minister to England. There are important negotiations now pending between that country and the United States, and the state of Mr. King's health was such that he had requested that, for that purpose, an extraordinary Minister might be united to go as special Minister. Before my nomination was sent to the Senate, Mr. King resigned altogether his place, and his resignation arrived in this country and was accepted. The President wishing to entrust me alone with the negotiation and unwilling to nominate at once a special Minister for that purpose and an ordinary Minister as successor to Mr. King, requested that I should go in the latter character, but with powers to negotiate, and with the understanding that I should be at liberty to return as soon as the negotiation was terminated, in the same manner as if I had been appointed on a special mission. . . . This cannot last longer than a twelvemonth."

The impending negotiations, if not " the most complicated and arduous ever entrusted by the United States Government in the hands of a single agent," were sufficiently important and difficult. They embraced not only those commercial questions so often and so fruitlessly discussed, involving the whole system of British colonial and navigation laws, but also the troublesome Maine and Oregon boundary disputes ; the Slaves Claim by the Treaty of Ghent ; and the renewal of the Commercial Convention negotiated in 1818 for ten years by himself and Minister Rush.[1]

[1] Henry Adams : *Life of Albert Gallatin.*

To his old diplomatic confrère Clay addressed a long letter of instructions (June 19), in which he told him :

" Your predecessor, Mr. Rufus King, purposes leaving London in the month of June, and on that account as well as on account of the important negotiations with which you are to be solely charged, the President wishes you to lose no time unnecessarily in proceeding to Great Britain.

". . . Owing to circumstances beyond our control, the negotiation has not been resumed as soon as the President had wished. Upon Mr. King's arrival last summer in England he found the members of the British Cabinet dispersed over the Kingdom and on the Continent. His Britannic Majesty was indisposed, as was Mr. Canning also. Mr. King has laboured under ill-health during the greater part of the time of his abode in England. It was not until the autumn that the British Cabinet assembled at London ; and the first object which engaged Mr. King's attention was the state of the mixed commission at Washington under the tripartite convention of St. Petersburg. He was for some time occupied by correspondence and conferences with Mr. Canning on that subject, until it was transferred to this city. Moreover, the British Parliament has recently passed laws affecting in a most important extent, the trade of the British colonies in our neighbourhood, the interpretation and practical operation of which it was desirable to test by some experience. These explanations of the causes of the delay which has arisen in the resumption of Mr. Rush's negotiation may be made, if you shall find it necessary, to the British Government. That of the United States has not been indifferent to the deep interests, and to the harmony between the two countries which are involved in the negotiation. And it is satisfactory to reflect that no prejudice to either party is believed to have accrued from the lapse of time, which, on the contrary, will have afforded to both a more ample opportunity of deliberately reviewing the past, and of entering again upon the negotiations under better lights, and with a spirit of mutual conciliation and concession, the best pledge for bringing them to a fortunate conclusion."

Gallatin was further instructed :

" If you should not be likely to bring your negotiations on the entire subject of the commerce between the two countries and their respective territories to a conclusion

in time to present the Convention in which it is expected
they will issue to Congress during its next session, it will
be desirable, and you are accordingly directed, to endeavour
to make a separate arrangement of the colonial question, so
as to enable the President at least to present that before
the adjournment. As to the duration of any general or
particular commercial convention to which you may agree, it
may be limited to a period of about ten years ; to which it is
advisable to add an article similar to the eleventh article of
our Danish treaty, stipulating that the convention shall
continue in force beyond the particular period agreed upon
until one party notifies the other in writing of his desire
to put an end to it."

Gallatin reached London in July and conferred at once
with Canning. During the following month he was received
by George IV, who, according to young Gallatin, was " most
gracious," adding, " But what a change since I last saw him !
He is fat, very red in the face and unwieldy."

The new Minister's first regret was that he had no longer
to deal with Lord Castlereagh as Foreign Secretary. George
Canning, in the language of Henry Adams, was doubtless a
greater man, but he was—

" one whose temper was not gentle towards opposition, and
whose old triumphs over Embargo and Non-intercourse had
not left upon his imagination any profound respect for
American character. Mr. Canning liked brilliant and
aggressive statesmanship. He was not inclined to admit the
new doctrines which had been announced by President
Monroe in regard to the future exclusion of Europe from
America ; he felt that the power of the United States was a
danger and a threat to England, and he would have been
glad to strike out some new path which should relieve the
commerce of England from its increasing dependence on
America. Unfortunately for Mr. Gallatin, the very moment
which Mr. Canning chose for experimenting on this subject
was the moment when Gallatin was on his way to England
in the summer of 1826. The object which he selected for
experiment was the West India trade." [1]

As has been already shown, the British Government both
in 1815 and 1818 had declined to accept the American

---

[1] Adams : *History of the United States.*

propositions on this subject. The trade between the United States and the West Indies was therefore left to be regulated by legislation as suited the interests of the parties. In proportion as England opened her colonial ports to American vessels, Congress relaxed the severity of its navigation laws, and, in spite of incessant dispute about details, this process went on with favourable results as fast as public opinion in England would allow. There was only one drawback to the policy. In the multiplication of restrictive and retaliatory laws the intercourse became so embarrassed that no man could pretend to say what was and what was not permitted or forbidden.

But an Act of Parliament passed in July 1825, which, while it offered the liberty of trading with the British colonies to all nations, limited that liberty—

" to the ships of those countries which, having colonial possessions, would grant the like privileges of trading with those possessions to British ships, or which, not having colonial possessions, should place the commerce and navigation of this country and of its possessions abroad upon the footing of the most favoured nation."

The United States had no colonial possessions, but they might have placed the trade of his Majesty's colonies in British vessels upon the aforesaid footing in American ports, and they had not done so.

" It would have been infinitely more agreeable to his Majesty's Government that the liberal disposition manifested by England towards the United States should have produced a corresponding disposition on the part of the American Government.

" But, finding themselves disappointed in their long-cherished hope that such would be the course of the Government of the United States, it remains for them only to let the provisions of the Act of 1825 take their course." [1]

The New England merchants were eager to get the whole matter settled. They demanded the privilege of shipping their merchandise to the British West Indies and bringing back West Indian molasses (the basis of New England rum)

[1] Vaughan to Clay, September 28, 1826.

in exchange. But being Protectionists, they refused to allow
British ships to share in the coastwise trade, and indeed no
substantial concession at all was offered in return for a
relaxation of the Navigation Acts. As Gallatin wrote to
Clay (September 22) when he had made a *coup d'œil* of
the international situation :

" On three points we were perhaps vulnerable : (1) The
delay in renewing the negotiation. (2) The omission of
having revoked the restriction on the indirect intercourse
when that of Great Britain had ceased. (3) Too long an
adherence to the opposition to her right of laying protecting
duties. This might have been given up as soon as the Act
of 1825 had passed. These are the causes assigned for the
late measures adopted towards the United States on that
subject, and they have undoubtedly had a decisive effect
as far as relates to the Order-in-Council, assisted as they
were by the belief that our object was to compel this country
to regulate the trade upon our own terms. But even this
will not account for the refusal to negotiate and the apparent
determination to exclude us altogether hereafter from a
participation in the trade of the colonies. There is certainly
an alteration in the disposition of this Government since the
year 1818, when I was last here. Lord Castlereagh and Mr.
Robinson had it more at heart to cherish friendly relations
than Mr. Canning and Mr. Huskisson. The difference may,
however, be in the times rather than in the men. Treated
in general with considerable arrogance till the last war,
with great attention, if not respect, during the years that
followed it, the United States are now an object of jealousy ;
and a policy founded on that feeling has been avowed."

Canning has been charged with " hair-splitting " on the
meaning of the words " right " and " claim " as applied to
the American trade with the colonies. For instance :

" When it is contended [he wrote to Gallatin, November
13, 1826] that the ' *right* ' by which Great Britain prohibits
foreign nations from trading with her colonies is the same
' *right* ' with that by which she might (if she thought fit)
prohibit them from trading with herself, this argument
(which is employed by the United States alone) implies that
the special prohibition is a grievance to the United States,
if not of the same *amount*, of the same *kind*, as the general

prohibition would be. This is a doctrine which Great Britain explicitly denies."

Canning was apparently bent upon making one more effort to save the Colonial system. He wished to ascertain by experiment whether the West Indies could be made independent of the United States by opening the colonial trade to all the rest of the world and prohibiting it to the United States alone.

It cannot be denied that Clay's diplomatic methods had not improved the situation or that President Adams himself had allowed expressions to escape from him which gave offence to Canning. Minister Gallatin, therefore, felt it necessary to warn the President at least to guard the privacy of his opinions.

". . . I received here a communication from a respectable quarter stating that, a few days before the publication of the Order-in-Council of July last, one of the King's Ministers had complained to a confidential friend of the general tone of American diplomacy towards England, still more so as respected manner than matter, and added that it was time to show that this was felt and resented. As to manner, the reproach cannot certainly attach either to Mr. Rush's or Mr. King's correspondence ; and I know from a conversation with Mr. Addington, that in that respect Mr. Clay's has been quite acceptable. On looking at your own communications, I am satisfied that those to the British Ministers can have given no offence whatever, and that what they allude to and which has offended them is your instructions to Mr. Rush, printed by order of the Senate, and which have been transmitted both to Mr. Canning and to Mr. Huskisson ; a circumstance, by the by, not very favourable to negotiations still pending. That they have no right to complain of what you wrote to our own Minister is obvious ; still, I think the fact to be so." [1]

The outlook was anything but cheerful and towards the close of the year Gallatin diagnosed it, again not to Clay but to Adams himself :

" Although all my faculties are exerted, and it is far from being the first time, in trying to accommodate differences

[1] Gallatin to J. Q. Adams, October 18, 1826.

and to remove causes of rupture, it is impossible for me not to see and feel the temper that prevails here towards us. It is perceptible in every quarter and on every occasion, quite changed from what it was in 1815–1821 ; nearly as bad as before the last war, *only they hate more and despise less*, though they still affect to conceal hatred under the appearance of contempt. I would not say this to any but to you and your confidential advisers, and I say it not in order to excite corresponding feelings, but because I think that we must look forward and make those gradual preparations which will make us ready for any emergency, and which may be sufficient to preserve us from the apprehended danger. . . . I must say, after my remarks on the temper here, that I have been personally treated by Mr. Canning with marked civility."

On November 14 the Convention of 1818 was renewed and signed. But the West India negotiations were suspended ; there was no hope for the navigation of the St. Lawrence ; the fixing of a definitive boundary in Oregon was postponed ; as was the settlement of the Maine boundary ; the only point settled was that of British payment in a gross sum for the captured slaves.

Meanwhile the Gallatins were mixing in London society, although there was less entertaining than usual, the King being at Brighton. Mrs. Gallatin joined her husband before Christmas. Her son notes in his diary :

" I met Mr. Greville the other night. He is Clerk of the Council. I was amused to see him making notes of the different things I told him. Rather a pedantic person. Princess Lieven is the Ambassador ; Prince Lieven is absolutely a nonentity. Lord Goderich is always the same delightful gentleman ; it is a pleasure to meet him. Lord Grey I suppose means to be civil, but his manners are not what they should be. Mr. Canning is always most gracious to father, who likes him very much but does not think him a very strong man."

Canning was indeed in wretched health : his end was not far off. The Gallatins gave several dinner-parties, but the Minister declined to make any presentations of Americans at Court, declaring that he was not resident Minister, but only special Ambassador. His son Albert records (December 21) :

" Dined at a large diplomatic dinner at Prince Jules de Polignac's at the French Embassy ; all men—we sat down thirty-six. I was delighted to meet Montmorency ; we had a good talk over our old days in Paris. He says things are much changed now, and that the King is much disliked. Our successors are not at all well received and do not entertain at all. After dinner, Montmorency and I went for a short time to White's and had supper late. London unutterably dull. Mamma is perfectly happy, as she has a perfect riot of churches to go to. It will be gayer after Christmas, but only among the Corps Diplomatique. Father will have to have some sort of reception for the Americans in the New Year. We really make quite a show. We are using all our old French State liveries—which are perfectly fresh." [1]

A few days later :

" We had a delightful Christmas with the Barings, who are hospitality itself. There are Barings of all shapes and colours, all sizes—tall ones, short ones, lean ones, fat ones, but all are so nice and cheerful. They seem indeed a united family. We played all sorts of silly games and became children again. We have a big reception of Americans on January 2."

London in that winter of 1826–7, especially after midnight, offered, it would seem, special opportunities for chivalrous young Americans.

" Driving home last night [wrote the Minister's son and Secretary], near the top of Park Lane we heard cries for help. I jumped down and found a hackney-coach which had been stopped by footpads. Two lonely females were in it. They had stunned the jarvey. I at once escorted them to our coach and we drove them home. They lived quite close to us. A Lady Lucy and her daughter. We had just come upon them in the nick of time and had disturbed the robbers. We never go out at night without at least two footmen and generally father's *chasseur* as well. It is extraordinary how unsafe London is at night, and in the very best quarters."

But the Gallatin household in London was always lively, as it had been in Paris. Young James lived and throve

[1] Vide *America's Ambassadors to France.*

in an atmosphere of adventures, assaults, escapades and midnight meetings. A few weeks later there is an uproar outside the Legation and the police are summoned.

January 20, 1827.—" We had some difficulty with our coachman. He committed an assault outside the Embassy but took refuge when they were about to arrest him in the Embassy. Of course no officers of the law can enter an Embassy. Father was informed of the matter. He inquired into the facts of the case and absolutely refused to give the man up. It has caused a great deal of correspondence and the matter is not yet closed."

Young Gallatin notes (January 25) that the Prime Minister, Lord Liverpool, " has seemed very odd in his manner lately, as if he were half-dazed." The negotiations meanwhile went on, but during February there was—

" a Cabinet crisis which has kept everything at a standstill— very annoying. We dined with the Duke of Devonshire yesterday, at his house in Piccadilly. He is a most gracious host. Snappy Charles Greville, always asking questions and taking notes, was there. A book called *Vivian Grey*, published by Colburn and immensely puffed, appeared last year. There were many surmises as to who the author was. Great names were mentioned and there was much speculation on the matter. It now turns out to be by a quite unknown youth called Disraeli, a Jew. Greville had the audacity to say that he knew who the author was from the first. Father thought well of the book."

The elder Gallatin had need of all the consolations to be derived from sprightly contemporary literature, for his diplomatic affairs were going badly, and already he was threatening to return home.

" Father [wrote his son James] is really despondent ; everything goes at a snail's pace. Mr. Adams, after promising him an absolutely free hand, is evidently irritated by Mr. Clay's continual interference and also influenced by him. Father looks upon Mr. Clay as simply an obstinate firebrand who is not capable of grasping or dealing with a subject without prejudice. The present negotiations are of a most delicate nature and have to be treated as such. Here it seems the custom for statesmen to conceal the truth. In France they do not pretend to tell the truth. The President has written a private letter to father begging him to remain in England. It is flattering to his vanity, but he has none. He is determined after this mission is fulfilled to give up political life altogether."

On February 17 Lord Liverpool had a stroke and died ten days later. Gallatin's " hopes that Mr. Canning will not be Prime Minister " were not destined to fulfilment, for early in April he took office.

" It seems [wrote James] to have put him into a good temper, and he is far more gracious, although his temper at times is very trying.   Father, much to his disgust, has been summoned by the King to Brighton—I go with him."

The Minister and his Secretary stopped only one night at Brighton.   Rooms had been prepared for them at a house close to the Pavilion, which the King maintained for certain of his guests.

" We were received by his Majesty, who was lying on a divan—he could hardly hold himself up. Lady Conyngham was present at first, but at a nod from the King, retired. She looks as if she had something of a temper. The King spoke on several political subjects, and for a wonder with great lucidity. He said suddenly, ' Canning is a damned old woman.' We were bid to sup with the Royal circle. I could see that father could hardly dissemble his disgust. The conversation was boisterous and indecent. Cards after supper, and on a plea of being very fatigued father begged leave to retire. He and I went for a walk by the sea. The only remark he made was, ' And that is a King '! We left in the morning without seeing his Majesty."

Young Gallatin notes that : " Mr. Canning's temper has become most uncertain, and it would seem that in his attitude towards his critics he was nourishing a grievance." Perhaps some comment in an American paper goaded him to one outburst at a dinner party on April 23.   The Minister wrote to Secretary Clay :

" At the dinner of the 23rd, Mr. Canning came near Baron Humboldt and me and told us, ' You see that the opinion universally entertained abroad, and very generally indeed in England, is that this Government is an aristocracy. It is not true. It is,' said he emphatically, ' a monarchy. The Whigs had found it out in 1784, when they tried to oppose the King's prerogative of choosing his Prime Minister. The Tories have now repeated the same experiment, and with no greater success.' [1] He appears certainly very confident, and speaks of any intended opposition in Parliament as if he had no fear of it. As all the leading newspapers are in his favour, I enclose the only pamphlet of note that has appeared on the other side.

"An infusion of Whiggism in the Ministry, by the accession of such a man as the Marquis of Lansdowne, might perhaps after a while have produced some favourable change in the policy of the Administration towards the United States. For the present, none can be expected. I do not believe that there is a single question between us in which the Ministers will not be supported by the public opinion of the country in taking rank ground against us. Our dependence for friendly arrangements rests solely on the superior sense of the Ministers. Unfortunately Mr. Huskisson [2] is less favourably disposed towards the United States, principally on the commercial subjects, than towards any other country. And, having to meet in other respects a formidable opposition to his plans, he may be disposed to regain some popularity with the shipping interest to pursuing with the United States measures inconsistent with his avowed general principles on that subject. If there is any reaction as relates to us, it must come from the West Indies, and perhaps at last, from the manufacturing interests.

"I have been compelled to remain perfectly quiet for the last months ; but now that a temporary Administration is formed, which will last at least as long as this session of Parliament, I will ascertain in the course of next week whether it is intended that our negotiations should be resumed. Mr. Canning, on the 23rd, again expressed great

[1] " Both father and Baron Humboldt were much surprised at this extraordinary outburst. They could not explain it. Some of the gentlemen sitting near, too, heard this remark and seemed much astonished. Later on the Duke of Wellington had a chair brought and placed between father and Humboldt. He made himself most agreeable, but seemed worried about something. He suddenly said, ' Do you find anything odd in Mr. Canning's manner ? ' "—Diary of James Gallatin.

[2] William Huskisson, Colonial Secretary 1827, responsible for the repeal of the Navigation Laws.

regret that they should have been so long interrupted, and intimated his intention of having, within a few days, a special conversation with me."

But the Prime Minister was doomed, and although work on this treaty was resumed, Canning died early in August. Gallatin always regarded Canning as an obstacle to his progress, and two days later his son could write :

" Lord Goderich, much to father's delight, is Prime Minister. All will now be plain sailing. When this treaty is signed it will be a final and, we hope, a lasting one. Certainly nothing has been left to chance, every detail has been discussed, assuring peace for years to come."

But four days later the Minister himself wrote to Clay in a far less optimistic mood.

" It is now understood that the new Administration of this country is to be but a continuation of that of Mr. Canning, to act on the same principles, and no new appointments to be made but those that are strictly necessary.

" There will, therefore, be no change in the policy of Great Britain towards us. The question of colonial intercourse was decided almost entirely by Mr. Huskisson's influence. He adheres to that decision, and immediately before leaving the country again committed himself in that respect by positive assurance to merchants interested in the subject. All the difficulties in renewing the Commercial Convention, and the determination not to renew it unless it might be rescinded at will, also originated with him. He has an undue and not very liberal jealousy of the increasing navigation of the United States. In other respects he cannot be said to be hostile to them ; and he would wish that causes of actual rupture might be removed. . . . I have reason to believe that he would be in favour of a satisfactory arrangement on the subject of Impressment.

" His views in regard to the country west of the Rocky Mountains are, on the whole, temperate, and the difficulties on the subject of the north-east boundary cannot be ascribed to him. Whether his reign will last is extremely doubtful, his general health is precarious, and he has an organic affection of the throat, so serious that he never made a long speech during the last session of Parliament without experiencing a relapse.

" The present Administration will, at all events, last till after the next meeting of Parliament in January."

An agreement was come to which continued the Commercial Convention of 1815 indefinitely, leaving either party at liberty to abrogate it at twelve months' notice. Also, another convention was signed by which the joint use of the disputed Oregon territory, as defined in the Third Article of the Convention of 1818, was indefinitely continued, subject likewise to abrogation at twelve months' notice. Finally, on September 29, a new convention was signed providing for the reference of the disputed Maine boundary to a friendly sovereign. That was as far as Great Britain would go.

Having secured this, Gallatin prepared to go home. He had failed to obtain for his country a share in the West Indian trade, and Adams had, in retaliation, shut out British goods. The retiring Minister wrote the new Foreign Minister, Earl Dudley, shortly before his departure :

" The right of Great Britain to regulate the intercourse with her colonies is not questioned, and it is not usual for nations to make any great sacrifice for the sake of asserting abstract principles which are not contested. She is undoubtedly the only proper judge of what should be her commercial policy. The undersigned has not been fortunate enough to be able to discover what actual advantages she derives from the measures in which she perseveres in regard to the colonial intercourse. He has apprehended that considerations foreign to the question might continue to oppose obstacles to a proper understanding. Nothing has been omitted to remove those which might have arisen from misconceptions of the views and proceedings of the American Government. It is gratifying to have received assurances that the decision of Great Britain was not influenced by any unfriendly feelings towards the United States. Their sentiments for Great Britain are those of amity and good-will ; and their Government is animated by a sincere desire to improve and strengthen the friendly relations of the two countries."

The strain upon the old man had been considerable. The truth was, as he said in one of his letters from London :

" The United States want here a man of considerable talent,

but he must be younger than I am and capable of going through great labour with more facility than I now possses. This is at all times the most laborious foreign mission. It is at this time, owing to the negotiations, one of the most laborious of public offices."

He had left behind, as Chargé, W. B. Lawrence, who, he believed—

" would prove a useful public servant. . . . I did not like French diplomacy ; I cannot say that I admire that of this country. Some of the French statesmen occasionally say what is not true (*cordon sanitaire*) ; here they *conceal* the truth. The temper also towards us is bad. After all, though it is necessary to argue well, you may argue for ever in vain ; strength and the opinion of your strength are the only efficient weapons. We must either shut ourselves in our shell, as was attempted during the Jefferson policy, and I might say mine, or we must support our rights and pretensions by assuming at home a different attitude. I think that we are now sufficiently numerous and rich for that purpose, and that with skill our resources would be found adequate."

BIOGRAPHICAL NOTE

Gallatin settled in New York, where he was President of the National Bank of the United States. He was one of the founders of New York University, and engaged in various scientific work until his death in 1849.

CHAPTER X

BARBOUR, McLANE, AND VAN BUREN (1828–1832)

GALLATIN had come home, disillusioned and burdened with public documents, leaving Secretary W. B. Lawrence in charge of a Legation strangely bereft of its archives. For it seems at that day to have been the common practice of retiring American envoys to carry off their official papers and records, generously leaving to their successors a clean slate undefaced by their failures and unadorned by evidence of their social and diplomatic activities. Yet this, as we shall see, might prove embarrassing. Gallatin was so distinguished a man and enjoyed such intimacy with the President and Secretary Clay that he was a law unto himself. But his London failure was, in truth, a notable one. The British Government had declined to pursue any treaty and were not, besides, in a very friendly mood. It became necessary for President Adams to do something. His term of office would expire in the following year and he might not be re-elected. To leave things as they were would be fatal to his political chances and his future fame. But who at this juncture would accept the English mission ?

It is odd that the only suitable man Clay could hit upon was the Secretary of War—James Barbour of Virginia. Diplomatic timber had generally come from Virginia. Barbour was a tall, lean, sturdy, roughish man—as great a contrast to Gallatin as could well be imagined. He had suffered a boyhood of privation in a sparsely settled region. At seventeen he was enrolled as a deputy sheriff and in this service acquired a working knowledge of the law, or that part of it current and active in the back country, so that only two years later he was actually admitted to practice. He had barely attained his majority than he was elected

180

to the Virginian House of Delegates, and there sat as a legislator for sixteen years. After a term as Governor he was advanced to the United States Senate, and after repeatedly serving as Chairman of the Committee on Foreign Relations, in 1825 President Adams chose him his Secretary of War. Such was the career of the statesman now sent to London. Should the Whigs fail at the coming Elections, his tenure abroad would probably be brief. Barbour was a fierce opponent to General Jackson and Jackson's presidential prospects were roseate.

Clay furnished his friend with a list of subjects he was to attempt to discuss with the British Foreign Office. It was the old list revived and brought up to date, but it was hardly likely that such a man as Barbour would succeed where King and Gallatin had failed. It consisted of:

1. The abolition of privateering.
2. Free ships, free goods.
3. Impressment.
4. The law of blockade.
5. Contraband.
6. Rights and duties of belligerents.

Besides these, there was of course the question of the Maine boundary, the recovery of fugitive slaves who had taken refuge in Canada, and a new grievance which had just arisen, a discrimination in British import duties prejudicial to American goods, especially cotton.

Unhappily, Clay neglected to instruct the new Minister very explicitly on these topics, and what made it worse was that on his arrival in London the valuable Secretary Lawrence announced his intention of resigning, and in fact did so. " I regret to find," wrote Barbour to Clay (Sept. 5, 1828), " that Mr. Gallatin carried his instructions to America without leaving a copy in the office of the Legation. I am referred to these instructions for the views of our Government on various topics." He was, therefore, for the present, helpless, and asked that the views of the Government be sent him as soon as possible.

Clay was shocked at this evidence of official laxity ; and it is probably due to his initiative that thereafter no papers were taken away by any Minister which had any bearing on the business of the Legation.

Barbour would have suffered much greater inconvenience from the defection of the Secretary had not he, too, like his immediate predecessors (and like several of his successors) possessed a son of suitable age and talents. All would go well," he wrote to his friend Clay. " I shall substitute my son, James Barbour, Junior."

From the first the state of British politics offered a great surprise to the new American envoy.

" From what has occurred since the death of Mr. Canning I apprehend that liberal principles have ceased to prevail in the councils of Great Britain. The present administration is completely Tory, and, judging from all I see and hear, I deem it the strongest which has existed for years. There seems to be a determination to fill every place from the ranks of the nobility, to the exclusion of all who are of plebeian origin. Mr. Peel is the principal exception to the rule, and rumour says he is about to retire from the Ministry. His Parliamentary talents apart, he is of little consequence ; separated from the people, his natural supporters, and humiliated by clinging to the aristocracy, he will be shaken off without hesitation or difficulty."

And yet, despite this, " the common people seemed pleased with the energy and decision of the new Prime Minister." The American envoy was unable to see the King, but the Duke of Wellington called upon him at the Legation and bade him welcome.

On October 1 he had his first audience of Lord Aberdeen and found him a broad-minded statesman and well disposed to America.

" I remarked to him that several interesting subjects as proper for conventional arrangement between the two Governments had been committed to my predecessors, some of which had been postponed on the ground that they were without interest except in time of war. But one, that of Impressment, was urgent, and the lead ought to come from Great Britain rather than from the United States."

In his (Barbour's) opinion the West Indian matter was on the same footing.

JAMES BARBOUR.

Aberdeen replied that " so far as he was concerned he was anxious to see every difference removed and equality secured for both." After this frank avowal:

" Lord Aberdeen adverted to our late tariff, saying that Huskisson had charged us with treating them scurvily in adopting that measure."

It was at this point that Minister Barbour gave a taste of his quality. He had not been a Senator and a member of the Foreign Relations Committee for years for nothing.

" I replied that Great Britain should be the last to refer to that step, especially as between us : that we had fallen far short of her example, that *she* had taxed our principal staples from 200 to 600 per cent., that our tobacco paid the latter sum, that our grain was interdicted except in times of imperious necessity, our rice, lumber, turpentine, etc., are labouring under the most onerous impositions, that cotton alone of our principal staples was exempt from these heavy burdens, *to the cause of which exemption it was unnecessary I should refer.*"

This was a shrewd *riposte*, causing the Foreign Secretary to remark it was a subject with which he was not conversant, " but he doubted not," he added, " that Huskisson could make a pretty ingenious case of it."

This allusion to Huskisson was what Barbour had been waiting for, and he let his lordship know what he thought of that statesman, who had so deceived Gallatin's trust in him.

" Mr. Huskisson [he said] professed very liberal principles and had established to himself the character of being an apostle of that school ; but so far as I was advised, his practice and his doctrines were entirely at points ; that one authentic deed was to us more valuable than all his professions, and I should be glad to be advised of one act of his, in reference to the United States, in any degree calculated to sustain his pretension to having liberalized our inter-course."

This was certainly forceful and well put. Aberdeen was impressed and must have felt that he could get on with such an envoy as Barbour. A fortnight or so later the Minister increased his character for originality. The Queen of Portugal came to London, and all the members of the Diplomatic Corps paid their respects and kissed the royal hand.

" Not perceiving the propriety of my doing so [he wrote Clay, October 17], I have abstained, and, being singular, the pretermission has attracted the more attention."

The more Barbour saw of the Ministry and public opinion in England, the further he became convinced that negotiations might be renewed with success.

" In a recent interview with the Duke of Wellington he took occasion in the course of the conversation to declare that he had no object more at heart than to cherish and strengthen the amicable relations between us and to remove every cause calculated to influence them prejudicially."

What troubled Barbour was that in the Presidential campaign now raging at home Adams would be beaten and go out of office before the negotiations had taken shape. But at least he made a start, the moment Clay's instructions arrived, which they did in November. From these he gathered that the Secretary was very angry about the differential duties. He wanted absolute equality for American merchandise.

" In other words [he wrote, October 15], when a British and an American vessel enter—for example, the port of Liverpool —laden with articles, the growth, produce or manufacture of the United States, precisely the same duties, and no others, are to be exacted in both instances, no matter from what place, colony or country the exportation of the articles has been made."

On the subject of Impressment, Barbour was instructed to renew the ancient protest to the British Government. Several cases had recently occurred where American-born sailors coming on shore and claiming the protection of their flag had been forced to return to a British vessel as part of its crew. It is true these mariners had joined the ship, but as the Minister told Aberdeen :

" It is scarcely necessary to remark that from the thoughtless character of seamen but little reliance ought to be placed on engagements to volunteer into the British service, loosely formed on shore, without solemnity and without any precaution to ensure the deliberate exercise of the sailor's judgment. In the case of one sailor, he testified that he remembered nothing—saying that he must have been drunk when he agreed to serve under the Union Jack."

As to the practice of Impressment generally, one of Clay's last acts was to re-state the American position as it had been propounded for more than a generation :

" The practice of withdrawing seamen from their service on board of American unarmed vessels by British ships of war, under whatever aspect it may be viewed, is one to which the American Government cannot submit."

Then in December came the expected blow : in America Andrew Jackson had been elected President and Minister Barbour's recall was certain.

The new President had chosen as his Secretary of State, Martin Van Buren of New York, and between them they decided on a totally different attitude in their relations with Britain. Perhaps Canning had, as one Congressman alleged, somewhat " raised their dander," but they could find no fault with the present Foreign Secretary, Aberdeen. And the prohibition by Adams of trade with the West Indies had been a mistake which was roundly denounced daily in New England.

Yet when Jackson came to make his first address to Congress, who would have expected the aged fire-eater (who had already entered upon a stiff quarrel with France) singling out Great Britain for compliment ? No words could have been more honeyed or more disarming :

" With Great Britain, alike distinguished in peace and war, we may look forward to years of peaceful, honourable and elevated competition. Everything in the condition and history of the two nations is calculated to inspire sentiments of mutual respect and to carry conviction to the minds of both, that it is their policy to preserve the most cordial relations. Such are my own views ; and it is not to be doubted that such are also the prevailing sentiments of our constituents."

To carry out this new policy it was decided to send the

suave Senator Louis McLane of Maryland to the British Court.

In the instructions with which Van Buren furnished him it was explained (July 20, 1829) that President Jackson was " not disposed to question the Adams policy," but

" Anxious not only to remove all actual differences between the two countries, but to enlarge the foundations of mutual harmony and mutual interests, and believing that a change of the course of the Government upon this point may be made consistently with the respect that is due to it, it is his wish that a different course should now be pursued. You may now therefore," he concluded, " tell the British Government that we are ready to conclude a new arrangement."

Minister McLane was particularly fortunate in his Secretary of Legation. The name and talents of the American writer, Washington Irving, had for some years been familiar in England. Irving himself was a favourite in London society. The Washington administration had been pressed to do something for a man whose genius had already cast a lustre upon his country. Irving was in Spain, in the shadow of the Moorish castle of the Alhambra, when he learnt of his appointment. Although some of his friends and admirers thought he should have been offered a higher post, Irving himself was flattered.

". . . If the world thinks I ought to be minister, so much the better ; the world honours me, but I do not degrade myself. I have the same feeling in this respect that I have always had on points of precedence : I care not who takes the lead of me in entering an apartment, or sits above me at table. It is better that half a dozen should say, Why is he seated so low down ? than any one should casually say, What right has he to be at the top ? So much for these objections."

There had been an interesting alternative to the Secretaryship, for some months before Irving wrote to his friend Everett, the American Minister to Spain, of a famous London publisher's proposal.

". . . Murray has offered me a thousand pounds a year to conduct a periodical magazine he is about setting up, to be devoted entirely to literature and the arts, without the least mixture of politics or personality, and to pay me liberally besides for any articles I may contribute to it."

But he resisted the temptation and wrote to Minister McLane :

" ALHAMBRA, GRANADA,
"July 22, 1829.

" MY DEAR SIR,

" I have just received intelligence of my being appointed Secretary of Legation to the Court of St. James, and that I am expected to join you in London as soon as possible. It gives me great satisfaction, sir, to be associated in office with one of whom public report and the private communications of my friends speak in the highest terms of eulogy. I shall make all possible dispatch in arriving at London, but must crave indulgence should I not be there as early as you could wish. This intelligence has been entirely unexpected, and has found me in the midst of occupations and engagements of a literary nature, from which it will require a few days to disentangle myself. The travelling in Spain, also, is slow, particularly at this sultry season. I trust, however, I shall be able to join you towards the end of August."

It was mid-September before he joined his chief, McLane, in London. From his letters we may derive considerable information concerning the new Minister and his life in the Legation. Mrs. McLane was a bright and cheerful woman, but not very robust, while her husband's health also suffered at first.

" Ever since my arrival in London [wrote the author of *The Sketch-book* to his brother, October 16, 1829], I have been so unsettled and so hurried about by various concerns that I have not had a moment to devote to literary matters. Mr. McLane being a stranger in London, and for a part of the time confined to his bed by illness, has needed my assistance incessantly. We have also had all our visits of ceremony to perform, which in this huge wilderness of a city take up a great deal of time. I trust the hurry and bustle are now over, and that I shall begin to have more time to myself. Mr. McLane is settled in a very commodious house, No. 9 Chandos Street, Cavendish Square, and I have taken lodgings immediately opposite in the same street, so that in half a minute

I can step from my own sitting-room to the office of the Legation, which is a very comfortable one and entirely at my command. There is likely to be but moderate scribe work in the Legation, and Mr. McLane seems disposed to take the greater part of that off my hands, by employing young Walsh, who is attached to the Legation, and whose father wishes him to be considered by Mr. McLane as a kind of private secretary."

During the ensuing six months negotiations went on between Aberdeen and the American Minister. No formal treaty resulted, but " an honourable understanding which worked just as well." On May 29 the British Government by an Order-in-Council at last gave permission to American ships to trade with the West Indies in return for the opening of American ports to British vessels, which had been interdicted by President Adams's proclamation in 1827.

On the heels of McLane's triumph came the death of King George IV. The new reign marked a new era in Anglo-American relations, so that Secretary Irving could write that—

" our diplomatic situation at this Court is as favourable and gratifying as we could desire, being treated with marked respect and friendliness by the Royal family, and by the various members of the administration, both of the old and new Ministry ; and all this appears to be spontaneous ; as, while we have fulfilled all the usual forms of mere civility and etiquette, we have never courted any favour or attention, but have rather held ourselves in reserve, and let the advance be made from the other party.

" I trust the general effect of our mission here will be to place the relations of the two countries on a more amiable footing, generally, and at the same time to establish freer intercourse personally for our diplomacy at this Court, where it was formerly received with coldness and reserve. Nothing can be more easy and frank than the manner with which at present we are enabled to carry on our business with the Ministers and at the public offices. These considerations in some measure reconcile me to the interruption this diplomatic episode has made in my quiet literary life, and console me amidst the official bustle, and the distractions of court pageantry and London life, which after all have no longer

LOUIS McLANE.

novelty or charm for me, and are a grievous tax upon my spirits."

So firm and cordial were these relations that McLane could bring up minor grievances with the certainty that they would be adjusted without animus or delay. It cannot be said that the new *entente* was understood or appreciated everywhere throughout the King's dominions and especially in the navy, where there were occasional " regrettable episodes," usually in connexion with the ancient Right of Search. For in September of this year Captain Price, of H.M.S. *Trinculo*, fell in with the American vessel *Providence* off the coast of Ireland and boarded her. The officer found the original manifest not signed, and, suspecting the papers, ordered the vessel to lay to while he sent for instructions. Notwithstanding this injunction, the *Providence* seized the first moment to make off. A shot across her bows followed. She was escorted into Cork harbour, where the Admiral decided that the ship should not be held and she was accordingly released. But what rankled in the American skipper's soul was not the search or detention, but the reprehensible conduct of the band of musicians aboard the *Trinculo*, which played *Yankee Doodle* with offensive gusto on his coming aboard.

He characterized this action as insulting, and the " insult " was reported to the American Minister, who called upon Lord Aberdeen for an apology. Aberdeen drew the Minister's attention to—

" that part of the affidavit wherein the master alleges that an offensive tune was played on his going aboard the *Trinculo*, in derision, as he conceived, of his character as a citizen of the United States. Captain Price states the circumstance to have arisen out of a mistake of the musicians, who being directed by him to play ' Hail, Columbia ! ' as a *compliment* to the American master, from ignorance began the other, but were warned and stopped by Captain Price."

It seems odd enough to-day to learn that *Yankee Doodle* was ever unacceptable to American ears, or that its playing could be construed into an insult.

As to the incident itself, the Admiralty, after a full consideration of the circumstances, caused Captain Price to be reprimanded for improper conduct. In future, it is probable that the gallant Captain was more precise in his choice of tunes for the ship's band on ceremonial occasions.

The new monarch, King William IV, himself an old sailor, was particularly entertained by this affair, and " Hail, Columbia ! " was often thereafter heard at Court.

" The King [wrote Irving] keeps all London agog : nothing but sights and parades and reviews. He is determined that it shall be merry old England once more. Yesterday morning there was a splendid review in St. James's Park, at which all the world was present. Then a royal breakfast at the Duke of Wellington's, attended by the dignitaries of the Court and several of the foreign Ministers, Mr. McLane among the number. In the afternoon there was held a chapter of the Order of the Garter, for the installation of the King of Würtemberg. Then a grand dinner at the palace, at which Mr. and Mrs. McLane ' assisted.' Mr. McLane and the King became so thick that some of the *Corps Diplomatique* showed symptoms of jealousy. The King took to him especially when he found he had begun the world by being a midshipman. The King and Mrs. McLane also had some pleasant discourse. In the evening there was a brilliant dress ball at the Duke of Wellington's, at which I was present. The King was there in great spirits, notwithstanding the busy day he had been through. He spoke to everybody right and left in the most affable manner, and I observe he has an easy and natural way of wiping his nose with the back of his forefinger, which I fancy is a relic of his old middy habits. Upon the whole, however, he seems in a most happy mood, and disposed to make everyone happy about him, and if he keeps on as he is going, without getting too far out of his depth, he will make the most popular King that ever sat on the English throne."

A pleasing picture, well worthy of being recalled.

About this time the American Minister to Russia, John Randolph, arrived in London. Randolph was a most eccentric personage, a hard drinker, hard swearer and a notorious duellist, but nevertheless a man of parts, whose forensic eloquence was the boast of many thousands of his compatriots. He was invited to a royal levée. McLane and

Irving called for him in a carriage, and found him prepared to accompany them wearing a black coat, and black small-clothes, with knee-buckles, white stockings, and shoes with gold buckles ; a huge sword, and a little round black hat. They gazed somewhat startled at his dress, which increased the extreme oddity of his figure. Randolph pointed to his gold buckles. " No sham about them. Rundell and Bridge, by God ! " To McLane's observation as to the propriety of his dress, he thundered out, " I wear no man's livery, by God ! " " But," ventured Irving, " the object of a court costume is to avoid awkwardness and challenge : there is a convenience in it : and at all events you don't want a sword." " Oh, now, Irving, as to the sword, you need not pretend to teach me about that ; my father wore a sword before me, by God ! " Irving explained that the huge sword belonged to a different costume, and was out of place in that dress. This seemed to strike Randolph, and he unbuckled his sword afterwards and left it in the carriage. As he was about to enter the antechamber, where the foreign Ministers were in waiting, he was, as Irving had feared, stopped by the usher. The Secretary of Legation immediately explained who he was, and he was permitted to pass. " There now, Randolph," said he, " you see one of the inconveniences of being out of costume."

In the antechamber the foreign Ministers eyed this amazing American curiously. Admitted to the presence chamber, he preceded Irving, made his bow to Royalty in his turn, and then passed before other members of the Royal family. As he went by the Duke of Sussex, the latter beckoned to Irving. " Irving," said he, with his thumb reversed over his right shoulder, and moving it significantly up and down, half suppressing a laugh at the same time, " who's your friend, Hokey Pokey ? " Irving, jealous for the honour of his country, replied with emphasis : " That, sir, is John Randolph, United States Minister at Russia, and one of the most distinguished orators of the United States."

But it is to be feared that the disclosure did not sufficiently impress this irreverent prince, for some time afterwards, when Irving was dining with his Royal Highness, he inquired after McLane, who had returned to America ; then, pursuing his inquiries, added with a significant smile, " And how is our friend Hokey Pokey ? "

By the following spring Mrs. McLane's rheumatism,[1] and the fact that he had accomplished all that he could expect to do diplomatically, made the Minister resolve to return home. When this was made known to the President, there came not only the required letter of recall, but likewise an offer of a seat in the Cabinet.   McLane arranged to sail July 1, instructing Irving to remain behind as Chargé d'affaires, although still on Secretary's pay.   " I trust, however," Irving wrote, " another Minister will be appointed with as little delay as possible, so that I shall be relieved by autumn at farthest."

For the present, then, London society beheld Mr. Washington Irving, the popular author, installed as the official representative of his country at the English Court, the first professional literary man to hold the post.   In that capacity he attended the Coronation of King William IV.   For the ceremony there were scores of Americans in London eager to obtain invitations, amongst them the Consul-General.   In the Embassy archives is a note in the cramped handwriting of the Master of Ceremonies :

" Sir Robert Chester presents his compliments to Mr. Washington Irving and will be much obliged if he will be kind enough, at his earliest convenience, to favour Sir Robert Chester with the names of the Persons, from the *Court of the President* of the United States of North America, for whom Mr. Washington Irving may wish to receive tickets of invitation to the ceremony of the Coronation of His Majesty in Westminster Abbey on the 8th September next."

Chester then takes occasion to point out that :

" Ambassadors, Ministers and Foreigners of Distinction are eligible for invitation, and that a Consul-General or Consul is neither considered a Foreigner of Distinction nor a Diplomatic Character."

Subsequent Consul-Generals seem to have been luckier ; this one did not attend the Sailor King's Coronation.

[1] " Poor Mrs. McLane," Irving wrote, " is confined to her bed with an attack of acute rheumatism, that deprives her of the use of her limbs, and subjects her to excruciating pain.   It throws quite a gloom over our home circle, for she is our sunshine."

That autumn Irving heard that McLane's successor was on his way—it was none other than the Secretary of State, Van Buren himself. Would he remain as Secretary of Legation ? No : the author in him was now calling for a resumption of creative work. He wrote :

" I trust the Government will perfectly understand that in declining to continue here as Secretary, I am influenced by no feeling of petty pride or mistaken etiquette. I have no idea of any derogation in returning from a casual and transient elevation as Chargé d'affaires to the duties of the secretaryship, and should have made a point of dis-countenancing such false punctilio by my example, did not other considerations, of which you are well aware, induce me to desire for the present a total emancipation from official duties.

" I am looking forward with great pleasure to the arrival of Mr. Van Buren, and to my release from London and its harassing life, as soon as I shall have put him up to the routine of affairs and the usages of the town."

If at the time of General Jackson's election any intelligent elector had been asked to name the most adroit and experienced politician in New York, he would have named Martin Van Buren. He was a little, bland, rosy-faced man who had from boyhood been noted for his precocity in the law and politics. A small farmer's son, of Dutch ancestry, at fourteen he was reading Blackstone, at eighteen he was member of a nominating convention, at twenty-one he was admitted to the Bar, at thirty he was a State Senator, and at thirty-nine a Federal Senator.

In the Upper House in 1824 he had opposed the ratification of President Monroe's Convention with England for the suppression of the Slave Trade, doubtless because a qualified right of search was attached to it. Although self-educated and accustomed to deal with mankind in the rough, Van Buren's manners were irreproachable and his diction refined even to stateliness. In 1827 he left the Senate to become Governor of New York, but threw himself so whole-heartedly into his friend General Jackson's Presidential campaign, that Jackson at once offered Van Buren the first post in his administration. As Secretary of State he had promoted several important measures, including America's share of the West Indian trade, but, like Jackson himself, he had incurred many enemies. It was Jackson's wish that Van Buren should eventually succeed him in the Presidency ; his holding the Secretaryship of State was a danger, and might compromise Jackson's administration and his own popularity. When, therefore, McLane resigned, he yielded his place to Edward Livingston and accepted the mission to England.

On September 14, 1831, Irving wrote to his friend the late Minister :

" Mr. Van Buren arrived in town last evening and put up at Thomas's Hotel, where I had engaged apartments for him. I have not yet seen him, as I dined last evening at the palace and did not get away until late. After dinner, when we had withdrawn to the grand saloon, I had a long and very interesting and satisfactory conversation with the King, who, I should observe, has always treated me with marked attention ever since I have had charge of the Legation. In the course of this conversation he alluded to Lord Palmerston, who was present, and said he believed we found him a very pleasant man to transact business with. I assented to the observation fully, but added that we might testify in the same way to the members of his Majesty's Government generally. And I took this occasion to speak in the strongest manner of the sense entertained by you and myself of the prompt, frank and friendly treatment we had experienced both in our official and private intercourse since we had resided at this Court ; of the great facilities it had given you in your negotiations, and the favourable effect it had produced in the relations between the two countries."

To this communication Irving added a postscript :

" . . . I have just seen Mr. Van Buren, and do not wonder you should all be so fond of him. His manners are most amiable and ingratiating, and I have no doubt he will become a favourite at this court, and will continue those amicable relations you have so advantageously established."

On September 20, Irving retired from the Legation, and on the following day the new Minister had an audience of

King William IV and presented his letter of credence. As he reported to Secretary Livingston :

" He received me in the friendliest manner . . . and said that he had succeeded to the throne at a period when the political condition of Europe was most critical and when its peace could only be preserved by the exercise of the utmost prudence on the part of those entrusted with the government of the principal Powers ; that for himself, if he had been ambitious, or willing to involve his country in war, there had not been wanting occasions when he might have done so, without subjecting himself even to the imputation of seeking to disturb the public tranquillity. But he was not ambitious, and believing, as he did, that the best interest of his country as well as the happiness of the world could only be promoted by the preservation of the general peace, he had exerted all the power with which he was invested to accomplish that great end. He said that his task had been a difficult one ; that Great Britain had endeavoured to exercise, and had exercised, an important influence on the side of peace. . . . As to the particular country from which I came, he had always been anxious for the preservation of the very best relations between it and Great Britain, that not only did their common interest point to that course, but their common origin and the kindred relations subsisting between them should stimulate both nations to practise forbearance towards each other.

" He added that he had served during the whole of the war and that he had endeavoured to discharge the duties he owed his country with fidelity and zeal ; but that on the return of peace he had laid aside all the feelings which war had given rise to and resumed with pleasure those which were more congenial to his disposition."

The King spoke with " frankness and feeling " and at unusual length, just as, it may be added, he had previously done and in very similar terms to McLane and Irving. He referred to President Jackson handsomely, observing that " all good men were traduced."

Van Buren attended a debate (it was on the Reform Bill) in the House of Commons ; he thought it " animated," but that part he heard " did not appear to me to be characterized by great ability." As to the Bill itself:

" The solicitude felt upon the subject by that portion of the aristocracy who believe that they foresee in the success of the measure the ultimate prostration of the privileged orders is obviously of the deepest and most painful character."

At that moment London was the scene of extraordinary diplomatic activity. An International Conference of five Powers was sitting and doing its best to avoid war in the matter of Belgium.

In the midst of it came a domestic political crisis. The Reform Bill was rejected by the Lords in October, and Van Buren reported :

" The feeling with which the result has been received by a great majority of the nation is intense . . . one of almost general and undisguised indignation. It shows itself by every means save open rebellion."

He mentioned that several peers had been openly insulted and their dwellings assailed. But as long as the King and Ministry had the confidence of the people, all was well. Should either change, then he could " conceive of nothing that could arrest a great convulsion of the Empire."

" A creation of new peers sufficient to carry the majority on the Ministerial side is confidently spoken of by reformers as the easiest if not the only remedy, and the King is urged towards the immediate adoption of it. . . . The current of public indignation against the Bishops is very strong ; and if it does not in the end prove overwhelming, must certainly seriously affect the temporal interests of the Church."

But his prognostications there were not fulfilled.

Two or three months later (January 14, 1832) Van Buren heard that " Lord Grey has at length been authorized to create a new batch of peers," although the King was reluctant to give his assent. Nevertheless, he would have to go with the Ministry and the wishes of the people.

Before this Lord Palmerston had put out a " feeler " to Van Buren with reference to the Slave Trade. He asked him " whether it was not probable that we might be induced to yield the right of search in a qualified form and at particular stations only."

MARTIN VAN BUREN.

" I told him [reported the American Minister] I thought not : that the Right of Search was so repugnant to the feelings of our people that I did not believe the Government would think of granting it to any extent."

In February Van Buren, at a family dinner with the Duke of Sussex, had an opportunity to converse freely with him upon the subject of the relations between the two countries. He found the Duke was " Whig from principle."

" He gave a sentiment at dinner very complimentary to the President and spoke of him and of our country in the most kind and liberal manner. His talents are of a much higher order than is generally supposed in the United States."

Which only confirms the opinion of other Americans, such as Rush, who met the Duke at close quarters.

All seemed to be going well with Van Buren and his mission when suddenly a bombshell burst. The Senate refused to confirm his nomination as Minister to London. The reason for this unprecedented action was that Van Buren while Secretary of State had been guilty of truckling to England in his instructions to Minister McLane concerning the West Indian trade. A passage was singled out which was regarded in the light of an " apology " for the Embargo measure of Adams and Clay. The latter, therefore, vigorously opposed Van Buren's nomination, which was defeated by the casting vote of Vice-President John C. Calhoun.

What course should the discredited Minister now take ? According to Washington Irving, who was still in London, engaged in his own affairs :

" Some of his friends were urgent for his immediate return to throw himself into the Senate and attack his foes sword in hand. We had long talks on the subject ; the result was that he determined to remain here a few weeks until he had put the affairs of the Legation in a fair train, then to visit some parts of the Continent, and to sail for the United States, so as to be there in June, by which time the public sentiment will have had time to express itself fully and sincerely, without any personal agitation on his part. This is certainly the most dignified course, and I think will be the most popular."

Van Buren himself wrote to Livingston (February 28) :

" I received on the 21st inst. your dispatches informing me

that the Senate of the United States had not confirmed my
nomination as Minister at this Court and leaving it discretion-
ary with me, according to my view of public good, to return
immediately or to continue in the discharge of my diplomatic
functions here until the constitutional termination of my
mission. . . . It does not appear necessary that I should
remain in England until the expiration of my commission ;
but my continuance here for a short time will be indispensable
to enable me to place the affairs of the Legation in a proper
train before committing them to the hands of Mr. Vail.
The period of my departure will be determined by the result
of an interview which I am to have with Lord Palmerston
in the course of the present week."

Irving tells us that the rejection by the Senate was unexpected by Mr. Van Buren, as it was by himself.

" We both thought there would have been talking and
threatening on the subject ; but that he would have been
confirmed by a bare majority. This news took him, therefore, by surprise, and when he was suffering under indisposition ; but he bore it with great equanimity. There were
just at this time levées, and drawing-rooms, and state dinners,
in honour of the Queen's birthday.   He was in doubt whether
to appear at them, as it had been represented in the papers
that the vote of rejection stripped him of his diplomatic
functions, and rendered all that he had done nugatory, unless
sanctioned by the Senate.   I advised him to take the field
and show himself superior to the blow levelled at him ;
at the same time I had the statement in the papers corrected
and the facts made known, that his appointment and all his
acts were valid until the end of the session of Congress,
unless he should be previously recalled by the President.
He accordingly appeared at all the court ceremonials ; and,
to the credit of John Bull, was universally received with the
most marked attention. Everyone seemed to understand
and sympathize in his case ; and he has ever since been
treated with more respect and attention than before by the
Royal family, by the members of the present and the old
Cabinet, and the different persons of the Diplomatic Corps.
This I consider an earnest of the effect that will be produced
by the same cause in the United States. I should not be
surprised if this vote of the Senate goes far towards ultimately
elevating him to the Presidential chair.

" The more I see of Mr. V. B., the more I feel confirmed in a strong personal regard for him. He is one of the gentlest and most amiable men I have ever met with ; with an affectionate disposition that attaches itself to those around him, and wins their kindness in return."

The rejected, but by no means dejected, Minister had his farewell audience of the King on March 19, 1832. He had at least accomplished something towards putting Anglo-American relations on a friendly footing. His one constructive act was an arrangement with Lord Palmerston (of whom he took leave on the last day of the month) for establishing American Consulates in the chief manufacturing towns of Great Britain, a much-needed measure.

Thus began President Jackson's quarrel with the Senate. He said he would subject no other statesman to a similar indignity. He did, however, make a nomination in 1834 ; but the Senate would not hear of it, and so there was no appointment of a successor to Van Buren for four years.

BIOGRAPHICAL NOTES

Barbour subsequently became the author of the Anti-duelling Act in Virginia and was President of the National Convention which nominated Harrison and Tyler. He died in 1842.

McLane returned home to become Secretary of the Treasury and, in 1835, Secretary of State. In the following year he returned to his estate in Maryland. He was, as will be seen later, re-appointed Minister to England in 1845. He died in 1857.

Van Buren was elected Vice-President on his return home, and so came to preside over the legislative body which had rejected him. In 1836 he was chosen President and four years later retired to his beautiful country-seat, where he long played an influential part in national politics. He survived until 1862.

CHAPTER XI

STEVENSON (1836–1841)

BUT if there was now to be for some years no regular American Minister at the Court of St. James, a remarkable Secretary of Legation had come over to take Washington Irving's place. As Chargé d'affaires he is so interesting a figure and his tenure was so lengthy and unusual that he well merits a place in these pages.

A few years before the battle of Waterloo, when Napoleon at the height of his power was capturing, sinking and confiscating American ships, there were few busier French seaports than L'Orient in Brittany. The American Consul there, Stephen Vail, was engaged in a perpetual struggle with the port authorities and an almost daily protest against the seizure of American ships, cargoes and seamen. At one time he had hundreds of shipwrecked sailors on his hands.

With the war of 1812 came a change ; it was the era of prizes, prize courts and prize money. This work, though lucrative, was even more arduous ; the Consul was advancing in years, and to help him he had apparently only his two small sons, Eugene and Aaron. Some day the story of life at an American Consulate in France during the turbulent Napoleonic wars, the greed, violence and robbery, the corruption of the officials and the suffering of the sailors, the night-long orgies in which an army of abandoned women participated, the frequent riots and scenes of bloodshed, will be fully narrated. Of all the American Consuls in France, Vail was the steadiest and most trustworthy. But, like the American Minister in Paris, Barlow, he too eventually sank under the strain.

Happily married, Consul Vail had reared a numerous family in a charming mansion belonging to an *émigré* Breton nobleman. On his death in 1815 his family returned to America, and Aaron, who attracted the attention of Barlow's successor, Crawford, was appointed to a clerkship in the American Legation in Paris.

Seventeen years passed. Young Vail seems in the interval to have wandered about Europe—in Vienna, at Madrid (where he eventually became Minister), and elsewhere—and in 1831 he is found at the American Legation in London. All this while he had been acquiring knowledge, experience and friends. At thirty-five and a bachelor, Vail had become what was then so sadly lacking in the American diplomatic service—a diplomat *par carrière*, devoted to his profession.

Such was the man who on Minister Van Buren's departure found himself called upon to take charge of the interests of the United States at the premier Court of Europe at one of the most critical periods in English, and indeed of European, political history. His term as Chargé d'affaires lasted full four years, from 1832 to 1836.

Within the previous similar period, no fewer than four Ministers—Gallatin, Barbour, McLane and Van Buren—had appeared like stars in the diplomatic firmament and had vanished, illumining little save their own shortcomings. Vail was not inclined to under-rate his promotion.

" Thus unexpectedly raised to a high and delicate station, [he wrote Secretary Livingston], I cannot, without great diffidence of my ability to do justice to it, contemplate its obligations and responsibilities, nor feel less sensibly the honour conferred upon me by this new manifestation of confidence on the part of the President. I can only promise that to deserve a continuance of it will be the constant object of my ambition and that I shall, with increased zeal and unsparing effort, endeavour to fit myself for a proper discharge of those obligations and responsibilities."

Being a bachelor, he could give his whole time to the work. He began by establishing order in the Legation archives, filing and indexing every paper, amassing every work of reference and newspapers. On his exiguous salary, although obliged to move into quarters in Regent Street and to keep no secretary, he managed to mix freely in London society while yet maintaining his dignity and independence. When he had to entertain, he did so at his club or in public rooms. He won the esteem of the King and Royal family, of Lord Grey, the Duke of Wellington, Palmerston and the leading politicians of both parties ; while his notes and dispatches to his own Government and to the British Foreign Secretary are so numerous and voluminous that, taken altogether, they might well serve as an abridged political history of England for the period.

Although the curious inquirer will look in vain for the name of Aaron Vail in any of the standard American biographical dictionaries, his name and services well deserve to be rescued from oblivion.

Amongst the archives of the Embassy there is a letter from Henry Jackson of Athens, Georgia, whom Minister W. H. Crawford had taken with him to Paris as Secretary of Legation in 1814 :

"ATHENS, GEORGIA,
"August 29, 1832.

" MY DEAR SIR,

"About twenty years ago, after an anxious voyage across the Atlantic, I became a temporary resident of your paternal mansion in one of the most delightful spots of the environs of L'Orient. At that period I, as Secretary of Legation, was accompanying the Minister of the United States to the capital of France ; you, a mere boy, but exciting, with your brother,[1] a lively interest in the happy family circle that surrounded you. I now address you in a more elevated rank as the representative of your country at the Court of a nation more nearly connected with our own and comparatively of more relative importance than any other on the globe, and in addition to this, commencing your political career under the most favourable auspices. Most sincerely, my dear sir, do I hope that every success may attend you and you will permit this expression of my feelings when you consider the claim I possess of sympathizing with the family at Washington in all the happiness that your prosperity will certainly afford them."

That Vail gave satisfaction is attested by a letter in the following February from Livingston, in which he says :

" The punctuality of your correspondence and the atten-

[1] Eugene Vail, later employed in the Department of State.

tion you have shown to the business of your mission have merited and received the entire approbation of the President and of the Department."

The year 1832 was one of political turbulence in both England and Ireland. With the defeat of the Reform Bill, Lord Grey resigned, the Duke of Wellington attempted in vain to place himself at the head of affairs, and at length the Tory Opposition was induced to yield by the threat of a wholesale creation of peers. There were riots in London and a great deal of seditious talk and writing. About the same time that the Catholics and the Jews were clamouring for emancipation in England and the negroes were demanding the same boon throughout the Empire, the Asiatic cholera broke out in London and society was in a panic. Vail's dispatches are full of these topics. He records the death of Napoleon's son, the young Duc de Reichstadt, and the arrival of Joseph Bonaparte in England. Of the latter he wrote :

" He is by no means an unconcerned spectator of the present political condition of France, and as inheritor by the death of young Napoleon of the pretensions of the Imperial dynasty feels most interest in the ultimate fate of the present occupier of the French throne than he is willing to avow. He has of his own accord freely conversed with me respecting his connexions with the people of France, and has left me under the impression that he would not be backward in answering any call that might be made on him."

Vail was indefatigable. While mingling freely in society, attending routs, receptions and dances, he kept his eye ever on the panorama of British and foreign politics. His dispatches on France, Holland, Belgium and Portugal are admirable. He was especially intimate with Señor Zea de Bermudez, the Spanish Minister, who later came to be appointed Foreign Minister at Madrid. They talked of President Jackson : Bermudez admitted he had formerly been prejudiced against Jackson on account of his actions in Florida, but had since come to admire him greatly, and this change of heart Vail duly reported to Jackson.

When Vail came to the Legation, he found that the chief London newspapers being sent to Washington were

The Times, the *Morning Chronicle* and the *Courier*. For the latter two he substituted the *Morning Post* and the *Globe*.

" The *Morning Chronicle* had ceased to be a leading journal and besides is on the same side with *The Times*, while the *Post* was the most able paper of the Opposition, and the *Globe*—an evening paper—is now considered as having the confidence and speaking in the sense of the Ministry."

It cannot be claimed that Vail's epistolary style had anything in common with that of the journals he read so assiduously. It is stilted, sententious and destitute of humour. But no doubt the President enjoyed reading Vail's compendious dispatches—they described persons and social and political conditions rather different from those prevailing in the Washington of 1833. For instance, the connexion between a Parliamentary prorogation and the " shooting season " must have awakened tender regrets in " Old Hickory's " mind.

" The approach of the shooting season [wrote Vail], which seldom fails to close the annual labours of the British Legislature, has, during the last week, given an impulse to the proceedings of both Houses which promises a speedy termination of their present session."

In the American capital, alas, the only " shooting season " they knew coincided too frequently with the maximum intensity of Congressional debates and in one or two instances had proved a great embarrassment to the Administration. And the quarry was generally antagonistic Congressmen.

At first, it is said, Lord Palmerston professed humorous terror of the young American Chargé d'affaires, who dressed and danced vivaciously, lived alone in Regent Street with a single man-servant, and wrote and copied his own dispatches. But later he came to feel for Vail a genuine liking and was always affable and communicative. As Vail put it in a letter to Livingston in 1833 :

" I have seldom omitted to avail myself of the opportunities afforded me by incidentally meeting with Lord Palmerston, to call his attention to the various subjects remaining unadjusted between the two Governments, in which I thought that my further agency might be usefully employed."

Occasionally, no doubt, this zeal was embarrassing to the Foreign Secretary, but with a diplomat like Vail there was no throwing off the cares of office, and even in the midst of a crowded ball-room, in the pauses of a State concert, he was not above "talking shop" with any attaché of the Foreign Office or any member of the Diplomatic Corps.

Between America and England just then, Impressment and the Maine Boundary were the dominant issues ; but other topics were constantly arising which demanded attention.

" When it was contemplated that Mr. Van Buren would have to open a negotiation here on the subject of Impressment, I prepared from the documents and books in the Legation an abstract of the former proceedings and negotiations upon the subject which I thought might save labour and time by facilitating reference by the Minister himself to voluminous State papers." [1]

Vail more than once varied his correspondence with the Secretary of State, by writing directly to the President. At this time Jackson, pondering on the high and special functions of his office, was beginning to be jealous of any invasion of its sovereign privileges. He was aware of the attention his character and administration attracted in Europe. When, therefore, he entered upon a second term, Jackson is seen to assume a more personal relation with his representatives abroad and his interest in foreign rulers becomes more intimate.

On March 28, 1833, the following was sent to Vail :

" It is observed that official communications from Foreign Powers intended for the Executive of the United States have been usually addressed to the President and Congress of the United States. This style was introduced under the old Confederation and was then perfectly proper. But since the Federal Constitution has been formed its inaccuracy is apparent—the whole Executive Power, particularly that of Foreign Intercourse, being vested in the President.

[1] Vail to Secretary of State, 1832.

" In future therefore the inscription should be to ' the President of the United States of America ' without any other addition in such communications *as pass from one Sovereign to another.*"

Backhouse, the Permanent Secretary at the Foreign Office, was not a little perturbed over this injunction and dashed off a private letter to Vail, asking :

" Did *we* ever use such a mode of address ? Is our present form of credential ' William the Fourth, King, etc., to the United States of America ' wrong ? Is it to be President in future ? Your own credential letter says that ' *He* has appointed the Minister with the advice and consent of the Senate,' but in which *He* desires that credence may be given to what our Minister shall say ' on the part of the United States,' and not on the part of Him, the President."

Vail explained, and an undertaking was given to address the President alone in all future correspondence.

Andrew Jackson was far more deeply interested in the figures and affairs of European royalty than his biographers have revealed. During his later occupancy of the White House the grim old soldier received many personal messages from Kings and Queens, Princes and Princesses overseas : none, however, held for him such an attraction as the heiress to the British throne, the little Princess Victoria. The attraction was, as we shall see, mutual.

On June 21, 1833, Vail wrote privately to the President :

" DEAR SIR,
" I beg here to communicate to you the substance of a conversation which I had with the Duchess of Kent, mother of the young Princess Victoria, heiress-apparent to the throne of Great Britain, with whom I had the honour of dining yesterday. Although that conversation was not of a character sufficiently official to be made the subject of a public dispatch, I feel convinced from the tone and manner attending it that it was intended or desired that you should be made acquainted with its import. Under this conviction I hope I shall be pardoned for the liberty I take of communicating it directly to yourself.
" In the course of the evening Sir John Conroy, the Duchess's private secretary, stated to me that she had

declared her intention of making inquiries respecting you and of apprising me of the interest she takes in your health and welfare, of the regret with which she had heard of the late outrage offered to your person and of her wishes for the prosperity of the United States, for which she entertains the most friendly feelings and great admiration. He said that the Duchess might possibly be prevented from communicating these sentiments to me in person ; but he desired that, if it so happened, I would take what he had said as coming from the Duchess herself, since he felt himself officially authorized to speak for her on the occasion. He adverted, in the course of conversation, to the attempts which had been made by a portion of the Press, to misrepresent the opinions and feelings of the Duchess, to give a false view of her political sentiments and to prejudice the public mind against the young Princess, her daughter, by representing her as *destitute of all moral and physical qualifications* for the station to which she was one day to be called.

" These remarks were likewise made in a tone which satisfies me of the existence of a desire that they should be understood at Washington ; and this circumstance led me to state in answer that, not a stranger to the misrepresentations of which Sir John had spoken, I had felt pleasure in discovering, as far as my general impression of things here and my opportunities of personal observation had enabled me so to do, that injustice had been done to those illustrious persons : that acquainted as I was with the friendly character of the feelings of my Government towards Great Britain, I felt persuaded that you took great interest in the welfare of the persons who are destined to rule the British Empire, and that the peculiarly interesting situation of the Princess Victoria and her mother could not but be viewed in the same light by the American Government and nation.

" Soon after I was desired to go up to the Duchess and she entered into conversation with me in which, with an affability which agreeably characterizes her intercourse with society and with a manner indicative of much interest, she made many earnest inquiries touching your health, your age, your public services and history, and spoke very much in the terms of Sir John Conroy of her admiration and friendly feelings towards the United States, refraining, however, from alluding to herself personally or the Princess, her daughter. To all this I answered in corresponding language, assured her of the desire felt amongst us to cultivate the most friendly relations with England, and I promised that I would communicate to you the substance of her remarks.

" The Duchess of Kent is designated by law as the person who on the death of the present King, an event which may not be very remote, would govern as regent during the minority of her daughter, which will not expire for four years. . . . Of all the members of the Royal Family no one sustains a purer character than the Duchess of Kent. Without ambition for herself, her most anxious care is that her daughter should be brought up under a proper sense of the responsibilities of her station and fitted by education for the discharge of the duties. That she succeeds in this is conceded, I believe, by all parties whether friendly or hostile to the pretensions of the young Princess, who is supposed not to be entirely free from enemies in the bosom of the Royal family circle.

" As this conversation must necessarily be of a private and confidential character, should you deem it proper to make some acknowledgment of the sentiments it conveys it will occur to you that such return would have to be made in a similar manner ; for which means may easily be afforded in conversation between the diplomatic agent of the United States here and the Duchess herself, or the proper officer of her household."

Jackson was naturally much gratified at this letter and wrote a long and complimentary missive in reply (August 15).

When the Duchess of Kent returned to town, Vail applied for an interview and on November 17 saw both the Duchess and the young Princess Victoria, to whom he read Jackson's letter and gave her a copy of it.

It only remains to add that Jackson sent his portrait to the young Princess and later received one of hers in return, and that when Victoria ascended the throne Jackson almost looked upon her as a protégée of his own. He perused greedily all the details of the succession, coronation, marriage and motherhood of his " little good friend," and before the old warrior's death in 1845 a *Life* of General Jackson had been read with interest by the Queen and the Prince Consort and afterwards by at least one occupant of the Royal nursery.

Vail could hardly have failed to note a certain physical

and moral resemblance between Old Hickory and the Iron
Duke. The American Chargé was on good terms with
Wellington and when his Grace came temporarily into office
in December 1834, he sent for Vail, who called at Apsley
House, wondering what business was afoot. But the Duke
only wanted to have a chat—to express his friendliness for
America and his desire to improve their relations.

Amongst Vail's dispatches is one dated May 22, 1833, in
which he describes a Reform riot. It has a special significance
of its own.

" Some individuals ascertained to be of obscure origin
and uninfluential standing had invited the people to meet
in a public square for the purpose of forming a National
Convention which would extricate the country from its
present difficulties. The Police having been apprised of the
design, the Home Secretary issued a proclamation cautioning
all persons against attending the meeting and threatening
the interference of the authorities to preserve the public
tranquillity. Notwithstanding this caution, a large assemblage of persons, chiefly, it seems, of that class which is always
attracted to similar scenes by idle curiosity, met at the
appointed place ; and on some low individuals making their
appearance to organize the meeting, strong detachments
of the Police Force, which had been stationed in the
neighbourhood, advanced to seize them ; and in doing so
came in contact with a party of men bearing flags and alle-
gorical banners and engaged in a scuffle in which three of the
police were stabbed, one of whom almost immediately died
of his wound. Incensed by this, the police began an
indiscriminate attack upon the unoffending populace in which
men, women and children were felled to the ground by blows
from their truncheons and the affrighted mob immediately
dispersed. . . . The murderer (of the policeman), who so
far has escaped apprehension, inflicted the wound in a scuffle
in which the policeman attempted to wrest from him a flag
which he had borne at the head of the procession.

" The flag, I am sorry to say [concluded Vail], was that of
the United States."

The American Chargé d'affaires was, of course, requested
to assist the police in tracing the identity of his desperate
fellow-countryman who had thus waged open war on law

and order : but Vail could only disavow the man and express
his indignation that his country's emblem should have been
dragged into the affair.   At a subsequent trial at the Old
Bailey, one George Forsey, accused of stabbing a policeman
and not convicted, was proved to have carried an American
flag.   He seems to have regarded it simply as a symbol of
liberty, like the Phrygian cap on a pole, also borne in the
procession.[1]

With Palmerston, as has been said, Vail was on the very
best terms and was also a favourite at Lady Palmerston's
parties.   In April 1835 Wellington had once more handed
over the Foreign Office to Palmerston.   There is a curious
letter from the latter statesman to Vail on the subject of
throwing open the archives to an American named Barry,
who had come to London to inspect documents relating to
revolutionary history.   Palmerston regretted that he could
not grant permission and gave his reasons.

" The period to which the search proposed by Mr. Barry
would relate is too recent and embraces the whole of the
contest which ended in the separation of the United States
from Great Britain.   It is obvious that the confidential
communications between the Government of the Mother
Country and its authorities in the colonies during such a
period of excitement, cannot for a great variety of reasons
be properly submitted to the unrestricted inspection of the
Government which has taken its origin from the successful
issue of the contest. . . . There might be many things in the
correspondence of that period unsuited to the present
relations so happily established between the two parties in
their capacity of Independent Powers."

The then state of the archives may be inferred from the

---

[1] It is rather entertaining to gather from the newspapers of the day that
the American flag or banner was regarded as a great novelty in London.   In
the account of the trial in the *Annual Register* for 1833 it is observed : " The
flag was produced.   It was a red and white striped flag with stars in one
corner and a blue ground."   How all in court must have craned their necks
to get a glimpse of the strange flag !   The other banners carried bore the
inscriptions, " Liberty or Death " with a skull and crossbones, and " Equal
Rights and Equal Justice," and " Holy Alliance of the Working Classes."
Only a year or two after Vail's departure from London, the American flag
was being carried in large numbers into the Queen's dominions by Fenian
agitators of the same stamp as Forsey, thereby making further trouble for the
American Minister in London.

fact that there were two hundred volumes concerning the period in the Record Office, and time could not be spent by the officials " to inspect them beforehand." Awkward assertions and incidents might be divulged which would be far from promoting Anglo-American goodwill. Public opinion in America and the science of history were not a century ago quite in the robust state both have since attained. However, the Foreign Minister was prepared to entertain any specific application for documents. It only remains to add that the George III, North, Shelburne and Germain correspondence would have to wait some decades before being accessible to the general public, although they were consulted in part by Sparks and Bancroft.

In President Jackson's quarrel with Louis Philippe's Government, which resulted in the closing of the American Legation in Paris, it was British mediation which restored the situation. Palmerston expressed his satisfaction and King William IV was delighted. The whole British public, the monarch told Vail, " shares in this feeling, which is not unmixed with pride at what is considered a new instance of British influence in regulating the affairs of nations." For a moment, indeed, it seemed as if the whole business might be nullified by the French Minister, Pageot's, indiscretions, but Palmerston thought it wiser for President Jackson to take no notice of these.

" 'The fact is,' said his Lordship in the free and familiar tone which characterized our interview, ' that in this affair France has ' knocked under ' to the United States, and that having yielded the main point in dispute it would be more generous not to press her too hard for further concessions.' "

Palmerston was happy that British intervention had been effective. " The United States," he said, " have never, in all this controversy, descended from the high and dignified ground it occupied at the outset and have acquired fresh title to the respect and confidence of other nations." [1]

Vail heard of the appointment of a regular Minister in April 1836, when Palmerston wrote him of his regret that this would put an end to their official relations. At least

---

[1] Vail to Secretary of State, March 14, 1836.

15

America's interests or the national dignity had suffered nothing in the long interval. Vail could have stayed on as Secretary, but the salary was too small; he accordingly resigned and returned to America, where his services were four years later rewarded by the mission to Spain.

The statesman whom Andrew Jackson had fixed upon for the English mission was another Andrew, surnamed Stevenson. The latter had been for some years Speaker of Congress, "a man most hateful to the Opposition from his strict partisanship in the appointment of Committees." [1]

Stevenson also was a Virginian, and one of Jackson's most trusted political henchmen. While Speaker in 1832 a disgraceful assault occurred upon a Congressman, William Stanberry. He had been set upon by the notorious Sam Houston and brutally maltreated. After a month's fiery discussion in the House, Houston received a reprimand from Speaker Stevenson, but a reprimand which clearly betrayed that Stevenson's sympathies were with the assailant rather than with the victim. The House felt that its dignity had been outraged. After nearly two years of agitation, Stanberry obtained a verdict against Houston for five hundred dollars and costs, besides the offender's imprisonment. But President Jackson promptly nullified the decision by remitting both penalties. Not only that, but he publicly announced that "after a few more examples of the same kind, members of Congress would learn to keep civil tongues in their heads."

Naturally, the politer communities of New York and New England, shocked and already hostile to the Administration, were hardly propitiated when "Old Hickory" sent in the name of Speaker Stevenson as Minister to England. It was rejected, and two years passed before a sufficient number of Senators could be persuaded to confirm the nomination.

It was Stevenson's first sea-voyage, and even for several days after his arrival, June 28, 1836, he continued prostrated by illness. The indefatigable Vail was more useful than ever. The new Minister was presented to the King and the Queen in the following month and then promptly entered upon

[1] James Parton : *Andrew Jackson.*

ANDREW STEVENSON.

business with Lord Palmerston. It was not altogether
felicitous that this business should concern slavery and
involve an official American defence of that institution.
The Minister himself felt this; but he was backed at
Washington by two statesmen—Southerners and slave-
owners like himself—who intended to push the American
claims to the uttermost. Stevenson's first letter to the
Foreign Secretary related to the Slaves Indemnity.

"I wished," he subsequently reported to Secretary
Forsyth, "to let them at once see that the President
intended to carry out the principles he laid down for his
Government in relation to foreign nations, to ask only
what was right and submit to nothing wrong." Therefore he told Palmerston "in strong, though respectful
terms, the painful surprise and regret of the President at the
delay which had taken place." His own opinion was that
"they wish to settle, notwithstanding the deep sensibility
excited throughout Great Britain upon the subject of slavery,
to which this matter is supposed, very improperly, to be
allied."

In his interviews and correspondence with the British
Foreign Secretary, however, Stevenson seems to have been
betrayed into a somewhat apologetic attitude, not at all to
the taste of "Old Hickory," who had just been giving an
exhibition of his uncompromising temper to Louis Philippe
and the French nation over other indemnities. He therefore
instructed the Secretary of State to administer a rebuke to
his envoy in London. Forsyth's letter was sufficiently
cutting.

"In your zeal [he wrote, September 14, 1836] to save
your country you have overlooked the consideration that any
defence anticipating imputation is a want of self-respect.
The consciousness of the position our Government occupies
should satisfy us that an attempt to impeach its honour
could not possibly be made. To say anything *by way of
vindication* is to admit that there is something which requires
to be explained or palliated. It would be very awkward
if Lord Palmerston should choose to discuss that part of your
note to him of which it is intended to show that the United
States have not been consistent."

He went on to observe :

" There is another point in your letter, which, if any discussion follows on the merits of the several claims, must not be forgotten. You argue the question of the claimants as if it were possible to apply to them the rules and principles of the recent British legislation for the West Indies.[1] You say correctly that they do not impair the right to redress : but two of the cases occurred *before* the Emancipation law was in force."

This was not the only matter upon which the President desired a direct and forcible expression of his views. There was Texas. Stevenson was enjoined not to fail to tell Palmerston that—

" any attempt at intervention from abroad for such purpose would impose upon us the obligation in self-defence to intervene. To us it is a matter of indifference whether the Texans forbid or permit domestic slavery, but it is not a matter of indifference that their domestic policy should be dictated to them on this, to us, most delicate subject, by any foreign Power."

Stevenson was not accustomed to be brow-beaten, and besides had no particular love for Forsyth. He was angry and wrote back indignantly that he was quite able to control the situation. The British Government were not attempting to take an unfair advantage, either about the Slaves Indemnity or Texas. Palmerston's attitude was friendly, and certain newspapers—

" do not vindicate the crude opinions nor seem to respect the impudently false assertions of those who have sought to involve Great Britain in the contest by imputing ambition to our Government and disgraceful speculations to its functionaries."

To this Forsyth replied :

" Nothing in my letter of the 14 September was intended

[1] In 1834 the British Government made the admission that " the servile character of the slaves in the British colonies was rather suspended than abolished by the West Indian Act of Emancipation, and that the relation between the slave and his owner was still capable of being renewed."—*Vide* Circular Dispatch of the Colonial Secretary, Spring-Rice, to the Governor of the West Indian Colonies, November 1834.

to call into question your motives or the object you had in view. The patriotism of neither was doubted. The particular cause you had judged it right to pursue . . . was objected to, as indicating an apprehensiveness of censure not consistent with a perfect self-respect and as liable to lead to an argument of no practical utility."

Palmerston, thought the Secretary, might have taken advantage ; was glad he had not done so. At all events he had put Stevenson on his guard. Later (April 17) he wrote :

" You inform me that you have had (February 22) an interview with Lord Palmerston on the North-eastern boundary and that you had suggested to his Lordship a mode of settlement. No intimation was made in your communication of the nature of the suggested mode. . . . You will therefore see the propriety of furnishing me, as soon as practicable, with a minute of the conversation between Lord Palmerston and yourself. . . . You suggest that the answer of the British Government regarding the boundary will be communicated through you. Why ?

" If such intention has sprung from a desire on the part of his Majesty's Government to transfer the negotiation to London, the President *wishes it to be discouraged,* as the reasons in favour of continuing it here, which cannot fail to occur to you, are of the *strongest character.*"

As indeed they were, as was demonstrated a few years later when Lord Ashburton was sent out to pursue the negotiations in Washington and was adroitly over-reached by Secretary Daniel Webster.

In June came the death of William IV and the accession of his niece, Victoria. In making the announcement the American Minister stated that he would have to put his whole official family into mourning and desired to know if he would be recouped for this expense by his Government. He made several applications on the subject, but the President was adamant. If Minister Stevenson desired to show formally his grief for the deceased monarch, the cost must be defrayed out of his own pocket. It was a hardship : but it was consistent. American diplomacy took no account of conventional forms of raiment.

" The accession of the young Queen to the British throne

[reported the Minister] may be regarded as having produced an important crisis in the affairs of this country. She and her mother (who, it is supposed and no doubt justly so, has great influence over the daughter) are believed to be strong friends to reform and popular rights. The greatest anxiety, of course, prevails on all sides as to the approaching elections, upon the issue of which essentially depends the character of the new reign. The contests throughout the whole kingdom will be severe and bitter, and everything that power, wealth and ambition and the highest state of excited feeling can effect may be expected. . . . My own opinion is that the Whigs will triumph by a majority of about forty. In the present state of Parties no administration can get on well with less."

The forecast proved almost exactly correct.

One of the first events of the reign was the Canadian rebellion, which was abetted by the Fenians on the American side of the border. The revolt was suppressed, but a band of filibusters seized Navy Island on the Canadian side of the Niagara River, while an American ship, the *Caroline*, was chartered to bring supplies thence from the American side. A body of Canadian militia landed on Navy Island in search of the *Caroline*, and not finding her yet arrived, crossed over to the boundary, towed out the vessel from her harbour and launched her to destruction over Niagara Falls. Instantly at such a bold violation of its territory the American Government were up in arms. The British contention from the first was that—

" the piratical character of the steamboat *Caroline* and the necessity of self-defence and self-preservation under which Her Majesty's subjects acted in destroying that vessel would seem to be sufficiently established. . . . Her Majesty's subjects in Upper Canada naturally consulted their own security by pursuing and destroying the vessel of their piratical enemy, wheresoever they might find her." [1]

But this episode did not at once come on the diplomatic *tapis* in London, and in the meantime Stevenson went on hammering Palmerston about the indemnity for the American slaves freed by the British in 1834 at Nassau. Palmerston

[1] H. S. Fox to Forsyth, February 6, 1838.

retorted, in effect : " How could England, feeling as she did about slavery, consent to pay the American slave shippers the value of the human freight landed in British territory? When they touched British soil they became free." " We will never," declared the President, " admit such a proposition ! " Stevenson did his best to convince Palmerston.

" You will perceive from my note to Lord Palmerston [he reported, December 27, 1837] that I did not admit that the claims were to be decided under British laws. On the contrary, I protested, as you will see, against any right on the part of Great Britain to apply her municipal laws on the subject of slavery to the citizens of the United States, or their property . . . and expressly declared that whatever her system might be in relation to slavery, whether abolished or not, it could interpose no bar to claims of indemnity of this character.

" But [he concluded, sadly] the whole subject is one of great delicacy."

Acknowledging a further dispatch outlining Jackson's views in relation to a proposed convention with Great Britain on the subject of " such American slaves as may hereafter be forced by stress of weather or other unavoidable contingency within British colonial ports," the Minister observes (July 4, 1838) :

" I owe it, however, to my Government and candour to say that the present state of public feeling in this country on all subjects connected with slavery and abolition is such as to indicate but little hope of my being able to negotiate any convention that would be acceptable to our country."

Yet Palmerston eventually agreed to settle the indemnity demanded by a cash payment of $115,999 and $27,360 interest from the time of detention.[1]

The Minister was glad to be quit of the business, although

[1] On the *Comet* were a hundred and sixty-four slaves, besides a child born on the voyage : of these eleven escaped as fugitives before the intervention of the colonial authorities ; five others returned to slavery in the United States, and three died . . . leaving a hundred and forty-six, for which an average price of $479 each slave was paid. Of the forty-five on board another ship, twelve returned to the United States.

he thought the sum small. He shocked Palmerston by reminding him that—

" some of the claimants, too, will probably expect that in estimating the damages in compensation for their slaves the probable profits which might have been made by working them, together with the losses have been sustained by being obliged to violate existing contracts which these slaves were intended to fulfil, ought to be taken into account."

It was not easy to induce Parliament to vote money for such a purpose, and several speakers were severe on the whole transaction, but an appropriation of £23,500 was finally approved.

By this time a new President had been elected. Martin Van Buren, the rejected American envoy of 1832, had reached the object of his ambition. On replacing Jackson at the White House, he retained Forsyth as his Secretary of State.

Although one dispute concerning slaves had been settled, there still remained in dispute between the two countries the proper method of suppressing the Slave Trade. An Allied fleet was patrolling the African coast, but its efforts would be nullified without the British Right of Search.

Clearly and picturesquely Palmerston summarized the whole difficulty in the course of a long talk with Stevenson. His words are thus reported by the Minister (February 29, 1840):

" It appears [said Palmerston] that when a Spanish, Portuguese or Brazilian slave ship sails from Cuba or Rio de Janeiro she is fitted up for the slave trade and with papers giving her fraudulently an American character. But she has a United States citizen on board who professes to be captain. If she is met on her outward voyage by a British cruiser the officer who boards her to inquire the country to which she belongs is shown the American papers and the American captain, and whatever the suspicions of the British officer may be he cannot search her, although if she then appeared in her real character of Spaniard, Portuguese or Brazilian he would on searching her find her equipped for the slave trade and would detain and send her in for trial before the proper tribunal, by whom she would of course be condemned. Such a vessel therefore, if met with on her outward voyage by a British cruiser, escapes by virtue of her assumed American character and the protection given by its flag. So, too, if she should be met by one of the United States cruisers she would equally escape because, having no slaves on board and being on her *outward voyage,* there is no law of the United States which renders it penal for a vessel to be equipped simply for the slave trade. She has then perfect impunity.

" Arrived on the African coast, the vessel proceeds to land her cargo of goods and take on board her return cargo of slaves, and the moment the slaves are secured on board she casts aside her American character and assumes her real character of Spaniard, Portuguese or Brazilian. The American papers are secreted and her other papers held ready to be produced. The American captain sinks into a passenger and her Spanish or Portuguese mate rises into command. The United States flag is struck and the Spanish or other substituted."

Why was all this procedure necessary ?   Palmerston explained.

" Having on board her slave cargo she is forced to run for it, because she is committing an offence against all laws ; but she chooses to do so in that character which will expose her to the least penal consequences. If with slaves aboard she were met with and captured by the American cruiser, she would be dealt with under American laws as a pirate and her crew would of course be liable to capital punishment. But if caught with slaves on board in her Spanish or Portuguese character, she would only be liable to the penalties stipulated by the treaties, and these apply only to the ship, which, if condemned, is confiscated and sold ; but the crew get off without any punishment whatever."

Was it any wonder the Treaties for the suppression of the Slave Trade were hard to execute ?   The British statesman suggested the confiscation by the United States of such vessels fitted up and equipped for the slave trade, even though no slaves were aboard.

" Why not help Great Britain and the other Powers with your American navy ? " he asked.

" I told Palmerston [reports Stevenson] that in any measures which the United States might be disposed to adopt, the Right of Search, however restricted or modified, would not be conceded. That right was regarded by my Government as entirely and exclusively belligerent and one which could only be exercised on the ocean and upon the belligerent claim, and that such had been the doctrine and practice of the British Government."

It appeared, however, that all Palmerston suggested was for America to authorize her own cruisers to board and examine such American vessels as might be supposed to be engaged in the trade.

Van Buren could hardly fail to see the reasonableness of this proposal, and at once took measures to terminate the abuse complained of. Stevenson was therefore instructed to convey the following to the British Government :

" The President, on learning the abuses which had grown out of it and with a view to do away with every cause for its longer continuance, having now directed the establishment of a competent naval force to cruise along these parts of the African coast which American vessels are in the habit of visiting in the pursuit of their lawful commerce and where it is alleged that this slave trade has been carried on under an illegal use of the flag of the United States, has a right to expect that positive instructions will be given to all her Majesty's officers to forbear from boarding or visiting vessels under the American flag. This expectation is now distinctly signified to her Majesty's Government, in the belief that it will see the propriety of confining the action of its agents to the vessels of nations with whom her Majesty's Government has formed stipulations authorizing a departure from the rules pre- scribed by the public law and thereby prevent the recurrence of circumstances inevitably productive of causes of irritation and deeply endangering the good understanding between the two nations." [1]

This was certainly a great step forward and it was hoped that the new arrangement would deal a death-blow to the Right of Search.

It was a pity the question of the Maine boundary still remained unsettled. The lumbermen of both nationalities were constantly coming to blows over the question of juris-

[1] Forsyth to Stevenson, July 8, 1839.

diction in the Aroostook Valley, and at last the Governor of Maine had called out the State Militia and occupied the district. Sir John Harvey, the Governor of New Brunswick, promptly put himself in a state of defence. The whole country rocked with excitement and the hot-heads made ready for war.

In the preceding April Stevenson called on the British Foreign Secretary and—

" Lord Palmerston with his usual frankness most readily yielded to my request and said that he would with pleasure communicate to me his views on the subject. He commenced by remarking that the late proceedings which had taken place in Congress had given a fresh proof of the close relationship of the two nations and showed that the English habit of not reading or of soon forgetting Parliamentary papers prevailed equally in Congress. . . . He said that if those that had taken part in the recent debates at Washington had borne in mind the papers which had been communicated by the President to Congress in 1829, they would not have asserted that the British claim to jurisdiction was a new one, nor construed it in the sense they had done. The grounds and nature of the claim of jurisdiction were explained by Sir Charles Vaughan in his note of September 16, 1827, and later by Sir Howard Douglas. The British Minister explained it in February 1828. . . . It would be seen that the British Government had not pretended to exercise any new act of sovereignty over any part of the disputed territory since the conclusion of the Treaty of Ghent, and the jurisdiction they claimed over the *unsettled* and unoccupied part of the territory was in reality only safe custody of the property for the benefit of the future and the prevention of the assemblage of lawless and disorderly persons therein, to the annoyance and injury of the neighbouring districts.

" They had not exercised that sovereignty which the Americans supposed them to contend for, and in proof of this he remarked that two years previously the British Government cheerfully put a stop to a plan for making a railway across to disputed territory from Quebec to St. Andrews, because the building of a new road would have implied an acknowledged right of sovereignty."

He reminded Stevenson that in December 1837 they had not found themselves at liberty to march troops across the territory from New Brunswick to Canada without a previous understanding with the United States Government on the subject.

Such abstinence, he declared, ought to be mutual, and neither party should trespass, make settlements, cut timber, make roads or establish military occupation.

In England the reported action of the Americans was much resented. *The Times* and *Standard* became " quite insolent and belligerent," although " the *Chronicle* was subdued and reasonable, as befitted a Government organ." The Duke of Wellington's and Peel's speeches in Parliament were " anything but pacific or conciliatory towards the United States, and we may at any time be plunged into a sudden war if this goes on." The Minister thought the " present Government pacific, but it may be overturned. We must," he concluded, " show a bold front and punish injuries." [1]

A temporary arrangement for the joint occupation of the disputed territory promised well. But by the following spring Stevenson reported (April 28, 1840) that—

" there are no indications on the part of the Government of a disposition to relax in their claim, or concede anything to us, and attempts may very possibly be made to prevent another reference of the subject."

He advised an immediate arbitration between the two governments. But two years passed before the negotiations began which ended in the Treaty of Washington.

One cannot omit mention here of Minister Stevenson's efforts on behalf of the American tobacco industry. What were then thought scandalously high duties seemed to him to be throttling the trade.

" Nothing [wrote Stevenson to Palmerston] tended more to counteract hostility and bind nations together than the adoption of a liberal and enlightened commercial policy. A duty of three shillings per pound on an article of four pence or six pence value is, not only a departure from the general principles of Free Trade and commercial reciprocity, but is a direct hostility to the just and liberal principles which characterize the commercial relations of the two countries.

[1] Stevenson to Forsyth, November 21, 1839.

" At the moment when the United States are admitting British manufactures as almost free of duty she is taxing one of the important staples of American industry with a duty of the most injurious and indefensible character."

To this Lord Althorp, then the Chancellor of the Exchequer, might reasonably have protested that it was not indefensible in that it brought in needed revenue.   But even that, it appears, was only a fraction of what it should have been.[1] Althorp agreed with the American Minister that the duty was too high and that a reduction to a shilling or eighteenpence would bring tobacco within the reach of a new and numerous class of subjects who could not at present afford to smoke, chew or snuff tobacco of even tolerably good quality.

It is to be feared that to his august sovereign, who could not endure even the odour of the most fragrant and exquisite examples of the weed, the prospect of a general extension of the smoking habit would hardly have been alluring.

In any case, to bring about an instant reduction of duty meant a loss of £2,000,000 a year and was not therefore practical.   The thing must be adjusted gradually.   Meanwhile, Althorp handsomely assured his Excellency the Minister (from Virginia) that the moment he could reduce the tobacco duties, " an additional motive and gratification would be the advancement of the domestic interests of a country which next to his own he regarded with the deepest respect and affection."

Stevenson sighed and reported to his Government (January 1839) that " we must await more propitious times."   What would he have said to a ten-shilling duty on the weed and a tenfold consumption, per capita, which we in this century have come to witness ?

This question of tariffs was a burning one in British

---

[1] It was the heyday of tobacco smuggling. In Ireland, according to a Parliamentary report, of 20,000,000 pounds only 5,000,000 paid duty. The revenue was therefore only £700,000 and it cost £750,000 to put down smuggling. In Great Britain 50,000,000 pounds were consumed and only 22,000,000 paid duty. Minister Stevenson thought a duty of three shillings per pound "fatal" to the industry. In 1837 the consumption of duty paid tobacco was 16,000,000 pounds. The United States exported 4,000,000 pounds of manufactured tobacco and Great Britain only 500,000 pounds.

politics just then, as the American Minister had ocular evidence in the Corn Law riots, the street crowds, the impassioned harangues and a general spirit of turbulence.

"That the excitement [he wrote, March 18, 1839] will continue to increase rather than diminish I am very confident. Having fairly put the ball in motion and arrayed the working classes against the landed interests, I see no probability of its being arrested until some signal change in the whole system of Free Trade shall be achieved. Indeed, it will be fortunate for the landed proprietors, who have so resolutely resisted all amelioration of the Corn Laws, if the struggle does not finally end in some *signal organic changes* not now anticipated by the most sanguine friends of Reform.

"My own opinion is very decided that this Government, as well as that of the French, will be forced to yield to the spirit of free representative Government which is abroad in Europe, or experience the fate that has overthrown so many of the Governments of the world."

President Van Buren went out of office in 1841 and was succeeded by William Henry Harrison. Minister Stevenson had previously signified his intention to retire and was in the midst of arrangements for departure when the once-famous McLeod affair galvanized international diplomacy. It was a sequel to the *Caroline* episode of 1837. Alexander McLeod was a Canadian who claimed to have been one of the party which had seized and destroyed the American vessel, and in the course of the exploit had slain one of the crew. As he made the boast on American territory, he was promptly arrested, charged and duly convicted of murder. When the news of his conviction and impending execution reached England, the London Press indulged in "the most revolting extravagance and violence, well calculated to agitate and influence the public mind already too much disposed for violent and rash measures."[1]

"It is proper that I should inform you [wrote Stevenson] of the state of public opinion here. There seems to be a general impression that war is inevitable."

He had heard that the British Minister, Fox, had been in-

---

[1] Stevenson to Secretary of State, March 9, 1841.

structed to demand the immediate release of McLeod and, if refused, to leave Washington and return home.

" Such is not my opinion [he added]. Yet pacific as the Government may be, it is impossible in the present excited state of the country to say what course they may not be forced to take under the influence of public opinion."

Palmerston had actually written Fox that " McLeod's execution would produce war, war immediate and frightful in its character, because it would be a war of retaliation and vengeance." Daniel Webster, now Secretary of State, shared these apprehensions, and did his best to get McLeod surrendered to the Federal authorities. But the Governor of New York was intractable, and refused a writ of habeas corpus, and seemed determined to execute the Canadian hero.

Palmerston now told Stevenson, privately, as a friend, that if McLeod were executed, war would ensue.

It is rather amusing now to read that Stevenson regarded Colonel Allan MacNab, the officer in command of the troops in Upper Canada and afterwards Governor, as the real culprit.

" From the moment," wrote the Minister, " that the Government conferred the honour of knighthood upon the individual who perpetrated this outrage, I felt persuaded that the proceedings would be avowed and justified. . . . Anxious then as our Government and people are for peace they cannot shut their eyes to the dangers that threaten the harmony of the two countries and the necessity of providing means best adapted to the nature of the case. . . . I have both officially and individually held but one language on the subject, and that has been to regard it as a most unwarrantable infraction of the neutrality of my country and a flagrant violation of its rights and sovereignty."

But the British people saw only a brave patriot being slaughtered, and were angry, and the demand of *The Times* was widely echoed : McLeod must be either surrendered if alive, or avenged if dead.[1]

Stevenson reported (April 7) that notwithstanding the peaceful professions of the Government, they have not seen

[1] *The Times*, March 9, 1841,

fit to relax their military and naval operations and that the dockyards were ominously active. He thought that his own country ought to put itself in a state of defence. " I have suggested to Commodore Hull in the Mediterranean his getting his squadron nearer home." It was really something more than a suggestion, as Stevenson's correspondence with Hull shows : he had his finger on Bellona's pulse and wished the gallant Commodore to take no risks.

In the midst of the crisis came news of the death of the aged President, after only one month of office. His successor, Tyler, announced that he intended to be firm with New York and insist on McLeod's surrender. But another and surprising solution of the difficulty presented itself. McLeod's counsel produced evidence that his client had not been present at all at the capture of the *Caroline*. The disclosure was tactfully accepted and the prisoner acquitted.

When the excitement had died down, Minister Stevenson became a target for American criticism. His correspondence with Commodore Hull was condemned as that of an alarmist. England never really intended war. The Minister again protested to Webster :

" I still entertain the opinion that if he [McLeod] had been condemned and executed by the authorities of the State of New York under the existing circumstances it would inevitably have led to a rupture between the two countries. Such is the general opinion here among all classes."

It cannot be denied that Minister Stevenson had been, during his five years' tenure of office, rather a stormy petrel on the diplomatic ocean, resembling in this respect the statesman who first appointed him. And his going was in keeping with the tenor of his whole mission. The Right of Search had only for a moment lost its pre-eminence as a burning question between the two countries. Countless notes had passed backwards and forwards from Downing Street, the American Legation and the Department of State for a period of fifty years. In its bearing on the efforts to suppress the African Slave Trade, Lord Palmerston had exerted much eloquence and many arguments. But all in vain. The American Government, whatever its political complexion, continued dogmatic. Recently, there had been fresh seizures off the African coast, and Palmerston, once more called upon for apology or disavowal, said, once and for all, that the British cruisers must have the right of stopping all vessels on the high seas and determining whether they were impostors or not.

In September 1841 Stevenson was at last packed up and ready to sail. But the chance was too good to be missed. The Melbourne administration had fallen and that of Peel had come in. It was high time that the long-repressed eagle should emit a scream. He therefore composed a lengthy paper in which he told the British Government that—

" the right asserted in these notes amounts to that of search and detention in a manner the most offensive and injurious to the Rights and Honour of our Country. I shall assert again the determination of my Government that its Flag shall cover all that sails under it ! "

The warning was issued : let the British lion take care.

And in this defiant spirit the Minister bade his farewell to English shores.

On Stevenson's return home the American papers stated that he had boasted that the most important part of his ministry had been the revival and prosecution of the question of the Right of Search, in which he had " fired very hot shot " and that his last act had been " to throw a bombshell into the English Cabinet on the eve of his departure."

A New York paper quoted in *The Times* said :

" Mr. Stevenson had written a very severe letter [on the Right of Search] just before he left England. . . . It was a Parthian arrow and the ex-minister, it is said, boasts that its *point was poisoned,* while Lord Palmerston considers the embroiled state of the negotiations as a delightful legacy for him to leave to his Tory successor."

" We must admit the possibility [declared the *Quarterly Review*] of Mr. Stevenson's having intended to embarrass the American administration which had recalled him, but we wholly disbelieve that Lord Palmerston, however factiously he may be disposed to deal with *internal* questions, could

16

have played such a part as Mr. Stevenson is said to have imputed to him on so serious a point of foreign policy." [1]

BIOGRAPHICAL NOTE

Stevenson on his return became Rector of the University of Virginia, devoting the rest of his life to that office, and to agriculture. He died in 1857.

[1] *Quarterly Review*, 1841.

CHAPTER XII

EVERETT AND McLANE (1841–1846)

DANIEL WEBSTER, the new Secretary of State, had a personal reason for being well disposed towards the English. Two years before he had visited England and wrote of his visit :

" I must say that the good people have treated me with great kindness. Their hospitality is unbounded and I find nothing cold or stiff in their manner—at least not more than is observed among ourselves. There may be exceptions, but I think I may say this as a general truth. The thing in England most prejudiced against the United States is the Press. Its ignorance of us is shocking, and it is increased by such absurdities as those to which, I am sorry to say, Captain Marryat is making an abundant addition. In general the Whigs know more and think better of America than the Tories. This is undeniable. Yet my intercourse, I think, is as much with the Conservatives as the Whigs." [1]

It was a gratification to him now as Secretary of State to secure the appointment to London of a totally different man from the last Minister. Edward Everett was a scholar, orator and man of letters, and like himself a New Englander. Everett had been Professor of Greek at Harvard and editor of the *North American Review*.

Anglo-American relations stood in need of delicate handling. The retiring Minister had not improved matters by " firing his parting bombshell into the enemy's camp." He, as Palmerston was alleged to have done with Aberdeen, had left an unpleasant legacy behind for his successor. And, moreover, negotiations were about to begin with regard to the Maine boundary. With this latter subject, indeed, Everett had long been familiar. If the negotiations should be carried

---

[1] Webster to Ketchum, July 23, 1839.

on in London, Webster particularly wished to have Everett take the leading part. In addition to Everett's great fitness for the post, their personal relations had for more than thirty years been of the most intimate and confidential character.

On the other hand, when Everett arrived in London in November 1841, he had been provided with no definite instructions and was entirely without diplomatic experience. Nor did he find at the Legation any Chargé or First Secretary to acquaint him with official customs and precedents. He was thus thrown wholly upon his own resources.

On November 29 he had his first interview with the mild and conciliatory Lord Aberdeen at the Foreign Office.

" He received me [reported Everett] with great ease and courtesy and placed me at once at my own ease. He is, I should think, about fifty-three years of age, of middle stature, slightly—very slightly—lame with one leg. He expressed great satisfaction at McLeod's acquittal. . . .

" He disclaimed all right of search, detention or interference with American vessels in African waters. All he claimed was the right to board vessels ' strongly suspected of being those of other nations unwarrantably assuming the American flag.' If a mistake was made, full and ample reparation should follow."

To this Everett made response that the United States had " never claimed that their flag should furnish protection to any vessel but their own." All therefore would be well, especially if Great Britain kept her promise to pay.

Aberdeen, to Webster's satisfaction, agreed to Washington as the meeting-place of the Joint Commission, and appointed Lord Ashburton as special commissioner, armed with full powers. " People," he remarked to Everett, " would call it a concession, but he would not be influenced." The decision to arbitrate in Washington released Everett from a heavy responsibility, but it is not certain that he appreciated the derogation from his diplomatic credit.

Webster's instructions at last came to hand, dated December 28, 1841 : and were very verbose and impressive.

" You are called to your present post, my dear sir, at a very important crisis, and it will require all that you can

EDWARD EVERETT.

do, as well as all that we can do here, to get honourably and peacefully through the subjects now pending between us and England.

" On the boundary question you are well-informed. You know that a negotiation is pending for a Joint Commission with an umpire. It has made little progress for a twelve-month, but it is intended to hasten it. There is much difficulty, however, in stating the proposition. It is my intention to send some confidential person to you in March (perhaps Mr. F. Webster), that the views of the Queen's Government may be informally sounded as to what would be their notion of a compromise line. But this is not to retard the negotiation of the convention for a Commission.

" Then there is the African question, and the *Caroline* question, in regard to both of which I shall write you as soon as possible, and there is another of slaves set free at Nassau, which is likely to give us new and great trouble. I know your ability and diligence will enable you soon to master these questions."

As regards the North-eastern Boundary negotiations Everett was left " to keep things running smoothly in London and to protest against the seizures by British vessels of American ships that were suspected of being engaged in the African slave trade."

The Minister settled down at first at 32 Upper Grosvenor Street. The house, however, proved impossible, and after the arrival of his wife from Paris they decided, after " a long and discouraging search," to take 46 Grosvenor Place, a tall and narrow house, " just behind the Buckingham Palace Gardens Mews, and commanding pleasant views of the Palace Gardens. It was on the corner of the street, with a little park space to the south-east which insured light, and what-ever sun there was." Here the American Minister dispensed a liberal hospitality, giving frequent breakfasts and always being at home to his countrymen on Sunday evenings.

He soon found himself in the midst of a distinguished coterie. Webster had given him a letter of introduction to the poet Samuel Rogers, with whom he instantly became intimate. Amongst others were Sydney Smith, Henry Hallam, Peel, Disraeli, the Duke of Wellington, Carlyle, Monckton Milnes, Dr. Holland. Whewell often came down from Cambridge and Wordsworth from his retreat in the Lake country.

A week or two before Christmas, Everett presented his credentials to Queen Victoria at Windsor Castle, where he dined and spent the night. In an entertaining letter Everett describes his embarrassment when after dinner the Queen's mother, the Duchess of Kent, invited Lord Aberdeen, the Neapolitan Minister and himself to form a whist party with her. Prince Castelcicala whispered to Everett that he knew nothing of the game.

" I told him I had not played a game of whist for thirty-five years, and but one game of cards of any kind in the interval. We concluded, however, that her Royal Highness's invitation was a command and could only hope that we might be partners to each other. So by great good luck it turned out. The Duchess and Lord Aberdeen, the Prince of Castelcicala and myself were mated. Lord Aberdeen, I soon saw, was a very good player. Her Royal Highness had Mr. Murray at her elbow to sort her cards and tell her how to play them ; and the Prince and I did better, I assure you, than might have been expected. Not so well, however, but that we had to pay six shillings sterling each at the end of the game, he to Lord Aberdeen and I to the Duchess of Kent. I took out a half-sovereign and Mr. Murray kindly made the change."

While these sportive and financial transactions were being negotiated between the three diplomats and the mother of the sovereign, Victoria herself and the rest of the company were making merry at another round table. The Harvard class-room and Boston Common seemed very far away !

Everett got on capitally with the Earl of Aberdeen, whom he also occasionally met at week-end country parties.

" Most of my public business is with him, and though people do not resort to the country to transact business, yet there are great opportunities in a morning's walk, or in a quiet corner of the library in the evening, to talk over matters to very good purpose. He is, besides, though of somewhat cold exterior and rather taciturn in a large circle, a person of most extensive information, straightforward character and goodness of heart. My intercourse with him, both official and personal, has been as agreeable as possible."

There were certain Englishmen who were not very popular in America just then, and amongst them was the rotund and witty Canon of St. Paul's, Sydney Smith, who had recently been very severe on the subject of American State debts. He spoke feelingly in the matter, being himself one of the sufferers. Everett accepted an invitation to spend Christmas with the reverend wit at his rectory at Combe Florey. His brief sojourn there attracted the attention of the American press, who thought that the American envoy should be better engaged than in hobnobbing with the clerical traducers of their country. Whereupon Smith addressed the following letter to the London *Morning Chronicle:*

" SIR,—

"The Locofoco papers in America are, I observe, full of abuse of Mr. Everett, their Minister, for spending a month with me at Christmas in Somersetshire. The month was neither lunar nor calendar, but consisted of forty-eight hours—a few minutes more or less.

" I never heard a wiser or more judicious defence than he made to me and others of the American insolvency ; not denying the injustice of it, speaking of it, on the contrary, with the deepest feeling, but urging with great argumentative eloquence every topic that could be pleaded in extenuation. He made upon us the same impression he appears to make universally in this country ; we thought him (a character which the English always receive with affectionate regard) an amiable American republican without rudeness, and accomplished without ostentation. ' If I had known *that* gentleman five years ago ' (said one of my guests), ' I should have been deep in the American funds ; and, as it is, I think at times that I see nineteen or twenty shillings in the pound of the face value.' However this may be, I am sure we owe to the Americans a debt of gratitude for sending to us such an excellent specimen of their productions. In diplomacy, a far more important object than falsehood is, to keep two nations in friendship. In this point, no nation has ever been better served than America has been served by Mr. Everett.

I am, Sir, your obedient servant,
SYDNEY SMITH.

But this was not the only charge in the press campaign against Everett. He was accused of being too English, an aristocrat, and fond of ostentation. When the eminent journalist Thurlow Weed came over to London he called on Everett, who apparently failed to accord him the warm reception he thought was his due. The result was seen in the following extract from an account of Weed of the prorogation of Parliament.

"I observed our Minister, Hon. Mr. Everett, with his daughter, in a bright yellow coach, with coachmen and outriders in rich livery, and Mr. Everett himself (instead of the plain republican garb with which Benjamin Franklin, John Adams, and John Jay used to appear on such occasions) in full Court dress, with gold embroidery. I don't half like this departure from the simplicity which distinguishes our form of government, though it is certain that the American Minister has acquired great popularity here, and perhaps augments his influence by his conformity in matters of display and etiquette."

This squib, of course, attracted widespread attention. Writing to a friend, Everett entered a protest.

"My carriage is certainly yellow; whether there is anything objectionable in that colour, I do not know. It is an old carriage which I hire; as it was already yellow (rather a favourite colour here for carriages) it was suggested to me that, in painting it anew, it would take the same colour better than a different one; that yellow was the colour that stood best; and that my predecessor's carriage was yellow. On these grounds I decided, and if, as Mr. Weed says, it is 'bright yellow,' after having been used more than eighteen months—summer and winter, day and night—one of the grounds of the choice seems justified. He says that I had 'outriders.' This is wholly imaginary. There are, I believe, no outriders to any but Royal carriages. My coachman and outriders (he says) were in 'rich livery.' My coachman and footman were in a very plain livery; as plain a one as was to be seen in the procession. 'Mr. Everett himself in full Court dress.' How this could be known, by a person seeing me in a closed carriage with the windows up, does not appear. I was not in what is called 'Court dress,' full or otherwise, but in my ordinary diplomatic uniform (not even the full uniform, which is worn at the Queen's Drawing Rooms) : my coat was rather less ornamented than that of my secretary, and was certainly the very plainest dress in the diplomatic box. That any gentleman, after seeing the really splendid equipages and uniforms of many of the foreign Ministers and officers of the Household and of State, should describe mine as Mr. Weed has done, is, I own, a matter of surprise to me."

Everett suspected that some of this misrepresentation was affecting his friend Webster, who was beginning to act rather strangely. Early in 1843 Everett was offered an Extraordinary Mission to China, which he refused. The offer, we are told, " never tempted Everett for a single moment. He did not like the ' trade ' aspect of the expedition for one thing, and in the second place he was very happy where he was."

Everett had previously written :

" I am fearful not only that Mr. W. has thoughts of supplanting me, but of discrediting me in the meantime by withholding all instructions upon matters of consequence, and thus putting it out of my power to show even a willingness to do my duty. Things have already been done, or rather left undone, which I would not have believed possible on any ground but my own personal knowledge."

As for Webster, we are told that he resented the constant implications that he was not treating Everett fairly and was plotting to supplant him, and there was serious danger of a breach between the two friends. Everett even wrote a letter to Winthrop complaining of Webster, and suggesting duplicity and unfair treatment. But he thought better of it, and tore up the letter.

In England, as we have seen, Everett was popular—too much so, perhaps, to commend himself to the mass of his own countrymen.

Lord Ashburton wrote to Webster (April 28, 1843) :

" I can give no information of what passes in the Old World that you will not have better from your friend Mr. Everett, who understands us thoroughly, and who is, as you may suppose, a marvellous favourite with us. I am frequently asked whether America furnishes many such

men. We were in some anxiety that he might leave us for
the Celestial Empire, but I find, as I anticipated, that he
will remain with the Terrestrials. He would be much too
fine an instrument for such a purpose ; it would be like
cutting blocks with a razor."

Yet at that time Everett's chief diplomatic task in England
was not a particularly grateful one. It was even disagreeable. He was perpetually in receipt of instructions to
present claims against the British Government on account
of American-owned slaves they had liberated. When the
claims were admitted and the money paid, it—

" put the American people and their representative in an
unfortunate and unfavourable light. For whatever else
might or might not be true of England, she was honestly
and actively trying to suppress a most shameful practice.
Moreover, there can be no doubt that Americans were directly,
but more often indirectly, connected with the trade." [1]

Bound up too with this question of slavery and the slave
trade was the impending annexation of Texas, which had
broken away from Mexico and set up as an independent
republic. The annexationists in the South wanted Texas
as a Slave State, which was obnoxious to the North and East.
President Tyler as a Southerner and a slave-owner approved
of this course, and Webster in consequence broke away from
the administration. It was hardly therefore to be expected
that Tyler would espouse very heartily Everett's Aboli-
tionist views or his intense reprobation of the traffic. To
Upshur, who had succeeded Webster as Secretary of State,
Everett boldly wrote in December 1843 concerning the
indirect participation of American citizens in the slave
trade.

" The evil undoubtedly exists, and might probably be
remedied to some extent by the application of existing laws.
I presume, however, that in order to secure its entire suppression further legislative measures are necessary. The
President, I am aware, has already asked the attention of
Congress to the subject. It is greatly to be wished that some
law might be passed which would put an effectual stop to the

[1] P. R. Frothingham : *Edward Everett.*

employment of American capital and the participation of American citizens in a traffic condemned by religion and humanity and revolting to the public feeling of the American people. The strenuous resistance of the United States to the methods by which Great Britain has been so long endeavouring to suppress the trade in slaves, and the great expense to which our Government is put in sustaining a squadron on the coast of Africa, make it equally our duty and our interest to resort to every measure within our competence to put an effective stop to the nefarious traffic."

This was certainly plain speaking. England, too, had made her own attitude clear. Lord Aberdeen told Everett plainly that it was—

" impossible for her Majesty's Government to make the slightest compromise on the subject of slavery; and that when slaves were found within the British jurisdiction, by whatever means, or from whatever quarters, they were *ipso facto* free."

When Secretary Upshur was killed by an accidental explosion in a warship early in 1844, the President appointed a Southerner, John C. Calhoun, his successor. Calhoun was pledged to Texas annexation and the maintenance of slavery. He also distrusted England's altruistic attitude towards abolition and her interest in the future of Texas. A certain General Duff Green was sent to Europe provided with secret funds to influence foreign opinion. Green was called " the ambassador of slavery at the British Court." President Tyler failed to get his Texan project through the Senate, but it was accomplished by his successor, Polk, a year or two later.

Meantime, Everett in London had suffered a great bereavement in the death of a beloved daughter, and during the whole winter of 1843–4 her loss hung heavily on him, and affected his social habits during the remainder of his English sojourn. He found little to cheer him in the political events which were happening in America, so that during the following summer he could write to a friend :

" It must be confessed that to be the American Minister at present is not the most enviable thing in the world ;

a conspicuous station with nothing to support it ; the representative of a country little respected and a Government not
at all ; faithfully and laboriously serving an Administration
who, so far from thanking and encouraging me, are vexed at
my very fidelity and assiduity, which leave them no decent
reason to recall me."

One of his social relaxations at this time was the entertainment of the diminutive being known to fame as General
Tom Thumb. On March 2, 1844, he records :

"Had 'General' Tom Thumb to lunch with us, to the
great amusement of the whole family and household. A
most curious little man. Should he live and his mind become
improved, he will be a very wonderful personage."

And again :

"The principal topic of conversation here for the last
few days is General Tom Thumb. He has been twice sent
for by the Queen and once by the Queen Dowager, and his
exhibition room is thronged with a row of carriages, blazing
with coronets, as far as you can see. He is really a very
curious specimen of humanity."

"April 7, 1844, General Tom Thumb and Mr. Barnum
took luncheon with us. Mr. Barnum showed us the Queen's
present ; quite costly and valuable enough, but far less
so than described by the reporters."

Less and less was Everett attracted by the usual social
diversions of London.

"The Season [he wrote, July 18, 1844], as it is called in
London, is drawing to a close ; but its dying efforts, like those of
a speared whale, are among the most convulsive and energetic.
We go to but few of the parties—especially I ; for I find it
beyond my strength to stand at a desk all day and in a
crowded and heated room all night, and if a man can't stand,
he is lost ; from which I suppose the proverbial mode of
saying a thing is intolerable is taken. One of my brother
diplomats says he has made a study of the mode of standing
on one leg at a time ; not absolutely drawing up the other
under him like a heron, but throwing the whole weight of
the body on each alternately. I believe the best way is,
however, to stand bolt upright on both."

But to how few of the world's diplomatists, even of to-day, is it given to be perfectly upright !

Admirer though he was of English institutions, Everett even reacted against some that he thought extravagant. When the Order of the Garter was given to the King of the French in 1844, he gave vent to his republican feelings in his diary, thus :

" Although I am decidedly of the opinion that a rational adherence to the past and an intelligent reverence of antiquity is all-important in England, yet I must confess that these orders of knighthood seem to me the silliest of things. The Order of the Garter—what does it mean ? According to Hume, the vulgar story of its origin is not unsuitable to the spirit of the times ; a standing memorial of the adultery of Edward III and the Countess of Salisbury. Such antiquity as this is, I think, not to be reverenced, nor such legends cherished."

Before the end of the year he received the news of Polk's election, which should have signified that the end of his mission to England was approaching. Yet he seems to have hesitated about requesting his recall. Perhaps he thought the new President might continue him in office. Certainly no decision came from Washington. James Buchanan was the new Secretary of State, and to him Everett addressed his congratulations. To his friend Winthrop he wrote (March 29, 1845) :

" I have been much embarrassed as to what I ought to do about asking for my recall. The clear opinion of yourself, Evans, and General Scott that I ought to, has great weight with me. The opinion of all my other friends, which has reached me, is the other way. My mind being thus to an equilibrium, as far as the judgment of my friends is concerned, I have decided (but with great hesitation) *not* to ask my recall. I expect, however, to receive it, and that without delay—very likely my successor is named. When I return I will mention one reason for my decision, which is of too confidential a nature to be put on paper. Another is, that if by not asking my recall I can prolong my stay here for even a few weeks, it is my duty to do so, in order to bring some long-standing claims to a favourable result.

" One matter of this kind I have within a few days succeeded in settling ; that is, procuring for our fishermen a right to fish within the Bay of Fundy. You may remember having sent some documents to Washington pertaining to a case of seizure for being found within the limits of that bay. Lord Aberdeen and Lord Stanley have at last agreed to yield it, not as a matter of right, but as an amicable concession to the United States. They do this against the opinion of the Crown lawyers. . . . It is a matter of very considerable interest to our fishermen."

So, as no word came from the President, Everett went on with his negotiations. A major subject—that of Oregon— was out of his hands and in those of Buchanan and Pakenham, the British Minister in Washington. For some time the Oregon dispute looked very serious. Polk in his inaugural Address had declared that the United States had a right to the whole north-west coast—and that the British claim to any portion of what was then called the Oregon country was an infringement on the Monroe doctrine. On his side, Sir Robert Peel was prepared to defend Britain's assertion to all the land north of the 49th parallel, including Vancouver Island.

" We trust [he told Parliament] still to arrive at an amicable adjustment of our claim ; but having exhausted every effort to effect that settlement, if our rights shall be invaded, we are resolved—and we are prepared—to maintain them."

This once more looked perilously like war—and war, indeed, might have come for the possession of Oregon but for the fact that Polk had Texas and a bellicose Mexico on his hands.

While the Oregon negotiations went on, in which he had little share, Everett had actually succeeded in securing the right of American fishermen to fish in the Bay of Fundy, which he afterwards referred to as—

" the most important result obtained by me in London in reference to the fisheries. I was in a fair way to have carried our point in reference to all the other outer bays. Sir Robert Peel's Ministry had determined to make the concession. Just as they communicated that purpose to the colonial authorities, I was recalled."

In July official word arrived saying that a veteran diplomatist had been appointed to succeed him, and would reach London early in August, and requesting Everett to continue to discharge his duties until the arrival of his successor.

Early in August Everett accompanied the incoming Minister to Downing Street and introduced him, after which the pair went on to Buckingham Palace. There was a sad parting from his many distinguished friends, some of whom had grown very dear to him. Sydney Smith was already dead, but there were others, Macaulay, Rogers, Dean Stanley and those two delightful old ladies, the Berry sisters.

Everett sailed away with a heavy heart. He had been charged with having been too friendly to England to be a wholly successful representative of his country. This was hardly just to Everett. He admired England and English institutions, but he held fast to his own fixed opinion of English policy. Years later he wrote :

" John Bull is very amiable in private life, and many of my best friends inhabit the ' fast anchored Isle ' ; but in his foreign politics he is selfish and grasping ; and where he dares, insolent. I saw him under favourable circumstances, as represented by Lord Aberdeen, who was a conciliatory and good-tempered man. He would at times put his name, in the press of business, to notes written by some of the underlings. I could detect the changed manner at a glance and I made it a rule to reply precisely in the tone in which I was addressed. We got on extremely well together."

President Polk had felt that the Oregon question demanded the services of the most experienced diplomatic agent the country could provide, one, moreover, whose sturdy Americanism would be proof against " the subtle social flattery of London." Such a one was found in Louis McLane of Delaware, a former Secretary of State, who had also been for a brief spell Minister in London sixteen years before. In consenting to step into the breach, McLane stipulated that it was to be for a specific purpose and that when he had achieved it he wished to retire.

The new Minister reached England July 31, 1845, and a week later presented his credentials to the Queen, then on the eve of paying a visit to the French King, Louis Philippe, accompanied by Lord Aberdeen.

McLane opened his batteries by flatly rejecting Aberdeen's idea of arbitration by a third Power.

" I assured him [he reported to Secretary Buchanan] that so far as public sentiment in the United States could influence the conduct of the Executive, arbitration would be the last expedient it would be politic to embark upon. We had never thought the subject one which admitted the interpretation of a third party ; and if it were otherwise, the present almost universal family alliance by marriage or otherwise among various Governments of Europe would render the selection of an impartial umpire, at least in the minds of our people, absolutely impossible."

Although President Polk was prepared, as Mowat says, to " fight for his view of the Oregon question," his Secretary of State was much more reasonably inclined.[1] He wished " to leave the door open for further negotiations," and would settle for the territory south of the forty-ninth parallel, not including Vancouver Island. He did not believe the country would " justify a war for the country north of forty-nine." In England, however, the Peel Government were taking no chances, and Minister McLane early noted the process of preparedness.

" It may not be improper to acquaint you that very extensive and indeed formidable naval preparations for active service are making in all the stations and dockyards of the kingdom. They consist in fitting for immediate service almost the whole of their present force of every description and in the addition of steam vessels upon the most improved plan ; and in engaging and collecting a large body of seamen and munitions of war of all kinds for the most formidable naval armament. I have no recollection of more extensive preparations in anticipation of any of the wars of former times, and they begin now to give rise to many speculations as to the real object of such large and extensive preparations.

" Upon two points opinions appear to be divided ; some referring it to an apprehended war with the United States,

[1] Mowat : *Diplomatic Relations of Great Britain and the United States.*

and others to contingencies which may arise out of the determination undoubtedly formed to maintain the dynasty of the present King of the French, in the event of his death, upon the throne. I think it not improbable that each of these objects may have its influence ; since notwithstanding the open menaces often made of the vigour and even ferocity with which a war with us would be prosecuted, I can scarcely believe they would, under present circumstances, incur so much expense in anticipation of that emergency ; whereas, in case they should encounter resistance to their schemes with regard to the French dynasty, not only is no time to be lost in preparing for an event which may happen at any moment, but no armament they could provide would be likely to prove too great for this occasion."

Just then the Mexican war was looming up. The American Government already looked upon Texas as being " virtually a part of our own country," and was reaching out to wrest California and New Mexico from Mexican hands.[1]

" You may consider it pretty certain [wrote McLane, September 26] that the design of this Government is and will be to keep the difficulties between the United States and Mexico in their present posture, at least during the pendency of the Oregon negotiation : so that Mexico may be in a position to be counselled to war or peace, as the result of this negotiation may render expedient. I need add nothing of the motive which would exist with the British Government to urge Mexico into active hostilities in case of a failure of the pending negotiation at Washington, or of the danger of irregular and premature outbreaks from its protracted continuance."

In Washington, the British Minister, Pakenham, had shown himself as unyielding as Polk, although afterwards certain phrases he used were disavowed by Aberdeen.

It was unfortunate that just then in England the prejudice against America should have been reinvoked and the country shocked to read a certain article from Gibraltar in *The Times*. It described the discovery in the wreck of the American frigate *Missouri*, burnt a year or two before, of several cartloads of slave shackles. Could there be more

---

[1] J. K. Polk : *Diary*, September 6, 1845.

17

damning evidence that this vessel was officially engaged in the terrible slave trade ?

It was rather a grave charge, and stung McLane and Americans generally to the quick. The American Consul at Gibraltar promptly investigated. He did indeed see thirty or forty pairs of shackles, large and small, but not so many as were then to be found on board of all vessels of war. He wrote as much to the Gibraltar *Chronicle*, but that paper refused, upon official pressure, to publish his letter. What made it worse was that the Governor of Gibraltar, Sir Robert Wilson, was charged not only with crediting the story, but with showing a distinguished French statesman, M. Thiers, then on a visit to the island, some specimens of the incriminating slave fetters. This the Governor denied; but in his denial he hinted that the number of these was greater than the Consul supposed.

In forwarding an account of the incident to Washington, McLane observed :

" It is very obvious that those who have maliciously propagated the base slander are not seeking for truth, but rather to gratify a bitter hostility towards our country and our people. . . . It deserves to be classed with the numerous instances of daily occurrence, so well calculated to lead us to look forward without regret to a different opportunity of vindicating the rights and honour of our country and of insuring better treatment and greater respect in future." [1]

This was very peppery language, but it cannot have escaped students of the period that if there was a lurking unfriendliness to America in England and a readiness to believe any stories to her discredit, it had been provoked by a knowledge of the speeches and writings of public men in America concerning Great Britain and British institutions. The Honorable Jefferson Brick was no simple figment of the novelist's imagination, any more than was Sam Slick,[2] who also flourished about this time : they lived, moved and had their being in Congress, in the press and on the hustings, and to these John Bull baiters and British lion's tail twisters

---

[1] Letter-book, September 26, 1845.
[2] *Vide* T. C. Haliburton : *The Attaché.*

the slogan " Fifty-four forty or fight ! " expressed a bullying land-covetousness as well as a sound national policy.

McLane reported that Aberdeen had in a moment of confidence shown him one of Pakenham's dispatches, in one of which he " questioned the sincerity of any profession on the part of our Government of compromising upon any basis short of the extreme claim."

Now, the British Government, commented Aberdeen sternly for once, would prefer any argument to war, but " if war is inevitable, it will receive the undivided support of the British people."

Even Polk could not remain unconcerned at the report of England's warlike preparations. The Minister was instructed to endeavour to ascertain " for whom all these gathering armaments were intended ? Were they for the United States ? " When questioned :

" Lord Aberdeen said very promptly and frankly that it would be improper to disguise that with the sincerest desire to avoid it, they were obliged to look to the possibility of a rupture with the United States, and that in such a crisis the warlike preparations now making would be useful and important ; but he stated at the same time very pointedly and distinctly that they had no direct reference to such a rupture, and would have been made in the same way and to the same extent without regard to the relations now existing between Great Britain and the United States." [1]

As a matter of fact it was, as we know now, simply part of a prudent system of national defence which events in Europe and the East made necessary.

McLane, however, was incredulous, and reported that England was putting herself into a position to strike the United States a " heavy blow."

Fortunately, the pacific efforts of Buchanan and Pakenham in Washington were beginning to bear fruit. Polk was anxious to get on with his cherished Mexican war and was easily induced to agree to the British offer concerning Oregon, and so on April 28 the treaty was drawn up and sent to Lord Aberdeen. A fortnight later war was declared between

[1] McLane to Buchanan, January 3, 1846.

America and Mexico. On June 3 McLane wrote from London :

" The commencement of the war with Mexico has been unexpected to all classes here ; and for that reason, perhaps, our participation in it is more unpopular. I fear, however, that we should have received no countenance and very little justice in this country, no matter under what circumstances or from what degree of provocation the war might have commenced. I will not attempt to dwell in detail upon the causes of the state of public opinion in England to which such a spirit of hostility to our country and its institutions and policy is to be traced, though I cannot resist the connexion, painful as it may be, that it exists ; and I am afraid that it may now and hereafter be expected to exert more or less influence in all our relations with this country."

How the political barometer swiftly rose and fell in Anglo-American relations ! Has it ever been " set fair " for more than a lustrum ?

It was McLane's firm conviction that there were Mexican agents in London seeking British financial support and disseminating anti-American propaganda, but he never succeeded in putting his hand on any of these. When Lord Aberdeen once offered British mediation, the American Minister could reply, " No ; you are too hostile to us."

With this distrust in his heart, McLane was ready to go home.

To Buchanan he wrote (July 3) that as the Oregon Treaty had been ratified by the Senate, there were no important matters outstanding, he desired to be recalled. " I can no longer be of service here and wish to return."

Yet before this Minister left he uttered a protest to the State Department which lets us see a little into the causes of his fits of petulance and his general social discomfort. He had recently lost his Secretary of Legation, Gansevoort Melville, whose death in London occurred May 12. McLane had been put to much trouble and expense in sending home the body, because he found burial was cheaper in America than in London. Melville's personal effects had been sold but had produced little, his small salary admitting only of bare necessities. It was a melancholy business. And now the Treasury was cutting down salaries and allowances in the diplomatic service still further.

Minister McLane had himself been Secretary of State, and his words, therefore, might carry weight in Washington.

" I regret that I cannot acknowledge in the persevering and vexatious attempts of the Fifth Auditor of the Treasury within the last few years to curtail and pinch down the scanty allowances of our agents in foreign countries any just regard of the public interest. The curtailment of the previously inadequate salary of the Minister at the Court of Great Britain, especially, at least nine hundred dollars per annum, has seriously aggravated the embarrassments always incident to a proper representation of the Government at this Court, and it would not be surprising if ultimately it should be found impossible to prevail upon anyone fit to represent his country abroad and not possessing the advantage of adequate private fortune, to encounter the annoyances to which the dignity of his office and his own pride would be constantly exposed." [1]

BIOGRAPHICAL NOTES

Everett was chosen President of Harvard College on his return. He was Secretary of State in 1852 and Senator in the following year. He enjoyed great popularity as an orator. He survived until 1865.

McLane retired to Baltimore and died in 1857. Long afterwards his son became Minister to France.

[1] McLane to Buchanan, August 5, 1846.

CHAPTER XIII

BANCROFT AND LAWRENCE (1846–1852)

DESPITE Minister McLane's warnings, there seemed to be an abundance of diplomatic material in America ready to be sacrificed for its country's good on the altar of the English Court. The danger was that these excellent men would, as in the recent case of Edward Everett, yield too readily to that potent force which every American politician was taught to despise from his cradle, but which so few, alas! had been able to resist abroad, English flattery.

Looking amongst his associates, President Polk thought he had discovered one distinguished man who was flattery-proof, a scholar and a statesman who had recently been exhibiting surprising vivacity and resource in Washington.

George Bancroft, who was just as old as the century, had at the age of thirty-five produced the first volumes of his *History of the United States*, which was believed, in Boston, to rival the finest productions of the Old World historians. Posterity has somewhat tempered this judgment, and Bancroft's presentation of revolutionary issues and persons has been rigorously revised since his death. Nevertheless, it still remains an American classic and its extension and recension occupied its author to the end of his long life. Bancroft had been brought by his admirers, very reluctantly at first, into politics. President Polk had appointed him Secretary of the Navy. Here the historian displayed unexpected initiative by founding the Naval Academy at Annapolis and subsequently persuading Congress to sanction that admirable institution.

Although Bancroft was a man of letters partially educated abroad whose training as an historian might be supposed to have given him a wide and impartial view of human affairs,

248

he yielded to no living American in his dogmatic patriotism, and competed with several who had not survived Revolutionary times. Just then, when the American Republic was in the throes of expansion and was putting forth her full strength on the Continent, patriotism, more than ever, meant an ostentatious assertion of political perfection, and his biographer speaks of Bancroft's " staunch belief in the superiority of the republican institutions of his native land over those of all monarchical governments."

There was one important abatement of the new Minister's professed and stalwart Anglophobism. He was accompanied on his mission by his wife, an intelligent, warm-hearted and vivacious lady, whose letters, long afterwards published, reveal on every page the affection she had for the Mother Country and the fascination its people and institutions had for her. It was really rather embarrassing. She had scarcely set foot upon its soil than the Liverpudlians elicited her praise.

" I like these people in Liverpool. They seem to me to think less of fashion and more of substantial excellence than our wealthy people. I am not sure but the existence of a higher class above them has a favourable effect, by limiting them in some ways. There is much less show of furniture in the houses than with us, though their servants and equipages are in much better keeping.

" On this railway I felt for the first time the superiority of England to our own country. The cars are divided into first, second and third classes. We took a first-class car, which has all the comforts of a private carriage."

One hopes that the Minister was spared the pain of reading these unbecoming disclosures.

The Bancrofts arrived on October 25, and London met the enraptured gaze of the Minister's wife. While Bancroft was calling stiffly upon Lord Palmerston, who was perfectly well-informed as to his visitor's private views and antecedents, but resolved to be agreeable, Mrs. Bancroft was writing home to America :

" To-day, to my surprise, came Lady Palmerston, which was a great courtesy, as it was my place to make the first visit. She is the sister of Lord Melbourne. Lord de Mauley has also been here.

". . . To-day I have been driving through some of the best streets in London, and my ideas of its extent and magnificence are rising fast. The houses are more picturesque than ours, and some of them most noble. The vastness of a great capital like this cannot burst upon one at once. Its effect increases daily. The extent of the Park, surrounded by mansions which look, some of them, like a whole history in themselves, has to-day quite dazzled my imagination." [1]

She goes out to dinner and meets a number of distinguished persons, who took to her at once.

" Of all the persons I see here the Marquis of Lansdowne excites the most lively regard. His countenance and manners are full of benevolence, and I think he understands America better than anyone else of the high aristocracy. I told him I was born at Plymouth and was as proud of my pure Anglo-Saxon Pilgrim descent as if it were traced from a line of Norman Conquerors."

Her admiration is no empty thing; it is informed with shrewdness and discrimination.

" And now, having given you some idea *whom* we are seeing here, you will wish to know how I like them, and how they differ from our own people. At the smaller dinners and *soirées* at this season I cannot, of course, receive a full impression of English society, but certainly those persons now in town are charming people. Their manners are perfectly simple, and I entirely forget, except when their historic names fall upon my ear, that I am with the proud aristocracy of England. All the persons whose names I have mentioned to you give one a decided impression not only of ability and agreeable manners, but of excellence and the domestic virtues.

" The chief difference that I perceive is this : In our country the position of everybody is undefined and rests altogether upon public opinion. This leads sometimes to a little assumption and pretension of manner, which the highest class here, whose claims are always allowed by all about them, are never tempted to put on. From this results an extreme simplicity of manner, like that of a family circle among us."

[1] Elizabeth Davis Bancroft : *Letters from England.*

And again :

" I like the English extremely, even more than I expected, and yet happy am I to think that our best portions of society can bear comparison with theirs. When I see you I can explain to you the differences, but I think we need not be ashamed of ourselves."

Later Mrs. Bancroft writes :

" We are endeavouring to become acquainted with the English mind, not only through society, but through its products in other ways. Natural science is the department into which they seem to have thrown their intellect most effectively for the last ten or fifteen years. We are reading Whewell's *History of the Inductive Sciences,* which gives one a summary of what has been accomplished in that way, not only in past ages, but in the present. Every moment here is precious to me, and I am anxious to make the best use of it ; but I have immense demands on my time in every way. . . .

" The furniture and houses are less splendid and ostentatious than those of our large cities, though they have more plate and liveried servants. The forms of society and the standard of dress, too, are very like ours, except that a Duchess or a Countess has more hereditary point lace and diamonds. The general style of dress, perhaps, is not so tasteful, so simply elegant as ours. Upon the whole, I think more highly of our own country (I mean from a social point of view alone) than before I came abroad. There is less superiority over us in manners and all the social arts than I could have believed possible in a country where a large and wealthy class have been set apart from time immemorial to create, as it were, a social standard of high refinement."

While the Ambassadress is thus gravely studying and endeavouring to tabulate the qualities and forces which had in the middle of the nineteenth century made England an example for the whole world, her distinguished husband's pen also was not idle. He wrote several long letters direct to the President, in one of which he acknowledged receipt of Polk's Message to Congress on the war with Mexico, which he thought " clearly and vigorously written."

" The comments upon it in many of the English papers spring from their consciousness of your success and of their own inability to interfere. It was a hard lesson for England to learn, but she has learned it, that America means to go on her own way, and that Europe, *though it might gaze with envy*, must give up the thought of swaying her destiny. . . .

" The news from America has been looked forward to with intense avidity. When the message came, they found it unanswerable. They saw that the Californias would certainly become ours, and they set up a savage, incoherent growl. The growl was the more fierce, because they intend only to be *lookers on.*

" The English people are already well aware of the rapid strides of America towards equality in commerce, manufacturing skill and wealth. They therefore look with dread on any series of events which tend to enlarge the sphere of American industry and possessions.

" It is on this account that the universal feeling of apprehension is awakened in England, not by one party, but by all, in reference to the increase of American territory, expected inevitably to ensue from the present war with Mexico. Added to this, the result of the negotiations about Oregon, on which, in America, there appears still to be a division of opinion, is here by all classes and the representatives of all nations felt to have been singularly honourable to America." [1]

In another epistle the Minister wrote (January 19) :

" Towards the United States the feeling is such as I have heretofore described to you. They do not love us ; but they are *compelled to respect us.* In *The Times* of the 18th you will see one of my dispatches as Secretary of the Navy cut up, though my name is omitted. But it all amounts to nothing. England sees that the Californias must be ours, and sees it with unmingled regret, but remains ' neutral.' You may rely on my conducting myself with circumspection ; and, what is of more importance, you may rely, I think, that the embarrassments of domestic affairs here, will forbid all British or French interference in Mexican affairs."

Of the Foreign Secretary, Bancroft reported (February 3, 1847) :

" Lord Palmerston is, I think, not very strong in his hold on the public affections. In social life he is very agreeable, but he belongs to the old school of British statesmen, who

---

[1] Legation Letter-book, January 4, 1847.

GEORGE BANCROFT.

think John Bull is everything, and that international law, treaties, and interests of all sorts must yield to British pretensions.   In the affair with France he is clearly wrong in his interpretation of the Treaty of Utrecht ; and in his declarations about Mexican privateers he has not shown the alacrity or the decision which Lord Aberdeen would have done.[1]   I hope that to his message, through Pakenham, to which he referred in the House of Commons, you answered as explicitly as possible.   You see that France at once declares that Frenchmen, under the circumstances described by the President, would be but pirates.   In conversation with Palmerston, with whom I am on very friendly terms, I gave him an opportunity of saying civil things about you, by observing that I had heard you speak of having seen him in England.   But in reference to our country, to the President, or to yourself, he has not wasted one civil word upon me. Lord John Russell is, I think, more alive to the importance of preserving the most friendly feelings with us ; but I think Palmerston has a good deal of sore feelings about our Mexican affair ; and as he cannot interfere, is disposed to manifest in some way, that, after all, he has not been frightened by our American doctrine of non-interference.

" I have become acquainted with Lord Aberdeen [he goes on to say], and I like him very much.   He has a frankness and openness, that lets you know what he means and feels. His resignation was openly deplored to me on the part of one of the principal Legations the other day.   But for us, there will be, practically, no difference, as Lord John is resolved on friendship with the United States ; and all England is conscious that such friendship is necessary.   We can do without England better than England can do without us. . . .

" America [concludes the Minister, in lyric mood] will be the happiest, most prosperous, most envied country on earth."

Meanwhile, the American Minister's wife was engaged in a practical denial of the proposition that *she* at all events could do without England.   She had fallen in love with England and English ways, and especially with London and Londoners. In her letters home she expatiates on the glories of her first

---

[1] This opinion of the superiority of Aberdeen to Palmerston in alacrity and decision sufficiently indicates Bancroft's want of perspicuity.

Court, her anxieties concerning her and—shades of Thomas
Jefferson !—her husband's first court dress !

" Mr. Bancroft's court dress had not been sent home, our
servants' liveries had not made their appearance, and our
carriage only arrived last night, and I had not passed judgment upon it.   Very soon came the tailor with embroidered
dress, sword and chapeau."

With what unregenerate ecstasy she gazed upon her
spouse's undemocratic flummery !

" But first let me tell you something of our equipages.
It is a *chariot*, not a coach ; that is, it has but one seat, but
the whole front being glass makes it much more agreeable
to such persons as have not large families.   The colour is
maroon, with a silver moulding, and has the American arms
on the panel.   The liveries are blue and red ; on Court Days
they have blue plush breeches and white silk stockings, with
buckles on their shoes."

Clearly a resplendent turn-out and one which must have
quite eclipsed Minister Everett's sadly-criticized yellow
coach and drab flunkey !

It was going to be hard for Bancroft, in such an atmosphere,
to resist the aristocratic contagion.   Besides, so many
brilliant people—in addition to the Court circle and Ministers
—laid themselves out to be agreeable.   To a friend he writes :

". . . You are right in supposing that we were very
cordially received.   We find ourselves already having a circle
of most agreeable acquaintants, among whom I am much
disposed to single out Milman as one of the most agreeable.
He is a man of unpretending excellence, cheerful, abounding
in conversation, and being yet more agreeable than learned.
Macaulay, too, I have seen very often ; and each day that
I see him makes me more and more admire the wonderful
extent and precision of his knowledge.   Mr. Hallam is
another of the same great class, having a delightful benignity
of expression and a mind richly stored with all kinds of
learning.

" Besides them, I have already met Lord Mahon, Babbage
the calculator, Lyell and a great many more ; Thackeray,
Kenyon, Bowring and many more whose writings are so
familiar to us in America." [1]

[1] To John Appleton, London, February 3, 1847.

In May he was able to report to President Polk—

" a very great and decided change in the views of England with reference to our war with Mexico, to our finances, and generally to the position of the administration and the country. The last news from the United States was too great, too important and too significant to permit of being concealed or undervalued. ' You are the Lords of Mexico ! ' said Lord Ashburton to me. ' How could you take the castle of Vera Cruz so soon ? ' ' You have been entirely successful,' said Lord Clarendon ; ' I hope your sacrifice will lead to a peace.' And even Lord Palmerston, who, more than any of them, has one system of politics for England and quite a different one for other countries, spoke to me in the very warmest language of the generosity of America towards the Irish, and of the *immense superiority of the Anglo-Saxon race* as displayed in our great number of victories over the Mexicans."

Oh this terrible English flattery ! And when " Pam " really wished to be agreeable he could be quite irresistible. Bancroft felt that his mission was indeed bearing fruit. So great was the progress towards a mutual friendliness that in October the Minister could write to the Secretary of State :

" A year's residence would convince you how entirely we are now beyond all danger of being interfered with injuriously by England."

There would be no serious trouble if the United States even annexed Mexico. Indeed, one of Bancroft's diplomatic colleagues had been told that " in the hands of America that country will be to English commerce and English capital of more value than Mexico in its former state."

But the continental revolutions of 1848 stirred up all Bancroft's old republican zeal. He wrote Secretary Buchanan (March 24) :

" Am I never again to have a letter from you ? Have you made peace with Mexico ? Is the country rousing itself for sound principles ? Has the echo of American Democracy which you now hear from France and Austria and Prussia and all Old Germany no power to stir up the hearts of the

American people to new achievements ? Can we show ourselves lukewarm, while the Old World is shaking off its chains and emancipating and enthroning the masses ? "

He protested that his residence in Europe had only " quickened and confirmed his love for the rule of the people." Poor Louis Philippe, who had always been a good friend to America, had fallen ; but Bancroft had no kind word for any monarchs, however just and benevolent.

He reported, moreover, that in London—

" the aristocracy are overwhelmed with gloom. In the Court circle I alone am the one to speak and think of the French republic with hope, with subdued exultation, with trust. The Queen was greatly agitated. The nobility are all the time congratulating one another, that here, at least, they are safe for some time longer ; but if France succeeds, there will not be a crown left in Europe in twenty years, except in Russia, and perhaps England may hold over a little while longer than the rest."

It was a pleasing prospect. Later in the year the Minister grew even more sorry for the future of the realm to whose sovereign he was accredited. It is true Englishmen were not alarmed, they were even apathetic.

" There is no movement : no cracking of the fabric : no rending of the wall. And yet there is a deep foreboding of the future. How it will come I cannot certainly foresee : but it seems to me, the form revolution will take here is through the finances. The questions about the income-tax and the war-tax will shake England pretty thoroughly, when the income-tax requires renewal, and when the corn laws reduce materially the price of corn. But as yet habits of subserviency to the aristocracy are so branded into the national character, that the people generally are satisfied with their institutions. They keep down pretty well their envy at our success, their consciousness that we are going forward full of hope, while their future is clouded ; but a growl against the results of your administration is sometimes heard ; and they dread the very name of Cass, as of one who would swallow Popocatepetl at a bite, make but one mouthful of Canada, and help the Irish every way he can. But after the seventh of November, they will speak of him in more kindly terms. The candidate of the Whigs may pass current with his party, if England's endorsement of him is sufficient."

His friend Cass's disastrous defeat by General Zachary Taylor at the polls was a blow to Minister Bancroft. He put it all down to European secret machinations and the perfidy of Van Buren. The idea that economics should have influenced the campaign and that the great commercial and industrial interests should have revolted against Democratic foreign policy was very distressing.

" If we could have foreseen the effects of European revolutions they might have been guarded against.
" Now what is to be done ? Shall I resign ? Shall I wait ? How are matters opening ? What prospect of the reorganization of our party ? " [1]

On January 5, 1849, President Polk wrote him :

" I congratulate you upon your success in the negotiation of the Postal Treaty. I submitted it to the Senate yesterday and to-day; that body advised and consented to its ratification."

To a friend he wrote :

" Had Cass been elected, I should have remained here a certain number of months, and then, from love to letters, have resigned a post in which I have been nearly long enough."

But the Minister's wife could not conceal her unhappiness over the prospect of so precipitate a return. To give up London where she was so enjoying herself—it was tragic ! She could hardly help feeling that, although wedded to a literary man who professed to find more pleasure in writing than in diplomacy, she was fitted by nature and education to be a distinguished ambassadress : and in this she was right. Bancroft, communing with himself on the eve of departure, was forced to admit that his English sojourn had been an " immense advantage " to him.

" The constant enjoyment of the most refined and cultured society, the change of scene, the opportunities of observing

[1] Bancroft to Buchanan, December 15, 1848.

statesmen and institutions, lords, commoners and ministers, have at once instructed me and have soothed and benefited me, when I most needed it."

If he had to go he might as well go in a blaze of glory, even—and especially if it were to be done at the expense of the Whigs. He discovered that the British Government were ready to grant to America a share in British colonial West Indian trade in return for the privilege of American coastwise commerce. It was a great chance—he drafted a convention, and if the Whigs would only let him stay long enough he would carry it through. Afterwards he would contentedly go back to his history and repay the generosity of his English hosts by portraying King George III as a blockhead and a tyrant, and his Ministers and administrators as the ruthless agents of hate and savagery.[1] So, on consideration, he would not resign. " The Executive, of course," he wrote, " can change its agents, if it will ; but I do not apprehend an interference with the business actually in hand."

Only, it appeared that the wretched New England shipowners were of another mind altogether as to the repeal of the Navigation Acts. They were angry with Minister Bancroft and put up Daniel Webster to attack him and his convention.

Webster introduced in the Senate (March 12) a resolution calling for information from the President on Bancroft's authority to arrange with the British Government for the

---

[1] Bancroft confided to a friend his plans for the next volume of his history. " I shall try to tell how Prescott defended Bunker Hill ; how Franklin swayed France to our assistance ; how Choiseul charmed the courts of Europe into a peaceful applause of our institutions ; how Lord North battled with his own ministry in which he was in a minority, and let himself be led against his judgment ; how the Empress Catherine humbugged the British Minister and favoured us ; how the inimitable Washington not only was the bravest in war, but the wise, loving, generous, creating father of our blessed form of Government. People here have heaped me full of documents. Lord North's daughter gave me all she had, and all her reminiscences to boot. The Duke of Grafton sent to my house a big box holding the most private papers of the old Duke with the key and unbounded licence to use the contents at my discretion ; Lord Dartmouth the papers of his pious progenitor. Then I have every letter written to every dog of a cut-throat that went into the wilderness to set the Indians upon us. What need of many words ? "—Life.

opening of the coasting trade of the United States to foreign vessels.

" All must agree [he said] that the subject is vastly important. And I confess I was a little startled to find that the American Minister, who is now remaining in England, has, at the present moment, and under existing circumstances, offered to act immediately in a proposition for a convention to throw open the whole coasting trade of the United States freely, and without discrimination, to British vessels."

Webster's resolution was adopted. Bancroft forthwith entered a protest.

" I hope you don't believe a word of the nonsense in the American papers about my having exceeded my instructions or acted without them. I had full authority for all I have done. And I hope you don't think I would embarrass the administration. On the contrary, losing the hope of finishing the business at which I have been at work these two years, I have, in the most disinterested manner and with singleness of purpose, been attempting to ensure the success of him who may follow me."

He was confident that he could have done the trick— actually secured the long-desired repeal of the Navigation Acts. And here were the short-sighted New Englanders —his own people—turning upon him and rending him !

"Webster's unprovoked attack on me in the Senate has had a very bad effect here. If I were with you, I could give you a thousand reasons why the President should sustain me. I could have had the whole British colonial trade and the indirect trade opened to our ships by the first day of September next." [1]

What base ingratitude ! Surely the President did not intend to throw him over ! " I know not why the President should wish to injure me," he exclaimed. Such a diplomatic achievement as his " would in the days of Washington have met a very different reception." Old Zachary Taylor was not Washington. But he was, like Washington, a sound Whig, and he told Bancroft to make ready to come home as soon as his successor could arrive. Bancroft regretted, now

[1] Bancroft to J. Davis, May 4, 1849.

18

that it was too late, that he had not resigned. " Had he [the President] treated me as any one of his predecessors would have done, I could have resigned with honour and satisfaction."

But now—" would it not be ridiculous for me to resign when I am already superseded ? The administration does not act frankly." In revenge, Bancroft would not wait his successor's convenience : not from any want of good-will to that gentleman, also from Boston and for whom he had a great regard, but simply to show his own independence. And so, nourishing a grievance, the eminent historian of the United States, with his trunks full of valuable papers, including a parchment from Oxford University signifying that he had been handsomely awarded a Doctorate of Civil Law, *honoris causa,* by that ancient seat of learning, the Minister and his brilliant wife about the end of August 1849 took passage for home.

Abbott Lawrence and his elder brother Amos were prosperous Massachusetts cotton manufacturers and philanthropists, Abbott taking an active part in the founding of the important industrial town which bears the family name. For some years as a young man the future Minister paid regular business visits to England and so acquired a considerable knowledge of English life and commercial and industrial conditions. In 1834 he entered Congress as a Whig, and fourteen years later was nearly nominated for Vice-President. This wealthy, sensible, dignified Bostonian refused a place in Zachary Taylor's Cabinet ; but the mission to Great Britain was another matter. He accepted at once and in his fifty-seventh year set out for London.

" It is difficult [wrote a friend at Lawrence's death] to find greater contrasts in the life of any man than these presented by his first and last visits to England—the first as a novice, confined to the operations of trade at Manchester and Leeds, and the last introducing him directly to Queen Victoria and the British Court and giving him free intercourse with the most distinguished statesmen of the land." [1]

[1] Nathan Appleton : *Memoirs,* 1856.

ABBOTT LAWRENCE.

Lawrence's personal and social qualities, which had not exactly been hidden in his own country, were now able to shine conspicuously in a larger sphere. On his arrival in the summer of 1849 he rented Cadogan House, Piccadilly, as his Legation. Here he delighted to bring together prominent Americans and the leading men in politics and the professions of Great Britain. "He was," says his biographer, "able to appreciate and admire all that was valuable or venerable in his surroundings without weakening his affection for his own country, or his preference for its political institutions." He was never blatantly American in spirit or utterance, and his reserved manner resembled that of the average well-bred Englishman.

The first diplomatic business to engage Minister Lawrence's attention concerned the projected ship canal across Central America. Secretary Clayton had written him (Oct. 31, 1894):

" The policy of the United States in regard to Tehuantepec is precisely the same as Palmerston regards necessary. You may say to Lord Palmerston that we encouraged and will certainly protect all routes, whether by canal or railroad, across the American Isthmus, and that we invite Great Britain to occupy the same ground, she to enjoy equal benefits with us, and *we* all the benefits of the ' most favoured nation.' "

Before Lawrence's arrival William Cabell Rives, the new American Minister to France, *en route* to his post, had had an interview with Lord Palmerston on the subject ; but his intervention does not seem to have cleared up matters, for Lawrence subsequently reported, " I found Palmerston still in error as to the policy of the United States."

Early in November Lawrence himself saw the Foreign Secretary, who told him that he had been shocked to hear that an American agent, Mr. Squiers, had actually made a treaty with Nicaragua. If this treaty was ratified, it would engage the United States to seek to compel the British Government to deliver up Greytown to Nicaragua. This would involve " an unprovoked aggression by America on England at a time when we were most friendly. We never expected so hostile a proceeding."

" The United States are acting [Lawrence explained]

with the best intentions. We are trying to clear away initial difficulties for the great work. A ship canal connecting the two oceans will do more to perpetuate peace between Great Britain and the United States, and in fact the whole world, than any other work yet achieved. After the lapse of centuries, during which various companies have been formed for its construction and have failed, we have the opportunity to exhibit anew the power and energy which have made us the two greatest commercial nations on earth."

" What you say is all very well," agreed Palmerston, " but this canal is going to cost a great deal of money. Before any private companies embark in it, let us ascertain the best route." Britain, he explained, did not ask or design to occupy or colonize any part of Central America. She was ready to enter into a guarantee with the United States for the neutrality of the canal. Lawrence, however, considered that these assurances were of no great value unless the British Government consented to abandon its protectorate over the Mosquito Indians. He wrote at length to the Foreign Secretary (December 15) :

" In order to give full confidence to the capitalists of Europe and America, neither the United States nor Great Britain should exercise any political power over the Indians or any of the States of Central America. The occupation of Greytown and the attempt to establish a protected independence of Mosquito throw at once obstacles in the way, excite jealousies and destroy confidence, without which capital can never flow in this channel. Nicaragua, too, stands in a position to *demand* the goodwill of all entering into this work. She holds the undoubted western key ; and should she refuse the right to traverse her territory, except on the recognition of its integrity, neither Great Britain nor the United States could take that right by force."

Palmerston never answered Lawrence's note, yet it is probable that in consequence of it instructions were sent to the British Minister in Washington which ultimately led to the Clayton-Bulwer Treaty.

" I suggested [wrote Lawrence at the close of his mission] a plan of settlement of the whole question which received the full approval of the President and, though never officially replied to, was made the basis of the subsequent adjustment. The negotiations were soon after transferred to Washington."

In 1850 President Taylor died and was succeeded by Vice-President Fillmore, who appointed Daniel Webster once more Secretary of State.

The great International Exhibition, the first of its kind, was held in London in 1851. Lawrence took a practical interest in everything connected with it, and his dispatches to the Secretary of State testify to his anxiety that his country should be properly represented. At a dinner given by the famous American banker, George Peabody, at the close of the Exhibition, Lawrence revealed the circumstances in which American exhibitors took part :

" The nations of Europe sent here men who in their respective countries were eminent in science and skill, and the expenses of these men were defrayed by their Government. But every man from America came here on his individual account and risk ; he paid his own expense ; and often paid for the transportation of his contributions ; and then freely gave his time to the exhibition of his products. It is due to you to state under what circumstances you came here."

Truth to tell, individual Americans, whether in or out of office, were expected to do a good deal in those days for international relations and international commerce at their own expense. The Legation was under-staffed and under-paid and its work was growing. In a report made to Secretary Webster in 1851 Lawrence notes a—

" great change in the current business and expenses of this Legation. The increase in the means of intercourse between Europe and North America has brought a corresponding increase in the calls upon the time of the Minister and of the Secretary. 1st, because the English people are beginning to regard American affairs with a greater interest, and 2nd a greater number of Americans are visiting Europe."

In the matter of passports the increase was striking.   Thus :

1831	.	170	passports issued	
1845	.	638	,,	,,
1850	.	1,167	,,	,,
1851	.	1,145	,,	,,	(for six months only)

As for the Legation correspondence, Lawrence and his Secretary sent out in one year four hundred and seven folio pages and dispatches to Washington, six hundred and sixty other official Notes and Dispatches, which had to be copied and re-copied, all in addition to private correspondence. The total of clerical work above amounted to 5,575 folio pages. No wonder that his Secretary of Legation, young Bancroft Davis, should have acquired a valuable training in diplomacy !

" The time of both of us is also additionally occupied almost daily by calls to various parts of London growing out of our positions which it would be almost impossible to avoid, such as calls at some one of the Government offices on business which can hardly be done by writing ; visits to our countrymen, attending some public meeting where the foreign Ministers are expected, etc. The distances in London are so great that (aside from expense) no little time is spent daily in travelling the streets."

With all this, it is surprising to read that—

" the only salaried persons recognized by the Government of the United States are the Minister and Secretary. It is easy to perceive, adds Lawrence mildly, that the business cannot be carried on without additional help. And in point of fact I have employed a clerk at my own expense ever since my arrival in London."

It was wonderful how the business was done at all. Indefatigable quill-drivers were the diplomats of those days ; they went without holidays, and their whole heart was in their work. Yet one does not envy the lot of the paid clerk who was employed, full time, at thirty shillings a week.

The Minister casually mentions that he spent " about £70 on books and pamphlets relating to Central America out of his own pocket."

Webster regretted this official parsimony, and had he lived doubtless some effort at amelioration would have been made. He wrote Lawrence asking what in his opinion the salary of a Minister ought to be. Lawrence replied :

" You are perhaps aware that, possessing private means, I have not been as exact in my expenses as I should have been. . . . The house I occupy is in a situation central and convenient for a Legation. I have esteemed it my duty to entertain my countrymen to a moderate extent and to maintain the hospitable courtesies of the great country which I have the honour to represent. The rent of a furnished house in London in a proper location would not be less than from seven hundred pounds to nine hundred pounds a year. Horses and carriage would cost from two hundred and twenty-five pounds to two hundred and fifty a year. To meet properly these and all the other expenses growing out of the position would require, in my judgment, an annual salary of twenty thousand dollars.

" I deem it proper to add that my own expenses have exceeded these sums." [1]

Postage was at that time a huge item, even though it had been reduced by the Postal Convention of 1848. It cost forty cents an ounce for American letters forwarded from Liverpool to Paris, although the United States only charged twelve and a half cents for British letters brought across Maine to Canada.

Lawrence especially urged cheaper ocean postage, which was then fourteen cents the half-ounce, whereas inland postage was only three cents in America and one penny in England. Yet water carriage was the cheapest form of transport. He thought America ought to take the first step in any readjustment, advice which was subsequently followed and a reduction brought about.

Lawrence was full of projects. He wished to establish a line of steamers from the United States to West Africa in imitation of Great Britain. This, he thought, would also " give us an opportunity to send to the coast numbers of our free coloured population to settle it and eventually to redeem it from the barbarism under which it has so long existed." There the mulattoes and quadroons " might enjoy the social position only to be gained in the country from which they sprang."

An excellent plan, but the free coloured population of America was passionately averse from repatriation.

In the course of 1851 the Minister made a tour of Ireland.

[1] Lawrence to Webster, December 10, 1851. The Minister's salary was $9,000.

His very able and lengthy dispatch on the condition of that country may to-day be read—if anything about nineteenth-century Ireland is ever read—with interest. He set out to ascertain the cause of the astonishing decrease of the Irish population since 1840, amounting to one million, six hundred thousand, besides a loss of over one million in natural increase. He thus recorded the cause of Ireland's decay :

" I place first in importance the fact that Ireland is a conquered country, and governed by the conquerors. Hence the legislation of the British Parliament has usually had reference to the especial interests of Great Britain and to those of Ireland as an integral part of the United Kingdom. Then come religious dissensions, absenteeism, ignorance, discouragement of manufactures, the repeal of the Corn Laws, emigration and starvation."

He found the wages of Irish labourers to be from four-pence to tenpence a day and farm-labourers from seven shillings to ten shillings a week, whereas in America labourers would receive one dollar a day. No wonder, then, that there was a huge emigration from Ireland on the part of all able-bodied men and their families who could get away.

If, just then, Ireland was harassing the British Government, another island, Cuba, was harassing the United States. To most political observers it seemed as though Cuba must follow the fate of Florida, Texas and California, and in spite of repeated American disclaimers the British, French and Spanish Governments watched proceedings in that quarter with a jealous and suspicious eye. In August 1851 General Lopez, a Venezuelan adventurer, raised a force in the United States and made a filibustering descent on the island, with the object of annexing it to the great republic. Lopez was defeated and he and many of his companions slain. British warships were about, and it was believed that the British Government was prepared, in conjunction with France, to support Spain's sovereignty of the island. To ascertain the truth of this, Lawrence called on Palmerston and had a lengthy discussion. Palmerston said that he had no objection to telling the Minister everything.

" At the time the Lopez expedition was thought to be about

to proceed to Cuba, there was an application on the part of Spain and France to obtain the joint action of the British fleet with that of France for the defence of Cuba. He [Palmerston] answered on behalf of the British Government that he believed the trouble would all blow over and there would be no need of action. The French, however, concluded to send their fleet, and did so. Some time afterwards Mr. Crampton [British Minister in Washington] wrote to the Foreign Office stating that he had good reason to believe that the Government of the United States would not oppose such a proceeding, and that the whole thing could be satisfactorily arranged; but if it were done it must be done with great care and caution, and that in no event must the commerce of the United States be interfered with by British vessels, neither could those vessels be permitted to come upon the coast of the United States. . . . Crampton intimated that the fleet would be employed to watch the coast of Cuba, not that of the United States. In the meantime information had been received in London that the Lopez expedition was going on."

When the British fleet was sent, Crampton explained that this was done in the most friendly spirit.

Lawrence asked whether there had been any stipulation to preserve the island of Cuba to Spain—to which Palmerston replied that Great Britain had made none.

"I wish [continued Palmerston] to ask you a question in perfect confidence. Suppose a proposition were made by France and England to the United States to enter into an undertaking, not in the form of a treaty, perhaps, but of an honourable understanding, that neither of the three Powers should take possession of Cuba, how do you think it could be received? What is your opinion?"

Lawrence replied that—

" there were persons in the United States without doubt who would entertain such a proposition and perhaps deem it wise to adopt it. He had no authority to speak for the Government, nor was he acquainted with its views. The policy of the United States had always been to keep itself free from alliances and undertakings of this character with foreign Powers. Personally, he would not wish to change that policy, even in a just cause. He would wish himself to see the United States, while observing the obligations of treaties, ever maintain its neutrality and keep itself from the political influences of foreign Powers." [1]

Ten days later Lawrence received a note from the Foreign Secretary in which he said that as regards Cuba his Government had " full confidence in American sincerity."

" But I deem it due to the frankness which ought to characterize the intercourse between the two countries to state that his Majesty's ships of war on the West Indian station will have orders to prevent by force *any adventurers of any nation* from landing with hostile intent upon the island of Cuba."

Naturally, these British intentions, which Lawrence reported, could hardly fail to shock President Fillmore, who protested vigorously. To him it was " a sort of British police over the seas in our immediate vicinity, and hence intolerable." Lawrence himself was indignant when he heard that a British ship had held up an American in Central American waters and that the British were more firmly fixed than ever in British Honduras.

"I think the time has arrived when strong measures should be adopted by our Government to compel the British authorities to abandon the coquetry that has been practised by British subjects in Central America, and, *as I believe*, sanctioned by the Cabinet Ministers in Downing Street.

" . . . I rejoice in the promptitude with which you have taken up the insult to our flag—the outrage committed upon the *Prometheus*." [2]

Secretary Webster wrote (December 29, 1851):

" Depend upon it, there will be no security for the continuance of peace in that quarter until the British retire from Greytown. The notion that British officers and agents hold that place only in behalf of the Mosquito King and as his agents strikes some people as being ridiculous and others as being an offensive and provoking pretence. I am quite at a loss to know what importance there is in the retention

[1] Private and Confidential Memorandum of an Interview between Mr. Lawrence and Lord Palmerston, November 12, 1851.
[2] Lawrence to Webster, December 19, 1851.

of this miserable town by England to justify all the hazards of collision which her continual possession of it will certainly entail upon her and us. When Sir Henry Bulwer went to England, I looked for his speedy return, and I thought we should be able to bring matters to a final and amicable settlement. I hope you lost no proper opportunity of urging the necessity of such a settlement upon the attention of Lord Palmerston. At the present moment, no part of our relations with England is so critical and so ominous of evil as this petty business."

However, it all led to nothing further just then, for Palmerston went out of office, and in America, Webster gave way to Edward Everett, as Secretary of State. Lawrence himself resigned in the summer of 1852, while the Cuban question was still causing anxiety. In London, the Spanish Minister told Lawrence that another filibustering expedition was being fitted out for Cuba and the British navy was warned to be on the alert.

Minister Lawrence's final activities were concerned with the North American fisheries and the share American fishermen claimed in these under the treaties. It was alleged that they were being restricted by the ill-will of the local population and that the too-frequent disputes about the three-mile limit were adjudicated by British naval commanders in their own nationals' favour. There had been several collisions on the fishing grounds and much excitement. Lawrence called on the new Minister, Lord Malmesbury, who showed himself sympathetic and promised that British naval vessels would be enjoined to be more lenient and not to make captures except in flagrant circumstances. He agreed that reciprocity ought to be practised, but that it was evident that the American fishermen were illegally encroaching within the three-mile limit.

With this understanding Lawrence took his leave of the Foreign Office and of his diplomatic work in London. His constant aim had been, he said in his last dispatch, to cultivate friendly relations with the United Kingdom.

"To this end I have mingled freely with people of all ranks, and I can say with truth in closing my connexion with the Legation that the relations between the United States and Great Britain have never in my judgment been so cordial or on so firm a basis of good understanding as at the present moment. I have found every administration of this Government animated with a desire to preserve this happy state of things and every class vieing with every other manifestation of respect and goodwill."

BIOGRAPHICAL NOTE

Bancroft prosecuted his history for years. In 1867 he was sent as Minister to Prussia, remaining at Berlin until 1874. His old age was spent in Washington, where he died in 1891 at the age of ninety.

CHAPTER XIV

INGERSOLL AND BUCHANAN (1852–1856)

WHEN Lawrence returned to America, he got news of the death of his old friend Daniel Webster, who had lately resigned the Secretaryship of State. One of the last letters written by this distinguished statesman was to Samuel Rogers, the venerable poet in London. It was dated from Washington, September 2, 1852, and ran :

" MY DEAR ROGERS,
" I give this letter to Mr. Jas. R. Ingersoll, who goes to London to succeed Mr. Lawrence, as American Minister to your Court. I introduce Mr. Ingersoll to you, not as a public man, but as a scholar, a gentleman and a personal friend of mine.
" I pray you, dear Mr. Rogers, accept anew assurances of our affectionate regards. Here, as elsewhere, everybody thinks and speaks kindly of you. Indeed, if good wishes are roses, then you are always ' on a bed of heaped Elysian flowers.' "

Thus did one dying octogenarian reach out in spirit to another across the widely sundering flood and invoke his kindness for an American newcomer.

President Fillmore had been forced to find a suitable person for the English mission content to undertake it for the brief remainder of his own term of office. Joseph Reed Ingersoll was a lawyer and a leading Whig Congressman from Philadelphia. His elder brother, another Congressman, Charles Jared Ingersoll, had been named Minister to France five years previously and rejected by the Senate. Ingersoll had been educated at Princeton and was a distinguished classical scholar. He was now in his sixty-sixth year.

The new Minister presented his credentials on October 16,

1852.   His first dispatches described the prevailing political situation in Britain, and his opinion of the members of the new Derby Ministry.   Lord Malmesbury had received him in Downing Street.

"He stated that he was desirous that we should become better acquainted and that he had invited the visit with a view to break the ice, rather than for any particular purpose.

"He inquired what I had considered when I left America the condition of the difficulty which had existed between the two countries.   I told him that in the last interview I had had with Mr. Webster I had inquired what answer I should make if asked in England as to the state of the Fishery dispute, and I had been told that I might say it was pacific—that it was hoped the month of September, which was the best fishing season, might go by without any accidental collision and that a negotiation would be opened, and he [Webster] had no doubt everything would be adjusted."

Malmesbury told Ingersoll that he supposed Webster wished to conduct the Fisheries negotiation himself.   The news of that statesman's death reached England at a time when the Ministry was tottering, and the *coup d'état* of Louis Napoleon on the other side of the Channel had already brought about Palmerston's downfall.

"Should this storm be weathered [reported Ingersoll] the evil day will probably only be postponed.   The course of Lord Palmerston, although directly acceptable to Ministers and the reverse to their antagonists, may be influenced in some measure by expectations of office for himself.   This nobleman certainly has a lofty standing with all parties. But his long possession of office has made the habit almost a second nature, and it is natural that he should feel inclined to resume power.   Yet it is said that there would be difficulties in giving him either the post of First Minister or the department of Foreign Affairs.   His ability and integrity are unquestioned.   His pen is said to be sometimes, however, dipped in gall, and foreign nations are supposed to be in dread of its habitual bitterness."

On December 17 the Minister reported—

"the probability of an assault of some kind from the other

side of the Channel. Military officers of great distinction considered it a probability. The trainings of militia and other movements of caution are induced by it. I mention the circumstance because it is often connected with remarks of a friendly character towards ourselves. . . . The idea is familiar that if the Powers of the Continent, relapsing, as they are supposed to be, into high-toned principles of Government, should manifest hostility to constitutional freedom by assailing it in its stronghold in England, the people of the United States would join in the defence of a common cause. There is certainly a tendency to cultivate good feelings with our country, which is worth cultivating in return."

At the same time, he added :

" The correspondence lately published in the Washington papers relative to the purchase of Cuba has called forth, as you will have seen, strictures from the English Press."

Palmerston's old place at the Foreign Office was now taken by Lord John Russell. In Washington, Webster had been succeeded by Edward Everett. When Ingersoll had his first interview with Russell he not a little surprised that statesman by giving him to understand that the Fisheries and other questions between the two countries might preferably be discussed in Washington rather than in London, inasmuch as a treaty " could be acted on at once by the Senate on the spot "—a domestic political consideration which Russell, and other British statesmen since, only imperfectly appreciated.

On February 8, however, Ingersoll and the Foreign Minister signed a Claims Convention under which all claims of corporate companies or private individuals of one State against the Government of the other, which claims had been presented since the Treaty of Ghent and had remained unsettled, were to be referred to two commissioners, and an umpire in case of a difference. The American commissioner was Nathaniel G. Upham, Judge of the Supreme Court of New Hampshire, while the British commissioner was Edmund Hornby, later Judge of the British Consular Court in the Far East. The umpire was Joshua Bates, American partner in Baring Brothers, the bankers. The Commission met September 15, 1853, and concluded its labours January 15, 1854. Awards were made to British claimants amounting to £55,420, and to Americans of £65,947.[1] Of the work of this Commission Seward declared that it had " the prestige of complete and even felicitous success."

About this time the scheme for a canal across the Isthmus of Darien was launched, creating a considerable sensation. Ingersoll's own opinion was that—

" while the Darien canal is the great work which the commerce of the world requires, the Nicaragua route seems to be of primary importance to the people of the United States, the communications with China, California and Oregon being shorter, and the railways by Panama and Tehuantepec are calculated for postal and passenger use. Each may come and each may promote its special ends."

Writing on April 8, 1853, Ingersoll observed :

" I have had occasion to notice the existence of an improved state of feeling in this country towards our own. The public journals, the general literature, and the uniform tone of remark in the common intercourse of society bear testimony to the fact. There is undoubtedly an existing sentiment of respect founded upon a belief of the increasing power of the United States. The progress of the nation is understood and appreciated. Its advancement in prosperity and in all the elements of improvement is freely acknowledged."

The Minister added that he had heard the pleasant remark, " The United States have annexed England."

In another dispatch he mentioned that he had a conversation with an experienced British naval officer, who said that—

" he had been familiar with the appearance and discipline of our American ships of war and that nothing could be more beautiful. He added that all this had been ruined by the law which prohibited corporal punishment. He did not believe there was danger of its being used to excess, and yet the consciousness that the power existed was indispensable both to the commander and the crew. He also advanced the argument that we have often heard at home, that the law is particularly severe on good seamen, as it throws upon

[1] Moore : *International Arbitrations.*

J. R. INGERSOLL.

them (*if* you enlist them) the burden of duty, and holds out a promise of immunity to the idle."

Secretary Everett passed this on to his colleague, the Secretary of the Navy, who was pleased at the compliment to the American naval force. All the same, instances of British friendliness would not persuade the American Government to make any undue concessions. Once the Duke of Newcastle, in a chat with Ingersoll, expressed his surprise that the United States preferred to make three different treaties, instead of a single one embracing all the points in dispute. It was probably because Washington felt that agreement would be simpler and safer if negotiated in detail. The British were certainly after concessions. At one conference the President of the Board of Trade turned to the American Minister and inquired whether America would not be willing to give England a share in her coasting trade.

" I do not think," was Ingersoll's comment, " any serious answer was expected to this. But it shows that the desire is still cherished." [1]

Lord Clarendon (who came into office on the fall of the brief Russell Ministry) was the third Foreign Secretary with whom Ingersoll had dealings within a few months. He had also corresponded with three American Secretaries of State, for Everett went out at the beginning of President Pierce's administration, making way for William L. Marcy. One of the suggestions Clarendon made to Ingersoll concerned the flags of the two countries on the high seas. He emphasized the utility and importance of hoisting the national colours whenever vessels of the two nations met. Hitherto, the practice of the British had been to send a shot across a stranger's bows and make her show her colours.

" It is very clear [wrote Ingersoll to Marcy] that if by a more prompt display of our ensign we can contribute to prevent mistake and deter from wilful wrong, much will be gained without the slightest compromise of dignity and honour. A forced demonstration would be a different thing. But a mutual understanding to the effect proposed would be consistent with the nicest sense of national honour. . . .

---

[1] Ingersoll to Everett, July 23, 1853.

19

The moment of hoisting the flag is apt to be matter of dispute: whether it was preceded or followed by the firing of a gun. If it should be elevated as a matter of course, those differences of recollection or assertion would be less likely to occur."

When this letter reached Washington, as if to point the moral, came a report of an attack by the British frigate *Vestal* upon the American barque *Martha Anna*. The latter had hesitated about revealing her nationality, and the Englishman, thinking she was a Portuguese pirate, risked a shot or two. However, Clarendon showed that the affair had been grossly exaggerated and that no real damage had been done.

As yet the status of American coloured men had not greatly troubled the London Legation. But before Ingersoll left, numbers of these, including some who were suspected of being fugitive slaves, appeared in London.

" Individuals of the coloured race, born in the Northern States and possessed of genuine papers to prove their condition and identity, occasionally present themselves. With regard to such persons the Legation is entirely uninformed of the views of the Department."

Naturally, visiting Democrats from the South were shocked at such presumption, and demanded that they be sternly discouraged. The new Minister, although also a Pennsylvanian, would be likely to discourage, for he was a Democrat, whose party was pledged to the repression of the negro race. He arrived to replace Ingersoll about the middle of August, and in his first dispatch to Secretary Marcy wrote :

" It affords me great pleasure that Mr. Ingersoll's kindness and attentions towards myself have been all I could have desired. He has conducted himself throughout his mission in such an acceptable manner as to leave a very favourable impression behind."

James Buchanan was a large-framed, blond Pennsylvanian, who by reason of his subsequent attitude as President on the outbreak of Civil War has had something less than justice done him in the American history-books. He was really a statesman of dignity, honesty and ability, and, as we have seen, had, as Polk's Secretary of State, done much to avert bellicose action in the affair of Oregon. He was now sent to London by the President, Franklin Pierce, and his instructions were framed by his successor in the State Department, a statesman after his own heart, bluff, downright and practical —William Learned Marcy.

In those instructions there was, in the new Minister's eyes, an important omission.

" Your instructions [wrote Buchanan to Marcy before he set out] do not seem to contemplate, at least for the present, any attempt to acquire the island of Cuba from Spain by purchase, and I should be glad to know the policy of the President in regard to the acquisition of this island as soon as it shall be definitely determined, and under your instructions to render any such incidental services in the accomplishment of this important object as may be deemed compatible with my position and duties as Minister at London. Ought I not to possess all the information in the Department bearing on the objects of these instructions ? "

It is, however, possible that the Pierce Administration was not as keen on the acquisition of Cuba as was the new envoy to London and his Southern friends, and would have preferred not arousing British opposition just then.

Buchanan arrived in August 1853. Twenty years before, on his return from the mission to St. Petersburg, he had passed a short time in England, and made the acquaintance of some of the public men of the reign of King William IV. Queen Victoria had now been on the throne for sixteen years, a reign in marked contrast to that of her immediate predecessor. The Cabinet, a Coalition " Ministry of all talents," seemed destined to a long lease of power.

There was then no hint of the Crimean War or those international obstacles to a settlement of the questions still pending between the two countries. Buchanan was presented by Lord Clarendon to the Queen at Osborne ten days after his arrival. He notes in a letter to his niece, Miss Lane :

" She has not many personal charms,[1] but is gracious and dignified in her manners, and her character is without blemish. The interview was brief. Mr. Ingersoll, who

---

[1] His predecessor, Bancroft, however, thought the Queen much more charming than her pictures.

accompanied me to take his leave, and myself lunched at the Palace with Lord Clarendon and several of the attachés of royalty. His conduct towards me is all I could have desired.

" You have lost nothing by not coming to England with me. Parliament adjourned on last Saturday, and this was the signal for the nobility and gentry to go to their estates in the country. There they will remain until next February, and in the meantime London will be very dull. All gaiety in town is at an end, and has been transferred to the estates and country seats throughout the kingdom."

In a letter he writes :

" You cannot conceive how dull it is, though personally I am content. The beau-monde are all at their country seats or on the Continent, there to remain until the meeting of Parliament. But what is worse than all, I have not yet been able to procure a house in which I would consent to live. I have looked at a great many—the houses of the nobility and gentry—but the furniture in all of them is old, decayed and wretched, and with very few exceptions they are *very, very dirty*. I can account for this in no other manner than that they are not willing to rent them until the furniture is worn out, and that London is for them like a great watering-place from about the first of March until the first of August. This hotel, which is the most fashionable in London, is not equal to the first hotels in Philadelphia and New York, and yet the cost of living in it, with two rooms and a chamber, is about $90 a week. The enormous expense (here) and the superior attractions (there) drive all the American travellers to Paris and the Continent. The London *Times* has taken up the subject, and is now daily comparing the superior cheapness and superior accommodations of the hotels in the United States with those of London. Here there are no *table-d'hôtes*, and the house may be full without your knowing who is in it." [1]

On September 22 he went to see Clarendon, and after a long chat about Russia and Turkey at length broached the chief topic of the President's instructions.

" I told him that my principal object in requesting this interview was to inform him that the President had confided to me the task of settling with him, if this were possible,

[1] G. T. Curtis : *Life of James Buchanan.*

the questions pending between the two Governments in relation to Central America."

Clarendon thereupon said " he feared we would have great difficulties in settling these questions—the two Governments seemed to differ widely on the subject. For their part they would gladly get clear of their Mosquito Protectorate—it was of no advantage to them—but for a period of two or three hundred years they had exercised this Protectorate and that the honour of Great Britain required they should not abandon the Mosquitos without proper attention to their interests."

To this Buchanan objected that even if the British Government had formerly any claims to the Mosquito Protectorate, they had entirely and explicitly abandoned them by their Treaties with Spain of 1783 and 1786.

" There are two opinions on that subject," observed the wary Clarendon. " We have since resumed our Protectorate."

Buchanan forbore to press his interlocutor further about the Mosquitos at the moment (" his lordship was evidently unprepared "), but immediately brought up the subject of Bay Islands and Honduras. Was not, he asked, the establishment of this new colony a direct violation of the Clayton-Bulwer agreement ? At least, he threw out shrewdly, there was no mention of such a British colony as Ruatan in the British Imperial Calendar for 1853. But Clarendon ignored this home-thrust and delivered one in the enemy's camp.

He said he was

" extremely sorry to remark that the speakers in both the Senate and the House of Representatives, particularly the latter, were in the habit of indulging in offensive remarks against Great Britain calculated to excite unfriendly feelings between the two countries, which ought always to be good friends. No member of the House of Lords or House of Commons indulged in similar remarks against the United States—it would not be tolerated."

This was certainly true, as a perusal of the *Congressional Record* will amply testify, but Buchanan told Clarendon that he " well knew how to make the proper allowance for freedom of discussion in a legislative assembly under a free Government," whatever he meant precisely by that, and that

the " continued succession of irritating questions between
the two Governments" was the true cause. Clarendon
admitted there was a " plentiful crop " of such questions, for
which he was sorry. " Well, then," rejoined the American,
" we wish to settle them and make a fresh and propitious
start."

As a chief irritant, Buchanan instanced the British attitude
towards negro slavery.

" Congress had no more power to interfere with or to abolish
the institution of slavery than had the Parliament of Great
Britain ; yet ever since the establishment of the British
Anti-Slavery Society and their associated societies in
America they had kept up an incessant war on this subject.
These fanatics ought to know that they were defeating their
own ends and exasperating the feelings of the citizens of the
slave-holding States by their violent abusive interference,
and had defeated all hopes of emancipation by the only
powers armed with authority in this matter, namely, the
several States. He instanced how Colonel Randolph, of
Virginia, had been discouraged from persisting with his
abolition measure by the ill-timed efforts of the Abolitionists
and now went about in danger of his life. The decision
ought to be left to the sovereign States."

This interesting interview was suddenly interrupted by the
Premier, Lord Aberdeen, who came into the room with the
latest dispatches from Constantinople—foreshadowing the
Crimean War—and the American Minister retired.

In Buchanan's opinion " Lord Clarendon is an experienced
and able statesman whose manners are frank, courteous and
agreeable ; but he did not appear to me to possess an intellect
of the highest order."

President Pierce was not prepared to protest against
Britain's colonization of the Bay Islands, although Buchanan
pointed out that all these colonies, including Honduras,
were both against the Treaty and the Monroe Doctrine.

When he tried to ascertain when British activities began
in that quarter he could find nothing from almanacs and
newspapers, and makes the remark : " Strange as it may
seem, I find it very difficult to obtain any precise information
about the colonies of Great Britain."

British legislators and publicists of that period doubtless had the same difficulty, which accounts a great deal for popular ignorance and apathy prior to 1870.

Meanwhile, the Minister was house-hunting in London, and his ill-success was beginning to colour his views of the capital and its inhabitants. He could find nothing suitable for less than $3,500 to $4,500. " The expense of living in this country exceeds even what I had anticipated," he noted. " I shall preserve my hotel bills as curiosities." To his niece he writes two months after his arrival (October 14) :

" I am sorry, truly sorry, that you look upon your trip to England as ' the future realization of a beautiful dream.' Like all other dreams you will be disappointed in the reality.

" I have never yet met an American gentleman or lady who, whatever they may profess, was pleased with London. They hurry off to Paris, as speedily as possible, unless they have business to detain them here. A proud American, who feels himself equal at home to the best, does not like to be shut out by an impassable barrier from the best or rather the highest society in this country. My official position will enable me to surmount this barrier, but I feel it will only be officially. Neither my political antecedents nor the public business entrusted to my charge will make me a favourite with these people, and I shall never play toady to them.[1] It is true I know few of them as yet."

He alluded to a lady friend of his who had just arrived with a glowing description of the delights of Paris and her saying, " She would almost be tempted to commit suicide, should she be compelled to remain long in London."

And now the harassed Minister is to be further harassed by an absurd ordinance promulgated by his own chief at the State Department, Secretary Marcy. The whole incident has a value and importance in the annals of diplomacy as illustrating the singular belief of democracy that special raiment has no ritual significance and that dignity, so far from being helped, is hindered by appropriate and traditional costume.

[1] Buchanan's biographer adds in a note : " This anticipation was not realized. He became a great favourite in English society, without any effort beyond the exercise of his social gifts in a natural way."

Marcy, of whom it was remarked that his " intercourse with the world, aside from American politics, had not been extensive," had issued a circular to the Ministers of the United States in Europe, directing them to appear at the Courts to which they were accredited " in the simple dress of an American citizen."

Previously, American Ministers at foreign Courts had, on occasions of ceremony, worn the simple uniform prescribed for them by the Department. The new order was to be operative " unless it should appear that non-conformity with the customs of the country would materially impair the proper discharge of their duties."

In Buchanan's case, he wore on nearly all occasions an antique and courtly dress, a tail coat, high collar and white choker, which, like that of a Presbyterian divine, was appropriate almost anywhere. But, although courtly, it was not Court dress, and the Minister was soon apprised of that fact.

On October 28 he wrote to Secretary Marcy :

" I deem it proper, however distasteful the subject may be, both to you and myself, to relate to you a conversation which I had on Tuesday last with Major-General Sir Edward Cust, the Master of Ceremonies at this Court, concerning my Court uniform. I met him at the Travellers' Club, and after an introduction your circular on this subject became the topic of conversation. He expressed much opposition to my appearance at Court ' in the simple dress of an American citizen.' I said that such was the wish of my own Government and I intended to conform to it, unless the Queen herself would intimate her desire that I should appear in costume. In that event, I should feel inclined to comply with her Majesty's wishes. He said that her Majesty would not object to receive me at Court in any dress I chose to put on ; but whilst he had no authority to speak for her, he yet did not doubt it would be disagreeable to her if I did not conform to the established usage. He said I could not of course expect to be invited to Court balls or Court dinners where all appeared in costumes ; that her Majesty never invited the bishops to balls, not deeming it compatible with their character ; but she invited them to concerts, and on these occasions as a Court dress was not required I would also be invited.

JAMES BUCHANAN.

" He grew warm by talking, and said that, whilst the Queen herself would make no objections to my appearance at Court in any dress I thought proper, yet the people of England would consider it *presumption*. I became somewhat indignant in my turn, and said that while I entertained the highest respect for her Majesty, and desired to treat her with the deference which was eminently her due, yet it would not make the slightest difference to me, individually, whether I ever appeared at Court."

Cust then intimated that in England an invitation from the Queen was considered a command. It seemed then probable that Buchanan would be placed socially in Coventry on the question of dress—

" because it is certain that should her Majesty not invite the American Minister to her balls and dinners, he will not be invited to the balls and dinners of her courtiers. This will be to me, personally, a matter of not the least importance, but it may deprive me of the opportunity of cultivating friendly and social relations with the Ministers and other courtiers which I might render available for the purpose of obtaining important information and promoting the success of my mission.

" The difficulty in the present case is greatly enhanced by the fact that the sovereign is a lady, and the devotion of her subjects towards her partakes of a mingled feeling of loyalty and gallantry. Any conduct, therefore, on my part which would look like disrespect towards her personally, could not fail to give great offence to the British people. Should it prove to be impossible for me to conform to the suggestions of the circular, in regard to dress, ' without detriment to the public interest,' and ' without impairing my usefulness to my country,' then I shall certainly and cheerfully be guided by its earnest recommendations and ' adopt the nearest approach to it compatible with the due performance of my public duties.' This course I pursued from choice while Minister in Russia, and this course I should have pursued without any instructions."

Buchanan resolved, after reflection, to wear neither gold lace nor embroidery at Court.

" The spirit of your circular [he wrote Marcy], as well as my own sense of propriety, brought me to this conclusion.

I did not deem it becoming in me, as the representative of a
Republic, to imitate a Court costume, which may be altogether proper in the representatives of royalty. A Minister
of the United States should, in my opinion, wear something
more in character with our democratic institutions than a
coat covered with embroidery and gold lace. Besides, after
all, this would prove to be but a feeble attempt ' to ape
foreign fashions ' ; because, most fortunately, he could not
wear the orders and stars which ornament the coats of other
diplomatists, nor could he, except in rare occasions, afford
the diamonds, unless hired for the occasion."

At the same time, having a sincere respect for the exalted
character of the Queen, both as a sovereign and a lady, he
expressed a desire to appear at Court in such a dress as would
be most agreeable to herself, without departing from the
spirit of Marcy's circular.

At this juncture it was then suggested to him by a pre-
sumably waggish American then in London that he might
assume the civilian dress worn by the illustrious Father of his
Country, General Washington. But after carefully examining
Stuart's portrait, he came to the conclusion that it would
not be proper for him to adopt this costume.

" Fashions had so changed since the days of Washington,
that if I were to put on his dress, and appear in it before
the Chief Magistrate of my own country at one of his
receptions, I should render myself a subject of ridicule for
life. Besides, it would be considered presumption in me
to affect the style of dress of the Father of his Country."

However, the conscientious Minister finally hit upon a
way out of the difficulty. Let him describe it in his own
words. The occasion was Queen Victoria's first levée of the
season in February 1854.

" The dress question, after much difficulty, has been
finally and satisfactorily settled. I appeared at the levée
on Wednesday last in just such a dress as I have worn at the
President's one hundred times. A black coat, white waist-
coat and cravat and black pantaloons and dress boots, with
the addition of a very plain black-handled and black-hilted
dress sword. This to gratify those who have yielded so much,
and to distinguish me from the upper Court servants. I

knew that I would be received in any dress I might wear ; but could not have anticipated that I should be received in so kind and distinguished a manner. Having yielded, they did not do things by halves. As I approached the Queen, an arch but benevolent smile lit up her countenance ; as much as to say, ' You are the first man who ever appeared before at Court in such a dress.' I confess that I had never felt more proud of being an American than when I stood in that brilliant circle, ' in the simple dress of an American citizen.' I have no doubt the circular is popular with a majority of people in England. Indeed, many of the most distinguished members of Parliament have never been at Court, because they would not wear the prescribed costume."

Many decades have passed since those days and the distinguished members of Parliament who baulked at Court costume have long been in their graves and members of a Socialist Government have attended the Sovereign's levées in cocked hat, laced coat and knee breeches without derogation of their extreme democratic principles ; and still further, an American Ambassador of the most uncompromising republicanism has not scrupled to don the terrible ceremonial uniform which was so repugnant to his predecessor of 1854.

The incident did not, as may be guessed, wholly escape adverse comment in the London Press, although none was quite so contemptuous as the *Morning Chronicle*, which remarked :

" There is not the least reason why her Majesty . . . should be troubled to receive the gentleman in the black coat from Yankee-land. He can say his say at the Foreign Office, dine at a chop-house in King Street, sleep at the Old Hummums, and be off as he came, per liner, when his business is done."

Which was smart, but not very respectful, to the representative of the United States.

Buchanan's " business " was soon arduous enough to cause questions of mere Court etiquette to relapse into insignificance. The Crimean War was at hand, and the British Government was deeply engaged elsewhere. Nevertheless, whenever Lord Clarendon and the American Minister met, they discussed the questions between the two countries " with great frankness and urbanity."

At first, these consisted of the Central American question, the Clayton-Bulwer Treaty, the Fisheries and Trade Reciprocity, Cuba and Slavery in that island, Slavery in the United States and European international relations. Later, with the Crimean War, there came Neutrality, Privateering and British Recruiting in America. In consequence of the views expressed by Buchanan to Lord Clarendon, on March 16, 1854, and communicated to the British Cabinet, the course of England towards neutrals during the war was affected. Clarendon had shown Buchanan a *projet* for a treaty between Great Britain, France and the United States, making it piracy for neutrals to serve on board of privateers cruising against the commerce of either of the three nations, when such nation was a belligerent, but the very impressive reasons which Buchanan opposed to it caused it to be abandoned.[1]

Clarendon on one occasion dared to characterize " the Monroe Doctrine " as merely the " dictum of its distinguished author." Buchanan replied that " did the occasion require, he would cheerfully undertake the task of justifying the wisdom and policy of the Monroe Doctrine, in reference to the nations of Europe, as well as to those on the American continent." The British Foreign Secretary might pertinently have inquired which of the two continents of the Western Hemisphere was the " American " continent *par excellence* ; and why one geographical division so widely separated from the other should assume special prerogatives. But any aggressive exposition on the part of the American Government was postponed to a long later day.

Cuba was an old bone of contention between the European Powers and America. As long ago as 1825 Canning had proposed a joint Anglo-French American Note to Spain relating to the future sovereignty of the island—a proposal which France rejected. Since that time there had been frequent agitation in the United States over Cuba, chiefly by Southern slave-holders looking to the annexation of Cuba, either with or without the consent of Spain. Such

[1] G. T. Curtis : *Life of Buchanan.*

efforts both Palmerston and Napoleon III's Foreign Minister did their best to foil. But just now a hot-headed Louisianian, French by birth, Pierre Soulé, was American Minister at Madrid and eager to bring the issue to a crisis. The result was high tension and very nearly war with Spain. But Secretary Marcy kept his head and a rupture which would have been fatal to Spanish possessions was narrowly averted. Soulé, however, pressed the State Department to put forth its views concerning Cuba to Europe, and in the end obtained permission from the President for a Conference of the three leading American Ambassadors to be held at Ostend. There Soulé, J. Y. Mason and Buchanan met to discuss " what line of policy it is desirable for the United States to follow with regard to Europe." It was an audacious idea, and the result was the famous and bellicose Ostend Manifesto, which startled some Chancelleries of Europe and amused others. The document signed by the trio of American diplomats set forth that—

" after we shall have offered Spain a price for Cuba, it will then be time to consider the question, does Cuba in the possession of Spain seriously endanger our internal peace and the existence of our cherished Union ?

" Should this question be answered in the affirmative, then by every law, human and divine, we shall be justified in wresting it from Spain if we possess the power ; and this upon the very same principle that would justify an individual in tearing down the burning house of his neighbour if there were no other means of preventing the flames from destroying his own home.

" Under such circumstances we ought neither to count the cost nor regard the odds which Spain might enlist against us."

This fiery pronouncement had a very mixed reception in America. The wiser heads in Congress derided it as fantastic. As for Secretary Marcy, his hand was not to be forced by the diplomat from Louisiana, and instead of the approval Soulé was waiting for, a dispatch was sent coldly observing that the United States were willing to purchase Cuba *if* Spain would sell, but that the transaction would not be pressed if Spain was adverse to it. " I am stunned ! " declared Soulé when he read Marcy's dispatch ; he could not understand such a feeble pacifism and incontinently resigned his post.

His colleague Buchanan took the rebuff less tragically. Clarendon had told him that the British Government sympathized with Spain and could not be a silent spectator if she were wronged, although he agreed that if Cuba were ever lost it would be because of Spain's wretched government of the island.

For the present, at any rate, the Cuban question relapsed into quiescence. Early in 1855 Buchanan wrote :

" England is now in a state of mourning for the loss of so many of her brave sons in the Crimea. The approaching ' season ' will, in consequence, be dull ; and this I shall bear with Christian fortitude. The duller the better for me ; but not so for Harriet. She has enjoyed herself very much, and made many friends ; but I do not see any bright prospect of her marriage. This may probably be her own fault. I confess that nothing would please me better than to see her married, with her own hearty good-will, to a worthy man. Should I be called away, her situation would not by any means be comfortable.

" We are treated with much civility here, indeed with kindness according to the English fashion, which is not very cordial. Such a thing as social visiting does not exist even among near friends. You cannot ' drop in of an evening ' anywhere. You must not go to any place unless you are expected, except it is a formal morning call. . . .

" It is said that the Queen is, and it is certain the British people are, deeply mortified at the disasters of her troops in the Crimea. If the men had died in battle this would have been some consolation, but they have been sacrificed by the mismanagement of officials in high authority. The contrast between the condition of the French and English troops in the Crimea has deeply wounded British pride. Indeed, I am sorry for it myself, because it would be unfortunate for the world should England sink to the level of a second-rate Power. They call us their ' cousins on the other side of the Atlantic,' and it is certain we are kindred."

It is a pity Buchanan was a widower and somewhat ponderous ; he would have enjoyed himself more. He was helped in his social duties by his pretty niece, Harriet

Lane, who certainly seems to have got more out of London and her position there than her uncle. She wrote to her sister (February 16, 1855) :

" London is looking up in the way of gaiety, though the war is still a sad weight upon many hearts. Yesterday I attended the second drawing-room. . . . It was a very full and brilliant one. I wore a pink silk petticoat, over-skirts of pink tulle puffed and trimmed with wreaths of apple-blossoms ; train of pink silk, trimmed with blonde and apple-blossoms, and so was the body. Head-dress, apple-blossom, lace lappits and feathers. There will be one more in celebration of the birthday on the 19th. Her Majesty was very gracious to me yesterday, as was also the Prince." [1]

It is to be gathered that Buchanan was not notable for his compliments, even in the bosom of his family. On their return home from the drawing-room, he remarked to his niece :

" Well, a person would have supposed you were a beauty to have heard the way you were talked of to-day. I was asked if we had many such handsome ladies in America. I answered, ' Yes, and many much handsomer. She would scarcely be remarked there for her beauty.' "

Perhaps under his niece's influence the Minister grew more mellow and less exacting. Or, it may be the reports from home concerning his roseate chances as a Presidential candidate brightened his horizon. Yet he affected to regard the great prize with something like indifference.

" There is a profound wisdom in a remark of Rochefoucauld with which I met the other day : ' Les choses que nous désirons n'arrivent pas, ou, si elles arrivent, ce n'est, ni dans le temps ni de la manière qui nous auraient fait le plus de plaisir.' "

However, Buchanan himself felt that his Presidential prospects made him an object of increased regard in London.

" . . . I dined with the Queen on Wednesday last, and had a pleasant time of it. I took the Duchess of Argyll in to dinner, and sat between her and the Princess Royal. With the latter I had much pleasant conversation. She

[1] G. T. Curtis : *Life of Buchanan.*

spoke a great deal of you and made many inquiries about you, saying how very much pleased she had been with you. The Queen also spoke of you kindly and inquired in a cordial manner about you. Indeed, it would seem you were a favourite of both. There has been a marked and favourable change of feeling here within the last month towards the United States. I am now made something of a lion wherever I go, and I go much into society as a matter of duty." [1]

As to current Anglo-American questions he was optimistic.

" The Central American question might now, I think, be easily settled with any other premier than Lord Palmerston. Since the publication of the correspondence here, and the articles in *The Times* and *Daily News* in our favour, there would seem to be a general public opinion that we are right. This, I think, renders it certain that serious difficulties between the two countries cannot grow out of these questions."

It was unfortunate that just then should come the awkward Crampton affair. John F. Crampton had long been Secretary of the Legation at Washington and was now British Minister. During the Crimean War he had conceived it to be his duty to encourage certain British officers to obtain recruits for the British army in the United States. This proceeding had shocked President Pierce and his Secretary of State. Crampton's recall was insisted upon, and meanwhile all relations with that zealous diplomat were suspended. To Buchanan, Marcy wrote (January 3, 1856) in his usual brisk style :

" I really believe he [Lord Clarendon] does not know how offensively British officers have behaved in this recruiting business ; but he had the means of knowing all about it, and when it was made a grave matter of complaint it should have been investigated. After the issues of fact and of law made in the case, and the refusal on the part of Great Britain to do anything which could be regarded as a satisfaction, it was not possible to avoid the recall of Mr. Crampton. " The people of the United States are not in a very good humour towards the British Government at this time, yet

To his sister, Mrs. Lane, February 29, 1856.

there is great calmness in the public mind which indicates a settled purpose to stand for their rights.

" The strengthening the British fleet in this quarter was regarded as a harmless menace. Our people rather admired the folly of the measure than indulged any angry feelings on account of it. The comments of the British Press and the miserable pretexts got up as an excuse for that blunder have provoked some resentment, which the course of the British Cabinet in regard to the Central American questions and recruiting in the United States will not abate.

" We are willing—more—anxious to be on friendly terms with ' our trans-Atlantic cousins,' but they must recollect that we do not believe in the doctrine of primogeniture. The younger branch of the family has equal rights with the older."

" For my own part [avowed Buchanan] I should have been inclined to cut the Gordian knot as soon as I possessed clear proof of Mr. Crampton's complicity, and I am persuaded this was expected at the time in this country. No doubt, however, yours is the more prudent course.

" You say [he went on] that if I can settle the Central American difficulty and you the Recruitment question, they may blow what blast they please on any of their organs. That you can perform the latter there can be no doubt ; the former is a sheer impossibility during the administration of Lord Palmerston. Any attempt of the kind will only more deeply commit this Government to do us justice. It is still my impression there will be no peace in Europe before the season for opening the next campaign ; and this will leave England in such a state of preparation for war as she has never been at any former period. This may act as a stimulus to the reckless and arrogant propositions of Lord Palmerston which have been so often manifested by him in his intercourse with other nations." [1]

The President's Message to Congress in the previous month had dealt with the interpretation of the Clayton-Bulwer Treaty and the Crampton correspondence. From London Buchanan wrote :

" The Central American questions are well and ably stated in the message received two or three days ago. I know from

[1] Buchanan to Marcy, January 11, 1856.

20

reliable authority that Lord Palmerston ' has very strong
views on the subject.' *The Times* is a mighty power in the
State ; and I have adopted means, through the agency of
a friend, to prevent that journal from committing itself
upon the questions until after its conductors shall have an
opportunity of examining the correspondence. These means
have hitherto proved effectual. The correspondence has
now arrived, and *The Times* may indicate its views to-morrow
morning. The tone of the other journals has not been satisfactory ; and the *Daily Telegraph* has been evidently bought
over, and become hostile to the United States within the
last four days, as you will perceive from the number which
I send. Should *The Times* take ground against us, it is my
purpose to have an edition of that part of the message relating
to Central America and the correspondence published in
pamphlet form, and circulated among members of Parliament
and other influential persons. Should the expense be great,
I may call upon you to pay it out of the contingent fund.

" The British people are now in that state of feeling that
I firmly believe they could be brought up to a war with the
United States, *if they can be persuaded that the territory in
dispute belongs to themselves*. This, absurd as it is, may be
done through the agency of a Press generally, if not
universally, hostile to us. I make these remarks because you
ought to know the truth and be prepared for the worst.
*Certainly not with a view of yielding one iota of our rights to
Great Britain or any other Power. Most certainly not.*

" I understand from friends that it is now stated by British
individuals in conversation, how easy it would be for them
in their present state of preparation, and with our feeble
navy, to bring a war with us to a speedy and successful
conclusion. In this they would be woefully mistaken."

The Times did not, however, take ground against the
American claim, and on January 25, 1856, the Minister
could report :

" From present appearances the Central American questions
can lead to no serious difficulties with England. Public
opinion would here seem to be nearly altogether in favour of
our construction of the treaty. Such I learn, is the conversation at the clubs and in society ; and with *The Times*, as well
as the *Daily News*, on our side, and this in accordance with
public sentiment, we might expect a speedy settlement of

these questions, if any statesman except Lord Palmerston were at the head of the Government. He cannot long remain in power, I think, after peace shall have been concluded.

"I still continue firm in the belief that peace will be concluded, though it is manifestly distasteful to the British people.

"I met Sir Charles Wood, the First Lord of the Admiralty, at dinner the other day, and had some fun with him about sending the fleet to our shores. He said they had only sent a few old hulks, and with such vessels they could never have thought of hostilities against such a Power as the United States ; and asked me if I had ever heard that one of them approached our shores. The conversation was altogether agreeable and afforded amusement to the persons near us at the table. He said : 'Buchanan, if you and I had to settle the questions between the two Governments, they would be settled speedily.' I know not whether there was any meaning beneath this expression."

Buchanan was now on the point of leaving for home. In his last dispatch (February 12, 1856) he wrote :

"I am happy to believe you that within the last fortnight public opinion has evidently undergone a change in favour of our country. The best evidence of this is perhaps the friendly tone of Lord Palmerston's speech on Friday night last. His lordship has, however, done me injustice in attributing to me expressions which I have never uttered, or rather which I never wrote, for all is in writing. All I said in relation to the matter in question was that I should have much satisfaction in transmitting a copy of Lord Clarendon's note to the Secretary of State. I never had a word with Lord Palmerston on the subject."

At the time of Buchanan's departure it was not known what action the American Government would take with regard to Minister Crampton.

BIOGRAPHICAL NOTE

Buchanan, who became President in 1857, was charged with too great leniency towards the Secessionist Movement, but was otherwise an able and active Chief Executive. He survived in eclipse throughout the Civil War and died in 1868.

CHAPTER XV

DALLAS (1856–1861)

GEORGE MIFFLIN DALLAS had himself been Vice-President under Polk, and an aspirant with his fellow-Pennsylvanian, Buchanan, for the Presidency. He was the son of a young Scots lawyer who had settled in Philadelphia in 1783, embraced politics and risen to be Secretary of the Treasury under Madison. Now sixty-four, a handsome, white-haired man resembling Macready the actor, he could look back upon a long official and diplomatic experience. Nearly twenty years before, President Van Buren had sent him as Minister to Russia. In March 1856, on the return of his rival Buchanan from London, Dallas became his successor.

In the five years which Dallas was to pass in England he succeeded in impressing himself on English public life far more forcibly and—in a sense—arrogantly than almost any one of his predecessors. Of the two important measures which he carried through, one was killed by the Senate and the other rendered nugatory by the outbreak of the Civil War. To-day, his chief title to remembrance is that he was a lively and prodigious letter-writer, and so proud of his compositions that he afterwards gathered them into a book, following in this respect the rather dangerous example of Lord Normanby on retiring from the British Embassy in Paris. It is true his communications to Secretary Marcy were often far more private than official, the two statesmen being personally very intimate. Moreover, Dallas kept a diary, which was published after his death by his daughter. Taken in conjunction they present a copious, detailed and highly prejudiced account of political, military and social life in London for the lustrum preceding the American Civil War.

294

When Dallas reached London the proclamation of peace with Russia was momentarily expected.   On April 4 he was received by Queen Victoria at Buckingham Palace.   As it was in the American tradition to say a word or two in his first dispatch concerning the British Sovereign's personal appearance, Dallas said it : " She is not handsome," he pronounced, " but her expression of face and her manner are engaging, and very soon put her visitors at ease."   We learn, besides, that the illustrious company on this occasion—

" were in no wise repelled from the American Minister by his plain suit of black, but, on the contrary, made his time, while waiting her Majesty's readiness, pass very pleasantly. My coat, which I am bold to say was as well made and of as good cloth as any in the Palace (except perhaps Prince Albert's !), came from the shop of a tailor in Philadelphia, Sixth above Arch, of the name of Kelly !   The truth appears to be that our common sense is gradually getting the better of traditional fooleries, in honest reality greatly improving social intercourse."

After this engaging piece of bunkum, the new American Minister becomes serious.   He has met his fellow-Minister from Haiti.   " What," he asks the Secretary of State, " is your Minister to do or say if he be placed at the royal table alongside of Soulouque's representative, whose fine ebony our friend Mr. Mason [the American Minister in Paris] had estimated at a thousand dollars ? "   But Dallas, coming from a free State, had no insuperable prejudices on the score of colour to overcome.

The Central American question had been shelved since the Crampton incident ; Lord Clarendon had formerly offered to arbitrate on the points in dispute, but now Dallas was against arbitration.

" Palmerston," he wrote of the Prime Minister, " must be looked coolly in the eye, so that he may gather from our composure as well as from our words that he can expect no substantial change in us."

Clarendon was shortly expected back at the Foreign Office from the Continent, and meanwhile Dallas made a public speech or two in which he expressed the hope of a speedy restoration of harmonious relations with England. But he vigorously disclaimed " all the balderdash about Mother Country, kindred and so forth," which was certainly refreshing.

" The truth is [he wrote Marcy] that such terms as ' mother,' ' daughter,' ' cousins,' etc. are *their own familiar ones.* I have resolutely and from principle eschewed any phrase of the sort."

This proud republican aloofness was perhaps carried to the verge of churlishness in the matter of the great Spithead Review, following the return of the British warships from the East.

" It will be a grand and ostentatious display of British naval power at which, as an American, citizen or Minister, I shall be reluctant to play the part of a wondering spectator. . . . I do not intend, unless *commanded* by a direct *invitation* from the Queen (which I have feared might come), to swell the exulting crowd at that demonstration."

He kept to this intention and afterwards wrote a letter pouring ridicule on the whole review—which appears, in truth, to have been sadly mismanaged.

Dallas early noted that Lord Palmerston was a man of great adroitness.

" Pray observe how in the distribution of the immense land and naval forces on hand, he is sending a larger force to Canada than they have ever yet had there ; other troops to Bermuda ; a most extraordinary supply of many millions of ball-cartridges, etc. We have in cotton, to be sure, pretty good bail for the peaceful behaviour of this country as a general thing ; but there are epochs and circumstances in which I should not think that bail sufficient. I have a strong mistrust of France ; but that is Mr. Mason's province, not mine."

He thought Palmerston was just then in " as victorious an attitude as any British premier had ever held . . . and has dexterously managed to postpone our American differences to a distant day."

" His majorities are large, and his party is full of exultation. Still, there is that thorn of America in his side—*hæret lethalis* —and if it does not bring him to the ground, it will be

G. M. DALLAS.

because you may come to his relief, or he may suddenly, by the indications in France, discover the expediency of greater conciliation in his relations with us. All men of opinions worth anything agree in saying—I should not be surprised to hear it from his own lips—that a conflict with the United States is the only thing he could not stand for six months, or even half that time. His power is immense, but that is a rock on which, if he touch, he founders."

By the month of May Dallas had installed his Legation in Portland Place, with the son Philip as Secretary. On the 16th he wrote :

" Politics are anything but satisfactory. I found on my arrival a fixed anti-American set in the ministerial and social classes, and entered upon a determination to break that down, first, by frankness and *conciliation*, if they would answer ; if not, then, second, by open defiance. Our countrymen here tell me that my success has been complete : but let us wait a little longer before too confident a conclusion. To go to war with us is an extravagance which I am certain would upset any Ministry in less than six months, if not on the instant ; but I doubt much their disposition to forgo their great luxury of treating us with insult and contumely. Their hospitality and kindness to me and my family have certainly been unmeasured ; but the region of national relations and policy is widely separated from that of mere personal intercourse. Should Mr. Crampton be dismissed by Governor Marcy I think we may look out for a series of retaliatory and recriminating acts between the two countries, which must lead, at no distant day, to the final trial of strength. When we are driven to that, *we must throw the scabbard away, and tie the hilt to the hand.*"

Meanwhile this very truculent Minister and his family continued to enjoy the gaieties of the London season at the Court of Queen Victoria. It was all very splendid, but effete, and Dallas's cold republican eye could detect the canker beneath the flaming petals.

" All this magnificence of ceremonial and pretension is fast being undermined, even among the proudest peers, by our republican principles, accompanied by our wonderful prosperity ; and before any one of your children reaches fifty it will have vanished, like the hues of a rainbow, for ever. Let them see it before it fades away."

His correspondent's offspring might be almost centenarians by now, and if they had preserved their eyesight they might still have a glimpse of a not too drab ceremonial at the Court of his present Majesty George V.

But exciting moments were in store for the Minister. Minister Crampton was at length dismissed at Washington, and now, in return, expulsion was hanging over Dallas's own head.

" If *The Times* and the *Post* are reliable organs, I shall probably quit England soon, *never* to return ; an undiscriminating retaliation amounts to an original insult, and will require many years to be forgotten. It will not surprise me if I should turn out to be the last Minister from the United States to the British Court, and that will certainly be fame if it be not honour."

A week later (June 7) he wrote in the same strain :

" My uncertain position is of course not without its inconveniences, and I am now and then tempted to exclude myself altogether from the world, until the world lets me know definitely whether I am to be decapitated or let go without day. The measure of dismissing me, as *in pari delicto* with that honourable gentleman, Mr. Crampton, savours of an undiscriminating vindictiveness which strongly marks an original insult. Indeed, I am disposed to think that the dignity of our country will make it necessary so to regard that measure, if it be resorted to, and that, without the amplest apology, we ought never to permit an American Minister, or diplomatic agent of any sort, even a consul, to show himself in her Majesty's dominions. My longing for historical fame would certainly be satiated if it were to turn out that I am to be the last of our Ministers at this Court. As it could not be ascribed to any fault of mine, and would unerringly indicate the moment at which the doctrine of *delenda est Carthago* began its practical operation, I should be borne down to future ages identified with the commencement of a great period. *Ultimus Romanorum* is better than merely Consul or even Imperator."

He had learnt that the offending Crampton had been sent his passports by the President and that the exequaturs of the three British consuls implicated were recalled. Marcy's dispatch was conciliatory, but it expressed an unchanged conviction as to the personal misconduct of Crampton and his coadjutors, who had acted in violation of American laws. But there was to be no retaliation on the part of the British Government. Palmerston announced in Parliament the decision " not to terminate their present amicable relations with Mr. Dallas." [1] What a signal triumph for American diplomacy !

" The breakers are avoided ; the Legation is in deep water again ; the Crampton squall has passed over, rather clearing the sky than otherwise ; and there is bright promise of a goodly day to-morrow. No time shall be lost to improve the returning swell of kindly feeling. It is not impossible that prompt negotiation may put an end to all controversy about the treaty." [2]

Alas ! Dallas's sturdy Americanism was almost too rigid. It could not countenance even trifling variants from its fixed principles. Thus, he presented himself at a levée at Buckingham Palace with three of his compatriots. The rules as to Court garb continued very precise in those quarters and were well known to the Minister. He himself and two of the party wore the approximation to Court dress which had been agreed upon between his predecessor Buchanan and the Master of the Ceremonies. But the third, who was a professor of civil and military engineering at West Point, and the father of the future Admiral A. T. Mahan, merely donned his official costume, a blue dress coat, with buttons of the Engineer corps, blue pantaloons, white vest, black stock and an ordinary hat.

It was objected, in a manner which Dallas avows was exceedingly kind and courteous, that as Mahan wore a black cravat, had no chapeau and no sword, he could not thus pass the Queen.

" I tried once, twice or thrice to surmount the difficulty by adverting to the *official* character of his dress ; but the

---

[1] Palmerston, however, showed his appreciation of Crampton's services by recommending him for a K.C.B.
[2] Dallas to Marcy, June 17, 1856.

rule was express, and there was no discretion to relax it.
Pained at the position in which my estimable countryman
was placed, among strangers, and in a place to which he
was entirely unaccustomed, I unhesitatingly offered to go
home with him, and in this suggestion his companions joined.
We retired. It was impossible to do less, and we did no
more."

It was a sad business. Naturally *The Times* and other
newspapers got hold of the incident and made the most
of it, intimating that the American had been actuated by
intentional disrespect to the Queen. It was as if an un-
mannerly individual had presented himself at a full-dress
party in street garb. Dallas professed himself unrepentant
and took refuge in satire.

" This really frivolous matter has worried me personally
more than I would be willing to admit ; but I have been
extremely guarded and forbearing to prevent its having any
influence whatever upon the discussions now proceeding as
to Central America. The French newspapers hailed its first
appearance in *The Times* with delight, and seemed to gloat
on a fresh opportunity of fanning discord between England
and the United States. They fired up incontinently at
the effort to advance another step in the usurpations of
democracy ! We may yet have a Congress of Sovereigns to
teach dress and manners, whose protocols will be accompanied
by photographic illustrations of the only tolerable ' shorts,'
' tights,' ' vests,' ' cravats,' ' rapiers ' and head-gear ! "

As a further example of Dallas's critical disposition,
his *nil admirari*, we find him writing to the Secretary of
State, after attending a review of the Guards :

" We have just had the Guards, returned from the Crimea,
some four thousand lads of nineteen, in bright red coats and
huge fur caps, pass through the highways and file in procession
before the Queen. One could not help thinking, as they
moved onward, ' hardly heavy enough for effective fight ! ' "

It may be mentioned that a large proportion of the Guards
were men of thirty and that all were chosen for their stature
and bodily fitness. But then, in Minister Dallas's eyes, the
English were a miserable, decadent race. Still, decadent or

not, there must be one specimen amongst them fit to be sent out as Minister at Washington.

" Give them time to recover from the galvanic shock of the Crampton smasher, and when they once resolve to let bygones be bygones I shall be mistaken if your Diplomatic Corps will not be adorned and strengthened by an Englishman of higher rank, greater ability, better temper and more winning manners, than any our terrible but resistless democracy has yet welcomed." [1]

How unfortunate that in 1856 Napoleon III was England's master.

" The ' prestige ' of this country, I consider gone, *fuit,* and no party on the Continent thinks her willing and competent to stand by and protect the cause of liberal government. She is essentially and practically chained to the footstool of a usurper more dangerous to the liberties of mankind, because more cunning to employ the vocabulary and arts of freedom, than would be a dozen Russian Czars. Steam, too, has brought her into such close proximity with her neighbour, that she dare not oppose him without being, what she knows she never is, ready to repel a sudden invasion."

Yet harbouring these feelings Dallas laboured on at and with Lord Clarendon towards a Central American Treaty. The Government was not inclined to make difficulties. The times were too difficult and the populace generally too discontented not to make sacrifices to gain American friendship. At last it was agreed that Great Britain should withdraw from her colony in the Bay of Honduras, give up her Mosquito Protectorate, admit Greytown to be a free port under the sovereignty of Nicaragua, and undertake never to overpass the limits of the Belize as defined under the Clayton-Bulwer Treaty.

What a welcome change in the international firmament ! And what another glorious victory for Minister Dallas !

" All, aye all, that I came here to do will be successfully accomplished, if indeed it has not been already achieved, in the course of a week. The two countries five months ago were at that critical stand of mutual and morbid defiance

[1] Dallas to Marcy, July 11, 1856

when a prolonged war might have sprung from a few more hot words, or the hasty discharge of a gun at sea. People watched with suspended breath the news of every hour. Americans, all over the continent of Europe, and in particular Commodore Breese, commanding our Mediterranean squadron, awaited a signal from this office to hurry home. Well ! it all changed in the lapse of a month or six weeks ; and the change has advanced, step by step, until now, before the entire expiration of five months, they who understand the condition and tone of international relations are satisfied that a sounder basis for mutual harmony and respect has not existed since the treaty of 1783. I cannot tell you how this has been brought about. There is the fact. I am, and always have been, just as ready to fight England as any man living, upon any adequate and honourable ground. Still, to have been accessory to the conversion of a ticklish state of reciprocal rage, springing from a mere bandying of diplomatic sentences, into calm and solid goodwill, is destined to close my political life with entire satisfaction to myself."

Was it not all magical, these diplomatic shiftings, like the transformation scene of a theatre !

And so on October 17 the treaty was signed by Dallas and Clarendon. At that moment a Presidential campaign was raging in America, with an election only a fortnight or so away. Dallas, however, could view the future with a tranquil mind.

" Having accomplished to the satisfaction of the American Government the adventurous and unpromising enterprises which brought me to England . . . I am ready to resume my niche of obscurity at home, be our new President whom he may."

So far as his treaty was concerned Dallas had, as we shall see, reckoned without his enemies and without the Senate. Albeit, Buchanan was elected and his retention of the mission was safe. Lewis Cass became Marcy's successor [1] as Secretary

[1] Cass, too, like Marcy, infinitely relished Dallas's communications from London. On one occasion in 1858 the Secretary of State wrote : " I thank you very much for your graphic letters. I read them all to the Cabinet, where they are listened to with great interest. Your facts and speculations are just what are wanted and what we can get nowhere else. . . . Since the days of Horace Walpole, I have seen no more successful effort of this kind." Sixty years later we shall find President Wilson expressing similar appreciation of the London letters of Minister Page.

of State. Dallas, then, was to stay on for four more years—into the administration of Abraham Lincoln. But his beloved treaty, the Central American Treaty that he had pushed so hard, lauded so highly and staked so much upon, was doomed.

As early as January 13, 1857, he wrote :

" It is not impossible that in removing all the points of controversy under the Clayton-Bulwer Treaty, I have crossed the grain of some who wished to get rid of that contract, and it is very likely that in both countries I have provoked large bodies of turbulent spirits by preventing them from coming to blows."

He wrote to Clarendon that, although there might be a resistance " aggravated by the debility incident to a retiring Administration," yet he was confident all was well.

Then came the distressing news : the treaty was being amended, slowly, vexatiously, and unless ratified by April 17 it expired by its own provisions.

" The amendments made to the treaty by the Senate are a series of miserable little criticisms, doctrinal and verbal, unworthy the dignity of the body and the gravity of the occasion."

On April 7 the amended document reached London, when it became abundantly clear that neither Government nor the Opposition (certainly not Gladstone) relished the American Senate's amendments and that they were glad of the excuse not to take action. So the treaty perished, its demise being unnoticed by the newspapers. Dallas was furious over the iniquity of the Senate :

" Our system constitutes, as the final negotiator of treaties, a popular body of sixty-two members ! They amend such instruments with all the freedom they amend ordinary bills, engrafting each his peculiar notion, and indulging claptrap and bunkum without stint. This is diplomacy run riot : and one must not be astonished at finding foreign Powers occasionally restive under its operation. As early as 1794 our Senate struck whole clauses from Chief Justice Jay's treaty ; in 1824, they so mutilated one made by Mr. Rush that this Government refused, just as they have now refused, to exchange the ratification. Whoever was the Senator to offer the amendment to strike out and insert the twenty words about the Bay Islands, he alone has the glory of killing the treaty." [1]

The failure was also taken deeply to heart by Marcy, who died suddenly a few months later. His friend the Minister was indignant that this event attracted no more attention in London than the passing of his darling treaty had done.

" Being at the Premier's drawing-room last night, I observed that it [Marcy's death] awakened about as much interest as would the decease of any sepoy in India."

Yet in the following year it seemed as if Dallas had succeeded in obtaining a concession from the British Government for which all his predecessors had striven in vain. It was in May 1858 that there burst upon the Legation news which revived the old American exasperation against the old British Right of Search in a worse form than ever. The American consul at an African port sent home a story " so transcendently outrageous as scarcely to be credible from the lips of one man only." And there were further misdeeds of British cruisers in the West Indies.

Dallas thought the situation justified the Secretary in requesting him to demand the issue of peremptory orders to British naval officers to cease visiting American vessels, and if not given in a fortnight, to request his passports and quit the kingdom. " My conviction is," he wrote in his diary, " that such a course would be successful and our relation of amity would at once be restored and strengthened."

But he feared his Government might not be prepared for so resolute a proceeding. Pending instructions from home, he sought Malmesbury and threshed out the whole matter with him. The British position at that time was thus officially stated :

" The United States having declared the slave trade to be piracy, he [Lord Clarendon] was convinced that the President and his Government were no more desirous than Great Britain that the trade should be extended. It could not be concealed that the American vessels had carried on

[1] To Colonel Murray, April 28, 1857.

the slave trade on the coast of Africa ; and he did not see how, unless some right of search was given, the real nationality of the flag of suspected vessels could be ascertained. Such a right had been admitted by all maritime nations for their common protection, and without it the most atrocious deeds might be perpetrated and yet remain unpunished. But the possession of such a right was a very different thing from the exercise of it. He was certain that no officer commanding a British cruiser, whatever his suspicions might be, would exercise the right of searching an American vessel if he was really convinced that it was *bona-fide* American. We are as proud as the Americans are of the honour and independence of our flag, but we should consider our flag tarnished if it were made a cover for nefarious transactions." [1]

The Foreign Minister stated that the accounts of the alleged outrages had been grossly exaggerated, but that he feared some unjustifiable acts might have been committed, in consequence of British naval practice. The Government had taken the advice of the law officers of the Crown, whose opinion was decisive that by international law we had no right of search—no right of visitation whatever in time of peace. That being so, they were prepared to disavow it. In other words, the old Right of Visit and Search in time of peace would be forthwith abandoned.

At a memorable interview on the same day, Clarendon told Dallas that her Majesty's Government were " not prepared to justify or excuse " the acts of naval officers complained of by the United States, but that it was " most indispensable, in the interest of civilization and the police of the Seas, that there should be a power of verifying the nationality of a vessel suspected on good grounds of carrying false colours." He then went on to say that the French had proposed that " a boat may be sent alongside of a suspected ship and may ask for papers, but not, unless invited, board the vessel." But pending negotiations about this, orders would be given to discontinue search of American vessels.

" My colleagues of the Diplomatic Corps [reported Dallas to Cass, June 11] have, one after another, expressed their congratulations. They seem to regard with pleasure every

[1] Parliamentary Debates: Earl of Clarendon, June 8, 1858.

check given to the maritime arrogance of England. Even Malakoff said he supposed I was now in good humour or softened. There is no country in Europe which does not look upon the Right of Search as a weapon in the hands of a single bully, especially since your famous letter which stopped Louis Philippe's signing the Quintuple Treaty." [1]

The French statesman Guizot complimented Dallas on having removed the last source of a quarrel between England and the United States. " He said he had tried the same thing while here as French envoy, but could accomplish nothing. It was a great *résultat* and would be felt everywhere."

The Minister himself first made the welcome announcement to an Independence Day gathering of his compatriots in London.

" I should like on the Fourth of July to announce to my fellow-countrymen that Visit and Search in regard to American vessels on the high seas in time of peace is frankly and finally ended [tremendous cheering, the whole company rising and manifesting the liveliest enthusiasm]. While, gentlemen, I am able to announce this gratifying fact, I think it ought also to be accompanied by the assurance that the termination of that for which we have struggled for nearly half a century has been brought about with a degree of honourable candour and fair dealing on the part of the British Government which is worthy of every acknowledgment on our part [loud cheers]." [2]

Dallas regarded himself as a hero, but it is difficult to see how his efforts had contributed in any way to the Government's action, which had been precipitated by a particularly flagrant naval indiscretion, the opinion of the law officers, and confirmed by the general feeling in Parliament, including the Opposition leaders. Disraeli said that the best answer to the inflammatory speeches in the American Senate was the dispassionate discussion in the House of Commons. The American Government had been told that their flag would surely be abused if the assumption that that flag covered any cargo were admitted, and they had been asked to suggest

---

[1] Cf. Willson : *America's Ambassadors to France.*
[2] *The Times,* July 5, 1858.

a mode of preventing such things. He believed existing misconceptions would soon disappear.

Lord Malmesbury returned to the Foreign Office with the short-lived Derby Administration.

Yet despite Malmesbury's conciliatory behaviour, Dallas rarely lost an opportunity of riding a high horse in the vicinity of Downing Street. He was always suspecting some official insolence or arrogance. Once he sent Secretary Cass a copy of his reply to " Lord Malmesbury's impudent note about Her Majesty's captains who visit suspected vessels." He felt anxious whether Cass should think it " too bitter " or else " too tame." But he heard that the Secretary was " delighted with its tone of rebuke, thinking it admirable and American." In his diary Dallas wrote :

" Malmesbury has had it for more than a month and I suppose he means to let the matter rest where it is. Possibly he is chewing the cud and intends another fling. Well, now that I have heard from home I am indifferent what *he* does."

It is to be feared that Dallas lived in a little world of his own—a world of perpetual jealousy, suspicion, insults and overweening pride. He once wrote :

" I am sometimes inclined to think that where people do not really wish to fight, they should proscribe the pen and confine their intercourse of views exclusively to conversation."

In conversation Dallas was considered a mild man. Was there not something symbolical in the fact that it was during his official lustrum that the Atlantic cable joining Europe and America was laid, operated and broke ?

On September 17, 1858, he wrote to Cass :

" The cable don't speak—the cause is yet undetected, not *in nubibus* but *in profundis,* and the electricians are at loggerheads. Everybody looks blank and croakers are beginning their bull-frog songs with, Well, you know, *I* always doubted ! '

" The absolutely perfect isolation which it is necessary to secure for the wire through the whole two thousand miles may remain for a short time—but can it in reason be expected

21

to last amid the lashings, grindings, abrasions and corrosions of our stormy sea ? "

Not for years—until after the American Civil War, when it was so much needed—was the Atlantic Cable made effective.

When Lord John Russell in 1860 complained of the continued inactivity of the American cruisers in the suppression of the slave trade, Dallas replied in effect that the British Foreign Office had better mind its own business. The Government at Washington did not require to be continually lectured as to its duty.

In his letter to the Secretary of State, Dallas added, " English statesmen generally have a complacent and irrepressible sense of moral superiority."

England had fought the battle for the suppression of the slave trade virtually alone. It had been a long and costly effort—and, unhappily, the slave trade still flourished.

But the traffic and the whole question of Negro Slavery was destined shortly to receive a fatal blow. In November 1860 Abraham Lincoln was elected to the Presidency. On February 5, 1861, Minister Dallas went to hear the Queen read her Speech in Parliament.

" Serious differences [announced one paragraph] have arisen among the States of the North American Union. It is impossible for one not to look with great concern upon any events which can affect the happiness and welfare of a people nearly allied to my subjects by descent and closely connected with them by the most intimate and friendly relations. My heartfelt wish is that these differences may be susceptible of a satisfactory adjustment.

" The interest which I take in the well-being of the people of the United States cannot but be increased by the kind and cordial reception given by them to the Prince of Wales during his recent visit to the Continent of America." [1]

Dallas, in common with his colleagues in Paris and elsewhere, was notified by a circular from the new Secretary of State, William Henry Seward, to " use all proper and necessary measures to prevent the success of efforts which

---

[1] The inaccurate terminology may be noted. There was no Continent of America. There was a Union of States called America on the North American Continent, and the expression now properly applies to that Union alone.

may be made by persons claiming to represent the seceding States to procure recognition."

Accordingly, on April 8, he had an interview with Lord John Russell, who assured him that "the coming of his successor, Mr. Adams, would doubtless be regarded as the appropriate occasion for finally discussing and determining the question" of the attitude to be taken by Great Britain towards America's schism. Dallas's dispatch containing this assurance was received at the State Department about a fortnight later. In the belief that nothing would be done until his arrival, Dallas's successor did not sail until May 1. Meanwhile, the startling news of the fall of Fort Sumter reached London on April 26, and during the following days the agents of the Confederate Government then in Europe, Messrs. W. L. Yancey, of Alabama, and P. A. Rost, of Louisiana, were seeking, though in an "unofficial" way, to obtain access to the British Foreign Secretary. On May 1 Lord John Russell sent for Dallas in consequence of the reports which immediately began to circulate as to "the intentions of President Lincoln regarding a blockade of the southern coast and the discontinuance of its harbours as ports of entry." He informed the American Minister of the arrival in London of the Confederate commissioners, intimated that an interview had been sought, and that he was not unwilling to see them "unofficially." An understanding had, he said, been reached between the Governments of France and England that the two countries should act in concert and take the same course as to recognition. Dallas informed Lord John that his successor would be in London in a fortnight, and the business could be left to him. The next day (May 2), in response to questions in the House of Commons, Lord John announced it as the policy of the Government—

"to avoid taking any part in the lamentable contest now raging in the American States. We have not [he declared] been involved in any way in that contest by any act or giving any advice in the matter, and, for God's sake, let us if possible keep out of it!"[1]

Dallas reported that at a party at Lord Palmerston's

[1] C. F. Adams.

one gentleman " confidently predicted that the South would capture Washington and give the Northerners the severest thrashing they have ever had." On May 11 the Minister received and communicated President Lincoln's Proclamation of Blockade to the Foreign Office, together with a copy of Secretary Seward's circular dated April 20, relating to the privateers against Federal commerce fitted out in accordance with Jefferson Davis's letter-of-marque notification. Two days later, the 13th, Lord John Russell got up in Parliament and announced that the Government had decided to recognize the Confederacy as a belligerent, " though not as an established and independent Power."

That very evening Dallas's successor arrived in London, and the next day both read in the *Gazette* of May 14 the astonishing and to one, at least, disconcerting Proclamation recognizing the Confederacy as belligerents.

Looking back now, after nearly seventy years, this Proclamation seems to us a very natural thing. It is difficult for all save the most bigoted sectionalists to look upon the people of the seceding States as " rebels." Rebels against what ? They had proceeded in an orderly and constitutional way. They believed, and they had the example of Jefferson in believing, in the sovereignty of the separate States and their right to withdraw from a federation which was disagreeable and completely unsympathetic to them and their sectional interests. The original colonists may have been rebels when they repudiated the dominion of the British Crown, the Irish were rebels, the Brazilians and Bolivians were rebels ; but the people of the Confederacy were their own masters, no sovereign held dominion over them, and if they wished to terminate the Union as originally constituted, could they be blamed, much less execrated, for that ?

The division and subdivision of nationalities has no power to excite us now—and we are only disturbed when racial interests are outraged. But no racial interests were outraged in 1861. It was from first to last a contest for and against slavery, and the English people should have perceived that from the first. What they plainly did see was a schism in the American Empire similar to the schism the British Empire had endured in 1776, with the South as under-dog appealing for English sympathy even as the American insurgents had appealed to France in 1776. It was, in their Victorian eyes, retribution. Looked at as simple human drama, divested of its underlying causes, it wears that aspect to-day.

BIOGRAPHICAL NOTE

Dallas retired to private life, after having formally denounced the policy of Secession. His death occurred in 1864.

CHAPTER XVI

C. F. ADAMS (1861–1868)

WHEN Charles Francis Adams of Boston, a short, upright, severe-looking gentleman of fifty-four, arrived at his hotel in London on the evening of May 13, 1861, a powerful new factor had intervened to influence the course of Anglo-American relations during the next seven crucial years.

Had the whole of America been searched, there was none who so precisely possessed the antecedents and moral and mental qualifications which the situation demanded. He was the third of the great Adamses; his father and grandfather had not only been Presidents, but they had both previously been Ministers to England. Though thus born to politics and public service, the grandson had not yet found his precise niche. Early called to the Bar, he had been a member of the Massachusetts Legislature; he had engaged in literature and journalism; had founded and edited the *Boston Whig*; had become actively interested in national politics and been elected to Congress. Universally recognized as an idealist, he was still unplaced—a man of refinement, learning and character. No one would have been surprised had Lincoln taken Adams into the new Administration, but the posts were all pledged, and Secretary Seward pressed his appointment to the Court of St. James. Lincoln good-naturedly agreed—as a personal favour to Seward—although it meant sacrificing another candidate. Strangely enough, Lincoln seemed to attach little importance to the appointment. In his Diary Adams recorded his single official interview with the then uncouth, inexperienced and harassed President, who was shortly to win immortality in the annals, not only of his own country, but of the world. The Secretary of State had summoned the new Minister to Washington to receive his verbal instructions:

" The country was in the midst of the most dangerous crisis in its history ; a crisis in which the actions of foreign Governments, especially of England, might well be decisive of results.   The policy to be pursued was under consideration. It was a grave topic, worthy of thoughtful consideration. Deeply impressed with the responsibility devolved upon him, Mr. Adams went with the new Secretary to the State Department, whence, at the suggestion of the latter, they presently walked over to the White House, and were ushered into the room which more than thirty years before Mr. Adams associated most closely with his father and his father's trained bearing and methodical habits.

" Presently a door opened, and a tall, large-featured, shabbily-dressed man, of uncouth appearance, slouched into the room.   His much-kneed, ill-fitting trousers, coarse stockings and worn slippers at once caught the eye.   He seemed generally ill at ease, in manner constrained and shy.   The Secretary introduced the Minister to the President, and the appointee proceeded to make the usual conventional remarks, expressive of obligation, and his hope that the confidence implied in the appointment he had received might not prove to have been misplaced.

" They had all by this time taken chairs ; and the tall man listened in silent abstraction.   When Mr. Adams had finished, and he did not take long, the tall man remarked in an indifferent, careless way that the appointment in question had not been his, but was due to the Secretary of State, and that it was to ' Governor Seward ' rather than to himself that Mr. Adams should express any sense of obligation he might feel ; then, stretching out his legs before him, he said, with an air of great relief as he swung his long arms to his head, ' Well, Governor, I've this morning decided that Chicago post-office appointment.'   Mr. Adams and the nation's foreign policy were dismissed together !   Not another reference was made to them." [1]

It is one of the oddest incidents in history.   Adams always held that Lincoln was an instance of a man growing to lofty moral and mental stature through the force of responsibility and experience.   But the man had within him an amazing potentiality of growth ; even so in 1861 there was only one such intense personality in America.

[1] C. F. Adams, Jr. : *Charles Francis Adams.*

As has already been stated, Adams reached London to find the international situation ominous. On the following day he read the Proclamation declaring the Government's recognition of the Confederacy as a belligerent, though not as an established and independent Power. This act, even though justified by international law, was in American circles " interpreted as unfriendly and seemed in fact to represent the feeling of suspicion and hostility of the ruling class in England towards the American republic." [1] This feeling found expression in a vague sympathy for the South, which was believed to be a more mannerly and " chivalrous " community, bent on obtaining independence of the cruder, commercial element inhabiting the Northern States.

It cannot be said that the language and deportment of the late Minister, Dallas, of Cass the Secretary of State, or of the Senate had altogether disposed the English people to be indulgent towards these States. Their diplomatic behaviour too forcibly suggested the behaviour of the Honorable Jefferson Brick not to provoke discomfort and resentment.

It is probably true that between May and November 1861, " the chances in Europe were as ten to one in favour of the Confederacy and against the Union." [2] The reports from America which were appearing in *The Times* and other newspapers definitely asserted that the bulk of Americans themselves were indifferent towards the impending schism. Russell, *The Times* correspondent, wrote in April:

" Practically, as far as I have gone, I have failed to meet many people who really exhibited any passionate attachment to the Union or who pretended to be actuated by any strong feeling of regard or admiration for the Government of the United States in itself."

This was not all. Seward himself, the Secretary of State, had actually repudiated not only the right but the wish even " to use armed force in subjugating the Southern States against the will of a majority of the people," and declared that the President willingly accepted as true the " cardinal dogma " of the Confederacy that " the Federal Government could not reduce them to obedience *by conquest.*" So, it

[1] C. W. Ford ; *A Cycle of Adams Letters.*   [2] C. F. Adams, Jr.

was reasonably argued in England, why not "friendly separation "?

The British Government was disposed to be especially suspicious and distrustful of the Secretary, William Henry Seward. There was a little story of him current which everybody believed to be, and which is now admitted to be, true. During the Prince of Wales's visit to America, Seward had remarked jocularly to the Duke of Newcastle that he expected shortly to be in charge of foreign affairs, when it would " *become my duty to insult England, and I mean to do so.*" It probably never occurred to Seward to doubt that in any such chauvinistic or Anglophobe demonstration on his part he would merely be following the old Senatorial tradition and the diplomatic example of Cass and his friend and disciple Dallas. In truth, Seward from the moment he was in office meant to go much further than any of his predecessors had done since 1812. As a means of distracting domestic attention from the Secession issue, he deliberately proposed to inflame the country into actual war against England, and, if necessary, France and other countries as well. It seems incredible, but we know now that he would unquestionably have carried out such a policy had it not been for President Lincoln's better judgment.

Adams, however, as yet knew nothing of all this, suspected nothing of Seward's scheme of flinging down the gauntlet to England and the whole of Europe.

On May 18 he drove out to Pembroke Lodge for his first interview with the Foreign Secretary. He found him " a man of sixty-five or seventy, of about the same size as myself, with a face marked by care and thought rather than any strong expressions. His eye is, I think, blue and cold." The conversation lasted more than an hour. His conclusion from it was that " the permanency of my stay is by no means certain."

In this interview he pressed Lord John " quite as far and as hard as circumstances justified."

" In truth [he reported to Seward], if I were persuaded that her Majesty's Government were really animated by a desire to favour the rebellion, I should demand a categorical answer ; but thus far I see rather division of opinion, consequent upon the pressure of the commercial classes."

He told the Foreign Secretary that " if Britain really designed to extend the struggle then going on in America, he had nothing further left to do " in London. This he said " with regret, as my own feelings had been and were of the most friendly character."

Nothing further happened until June 10, when Adams received a dispatch from Secretary Seward, dated May 21, which gave him a shock. But the shock he received was nothing compared with what he would have felt had he known the terms which Seward had originally drafted. The inner history of this dispatch was first revealed by Lincoln's biographers thirty years later. It informed Great Britain that if she " shall recognize the bearers of Confederate letters of marque as belligerents, we from that hour shall cease to be friends and become once more, as we have twice before been forced to be, enemies of Great Britain." The same threat was made to France. But this bellicose dispatch, which would certainly have produced war " almost before the carriage of the American Minister had rattled out of Downing Street," had been not only amended by the President, but was now marked " Confidential—not to be read or shown to any one." In this form it reached Adams. Yet its language was still so " indecorous and threatening " as to startle the Minister.

" The Government seems ready to declare war with all the Powers of Europe, and almost instructs me to withdraw from communication with the Ministers here, in a certain contingency. I scarcely know how to understand Mr. Seward. The rest of the Government may be demented for all that I know ; but he surely is calm and wise."

Whatever he afterwards became, under the stress of the conflict, " calm and wise " just now Seward was not.

" My duty here is [wrote Adams in his Diary], so far as I can do it honestly, to prevent the mutual irritation from coming to a downright quarrel. It seems to me like throwing the game into the hands of the enemy. . . . If a conflict with a handful of slaveholding States is to bring us to our present pass, what are we to do when we throw down the glove to all Europe ? "

Again he sought an interview with Lord John, and told him " in all frankness " that any further protraction of relations, unofficial or not, with the " pseudo-commissioners " from the Confederate States " could scarcely fail to be viewed by us as hostile in spirit and to require some corresponding action accordingly." Put to him in that way, Lord John denied any intention to give offence. He discouraged the visits of the Confederate commissioners, who were eventually superseded (September 23) by a single emissary, John M. Mason.

So far Seward's " crazy dispatch " had borne fruit. But, as the Minister's son, Henry Adams, wrote home, if his father had obeyed it literally he " would have made a war in five minutes and annihilated our party here in no time at all."

In the younger man's opinion :

" America seems clean daft. She seems to want to quarrel with all the world, and now that England has eaten humble-pie for what was, I must say, a natural mistake from her point of view, I cannot imagine why we should keep on ' sarsing ' her." [1]

Henry Adams was his father's secretary, a highly intelligent, somewhat introspective youth, who had not yet decided upon a career—who, indeed, never decided, but drifted through life for the next fifty years, one of the ablest, most independent and most solitary figures of his time.

To disprove the impression that all the English were unfriendly at this juncture, we have Henry Adams's testimony. Writing July 2, 1861, to his brother, he says :

" The English are really on our side ; of that I have no doubt whatever. But they thought that as a dissolution seemed inevitable and as we seemed to have made up our minds to it, their Proclamation was just the thing to keep them straight with both sides, and when it turned out otherwise they did their best to correct their mistake."

American historians now admit that the British Proclamation of May 13 was justifiable.[2]

[1] Ford : *A Cycle of Adams Letters.*
[2] *Vide* Rhodes : *History of the United States.*

The Minister first took a house close to Portland Place (5 Mansfield Street) belonging to Sir Vesey Fitzgerald, and there established his Legation. In his social duties he was admirably assisted by his wife. On July 18 he wrote to their son Charles :

" I think I have attained a tolerable idea of the texture of London society. I have seen most of the men of any reputation, literary or political. The conclusion is not favourable, so far as the comparison with other periods is concerned. . . .

" The general aspect of society is profound gravity. People look serious at a ball, at a dinner, on a ride on horseback or in a carriage, in Parliament or at Court, in the theatres or at the galleries. The great object in life is social position. To this end domestic establishments are sustained to rival each other. The horses must be fine, the carriage as large and cumbrous as possible, the servants as showy in livery as anybody's, the dinners must be just so, the china of Sèvres and the plate of silver, the wines of the same quality and growth, not because each person takes pleasure in the display, but because everybody else does the same thing."

Adams was soon called upon to transact a delicate business. In 1856, as a result of the lessons gained in the Crimean War, the leading nations of Europe had assembled in Paris and agreed to four principles regulating neutrality at sea.[1]

To this Declaration, America was, with the rest, invited to accede. But Secretary Marcy stated that his Government could not abandon the right to use privateers, without the exemption of all private property, not contraband, at sea. His proposed amendment was not satisfactory to England, and so America remained outside. In 1861 Seward thought it desirable for his country to join in the pact, and so sounded the various Ministers abroad. Adams, for one, decided that the articles of the Declaration of Paris were sound in principle

1. Privateering is and remains abolished.
2. The neutral flag covers enemy's goods, with the exception of contraband of war.
3. Neutral goods, with the exception of contraband of war, are not liable to capture under enemy's flags.
4. Blockades in order to be binding must be effective—i.e. maintained by forces sufficient really to prevent access to the coast of the enemy.

C. F. ADAMS.

and that America " would commit itself very badly if it
should turn its back to them."

But when he came to discussion with Russell, he quickly
perceived that there were difficulties in the way. The truth
is, Russell was suspicious of Seward's motives, having been
warned by Lord Lyons, the British Minister in Washington,
not to take any step " without an explicit understanding as
to the effect which America's proposal to accede to the
Declaration was intended to have with regard to the Confederacy." To expedite matters, Adams said it was his
Government's intention to accept the Declaration " pure and
simple." But the Foreign Secretary suspected a trap of
some sort and asked for the insertion of a special clause
stipulating that the proposed arrangement should have no
bearing " direct or indirect on the internal difficulties now
prevailing in the United States."

Adams was affronted : the negotiation was immediately
broken off and never renewed.

From that time forward Adams never fully trusted the
Palmerston-Russell Ministry. He suspected, what was
doubtless the fact, that both statesmen, as also some of their
colleagues, were " no true friends of the North or of the
cause of democracy."

Nevertheless, the Legation and its occupants, in spite of
the impression given a couple of generations later by Henry
Adams's autobiography, were by no means filled with gloom
or boredom at this time.

" *Enfin* [Henry Adams writes his brother], it is an exciting,
hardworking life here, and the Chief and I are as merry as
grigs, writing in this delightful old study all day long, opposite
to each other. When I say ' delightful ' I stretch a point ;
but it is not bad."

Long afterwards Henry Adams had some hard things to
say of his London diplomatic experiences—lasting seven
years—and of Lord John Russell especially, whom he roundly
accuses of being a consummate liar. But in 1861 he could
write (September 28) :

" Lately, England has behaved very well. Lord Russell
was very open and confidential towards the Chief and showed

him confidential dispatches proving the truth of the matter with regard to Spain, besides treating him in every way extremely kindly and confidentially."

And again (November 7) :

" There is no danger from England, of that you may be sure, and I have done my best to induce the New York press to change its tone towards this country ; but they *are* damned fools, I suppose, and make our difficulties as great as they possibly can be. The English Government are well disposed enough."

Then that same month came the celebrated *Trent* affair, when the hot-headed Captain Wilkes stopped a British steam-packet on the high seas and forcibly took off Mason and Slidell, the two accredited Confederate emissaries to England and France.

Instantly two countries were aflame—the United States with joyous triumph and England with resentment. Adams was staying with Lord Houghton in Yorkshire when the news reached him. At first, his conclusion was that the *Trent* seizure had been directed from Washington and that Seward again intended to provoke war. But for the moment he was helpless : he could do nothing. There was no trans-atlantic telegraph in operation ; otherwise, as his son says, the incident could not have failed to involve the two nations in war. He therefore maintained a dignified silence. But his son and secretary reveals how they both felt :

" We are dished . . . our position is hopeless. If the Administration ordered the capture of those men, I am satis-fied that our present authorities are very unsuitable persons to conduct a war like this or to remain in the direction of our affairs. It is our ruin. Do not deceive yourself about the position of England. We might have preserved our dignity in many ways without going to war with her. . . . But now, all the fat's in the fire."

What made it worse was that a fortnight before (November 15), to the Minister's surprise, he had received a note from the Prime Minister, Palmerston, asking him to call on him at his residence, Cambridge House, Piccadilly. His reception was " very cordial and frank." He did not, says Adams's biographer, fully explain his reasons for this unusual interview, which were " highly creditable to him." He was going out of his way to give the American Minister an intimation of possible impending difficulty with a view to obviating it. There followed a lengthy interview, in which Palmerston mentioned that he had heard that Mason and Slidell were on their way to Europe and were expected to sail from Nassau on the *Trent*. He had also heard that an American war vessel in British waters had received instructions to board the *Trent* and take off these commissioners. Apart from the legality of such a proceeding, Palmerston merely desired to tell Adams that he thought the step would be highly inexpedient in every way. He thought it would occasion great popular prejudice against the Northern cause, without any compensating advantages.

In reply, Adams discredited the story and warmly disavowed the existence of any such orders from his Government.

Now, the very thing Palmerston had forecast and he had repudiated had happened ! For three long weeks he awaited dispatches from Washington. When they came, there was no mention of the *Trent*.

" Mr. Seward's ways are not those of diplomacy. Here I have been nearly three weeks without positively knowing whether the act of the officer was directed by the Government or not."

The exultation of his countrymen over the affair was an extra source of humiliation to Adams. His son wrote :

" They have given us no warning that such an act was thought of and seem almost to have purposely encouraged us to waste our strength in trying to maintain the relations which it was itself intending to destroy. I am half mad with vexation and despair."

In the midst of the excitement caused by the *Trent* affair came the death of the Prince Consort, who had on his deathbed suggested a revision of Lord Russell's dispatch to Washington.

It was December 17 before Adams heard from Seward,

who then mentioned casually in the course of his dispatch that Captain Wilkes had acted without instructions and trusted that the British Government would consider this " new incident " in a spirit of forbearance. Adams took it to Russell, who discussed it amicably. " His lordship," wrote the Minister, " did not desire war ; but he was likely to be pushed over the precipice by his desire to walk too close to the edge."

A month later the tension was over and the surrender of the commissioners announced. This result was unquestionably due to the strong representations which Adams made to Seward, which triumphed over the hot-heads in Congress, who had actually voted congratulations to Wilkes on his exploit !

" What a bloody set of fools they are ! [wrote the Second Secretary of Legation in London]. How in the name of all that's conceivable could you suppose that England would sit quiet under such an insult ? *We* should have jumped out of our boots at such a one."

The Minister himself, in a private letter, expresses his feelings towards his own countrymen (December 27) :

" I have never before met with an instance so striking of provoking simplicity in a nation. You do not even resort to the most ordinary habit of judging others by yourselves. Here is all Europe from end to end arrayed in opinion against you and not a shade of suspicion that you may not be right yet rests upon your brows ! "

The Legation was soon afterwards moved to No. 5 Portland Place, far more commodious and agreeable premises.

Having plenty of time on his hands, a young man with the literary talent of Henry Adams naturally longed to give it expression. But as a Secretary of Legation he could only publish his efforts clandestinely—itself a proceeding not free from danger. He began sending bright London letters to the *New York Times*, which printed them anonymously and paid for them. For a time all was well. One day, however, early in 1862, a lively article was published in the *New York Courier*, to which the editor inadvertently added Adams's signature. A copy of the paper reached London and was promptly reprinted with severe comments. Adams found himself—

" in a scrape that is by no manner of means agreeable. . . . To my immense astonishment and dismay I found myself this morning ' sarsed ' through a whole column of *The Times*, and am laughed at by all England. You can imagine my sensations. Unless something occurs to make me forgotten, my bed is not likely to be one of roses for some time to come. There is nothing to be done but to grin and bear it. But for the present I shall cease my other writings, as I am in agonies for fear they should be exposed."

Of the embarrassment caused to his father, the Minister, nothing is said, but he must have intensely disapproved of indiscretions of this sort.

In young Adams's letters there is a passage which displays considerable prescience :

" For England [he wrote, April 11, 1862] there is still greatness and safety, if she will draw her colonies around her, and turn her hegemony into a Confederation of British nations. . . . You may think all this nonsense, but I tell you these are great times."

The social atmosphere in London could not be exactly cordial in 1862 and grew chillier month by month. No wonder the Minister became touchy—that he was under constant temptation to retort upon the English traducers of his country, to deny the libellous reports and gossip rife in London on every side.

He was hardly prepared to find Lord Palmerston himself credulous of these charges of Northern outrage and tyranny. One of these was directed against General B. F. Butler, the Military Governor of New Orleans. The Federal troops in occupation of that city had suffered much from the white female population, who treated the victors with spite and contumely. Their behaviour at last reached such a pitch that, as the Federal Governor said, " flesh and blood could stand it no longer " ; he thereupon issued an order declaring that any women " who insult our soldiers are to be regarded and treated as common women plying their vocation."

When a copy of this order reached England, it created in

22

certain circles a tempest of indignation. Palmerston read it, and it made his chivalrous blood boil. Forgetting that he was Prime Minister, and that protests of any sort should properly emanate from the Foreign Secretary, the aged statesman sat down and dashed off the following to the American Minister :—

"BROCKET, 11 *June*, 1862.

" MY DEAR SIR,—

"I cannot refrain from taking the liberty of saying to you that it is difficult if not impossible to express adequately the disgust which must be excited in the mind of every honourable man by the general order of General Butler given in the enclosed extract from yesterday's *Times*. Even when a town is taken by assault it is the practice of the commander of the conquering army to protect to his utmost the inhabitants, and especially the female part of them, and I will venture to say that no example can be found in the history of civilized nations, till the publication of this order, of a general guilty in cold blood of so infamous an act as deliberately to hand over the female inhabitants of a conquered city to the unbridled licence of an unrestrained soldiery.

" If the Federal Government chooses to be served by men capable of such revolting outrages, they must submit to abide by the deserved opinion which mankind will form of their conduct.

" Yours faithfully,

"PALMERSTON."

Adams was naturally staggered by this surprising attack. His first thought was that Palmerston wished to provoke a quarrel and had chosen this as an excuse. It was essential to know whether the letter was official or " purely as a private expression of sentiment between gentlemen." Palmerston evaded the point, in his reply stating, however, that Adams could make any use of his first letter that he chose. He was, he said, " impelled to make known to you my own personal feelings about General Butler's Proclamation before any notice of it in Parliament should compel me to state my opinion publicly."

To this Adams replied with great dignity next day :

" I trust your lordship will at once understand how impossible it is for me, with any self-respect, to entertain as private any communication which contains what I cannot but consider most offensive imputations against the Government which I have the honour to represent at this Court—imputations, too, based upon an extract from a London newspaper on which the most unfavourable construction is placed without a moment's consideration of any other, or any delay to understand the action of the Government itself.

" I am quite certain that that Government did not send me to entertain any discussions of this kind here. It is, in my view, fully competent to the care of its own reputation, when attacked either at home or abroad. But I know it would visit with just indignation upon its servants abroad their tame submission to receive under the seal of privacy any indignity which it might be the disposition of the servants of any Sovereign, however exalted, to offer to it in that form."

It is possible that Palmerston had intended to make political use of the incident in Parliament and to allude to his rebuke of General Butler, addressed to the American Minister, as the latter's son and biographer seems to think. If so, the intention was frustrated. His next letter to Adams expresses his own justification. The Foreign Secretary was the regular official organ—true—but it was part of the functions and might sometimes be the duty of the Prime Minister to communicate with the representatives of foreign States upon matters which had a bearing upon their mutual relations.

" I conceived, therefore, that I was doing good service to both [nations] by enabling you in such manner as to you might seem best, to let your Government know the impression which General Butler's Proclamation had produced in this country. I at the same time implied a hope that the United States Government would not allow itself to be represented in such matters by such a person as the author of that Proclamation. This hope, I am glad to say, has proved to be well founded ; for we have learnt from dispatches from Lord Lyons that all power over the civil inhabitants of New Orleans has been taken away from General Butler and has been placed in other hands. . . . The Government have shown by superseding him in his civil command that they shared the sentiments which I have expressed, and have thereby done themselves honour."

Adams, however, was in a huff from which he was not to be withdrawn. He was indignant that Lord Palmerston should thus have gone out of his way to read his countrymen a lesson in humanity and decorum.[1] He wrote a final letter to say that he understood the Prime Minister had retracted his first precipitate charges, and added that—

" the difficulties in the way of this anomalous form of proceeding seem to me to be so grave, and the disadvantage under which it places those persons who may be serving as diplomatic representatives of foreign countries at this Court so serious, as to make it my painful duty to say to your lordship that I must hereafter, so long as I remain here in a public capacity, decline to entertain any similar correspondence."

It is a most curious episode in diplomacy and the letters deserve to be read at length. For a time the Adamses gave up going to the Palmerston receptions ; but Lady Palmerston managed that the quarrel should not last long, and the Prime Minister and the American envoy were soon friends again.

The year 1862 was marked by the spread of the Cotton Famine, caused by the blockade of the Southern ports, when hundreds of British mills were closed and their operatives were idle and hungry ; the crisis lasted well into the following year. Naturally, the friends of the Confederacy were not slow to use this grave situation to promote the cause of official recognition. Many members of Parliament were already pledged to support a measure which would " place the Confederate States amongst the Governments of the world." But not all of them were of the weight and standing of W. E. Gladstone, then Chancellor of the Exchequer.

What happened was this : On September 14, Palmerston, conceiving that McClellan was beaten and Washington captured, admitted British intervention to be possible. Russell proposed to call a Cabinet meeting to consider intervention. Granville protested ; whereupon Gladstone felt that the time was come to force Palmerston's hand. He was

[1] As a matter of fact General Butler had by no means intended to deliver the ladies of New Orleans over to the " unbridled licence of an unrestrained soldiery." He had merely wished to frighten the viragoes amongst them, young and old, into more seemly behaviour.

engaged to speak at Newcastle on October 7; the occasion
seemed a good one to foreshadow the policy of the Government of which he was a member. He therefore made his
celebrated speech in which he virtually told President Lincoln
and the Northern leaders that they might as well admit
defeat—all the world saw that the Union was ended.

" Jefferson Davis and other leaders of the South have
made an army; they are making, it appears, a navy, and
they have made, what is more than either, a nation."

One can imagine Adams's feelings when he read that
deliverance in *The Times* the following day. But not he
alone was outraged. Palmerston himself, who had previously
refused to have his hand forced by Russell, was equally
indignant. Sir George Cornewall-Lewis arose in the House
and repudiated the Chancellor of the Exchequer. As for
Russell, while publicly deprecating Gladstone's indiscretion,
he was privately urging the Cabinet to intervene. The
Cabinet met on October 23, and again on November 11,
and decided not to intervene.

" Russell [wrote Gladstone in his diary] rather turned tail.
He gave way without resolutely fighting out his battle.
However, though we decline for the moment, the answer is
put upon grounds and in terms which leave the matter very
open for the future. . . . Palmerston gave to Russell's
proposal a feeble and half-hearted support."

The odd thing is that on October 23, when Russell and
Gladstone were doing their best to persuade their colleagues,
the former told Adams that it was—

" still their intention to adhere to the rule of perfect neutrality
in the struggle and to let it come to its natural end without
the smallest interference, direct or otherwise.
" But he could not say what circumstances might happen
from month to month in the future. I observed that the
policy he mentioned was satisfactory to us, and asked if I
was to understand him as saying that no change was now
proposed. To which he gave his assent." [1]

[1] Adams to Seward.

It is doubtful, however, if Russell quite deserves the opprobrium forty years later cast upon him by the Minister's son in *The Education of Henry Adams*. Russell and Gladstone did believe that the time for intervention was ripe ; but they could not carry their colleagues with them and so had to put the best face on the matter with the American Minister they could. Russell did not immediately abandon his position : he had distinctly intimated that official action would be governed by circumstances " which might happen, from month to month "—and another victory by Lee might completely change the outlook.

All this time Adams had not been without warning. As far back as July he had intimated to Seward the possibility of a joint Anglo-French proposal for intervention or mediation. To this Seward had returned as firm an injunction as ever came from his pen. Adams was forbidden to debate, hear, receive, entertain or transmit any communication of the kind.

" If, contrary to our expectations, the British Government either alone or in combination with any other Government should acknowledge the insurgents . . . you will immediately suspend the exercise of your functions."

Meanwhile, Lincoln's Emancipation Proclamation had reached London, receiving anything but a flattering press. It was held to be merely a political dodge, intended to deceive Europe, a mere menace to the South and without any real value or importance—a strange reception for one of the greatest acts and documents in human history ! [1]

This misunderstanding, however, was not of long duration. As soon as the Proclamation was really understood, addresses began to pour into the Legation " in a steady and ever-swelling stream." The heart of the English masses, especi-

---

[1] A single sample of invective will suffice. " Mr. Peacock, M.P. for North Essex, said at Colchester that the Emancipation Proclamation, even if it had been in the interests of the negro, would have been a political crime ; but when we reflect that it was put forth, not in the interest of the negro or of civilization, but that it was merely a vindictive measure of spite and retaliation upon nine millions of whites struggling for their independence, it was one of the most devilish acts of fiendish malignity which the wickedness of man could ever have conceived."—*The Times*, October 1862.

ally those who worshipped in the temples of Nonconformity, began to expand. A great meeting at Exeter Hall in January 1863 afforded a conclusive manifestation, which the Government could not ignore, of sympathy with the North. As Richard Cobden wrote to Sumner :

" That meeting has had a powerful effect on our newspapers and politicians. It has closed the mouths of those who have been advocating the side of the South."

Yet although the English people were won over, it was otherwise with the upper classes, whose attribution of base motives to Lincoln and the Northern leaders was afterwards atoned for in shame and contrition. England had long pointed the figure of scorn at America for not freeing her slaves ; now that she had freed them, it was denounced as a danger and a cruel injustice to the brave slave-owners of the South !

No wonder Adams could write in his Diary :

" Thus it is that the utter hollowness of the former indignation against America for the upholding of slavery is completely exposed. The motives of that censure, as for the present emotion, are jealousy, fear and hatred. It is impossible for me to express the contempt I feel for a nation which exhibits itself to the world and posterity in this guise. It is a complete forfeiture of the old reputation for manliness and honesty."

The story of the *Alabama* and the " Laird rams " is a familiar one to the student of Anglo-American history. It is the theme of numerous volumes and so need be no more than briefly summarized here. The Confederacy in 1862 sadly lacked war vessels, and Messrs. Laird of Liverpool were prepared to furnish them, if it could safely be done. Lawyers were found who put such a construction upon the British Neutrality Act as seemed to enable such vessels to be built for a foreign Power. So a large commerce destroyer provisionally known as the " 290 " and afterwards world-celebrated as the *Alabama* was forthwith begun at Liverpool. But whatever the Crown lawyers thought, Minister Adams was convinced that the Neutrality Act was being violated, and also that the " 290 " would sail out to sea on completion and inflict vast damage on Northern shipping if he did not somehow prevent it.[1] There thus ensued a protracted series of incidents which, as one American historian has remarked, would have appealed to "the writer of opera-bouffe libretto or to Dickens for his account of the Circumlocution Office."[2]

Minister Adams, however, protested in vain, and so, on July 28, 1862, the *Alabama* steamed down the Mersey on a pretended trial trip and never returned to dock. She was manned, gunned and equipped on the high seas—and thereafter no Northern vessel was safe.

Simultaneously, orders had been placed by the Confederacy for a couple of ironclad "rams" at half a million dollars apiece, to be ready in the spring of 1863. Adams again protested, and this time his protest had an ominous ring. If these Confederate ironclads were allowed to steam out, it would certainly mean war. The *Alabama* was now full on her course of destruction. But these rams must be stopped. Only, how was it to be done? A long contest ensued between the agents for the Confederacy in Europe (Mason in London was but a weak tool in their hands) and Minister Adams, for the favour of Lord Russell.

It has never been explained why Jefferson Davis chose Mason as his agent for London when he made so good a choice as Slidell for Paris.[3] As Henry Adams afterwards wrote:

"The Confederacy had plenty of excellent men to send

---

[1] Rhodes : *History of the United States.*

[2] Henry Adams wrote on June 27 : " What will be the result of yesterday's work I can't say, but I can guess. Our present position is this : There is no law in England which forbids hostile enterprises against friendly nations. The Government has no power to interfere with them. Any number of *Alabamas* may now be built, equipped, manned and dispatched from British ports, openly for belligerent purposes ; and provided they take their guns on board *after* they've left the harbour, and not while in dock, they are pursuing a legitimate errand. Of course, this is crowner's quest law ; crazy as the British Constitution ; and would get England soon into war with every nation on the sea. The question now is whether the Government will mend it. Mr. Cobden told me last night that he thought they would."

[3] One can divine how small a figure Mason cut in London. Henry Adams wrote (June 6, 1862) : " I hear very little about our friend Mason. He is said to be very anxious and to fear a rebellion within the rebellion. He has little or no attention paid him except as a matter of curiosity, though occasionally we are told of his being at dinner somewhere or other."

to London, but few who were less fitted than Mason. . . . He enjoyed a great opportunity ; he might have figured as a new Benjamin Franklin, with all society at his feet ; he might have roared as a lion of the season and made the social path of the American Minister almost impossible."

Henry Adams wondered that such a man as J. Q. Lamar of Mississippi had not been sent : a man of—

" presence, tact and honour. London society would have delighted in him ; his stories would have won success ; his manners would have made him loved ; his oratory would have swept every audience ; even Monckton Milnes could never have resisted the temptation of having him to breakfast between Lord Shaftesbury and the Bishop of Oxford."

As it happened, Adams's chief antagonist was John Slidell in Paris. He had gained over France to his side, and a French firm ostensibly became the owners of the British-built rams. A Cotton Loan of £3,000,000 was floated. All was ready for the *coup* of forcing the Government to recognize the Confederacy. A member of Parliament, Roebuck, drafted his famous resolution alleging that Napoleon III was ready to acknowledge the South, and on July 4 Mason publicly stated his opinion that General Lee was already master of Washington. On that very day the first of the Laird rams took the water at Birkenhead. Then events went wrong for the Confederacy. The Parliamentary debate revealed the falsity of the intervention conspiracy and the conspirators. Roebuck, disavowed by the Emperor and demolished by John Bright, withdrew his motion for recognition on the 13th ; on the 16th arrived news of a " three days' battle at Gettysburg " ; and on the morning of the 19th Adams wrote :

" When I came down I found on my table a private telegram, which, as usual, I opened with trepidation. It proved to be an announcement from Mr. Seward that Vicksburg had surrendered on the 4th."

Few had expected Vicksburg to fall. News of victory was sadly needed. But although it strengthened Adams's hand, it did not solve his difficulties. Lord Russell had not yet acted officially and the rams were almost ready to steam down the Mersey. Again and again Adams launched his protests and warnings, efforts to avert the danger. Actual menace he avoided until the last moment, when he telegraphed Russell (September 5) the sentence : "*It would be superfluous in me to point out to your lordship that this is war.*"

It was decisive. Three days later the Government issued orders that the vessels should be detained. Adams had won the battle, and his opponents, Slidell and Mason, had lost. Adams afterwards wrote :

" Friday (September 4th) I gave up all for lost, and made preparation for the catastrophe. On Saturday I got news of a prospect of a change. . . . This is rather close shaving. Even now I scarcely realize the fact of our escape."

" The tribulation of fourteen months," remarks his eldest son, " had come to an end, and thenceforth all went well. Mr. Adams had now established his own position, as well as the position of his country, at the Court of St. James ; nor was either again challenged."

Poor Mason abandoned the field ; less than two weeks after the detention of the rams was officially announced, he addressed a farewell letter to Lord Russell, and shook the dust of England from his feet and withdrew to join Slidell in Paris.

"*The Times* [wrote Adams to Seward] distinctly admits this to be a relief to the Government ; though I confess myself at a loss to understand how he annoyed them. The selection of Mr. Mason to come here was an unfortunate one from the outset. I can scarcely imagine an agency to have been more barren of results." [1]

During all this time of ordeal Adams as American Minister had suffered from the presence in London of numerous amateur diplomatists who had come over or been sent over from Washington to aid him in its duties. His son describes these emissaries as belonging to four distinct types :

" (1) The roving diplomat, irregularly accredited by the

[1] Mason's career was over. Remaining in Europe until the close of the war, he then returned to Virginia by way of Canada, and, broken in spirit and fortune, died there in 1871. Slidell died in England the same year, surviving his brother envoy by only three months.

State Department; (2) the poaching diplomat, accredited to one Government, but seeking a wider field of activity elsewhere; (3) the volunteer diplomat, not accredited at all, but in his own belief divinely commissioned at that particular juncture to enlighten foreign nations generally, and Great Britain in particular; and (4) the special agent, sent out by some department of the Government to accomplish, if possible, a particular object." [1]

It was nothing, of course, to what the Embassies at London and Paris had to put up with half a century later, during the Great War; but it was enough to move Adams to remonstrance.

"It cannot be denied [he wrote privately] that ever since I have been here the almost constant interference of Government agents of all kinds has had the effect, however intended, of weakening the position of the Minister. Most of all has it happened in the case of Mr. Evarts, whom the newspapers here have all insisted to have been sent to superintend my office in all questions of international law. I doubt whether any Minister has ever had so much of this kind of thing to contend with."

But with the formal rupture between the Confederacy and the British Government and Mason's departure from London all this annoyance ceased. During the remaining period of Adams's mission he enjoyed a position unequalled in prestige by that of any of his predecessors. He had finally succeeded in winning the confidence of both the British Government and the people, and the success of the Federal Government in the field only confirmed his own secure status.

The correspondence relating to the American claims for losses in respect of the *Alabama* was taken up with Lord Russell in 1864 and conducted voluminously throughout the following year. The publication of Adams's arguments greatly added to his reputation, and these eventually became the basis of the American case in the arbitration years later at Geneva.

At the beginning of 1865 Henry Adams wrote:

"In one sense society is much more agreeable now than it used to be. I no longer feel any dread of conversation

[1] C. F. Adams, Jr.: *Charles Francis Adams.*

about our affairs. The name of Sherman has of late placed us who are abroad in a very commanding position, and our military reputation is at the head of the nations. You can imagine that this relieves us of our greatest discomfort ; and in fact we now receive compliments where we used to hear nothing but sneers."

When the death of President Lincoln was known in England it evoked universal sorrow, and tributes to his noble character now came from quarters which had formerly distinguished themselves by abuse and disparagement. For weeks the Legation was kept occupied in acknowledging addresses and letters of condolence.

According to the younger Adams—

" the last year in England [1867] was the pleasantest. He himself was already old in society and belonged to the Silurian horizon. The Prince of Wales had come ; Mr. Disraeli, Lord Stanley, and the future Lord Salisbury had thrown into the background the memories of Palmerston and Russell. Europe was moving rapidly, and the conduct of England during the American Civil War was the last thing that London liked to recall. The revolution since 1861 was nearly complete, and for the first time in history the American felt himself almost as strong as an Englishman. He had thirty years to wait before he should feel himself stronger." [1]

Throughout, at the Legation, Mrs. Adams's success and popularity equalled, and at times surpassed, that of her husband. One of her remembered sayings was that " every woman who lived a certain time in England came to look and dress like an Englishwoman, no matter how she struggled." Life at the Legation and for the Adams family—

" grew more and more agreeable and amusing. Minister Adams became, in 1866, almost an historical monument in London ; he held a position altogether his own. His old opponents disappeared. Lord Palmerston died in October 1865 ; Lord Russell tottered on six months longer, but then vanished from power ; and in July 1866 the Conservatives came into office. Traditionally the Tories were easier to deal with than the Whigs, and Minister Adams had no reason to

[1] *The Education of Henry Adams.*

regret the change. His personal relations were excellent and his personal weight increased year by year."

True, in one direction he made enemies at home. The Fenian disturbances after the war gave the London Legation much trouble and anxiety. Minister Adams's view of Irish-American dynamiters and murderers being precisely that taken by the law everywhere, his lack of sympathy with these criminals did not increase his popularity with the Fenian agitators, whether in England, Ireland, Canada or his own land. He was charged with being pro-British, and one Congressman actually proposed his formal impeachment!

Adams insisted on President Johnson's acceptance of his resignation in the spring of 1868.

A generation later James Russell Lowell said of Adams :

" None of our generals in the field, not Grant himself, did us better or more trying service than he in his forlorn outpost of London. Cavour did hardly more for Italy.

" Peace hath her victories
Not less renowned than war."

BIOGRAPHICAL NOTE

C. F. Adams narrowly missed a nomination to the Presidency in 1872. After his great labours during the *Alabama* Tribunal at Geneva, he retired to edit his father's *Memoirs*, to which he devoted several years. He died in 1886.

CHAPTER XVII

JOHNSON AND MOTLEY (1868–1870)

When Adams went home, the President, persuaded that the impending litigation between the two countries called for an eminent legal mind, chose for his successor the veteran Maryland lawyer, Reverdy Johnson.

To Johnson, born in 1796, belongs the distinction of being the oldest Minister, at the date of his original appointment, of any who have ever held the post. He was the son of the Chancellor of his State, and had actually been practising law for over half a century. At twenty-five he had been elected to the State Senate and had been Attorney-General in President Taylor's Cabinet. Subsequently he became a Federal Senator. Johnson was a fearless, sagacious man, who never hesitated to express his opinions and chafed under party shackles. Fifteen years before Reverdy had come to London to argue a case before an Anglo-American Commission, and had made a distinctly favourable impression on the English Bar by his forensic knowledge and dignified bearing.

When Reverdy Johnson reached London (August 18, 1868), Queen Victoria was absent with the Foreign Secretary, Lord Stanley, on the Continent, and so, with time on his hands, he went down to visit the British Premier, Disraeli, at Hughenden Manor, where he met a distinguished party, including Cairns, the Lord Chancellor. Disraeli was glad of the opportunity to greet the new American Minister and give him a cordial welcome. The *Alabama* controversy was fast rising on the horizon, and the atmosphere should be kept as genial as possible. When, a month later, Johnson was received by the Queen at Windsor Castle, he said :

" If (as I am persuaded will be the case) my efforts are

REVERDY JOHNSON.

met in a corresponding spirit by your Majesty's Government, I do not doubt that the few causes which have for a time somewhat disturbed our relations will soon be removed and they will be placed on a more firm and enduring basis than ever."

The chief item in his instructions was to arrange a Convention for the consideration of the *Alabama* claims ; but there was also the Naturalisation measure, which he was charged to press, current conditions rendering it urgent. In Johnson's communications with the Department of State he enjoyed a facility which had not been available to his predecessors—one which was gradually to revolutionize the practice of international diplomacy—the Transatlantic telegraph. It has not always since proved an unmixed advantage—its tendency has been to throw more immediate responsibility on the State Department and less on the man on the spot—but there is no doubt that had the ocean cable existed in times of grave international crisis it would have averted many perils and much evil, if only by informing both the rulers and the ruled of conditions which had altered since a given opinion had been formed or a decision taken. On the other hand, facts are not always paramount—there are states of mind, a moral atmosphere, mutual impressions and personal dispositions which cannot be conveyed instantaneously, and it is well to remember that some of the greatest diplomatic triumphs in the cause of peace and of the national welfare had been carried through without the aid of the trans-oceanic cable—just as some of the worst failures have since been attributable to discussions conducted with greater speed than light.

In the present case Seward would have done better, as the sequel showed, to allow Reverdy Johnson to carry through his negotiations quietly and without interference, without revealing any of the intermediary processes to a highly critical Senate and popular Press. Johnson was making a good impression and creating a favourable atmosphere. On October 7 he reported :

" I continue to receive the strongest evidence from other members of the Government, as well as Lord Stanley and from the English public generally, of the friendly feeling entertained by them all for the Government and citizens of the United States."

He was, therefore, able to arrange a Protocol for Naturalization, and on October 29 cabled Seward that he expected to sign an Alabama Convention in the following month.

He realized, as Seward did not, that the existing Government was precarious and was anxious to complete his arrangements before any political change took place. Seward wanted the proposed Commission to meet in Washington, but Minister Johnson telegraphed him : " London best for *Alabama* claims. All proof here. If umpire is to be European, Washington would much delay settlement." In reply Seward insisted upon the prevalent anti-English prejudice in America—" a highly disturbed national sensibility which would influence public judgment on your action in agreeing to London." The Minister discounted this ; he was confident, he said, of " the good sense of our people and that they would be satisfied with what I have done."

Nevertheless, in the end he was obliged by his Government to go to Stanley and request that the meeting-place should be Washington. To this request the Foreign Secretary agreed. There ensued a difference as to the arbitrator to be chosen, and here agreement was suddenly interrupted in December by the fall of the Disraeli Ministry. Gladstone came into office and Lord Clarendon returned as Foreign Secretary. This was very awkward for the American Minister, who cabled on December 24 :

" Lord Clarendon tells me that he brought your amendment before the Cabinet and that they refuse to convert the Convention into a Protocol and to have it signed at Washington instead of London. They think that this would be disrespectful to the late Government and wholly unnecessary. . . . The provision in your amendment which looks to the contingency that the two Governments might not agree upon the head of some foreign friendly nation as an arbitrator, if the appointment was referred to them, would be to call in question their good faith. Also, the appointment of such an arbitrator of the commissioners would be esteemed so discourteous that no head of a foreign Government so appointed would consent to act and that thereby the Convention would be rendered futile."

"His lordship's long diplomatic experience," added Johnson, "gives to his opinions great weight," and he otherwise made it clear that he agreed with Clarendon. But a fortnight later he cabled that he thought the Government would consent to Seward's amendments, and on January 14, 1869, the Conventions were signed. In forwarding them he wrote :

"This Government have yielded in regard to these claims two grounds heretofore positively assumed by them. First, during the period that Lord Russell was in the Foreign Office, that they would not refer to arbitration at all, our demand in regard to them. And, secondly, during the administration of that office by Lord Stanley, that they would so refer the question of the right of this Government to have recognized the late Confederates as belligerents. Both questions, by the Convention just signed, will be before the commissioners, and on their failure to agree, before the arbitrator.

"I have reason to believe that the abandonment of the grounds originally taken to which I have referred, has been owing in a great measure to the growing friendly feeling for the United States which has been so strongly exhibited since my arrival in this country. Anticipating that that would be the effect, I determined to lose no time in cultivating such a feeling, whilst never forgetting scrupulously to regard the rights and honour of our country. This has been my sole motive in the speeches which I have delivered since reaching England."

Seward wrote that Johnson had attended with "perseverance and fidelity" to his instructions and that the President also approved. In addition to his regular diplomatic labours (which included also a discussion of the San Juan boundary), Johnson had delivered several addresses at public gatherings which attracted considerable attention in the Press. Moreover, he was making many new English friends in addition to the old ones.

When the Queen held her Court there was some curiosity evinced as to what costume the American Minister would wear, and Johnson wrote to the Master of Ceremonies to learn

23

whether he and the members of the Legation would be authorized to appear in the plain evening dress which had been enjoined by Congress in 1867. He was told that her Majesty would make no difficulties, and so the venerable Minister donned at mid-day the costume European fashion prescribes for his sex at nightfall and drove—another sartorial and sable pioneer—to the palace, the cynosure of an amused Cockney populace, who raised three cheers for " Reverend " Johnson. As for the Queen, she only smiled pleasantly ; the courtiers probably thought that, if Reverdy's colleagues of the Diplomatic Corps in their historic and becoming uniform could stand it, they could. Only—if officers, whether diplomatic or naval and military, can pursue their duties in tweeds and bowler hats, why have uniforms at all ? As Ambassador Choate remarked a generation later, " This republican simplicity dodge of ours about ' plain clothes ' is the most impertinent piece of swagger in the world. . . . We single them out from everybody else in a room with a thousand people." [1]

Meanwhile, the Presidential election had been held in America and General Grant had been chosen President. Seward's long régime at the State Department was nearly over, and naturally he and the Chief Executive and the Minister in London were concerned over the fate of the Convention at the hands of a new Senate. Reverdy sent to Washington a long and able résumé of the course he had taken and the frank and friendly manner in which both Stanley and Clarendon had discussed the question.

" I am satisfied [he wrote, February 17] that if the Convention goes into operation, every dollar due on what are known as the *Alabama* claims will be recovered."

But two days later there was an ominous leading article in *The Times* pointing out objections to the Convention, which had just been signed. Johnson sent the article to Washington, where it was read by a new Secretary of State, Elihu B. Washburne, who, however, only filled the post for a few weeks before being transferred as Minister to France. To him Johnson wrote on March 29, resigning the London

[1] Cortissoz : *Whitelaw Reid.*

mission, the resignation to take effect the following July or
August. He was to depart even sooner. The Senate was
clearly hostile. First it objected to the Claims Convention
in that "it only provided for the settlement of individual
claims and not for any that either Government at its own
right might have upon the other." Johnson saw Clarendon
and proposed a modification. But the Foreign Secretary
declined unless Johnson had "express instructions from his
Government," and so the Minister inquired if Washington
would agree to an amendment including all mutual claims.
But that was precisely what the Senate would not do. So
they promptly killed the Convention which he and Clarendon
had drawn up with so much care. The American Minister
advised Clarendon (whose disappointment nearly equalled
his own), adding—

"what I know to be true, that my residence in this country
must have satisfied me ' that it was the desire of the Government and people of England that all differences between the
two countries should be honourably settled and that their
relations with the United States should be of a most friendly
character '—I say that I know this to be true, because
I have seen conclusive evidence of it wherever I have been
since my arrival." [1]

If Minister Johnson entertained further hopes of obtaining
any modification in the Convention they were frustrated by
an unfortunate speech delivered by Senator Charles Sumner,
of which a report was cabled to England.

" If [was Johnson's comment] an opinion may be formed
from the public Press, there is not the remotest chance that the
demands contained in that speech will ever be recognized
by England. It would be an abandonment of the rights and
a disregard of the honour of the Government."

Reverdy Johnson was now impatient to be gone, and sailed
on May 22, without waiting for his letter of recall. He was
ill and dispirited over his failure. To the new Secretary,
Hamilton Fish, he wrote :

" Thus terminates a mission which has been conducted
on my part with zeal and fidelity, which has fulfilled to the

[1] Johnson to Secretary of State, May 4, 1869.

letter all the instructions received from my Government, which has aimed to protect the rights, preserve the honour and promote the interests of our country."

The aged Minister, in truth, had done his best; but the politicians were too much for him.

There was thus, at this juncture, an unhappy tension in Anglo-American relations. Professor Bassett Moore goes so far as to say that "at no time since the war of 1812 had the relations between the United States and Great Britain worn so menacing an aspect as that which they assumed after the close of the Civil War."[1] But if resentment and ill-will existed, it came chiefly from the side of the United States. There was, for one thing, the Fenian agitation and there was the unsettled Fisheries dispute. Above all, in America it was the memory of England's early favour to the Southern Confederacy and the depredations of the *Alabama* which rankled. Lord Stanley had, as we have seen, been perfectly ready to arbitrate on the pecuniary claims for damages, but Seward had insisted on introducing the question of British neutrality. His successor at the State Department, Hamilton Fish, was enough of a statesman to wish the whole business settled amicably, and on the British side Lord Clarendon was of a like mind.

A new Minister, one who enjoyed the friendship of Charles Sumner, who still led the hostile faction in the Senate, might therefore yet stand a chance of success.

John Lothrop Motley was a famous American author, known far and wide for his history of the old Dutch Republic. He was a member of that brilliant group of Boston literary men which comprised Edward Everett, Bancroft, Longfellow, Prescott, Holmes and Lowell. To a handsome person (Lord Byron's widow said he resembled her husband more than any man she had ever met), distinguished manners, literary talent and diligence, Motley joined other qualities, unhappily those which hardly ever make a success in politics or diplomacy. He was impulsive, indiscreet and incurably opinionated. These undesirable traits also distinguished

[1] J. B. Moore : *International Arbitrations.*

his friend Sumner, who, for his part, added a combativeness
bordering on fanaticism.

As a youth of eighteen, Motley had been a fellow-student
with Bismarck at Göttingen, where he learned to speak
German like a native. Nine years later, in search of a career,
he entered the diplomatic service as Secretary of Legation at
St. Petersburg. But he changed his mind after a few
months ; St. Petersburg was too cold, too cheerless, too
expensive. So he came home and embarked upon literature,
conceived the idea of a vast historical work similar in plan
to his friend Prescott's Spanish histories, and by 1856 had
published, at his own expense, his celebrated *Rise of the
Dutch Republic*, which placed him at a bound in the world's
favour. At the height of his literary fame in 1861 his friends
procured him the appointment of Minister at Vienna. Motley
spoke German faultlessly and was a graceful waltzer. He did
very well at Vienna and might have remained there as long
as he chose had he been a little more circumspect and somewhat less petulant. He had a poor opinion of Secretary
Seward and still less of President Andrew Johnson, and he
made no secret of either opinion. When he was taxed with
indiscretions, the Minister promptly mounted his highest
horse. The resignation he needlessly offered was, to his
astonishment, accepted, and he came home to receive the
sympathy of his friends and admirers. Sumner was especially
indignant, and after General Grant's election succeeded in
obtaining from the reluctant and doubtful new President
the appointment of Motley to the Court of St. James.

On the very eve of Motley's departure for London Charles
Sumner arose in the Senate and made a speech which in-
flamed the whole controversy, and caused bitter resentment
in England and amongst the friends of peace in both countries.

According to Sumner, the Queen's Proclamation of May
13, 1861, was the fountain-head of all the disasters that
followed, that in consequence the war was doubled in duration. England therefore had been instrumental in involving
America in an expense exceeding two billion dollars.

Such a doctrine, if supported by President Grant and his
Administration, would have shut the door to any future
negotiation, for England would have risked war rather than

admit its validity. But they did not support it. They believed the Queen's Proclamation had been hasty and unnecessary, but quite within the competence of an independent political Power. Nor was this the extent of Sumner's Jingoist utterance. He insisted that as further reparation and as a preventative of future friction Canada should be ceded to the United States. As Canada had just then formed itself into a Confederation under the British Crown and was entering on a career of autonomous prosperity, the extravagance of the proposal could only excite Canadian derision.

The new Minister being a close friend of Sumner's, whose views bade fair to embarrass the Administration at the outset in its desire to reopen the negotiations frustrated by the rejection of the Johnson-Clarendon Convention, Secretary Fish was at some pains to instruct Motley carefully in writing before his departure. He first courteously showed these instructions to Sumner, who said, on reading them:

"I regret that Mr. Motley's own programme has not been adopted. . . . I wish he were allowed to speak according to his own enlightened discretion."

But Fish declined either to trust to Motley's enlightened discretion or to accept Sumner's emendation of Motley's instructions as regards belligerency.

The instructions read:

"The necessity and the propriety of the original concession of belligerency by Great Britain at the time it was made have been contested and are not admitted. They certainly are questionable, *but* the President regards that concession as a part of the case *only so far* as it shows the beginning and the animus of that course of conduct which resulted so disastrously to the United States."

Thus the Proclamation of Belligerency, from which Sumner dated all the trouble, would disappear from the controversy, save as evidence along with other evidence of injury. Motley was directed "in his social and private intercourse and conversation" to let it be understood "that the United States make such recognition by them [the British] *no ground of complaint.*" [1]

1 Fish to Motley, May 16, 1869.

It is possible that the talented and headstrong historian did not quite take the measure of the elderly, respectable gentleman who was now at the head of the State Department. He seems to have imagined that, with his friend Sumner's backing, he would be able to settle matters in his own way. When he took up any theme or opinion, his practice was to pursue it whole-heartedly, to drive it home with picturesqueness and fervour. Although he had dwelt in England and had many eminent friends in that country, he believed that an assertion of uncompromising patriotism and a demonstration of England's guilt was the best way to achieve what his heart was set upon—a diplomatic *tour de force*. In this way he had, in his notable history, brilliantly attacked Alva and the Spanish Government and ineffaceably blackened the character of every Spaniard, Austrian and Dutchman who had dared oppose his hero, William of Orange. Carefully select the evidence, heighten the colouring, darken the shadows, omit all mitigating factors, and then, framed in splendid rhetoric, hold up the damning picture, confound the culprit and ask the world for its plaudits. It was all quite in his line and seemed to Motley a superb chance.

" I feel [he wrote to Oliver Wendell Holmes, who was afterwards to pen his biography—a melancholy performance for so gentle and trusting a nature] that I am placed higher than I deserve, and at the same time that I am taking greater responsibilities than ever were assumed by me before." [1]

At Washington, while waiting for Secretary Fish to draw up his instructions, the newly-appointed Minister requested permission to examine the archives of the Department. Amongst these he spent weeks. He was in his element, and finally emerged with a voluminous Memoir, embracing every detail and circumstance, every illegality and affront, every speech and offensive gesture of every British skipper during the Civil War that he could cram into its pages. This document he showed to Fish, who glanced through it in surprise, and returned it with the brief remark that " discussion of these points had better be postponed."

Motley was disconcerted; he probably reflected that the Secretary of State was a politician and not an historian.

[1] O. W. Holmes : *John Lothrop Motley : A Memoir.*

Arrived in London early in June, having been cordially received at Liverpool and making a couple of graceful speeches on the way, Motley, without waiting to present his credentials to the Queen, at once plunged into business. At the Legation he found, in the person of First Secretary and Chargé d'affaires Moran, a diplomat whose counsel might have been useful had he taken it; but Motley was impatient and carried things *en grand seigneur* from the first. He sought and obtained an interview with the Earl of Clarendon.

This interview of June 12, 1869, was destined to be memorable in the story of Motley's fortunes. He began by informing the British Foreign Secretary that—

" the refusal of the Senate to give its consent to a convention implied no discourtesy, and that the magnitude of the pending questions and claims required more than the brief statement to which the peculiar delicacy of the circumstances had limited the first announcement."

To which Clarendon observed that his Government had had only " a dry notification of the fact, and they had heard nothing more until Mr. Sumner made his speech."

" It was [he added] an awkward situation and would induce more caution in future, as when dealing with plenipotentiaries from the United States it would be necessary for a Government to remember that there was a greater power behind them—namely, the American Senate."

Motley thereupon reminded his interlocutor that the Senate had always been there and in power from the first, but always used their—

" veto from the best and most patriotic of motives. In the present case they had to deal with an attempt of an expiring administration to settle a momentous affair within six weeks of the incoming of a new President and Senate."

In accordance with his instructions, he then proposed " an interval of calm—so that the public mind might recover from its excitement." Clarendon said he had no objection to a lull, although he thought it " highly objectionable that the question should be hung up on a peg, to be taken down at some convenient moment " for the American Government.

JOHN LOTHROP MOTLEY.

Motley repudiated any underhanded designs on America's part. He did not refrain, however, from mentioning that the President thought that the proposed throwing of dice for umpires might bring about opposite decisions in cases arising out of identical principles, and was objectionable. But, said Clarendon, the throwing of dice or the drawing of lots was no new invention—it was not an uncommon method in arbitration. Motley retorted that " such an aleatory practice was unworthy when disposing of such mighty issues involving the welfare of nations." [1]

The talk then drifted to a reform of the Neutrality laws and by degrees to the Queen's Proclamation of Neutrality of May 13, 1861. This was Motley's chance. He described it as the fountain-head of the disasters caused to the American people by the hands of Englishmen during the war.

" I then stated the opinion of the President in regard to the recognition or concession of Belligerency, saying that the President recognized the right of a sovereign Power to issue proclamations of neutrality between an insurgent portion of a nation and the lawful Government . . . *but that measure must always be taken with a full view of the grave responsibilities assumed.*

" As regarded the Proclamation ' the President wished it to be used when our case should once more be presented only as showing animus *and as being the fountain-head of the disasters which had been caused to the American people*, both individually and collectively, by the hands of Englishmen. Other nations had issued proclamations, but only in the case of Great Britain had there come a long series of deeds injurious to the United States *as the fruits of the Proclamation.'* "

Thus did Motley " ingeniously contrive to inject into his speech to Lord Clarendon the ideas which Mr. Fish had carefully eliminated from his instructions." Clarendon, on the contrary, warmly maintained that the English neutrality had been a fair and sincere neutrality. Motley prudently refused to argue the point just then, but he re-

---

[1] In this he was using his friend Sumner's own words. The objection to drawing lots in choosing an umpire was purely academic.

J. C. Bancroft Davis : *New York Herald*, January 4, 1878.

minded the Foreign Secretary of the responsibility that lay
upon them both to allay international passions and avoid war.
Clarendon became deeply moved.

" He could contemplate [he said] the possibility of war
between Great Britain and any other foreign Power, but
war with America inspired him with abhorrence. He regarded it as a *crimen non nominandum inter Christianos*.
He never could bring himself to look upon Americans as
foreigners." [1]

Motley sympathized with the sentiments, but " confessed
to a despondent feeling sometimes as to the possibility of the
two nations *ever* understanding each other—of the difficulty
at this present moment of their looking into each other's
hearts."

" Yes," agreed Clarendon, " we both have the same Saxon
stubbornness and absolute confidence in ourselves and each
in our own cause. When we quarrel, it is Greek meeting
Greek."

The protracted interview over, Motley returned to the
Legation and penned a full minute of it, which he was very
imprudently moved to send to Downing Street, so that
Clarendon might be under no sort of doubt as to the views
he (Motley) had expressed as being those of the American
Government. The minute was then forwarded to Washington. The disgust and dismay of both the President and
Secretary Fish when they read Motley's statements may
readily be conceived. Grant is said to have uttered a re-
grettably profane ejaculation and to have insisted on Motley's
being recalled at once.

Long afterwards, Grant made a statement about the
incident :

" Mr. Motley [he said] had to be instructed. The instructions were prepared very carefully, and after Governor Fish
and I had gone over them for a last time I wrote an addendum
charging him that above all things he should handle the
subject of the *Alabama* claims with the greatest delicacy.
Mr. Motley, instead of obeying his explicit instructions,
deliberately fell in line with Sumner, and thus added insult
to the previous injury. As soon as I heard of it, I told Fish

[1] Motley to Fish, June 12, 1869.

to dismiss Motley at once. I was very angry indeed, and I have been sorry many a time that I did not stick to my first determination. Mr. Fish advised delay because of Sumner's position in the Senate and attitude on the treaty question. We did not want to stir him up just then." [1]

The Secretary of State was of opinion that, as nothing in writing had passed between the London Legation and the Foreign Office, no harm had been done which could not be rectified by speaking to Thornton, the British Minister at Washington. But there must be no further risk, and future negotiations must be transferred to Washington. Motley might, and probably would be, deeply offended, but that could not be helped. On June 28, therefore, he replied to the Minister and, after mildly approving of his general presentation, mentioned that the President's view with regard to the right of deferring its relations with a warring State " was not conveyed in precise conformity " to his instructions, or " as it would doubtless have been conveyed by you had your communication been made in writing."

" In the meantime [he went on] you may be content to rest the question on the very forcible presentation you have made of the American side of the question. It was strongly done, and if there were expressions used stronger than were required by your instructions, the excess was in the right direction, and, stopping where they do and uttered as they were, it may well be hoped that they may tend to impress the Minister with the seriousness of our application and the grievances we have sustained."

It was, he added, the President's wish that when the negotiations or discussions should be renewed, they should be conducted in Washington.

" I supposed [President Grant stated afterwards] that Mr. Motley would be manly enough to resign after that snub."

The fact that Motley had sent his minute of the interview with Clarendon to the Foreign Secretary himself was then wholly unguessed by the Secretary of State. He learnt this only when (seven weeks later) Motley wrote :

" I find that I have inadvertently omitted to inform you

[1] Interview in *New York Herald*, September 11, 1877.

that my dispatch of June 12 containing a minute record of an official interview with Lord Clarendon was confidentially submitted by me to his lordship."

This was too much to be borne. But Fish had gone away on holiday and did not read Motley's avowal till October. Before this time other dispatches had been received from the Minister in London—dispatches which do not appear to have been cited by any of those who have narrated the story of Motley's dismissal. In one of these, dated July 9, he calls attention to an article in *The Times* on the postponement of negotiations.

" You will [he tells Fish] be struck by the gravity with which that journal assumes that the Neutrality Proclamation, or, more properly speaking, the concession of belligerent rights, has been gradually allowed to drop out of sight by the Republican party and with which it hopes that the question will in time be tacitly abandoned."

But it would not be abandoned by Motley if he could help it.

" When the time arrives for reopening the discussion [he goes on to say] it will probably be found that the emphatically announced concession of belligerency in May 1861—the hurried and unprecedented elevation of an insurrection to equality with an established and friendly Government, and the almost simultaneous invitation to rebels to negotiate . . . are matters *not likely to be dropped out of sight* by the Republican party or by the Americans of any party."

Small wonder if Grant fumed and Motley kept on harping on this forbidden string, actually writing to Fish that he " spoke of it on all possible occasions "—so infinite was his zeal.

" The idea that Mr. Sumner and his speech have been abandoned at home and answered abroad by mere misrepresentations, suppression of text and denunciation, is too erroneous to be suffered to take root. . . . The English people must look steadily at the subject, not as *they* choose to regard it, but as *we* present it to them."

This London envoy was going to be stern and uncompromising with the English. They fancied they were being humiliated. They should know what humiliation meant. Their offence must be brought home to them. Above all, no concessions must be made. It was thus, he reported blandly, that " I am in the habit of conversing with influential persons as opportunity offers."

And before the Secretary's initial rebuke had reached him he wrote (July 15): " The extensive disasters resulting from that hurried recognition of belligerency have always impressed me," and then proceeded to demonstrate it all over again.

In the meantime (September 25) Fish, believing that sufficient time had elapsed to begin discussions in Washington, forwarded to Motley " a dispassionate exposition of the American complaint against Great Britain," covering many pages of foolscap, closing thus :

" At the present stage of the controversy the sole object of the President is to state the position and maintain the attitude of the United States in the various relations and aspects of this grave controversy. It is the object of this paper (which you are at liberty to read to Lord Clarendon) to state calmly and dispassionately what this Government seriously considers the injuries it has suffered. It is not written in the nature of a claim, for the United States make no demand on account of the injuries they feel they have sustained. In effect, they left the question of a settlement in the hands of the Queen's Government, and would be ready at the proper time to entertain any proposition for a solution."

Fish further expressed the hope that the British Government would be willing to open a discussion at Washington.

Clarendon explained that her Majesty's Government " cannot make any proposition or run the risk of another unsuccessful negotiation " until they know a little more clearly the basis upon which America was disposed to begin negotiations. This was only natural, considering the views Motley had expressed and which Senator Sumner was continuing to urge in the United States.

At last, after an unusual delay, Fish read Motley's avowal about his Clarendon minute. He wrote (October 11):

" When on June 28 last I acknowledged the highly

interesting account of your interview with Lord Clarendon and of the views which you there presented to him as the views entertained by the President upon the subject of the recognition of the late insurgents as belligerents . . . I was not aware that your statement of the conversation had been submitted to his lordship for his verification.

"As without an explanation his lordship may naturally be surprised at finding some of the views purporting to come from the President inconsistent with the views contained in the paper dated September 25 last, I must ask you to explain to him that your presentation and treatment of the subject discussed at that interview were in part disapproved by me in my communication of June 28 last."

This ought to have been enough to awaken Motley's suspicions and to put him on his guard. Nothing further reached him from the State Department about the *Alabama* claims. But Motley was a restless soul, and it may be that Sumner was urging him to an unauthorized activity.

During the autumn Motley's talk in society was such that Sir John Rose, a Canadian statesman in London, felt impelled to write Secretary Fish " expressing fear and regret that Mr. Motley's bearing in his social intercourse was throwing obstacles in the way of a future settlement." Fish mentioned this to Sumner, who disregarded it, and Fish " felt unwilling to push an inquiry and thought it better to submit for a while to misrepresentation at London " rather than arouse Sumner to increased opposition to the San Domingo Treaty, which the President was just then anxious to negotiate.

All along, Motley in London had not been without many distractions. His mind and interests were fully occupied. He was presented to Queen Victoria at Windsor on June 18, the anniversary of Waterloo, and reported that it was " impossible for any sovereign to receive a foreign envoy with more marked manifestations of friendly disposition."

Perhaps her Majesty would have been a little less cordial if she had suspected the extent of the American historian's vindictiveness and the design he harboured of punishing and humiliating her subjects for the Royal Proclamation of eight years before. But, at least, in making his bow at Court, Motley was sound on the dress question.

"It is for Congress [he wrote] to decide whether on the whole it is better that an American representative should be rendered somewhat uncomfortably conspicuous abroad on State occasions by wearing a dress in sharp contrast to that of all other persons present ; or whether it might be considered a mark of respect to our own Government that its diplomatic agents should wear some uniform on public occasions, showing them to be in the service of the Republic ; for the same reasons which make it decorous for officers of the army and navy and for consuls to wear the insignia of their country and profession when they meet at official ceremonies with foreigners of the same official rank."

At any rate, small-clothes, silk stockings and shoe-buckles were insisted on for drawing-rooms, and Motley said he would wear these unless ordered not to do so. And he wore them.

Motley once, with Henry Adams, ventured upon the dictum that the London dinner and the English country-house were "the perfection of human society." In recalling this, the younger man, who had spent seven years in London, reflected :

"Motley could not have thought the dinner itself was perfect, since there was not then—outside of a few bankers or foreigners—a good cook or a good table in London, and nine out of the ten dinners that Motley ate came from Gunter's and all were alike. . . . He could not think that Motley meant to praise English *cuisine.* . . . Equally little could Motley have meant that dinners were good to look at. Nothing could be worse than the toilettes : nothing less artistic than the appearance of the company. One's eyes might be dazzled by family diamonds, but, if an American woman were present, she was sure to make comments about the way the jewels were worn. If there was a well-dressed lady at table she was either an American or ' fast.' " [1]

Again :

"The manners of English society were notorious, and the taste was worse. . . . Probably he [Motley] meant that, in his favourite houses, the tone was easy, the talk was good and the standard of scholarship was high. . . . To the literary American it well seemed perfection since he could

[1] *The Education of Henry Adams.*

find nothing of the sort in America. Within the narrow limits of this class, the American Legation was fairly at home : possibly a score of houses, all Liberal and all literary."

Hearing nothing further from Washington about the *Alabama* claims, the Minister passed his winter and spring agreeably, although, as Sir John Rose testified, his mind and talk was still full of the interdicted subject. There were other diplomatic matters, however, to occupy him—the Naturalization Treaty, the proposed Consular Convention and the release of American Fenians in British prisons. But Motley had not been forgotten by his Government. In June 1870 Lord Clarendon was ailing, and on the 27th he died.[1] A fortnight later Motley received this letter from the Secretary of State at Washington, dated June 30 :

" I am instructed by the President to say that he finds it desirable to make a change in the mission to England and that he wishes to allow you the opportunity of resigning in case you feel inclined to do so."

Motley at once telegraphed :

" I respectfully request you to inform the President that I feel compelled to decline the offer."

Next day (July 14) the London newspapers informed the world that General Schenck had been appointed Minister to London and was confirmed by the Senate—the whole sequence only occupying forty-eight hours !

It was a stunning blow ; Motley rallied from it sufficiently to write to Secretary Fish the same day :

" It is not my wish to embarrass an Administration which I have always faithfully supported, but I owe something to myself.

" Were I now to make use of the permission accorded me to resign it would seem that I did so in order to avoid a removal which I knew to be just and to escape a stigma

---

[1] When the news of Lord Clarendon's death reached Washington, President Grant telegraphed that " his death removes a statesman whose fame belongs to the world, and whose loss will be felt by other nations than that in whose behalf he laboured for the advance of civilization and in the interests of peace." Grant seems throughout to have had every confidence in Clarendon ; his death undoubtedly removed one reason for Motley's retention.

which I felt to be deserved. It would be difficult to treat an envoy of the United States accredited to the Sovereign of a powerful Government with a more marked disrespect for his official position or for his feelings as a loyal citizen of the Republic than has been done in my case. . . . No Minister at this Court was ever removed by the President who appointed him.

" It has generally been admitted in our country that power and responsibility are inseparable, and that republican institutions are founded upon reason, justice and honour, not upon arbitrary will. Yet the Government of the United States has deliberately wrought as much injury to my reputation in an honourable profession as it could do, and there is not a charge against me.

" The egotism of this dispatch is not in accordance with my taste or my feelings, but the Government has placed me in a position in which self-defence is imperative. This much I owe to the dignity of an office which has been insulted in my person, and to my own character, which has been subjected to malignant and anonymous attacks."

The upshot was that Motley flatly refused to resign. As his expostulations on the subject were not answered from Washington, he went on with his business at the Legation for several months until at last in December the President ordered him peremptorily to place the Legation in Secretary Moran's hands and retire, " an indignity, I believe, to which no public Minister of the United States has ever before been subjected. History will decide upon whom the discredit of the transaction rests."

History—had not Motley always relied too much on History, whose oracles he had the splendid but dangerous gift of interpreting according to his own fashion ?

The President furthermore wrote to the Queen announcing his Minister's recall, and sent the letter to Motley, who was advised by Lord Granville, the new Foreign Secretary, to await her Majesty's return from Scotland.

So Motley and his devoted wife [1] and daughter left the Legation and sought seclusion while he prepared a lengthy apology for the State Department and the world, which never

---

[1] To Mrs. Motley, who was the daughter of Park Benjamin, her husband's dismissal was a shock from which she never recovered.

24

saw the light.   It was to be his last dispatch ; it covered many pages of foolscap and is a pathetic, unread document.

" It would be impossible [he wrote] for any diplomatic agent to believe himself as more thoroughly possessing the confidence of the Government which he had the honour to serve than I supposed myself to enjoy at that moment. No intimation of a contemplated change had been made to me, no shadow of a difference of opinion existed between the President and his Government and myself as to our relations with Great Britain or any other Power, as to the general policy of his administration, and I was at that very period engaged in as delicate and confidential a diplomatic correspondence with yourself and the British Government upon several important matters as could well be confided by a Government to its foreign agent."

How, then, could such " monstrous injustice " be ?   He could not tell.

What added to the pathos of this last dispatch was that, in his agitation, Motley neglected to sign it and the Chargé d'affaires sent it on to its destination, unsigned.

Motley's faculty for self-deception was notable.   To his friend Oliver Wendell Holmes he wrote (December 27) :

" I truly believe that I found myself exactly at the moment when I was expelled from my post in a position in which I could do much good. . . . I know that I could have done as well as any man to avert war and even animosity between two great nations and at the same time guard the honour and interests of our nation."

On the whole, the world may be content to accept the summing up of the Assistant Secretary of State, Bancroft Davis, who knew all the facts :

" He [President Grant] had already determined upon the removal as far back as October 1869.   Motley no longer enjoyed the official confidence of the Secretary of State.   He was worse than useless in London, should the desired resumption of negotiations take place.   He had been retained in office after a great breach of duty, only at the request of the Secretary of State—a request made partly in the hope of eventually gaining Sumner's support to the English policy, partly in the desire of not offending him, and, in my judgment, in no small degree from the high personal regard which the Secretary had for Motley."

This, then, answers the questions asked by the historian and his partisans, "Why had he been suddenly dismissed from office thirteen months after the Clarendon dispatch? Why had the Government gone on employing him?"

BIOGRAPHICAL NOTES

Johnson resumed the practice of law, dying in 1876. His successor Motley remained in Europe engaged in literary work, but broken in spirit, especially after his wife's death. He himself died in 1877 and is buried at Kensal Green. His daughter Lily married Sir William Harcourt and survived until 1928.

CHAPTER XVIII

SCHENCK, PIERREPONT AND WELSH (1871–1879)

A few weeks after Motley had left the Legation in London the Canadian, Sir John Rose, turned up in Washington (January 9, 1871) and on the very evening of his arrival dined with Secretary Fish. He stated that he had been requested by the British Government unofficially, as being " half-American and half-Engish," to ascertain what could be done for settling the *Alabama* claims. After a lengthy conversation, Rose cabled to London and got further instructions from the Foreign Office.

As a result, a Joint High Commission was agreed upon to meet in Washington, and this was organized February 27, 1871. Amongst the members to be appointed to this commission was an affable, bearded, middle-aged Congressman, named Robert Cumming Schenck.

It had long been the custom for English writers to descant upon the gifts, moral, intellectual and political, of the Mother Country to America, with little or no appreciation of the fact that there could be any reciprocal contributions from the opposite side of the Atlantic. Yet by the middle of the last century American authors were being widely read. American inventions were invading British industry and the wealth of a philanthropic American, George Peabody, was relieving the severer hardships of the London poor. Barnum had come, and Artemus Ward, to illustrate the lighter, though characteristic, traits of American life. In the appointment of General Schenck to the Court of St. James, the President was not only sending a personal friend he could trust to represent the policy of the Administration, but he was instrumental in conveying a further boon from America to a London society in search of novelty.

The connexion between diplomacy and draw-poker is

R. C. SCHENCK.

not very recondite. General Schenck was one of the pioneers and the leading exponent of the game in its native haunts. What " Cavendish " was to whist, " Schenck " was to poker. He was the author of the standing exposition in which he laid down principles which, incredible as it may seem to-day, caused a sensation in London in 1871 and evoked the mild reprobation of several Nonconformist clergymen and ultra-moralists. But to the race of diplomatists the code offered nothing unfamiliar.

" In the game of poker [Schenck stated], every player is for himself and against all others ; and to that end will not let any of his cards be seen nor betray the value of his hand by change of countenance or any other sign. It is a great object to mystify your adversaries up to the ' call,' when hands have to be shown. To this end it is permitted to chaff or talk nonsense, with a view of misleading your adversaries as to the value of your hand without unreasonably delaying the game.

" To ' bluff ' is to take the risk of betting high enough on a poor hand, or a worthless one, to make all the other players lay down their hands without seeing or ' calling ' you.

" A skilful player will watch and observe what each player draws, the expression of the face, the circumstances and manner of betting, and judge, or try to judge, the value of each hand opposed to him accordingly.

" The player with a worthless hand had generally better begin by ' raising ' when he goes in, or else nobody will be likely to believe in his pretended strong hand." [1]

But enough has been quoted to demonstrate the close affinity between this exciting Western pastime and the game of diplomacy.

When the High Commission had finished its labours in Washington, and a Treaty of Arbitration had been agreed upon, General Schenck sailed for England, and on June 6 arrived in London. Exciting European events had been happening during the previous six months to engage the attention of the American Chargé d'affaires. There had been

[1] *Draw-Poker*, by the Hon. Robert C. Schenck, Envoy Extraordinary and Minister Plenipotentiary from the United States near her Britannic Majesty.

the Siege of Paris by the Germans, and the constant communication with the besieged American Minister, Washburne. Then had come the Capitulation, followed by the
terrible episodes of the Commune. There was also further
trouble about the Fenians, and negotiations with Spain
which had necessitated the sending of the First Secretary,
General Adam Badeau, to Madrid. Schenck's arrival was
followed by that of Bancroft Davis of the State Department
with the copy of the treaty, which now only awaited exchange.
In his chief, Lord Granville's, absence Lord De Grey (afterwards Marquess of Ripon) called on the new Minister at his
lodgings and told him that opposition to certain clauses had
developed and that the Government would be interrogated
in Parliament.

Roundell Palmer and other lawyers held, for example, that
the second rule in Article VI would restrict or forbid the sale
by a neutral of arms and other military supplies in the
ordinary course of commerce.

Sir Stafford Northcote, however, had assured the Government that the rule was never so construed by the Washington
negotiators, and Secretary Fish cabled his surprise that there
should be any question or hesitancy about ratification in view
of her Majesty's solemn engagement and promise in the
powers given to the High Commissioners. Schenck shrewdly
showed this private message to Granville, quietly begging him
to pay no attention to its querulous tone, and Granville
" promised to forget it."

When the Washington Treaty came up in the Lords
Schenck was in his place in the Diplomats' Gallery. The
debate was opened by Earl Russell in a speech " nearly
two hours long, uttered in a low voice, heard with difficulty,
tedious, fault-finding, and tending to dampen rather than to
fire up the opposition. I suppose that age must have taken
from this able and eminent man much of his former energy
and force."

Publication of ratification was held back for a fortnight or
so owing to Canadian susceptibilities regarding the fisheries.
But on June 7 the exchange of ratifications took place at a
quarter past two o'clock p.m. at the Foreign Office.

" I note the exact time and place [Schenck reported], as

marking an interesting and momentous point in the history of the two countries and their Governments."

There was no particular ceremony, but "there was an interchange of hearty mutual congratulations that we had completed an act which has not only removed our present serious difficulties, but established, we hope, lasting peace and better understanding between the two countries."

Schenck had not yet been presented to the Queen, and his presentation, when it took place, was an unusual one. It was fixed for one o'clock on June 23 at Buckingham Palace, to be followed by a royal garden party. But just as the Minister was ready a message came from Lord Granville saying that he had just received a telegram from the Queen regretting that she would not be able, after all, to receive the American Minister on that day.

" This seemed singular, and I replied by a private note to Lord Granville, expressing my surprise. The subsequent explanation was that her Majesty had a headache. Giving up, then, the prospect of attending a party in the garden at Buckingham Palace, with my daughters . . . their presentation depending on my first being officially received, and supposing that all was postponed indefinitely, I went off to other engagements."

The Minister got into his carriage, and was driving out, when a message came in hot haste from the Foreign Secretary. The Queen would, after all, receive General Schenck at the garden party and cards were enclosed for the young ladies. And so, amidst the crowd on the lawn and in the rain (which, the Minister adds, " was falling as usual "), the representative of the United States, in the blue uniform of a general, stepped forward and presented his letter of credence to the little, middle-aged lady in widow's weeds, who, despite her headache, was " very affable and gracious." General Schenck made his speech, and the Queen responded, not forgetting to make an allusion to the satisfactory agreement just concluded.

His military uniform spared Schenck any of the usual heart-burnings at the Legation on the subject of diplomatic dress.

And now came the business, which proved to be enormous,

of preparing the American case for the arbitration at Geneva, provided for by the treaty. It was Schenck's idea to pump systematically all the friendly English who knew, and might consent to reveal, the secret history of the *Alabama* affair. He wrote to Washington asking especially for " a sharp lawyer to take such testimony." While the Minister was bending his energies to this work, there came an interruption from that troublesome South American republic, Venezuela. Owing money to European countries, she was seeking shelter behind the United States. Germany wished Great Britain to unite in a diplomatic declaration to Caracas, coupled with a demand for reparation. But Schenck was convinced America would not countenance such a European combination. He was intensely suspicious of Germany's motives, and wrote (July 29) :

" She is flushed with recent military successes. She aspires to become the leading Power in Europe and in the world. She has a navy now, larger and stronger than ever before, and . . . casts her eyes even across the Atlantic in search of something that shall help to mark her influence and exhibit her naval strength and give it employment."

An opinion which was exactly applicable just forty years later.

Under the Treaty of Washington, the Emperor of Brazil had been named to select one of the arbitrators, and being just then in London, Schenck called on him. To his surprise Dom Pedro informed him :

" I have nothing now to do with public affairs. I am not Emperor of Brazil while away, but only a private citizen travelling."

Such an attitude was unexpected, and both Lord Granville and Schenck were greatly taken aback. It involved delay, but there was no help for it.

" If [wrote the American Minister to his Government] the Emperor is resolved *not* to exercise any act or duty whatsoever as a sovereign during his absence abroad, enough has been said. We cannot argue with him, but must await his return to Rio."

When the Washington Treaty had been debated in the Lords the American Minister had been present, had listened to Lord Russell's exposition of it and offered no protest. It was now held at Geneva that there was an "implied acquiescence in the meaning then given to the instrument."

"It would [commented Schenck scornfully] keep the diplomatic agents of the United States in London and of Great Britain in Washington rather busily occupied, during the sessions of Congress and of Parliament, if they were required to state and report whatever might be said in those assemblies at the risk otherwise of being bound by all the declarations made by legislators!"

The Arbitration Commission began its sessions at Geneva on December 15, 1871. When they had been sitting for weeks a rock was encountered which nearly caused the ship to founder. Secretary Fish, in his instructions to the American agent, Bancroft Davis, did not urge the extravagant Sumner claim for the whole costs of the war, but stipulated for all the other indirect claims.

Disraeli characterized such American claims as "preposterous and wild"—they were like the exaction of "tribute from a conquered people." Gladstone said they transcended every limit hitherto known or heard of, which not even the last extremities of war would force a people with a spark of spirit to submit to, at the point of death.

"The American Government [says Mowat] did not wish to press the indirect claims, but it was compelled to do so by public opinion. . . . The indirect claims were quite logical, but they were not sensible."

During the whole spring of 1872, while the American claims were being argued at Geneva, Minister Schenck was indefatigable. He kept the cables incessantly throbbing with his messages, and the corresponding tolls made old-fashioned diplomatists stare.

"Our policy is clearly [he reminded Fish] to show in every way and in all departments of the Government our willingness and determination to abide by and carry out the treaty and leave Great Britain the whole responsibility of any rupture or repudiation."

On April 23 Fish wrote to Schenck that the American Government " would at any time willingly have waived the indirect claims for *any* equivalent."

Schenck's suggestion was that, in consideration of the United States agreeing not to press these claims, Great Britain should withdraw her pretensions of title to the island of San Juan under the Treaty of 1846 and accept the Canal de Haro as the boundary line, which would still give her the whole of Vancouver Island according to the intention of that treaty. But the British Government would make no concession.

On April 24 Lord Granville called on Schenck and told him flatly that, if the American answer should persist in the claim for indirect damages, the British Government would ratify their commissioner's refusal to proceed with the arbitration—the claim must be withdrawn before June 15. Schenck cabled that he thought it only too probable that the Government would yield to the popular clamour and take a course that would put an end to the treaty. At the same time, he observed :

" If there is to be a disastrous termination of all our work, from which we had hoped so much good for the two countries and for the world, it will be not a little owing to the course of some of our own citizens."

Great Britain was being patently encouraged by the tone of some of the American journals, by the inconsiderate declarations of some public men, and by much writing, telegraphing and conversation, though not mischievously intended. All this talk had led Britain to think that the best men in America wished their own Government to recede from its position.

At last, on May 9, Schenck asked Lord Granville—

" to agree, in order to save time, that negotiations on this point might be considered at Washington, but he declines. It would relieve me from a painful responsibility. His lordship's last words, after more than two hours' conversation, were as follows :

" ' I carefully avoid anything like menace, but in consequence of the views and information you have presented to me yesterday and to-day, I take an unfavourable view of the chances of any settlement.' I told him [added Schenck sorrowfully] I was getting to be of the same mind."

During the height of the crisis there occurred almost daily and sometimes semi-daily interviews, hours long, besides notes, letters and telegrams, between Lord Granville and the American Minister.

On the evening of May 9 it seemed as if all hope of agreement were indeed over, and Schenck reported :

" Failure, disappointment and estrangement, instead of Success, Friendship and Peace. I have not slept well on this conclusion of our interview.

" But next morning came Granville's message asking me to see him upon the Cabinet meeting."

Again full of hope, the American had drawn up a portentous résumé which he carried to Downing Street and read to Granville, who appears to have been impressed.

On the last day of the month the sky brightened, and Schenck notes an intense and general desire to save the Washington Treaty.

How the treaty was saved may be read elsewhere. After a struggle lasting for five months, Charles Francis Adams, the American arbitrator at Geneva, took the responsibility upon himself of abandoning the indirect claims. Finally, on September 14, 1872, the tribunal awarded the United States the sum of $15,500,000 in gold.

Little has been said or written in all the vast literature of the *Alabama* award at Geneva of the part taken in London by the American representative and by Lord Granville— the anxious strain to which both were subjected, the constant surprises and excitements and the highly-charged atmosphere of their surroundings.

General Schenck had played many thrilling and intense games of poker in his life, but never had he played any so thrilling or for stakes so vast. It may seem unfair, indecorous, to push the analogy too far—but America had staked a fabulous sum on a single card, and then—fortunately for international peace, her bluff—Sumner's bluff—had been ' called.'

After that all became serene at the London Legation,

and the Minister was free to follow the pleasant social round, in which his two interesting daughters and the great western card game, of which he was the high priest, constantly figured.   When President Grant was re-elected, there was no thought of replacing General Schenck, and he might have continued undisturbed during the whole term of his administration but for his own imprudence.   There were, as all the world knows, other things characteristic of the Far West besides draw-poker; there were gold and silver mines and mining stock.   Half a century ago the name of the Emma Mine was on everybody's lips.   It was a famous financial scandal, and alas! Schenck was involved in it.   He himself came to confess to the President: "A few months after my arrival here I invested in the shares of a mining company in which I allowed my name to appear as director." He said he was led to do this because he was a poor man and the expenses of the post which he then expected to hold for only two years were great.

"If this was unfortunate, it is to be remembered that I yielded to the representation that it would be well for me to be in a position to help protect my own interests and that of other American shareholders."

He went on to say that, when criticism was evoked in the Press, he had telegraphed Grant that he had perhaps made a mistake and proposing to withdraw from the board of directors.   Grant replied that Schenck "had a right to invest his money in anything he chose, if it were honest," but advised his withdrawal from any management of a company in the country to which he was accredited.

That was in December 1871.   When, some years later, the company foundered, a hue and cry was raised by the victims and their friends.   The New York *Tribune* published an article attacking Schenck and reproducing a letter written by the Minister to a shady character amongst the mine promoters.   In February 1876 the House of Representatives passed a resolution instructing the Foreign Relations Committee to ascertain what action the President had taken in relation to General Schenck's connexion with the Emma Mine.

When this was announced in the London *Times* it became clear to the Minister that his position was untenable, and on February 19 he resigned. By this time the Senate Committee was investigating the charges against him and the defamatory evidence of witnesses was being published in the London newspapers.

It is all forgotten now : it was a sorry business, and was very undignified for the Legation. Schenck sailed for home on March 4 without waiting for diplomatic formalities. On the eve of his departure a police officer actually came to the Legation and served a writ on the Minister. The faithful First Secretary, Wickham Hoffman, was shocked. He carried the writ instantly to Lord Derby, leaving it with an explanatory note. The next morning the writ was withdrawn and an apology sent for this unwitting invasion of a foreign envoy's extra-territoriality.

It was a melancholy ending to General Schenck's diplomatic career. Nor was this all; a smart London society weekly announced that the game of draw-poker was temporarily *tabu* in the best stock-jobbing circles !

It was bad enough for the Grant Administration that one of its English envoys should have met with disaster. Two really seemed excessive. To avoid any further mishaps due to over-zeal either for history or commercial speculation, the President felt that a quiet, obscure person would be the safest choice. The difficulty was to discover a nonentity of good manners who could support the honour, for political nonentities in America are generally poor men. Two or three offers were made and refused. At last it was announced that a highly respectable New York lawyer, Edwards Pierrepont, who had lately been Federal Attorney-General, had been chosen for the English mission.

The new Minister arrived, by a happy chance, on the Fourth of July, the hundredth anniversary of the Declaration of Independence. At Liverpool he was given a civic luncheon and made a brief speech (" signifying nothing," he hastened to assure the apprehensive Secretary of State), and reached London just in time to preside at the Centennial banquet at the Westminster Palace Hotel. It was all rather a strain on a new arrival, but he acquitted himself to the satisfaction of his countrymen, who, however, rather missed General Schenck's oratorical humour and breeziness. The loudest applause of the evening, it is diverting to learn, after the greeting to the Chairman and the chief patriotic toast, was accorded to an allusion to the game of poker. One humorist lamented that, as in the case of the British naval hero, Nelson, a certain female named " Emma " had exerted a baleful effect on the kindliest gentleman, the ablest diplomat and the shrewdest poker player of his time.

At the time of Pierrepont's arrival, English industry was in a far from prosperous state—which was doubtless a reaction to the condition which had for some time prevailed in America. In the Minister's first dispatch he observed, with a concluding touch of irony :

" I am not a little surprised to find the commercial depression in England, so exactly like our own in kind, varying only in degree. The two nations *surely sympathize in trade and finance, if in nothing else.*"

A few days later, he met the Queen and had no fault to find with the cordiality of his reception, either at Windsor or on the following day at a party given by the Prime Minister. The latter's goodwill, it appears, was unexpected.

" Last night I attended a reception of the Prime Minister. I had been told by one Cabinet Minister that Mr. Disraeli was not very cordial towards the American representatives. I think he must have changed, as a more friendly reception could not have been given than I received from him."

Before the London season was over Pierrepont was thoroughly enjoying himself, although the expense of returning the hospitality of his hosts rather terrified him.

" I can see [he reported] that valuable information comes through social life, and that such life in London cannot be taken up without large expense. A Minister cannot live here on less than $45,000 a year."

In the American Presidential election of 1876 the Republican candidate, General Hayes, was successful, and Pierrepont

EDWARDS PIERREPONT.

was not disturbed in his tenure and might even have remained on through the new Administration. But he found it a burden too great to be borne, and in the following summer sent in his resignation. Before he retired, however, he had to bear the brunt of the odium with which the English people regarded certain financial measures in America, which put silver on a parity with gold. So far from defending these measures, they filled him with resentment and humiliation. " Our financial credit here was good until repudiation cast its shadow over our international transactions." In his last dispatch (December 22, 1877) he spoke very plainly :

" No disguise under cover of a statute which proposes to pay a silver dollar where a gold one was promised will be regarded as other than a fraud ; any such course must tarnish and damage our prosperity.

" *The greatness of England is largely due to her unshaken credit ;* it is so firm that where gold flows out in a very short time they can fill their vaults again by raising their rate of interest. The world knows that principal and interest will be paid according to the implied contract."

Europe, he told the Secretary of State, was watching America more closely than ever.

" The enemies of popular Governments have a theory that delicate honour and commercial integrity soon perish in a democracy, and they will jeer and rejoice if we ourselves prove the truth of this theory."

These wise words doubtless had their due weight with the Administration at Washington.

Pierrepont waited for his successor to arrive in December : he accompanied him at his presentation to the Queen at Windsor, and they spent Christmas together before he himself sailed for home.

The new Minister was a well-known and wealthy merchant of Philadelphia, John Welsh, one of two brothers who had made a vast fortune out of the West India trade. He held a position in the community similar to that later held by another eminent Philadelphian, John Wanamaker. Welsh had been President of the Centennial Exposition Board of

Finance, and in that capacity had perhaps done more than any other man to render the great commemorative enterprise a success.   It had brought him into official contact with the representatives of many foreign countries, who had bestowed their decorations upon him.   A grateful city had presented him with a gold medal and $50,000, with which sum he immediately endowed the John Welsh Chair of English Literature in the University of Pennsylvania.

But his arduous labours over the Exposition had affected his health, and, besides, he was now over seventy.   Nevertheless, Secretary Evarts, one of his most intimate friends, urged his acceptance of the post, and the aged Welsh, conscious of the great honour offered to him, consented.

The new Minister's dispatches from England now read more like personal and intimate letters to a friend rather than official documents.   Even on board ship he penned a minute account of all that happened, giving the captain's name and the names of the chief passengers, and he rarely, in his reports to the State Department, forgot to inquire after the health of Mrs. Evarts and to send her his compliments.

Welsh was, first and foremost, a business man, and from the date of his presentation at Windsor and the taking over of the Legation his chief interest was in the financial, industrial and economic conditions of the country to which he was accredited.   Politics were a lesser consideration—he wished the Hayes Administration to know the exact truth about matters which were then the subject of many rumours in America, especially about the economic state of the Mother Country.   Many banks had failed and exports had fallen 20 per cent. since 1873.   But—

" Whilst the industrial troubles of Great Britain are certainly very serious and will require the exercise of much judgment to keep them from causing suffering and disturbances, I regard them as temporary. The enterprise and intelligence of the nation have frequently in the past overcome more serious interruptions of prosperity."

Externally, he found England prosperous in 1879.

" Its cities, towns and villages and hamlets present a most attractive aspect.   There is an absence of all indications of dilapidation. The buildings and out-houses are well-kept, in good repair, exceedingly neat, with many ornamental flowers, particularly among the humbler classes. New buildings are rising in almost every suburb, many being villas for successful tradesmen and more for the industrial classes."

He saw few beggars in England, and in general good order and security prevailed.

" The most offensive feature is that connected with the ' public-houses ' . . . and in those parts where the most depraved dwell the scenes connected with them are very revolting. Drunkenness is the besetting sin of the lower classes, and here women participate in it more numerously than in any other country." [1]

Minister Welsh found the British landlord system surprising.

" One of the greatest peculiarities of Great Britain is the very small number of its land-owners and their continual tendency to diminish in number. . . . Out of a population of 36 millions, 10,888 individuals own two-thirds of the land and 2,184 own considerably more than one-half of the land in the kingdom."

This might be an injustice and a future danger, but although the British aristocracy owned and ruled, the administration of Government evoked his admiration. In strong contrast to the United States, too, was the system of the Civil Service. " There is no such class here as office seekers. Elections are conducted without their interference and members of Parliament are free from this annoyance." He also paid his tribute to the purity of English elections and the high moral and social standing of the members of Parliament.

In his report to Evarts, Welsh goes on to observe :

" The Conservative party has now a strong hold upon the country. Its course for a year or more has met with the approbation of the people, in the restoration to the country of its national prestige as a leading Power. It is respected everywhere."

[1] Welsh to Evarts, January 18, 1879.

25

As for Lord Beaconsfield, the American Minister thought it was doubtful whether he would again appeal to the electorate or serve out his term and retire.

" His physical vigour has materially abated and his years are approaching that period when labour becomes a burden. It is possible that an unfavourable Budget and the embarrassed conditions of the moment may yet cause difficulties."

The forecast was fulfilled ; the Conservatives went out of power the following year and Disraeli died in 1881.

In 1879 Minister Welsh reported the British Navy and Army to be in " the highest state of efficiency." But he thought that—

"costly and unwieldy ships might be unequal to cope with smaller cruisers of greater activity. The wisdom of our Government in allowing others to experiment has already been most satisfactorily shown."

The Minister paid his tribute to the Mother Country in the sphere of philanthropy and religion, although he felt impelled to state :

" There is a portion of the people here steeped deeper in depravity than can be equalled in any other part of the world within my knowledge."

He had seen the gloomy horrors of the slums of London and Liverpool—and wondered that human beings could be found to endure such a negation of all comfort, beauty and happiness. In spite of these local conditions, he thought the general state of England was improving. As to his own country, nothing could prevent the United States from becoming the leading commercial nation of the world before another century had rolled by.

Half of that period has now elapsed : the prediction has already been fulfilled. There is no other country so rich in the aggregate or where the average of individual wealth is so high. Yet, even so, as Welsh wrote to Secretary Evarts, America and Britain could always continue friendly rivals in material progress, for " the world is large enough for both."

JOHN WELSH.

There was one English condition, the weather, which, differing from his successor, Minister Welsh found intolerable, at least in winter. He suffered severely from bronchitis during the first winter, and during the second the eminent physician, Sir William Jenner, became a daily visitor at No. 37 Queen's Gate. The Minister kept at his post pluckily till spring and then (May 10, 1879) wrote Secretary Evarts :

" My health renders it unwise for me to reside in London during another winter."

He therefore formally resigned the Legation and returned, at the close of the ensuing summer, to his Philadelphia home, where he died in 1886.

BIOGRAPHICAL NOTES

Schenck was subsequently cleared of the charge of complicity in the Emma Mine fraud, and resumed the practice of law in Washington. He survived until 1890.

Pierrepont on his return engaged actively in his profession, besides publishing many pamphlets on financial affairs, in which he took a deep interest. He died in 1892.

CHAPTER XIX

LOWELL AND PHELPS (1880–1889)

"What if I sent him, Uncle S., says he,
To my good cousin whom he calls J. B. ?
A nation's servants go where they are sent :
He heard his Uncle's order and he went."

O. W. HOLMES.

THE two Ambassadors whose sojourn had been so brief and uneventful, and whose characters rather reflected the colourlessness of the Hayes Administration, were to be followed by one whose name and talents were famous on both sides of the Atlantic. James Russell Lowell was not only a poet, and a cultured essayist, but a humorist whose shrewd political satire in the *Biglow Papers* was immensely popular. Lowell, like his predecessors and fellow-Bostonians, Everett and Motley, had been drawn into diplomacy as a convenient means on the part of the Administration of rewarding literary eminence. He had first been sent to Spain, where he had acquitted himself admirably ; and on the vacancy occurring in the London mission his friends in America exerted themselves to procure Lowell's appointment.

So, on January 20, 1880, when the Minister was seated in his Legation at Madrid he was, he says, " startled with a cipher telegram. My first thought was ' Row in Cuba ; I shall have no end of bother.' " But the message turned out to be this :

" President has nominated you to England. He regards it as essential to the public service that you should accept and make your personal arrangements to repair to London as early as may be. Your friends whom I have conferred with concur in this view."

Lowell lost little time in making up his mind, and although his wife's health was then too precarious for her to accompany him, he set out at the beginning of March for his new post.

The two and a half years that he passed at Madrid had been as an excellent preparation for the more important mission.

" . . . He had [remarks his biographer [1]] practised the diplomatic art in a country where the language was foreign and the race unfamiliar, and if in his short residence he could, with some assurance, analyse the internal political conditions, he might hope more quickly to be able to apprehend nice discriminations in the current politics of a country where he was at home in language, literature and history. . . . The educated men of America were delighted with the appointment. They felt at once that they had a spokesman, and it may fairly be said that Americans generally were gratified."

On the other hand, in some of his writings and in his general habits of mind, Lowell had been, though " at home " in England in the sense of familiarity, yet a rather outspoken and occasionally petulant critic of the English. He had a corresponding touchiness concerning American shortcomings which he would allow no Englishman to abuse or even to mention. His well-known essay, " On a Certain Condescension in Foreigners," illustrates this trait of super-sensitiveness and pugnacity, common, however, to most, if not all, of the American representatives in England up to the time of Bayard, and from which Hay, Choate, Whitelaw Reid and Walter Page were happily free. Of this trait in Lowell, Professor Max Müller tells us that—

" sometimes, even the most harmless remark about America would call forth very sharp replies from him. Everybody knows that the salaries paid by America to her diplomatic staff are insufficient, and no one knew it better than he himself. But when the remark was made in his presence that the United States treated their diplomatic representatives stingily, he fired up, and discoursed most eloquently on the advantages of high thoughts and humble living."

Contentment with his salary ought surely to be regarded as the supreme test of patriotism in an American diplomat.

---

[1] H. E. Scudder : *James Russell Lowell.*

The new Minister presented his credentials at the Foreign Office on March 11, and ten days later he had an audience of the Queen. It had been arranged that Mrs. Lowell was to follow him to London at a brief interval, but he had scarcely settled down at the Legation when he heard that his wife had suffered a relapse in Madrid. He rejoined her. She grew better and they both came to England about the middle of May.

It was perhaps fortunate for Lowell that his wife's health during the whole period of his mission confined his hospitality within narrow limits and yet did not prevent him from accepting the hospitality of others. For otherwise it would have been difficult for him to have supported the position on his official salary and slender private income. The acceptance of the social invitations which were so lavishly showered upon him had, however, to be paid for. His popularity as a writer and speaker soon exhausted his spare time and energy. He was called upon to attend public dinners, unveilings, corner-stone layings and meetings of all kinds, and confidently expected by his admirers " to scatter broadcast pearls of wit, wisdom and rhetoric on the shortest notice." Lowell rarely, if ever, failed his auditors. " It was but a slight remove from his lecture-room at Harvard or his study at Elmwood to an English table and the themes on which he was called upon to speak were very familiar to him. Literature, the common elements of English and American life, the distinctiveness of America, these were subjects on which he was at home. He brought to his task a manner quiet yet finished by years of practice.[1]

In the first days after his return from Spain, he wrote :

" I am overwhelmed already with invitations, though I have not put my arrival in the papers."

And a few days later :

" I lunched with Tennyson yesterday. He is getting old and looks seedy. I am going in to take a pipe with him the first free evening. Pipes have more thawing power than anything else."

Lowell was now, it may be recalled, in his sixty-first

[1] Scudder : *James Russell Lowell.*

year. For the greater part of his life he had been simply
a college professor, a scholar and a good deal of a recluse.
Nevertheless, he had always been fortunate in the quality of
his social acquaintances, who had been, both in America and
England, the picked men of literature and affairs, and all of
these were cosmopolitan men who had travelled widely, so
that in their appearance, speech, culture and manners the
members of the Harvard College circle had little to distinguish
them from the poets, statesmen and scholars who attended
Lord Houghton's famous breakfasts or met at the Athenæum
Club. Anything, therefore, less like the proverbial Yankee
than Lowell can hardly be conceived, and in the perfection
of his urbanity, thought and diction he was able to make a
real contribution to English social life, according to accepted
English social canons.

At the outset his official business was chiefly confined to
disputes in connexion with the North American fisheries;
but it was not long before the United States were drawn,
very reluctantly, into the quarrel just then raging between England and Ireland, in consequence of the Coercion
Act. Lowell followed and reported political affairs in
Great Britain very closely in his letters to Secretary Evarts.
But his own opinion of the Irish question and Irish agitators
had been formed in America a generation before. In 1848,
when the Irish leaders, Smith O'Brien, Meagher and others,
were striving to stir up trouble, Lowell wrote in a periodical
he then edited:

" The only insurrection which has done Ireland any real
service was the one headed by Father Mathew. The true
office of the Irish Washington would be to head a rebellion
against thriftlessness, superstition and dirt. The sooner
the barricades are thrown up against these the better.
Ireland is in want of a revolution which shall render troops
less necessary rather than more so."

In a dispatch to the Secretary (January 7, 1881) he wrote:

" Seldom has a session of Parliament begun under more
critical circumstances. The abnormal condition of Ireland
and the question of what remedy should be sought for it
have deeply divided an embittered public opinion. Not
only has the law been rendered powerless and order dis-

turbed (both of them things almost superstitiously sacred in England), but the sensitive nerve of property has been rudely touched. The Opposition have clamoured for coercion, but while they have persisted in this it is clear that a change has been gradually going on in their opinion as to how great a concession would be needful."

He thought that Parnell had been unpleasantly surprised by the Land League and had been compelled to identify himself with a movement rather more desperate in its aims than he privately approved.

" So far as can be judged, a great deal of the agitation in Ireland is factitious, and large numbers of persons have been driven by timidity to profess a sympathy with it which they do not feel. . . . I am sure that the reasonable leaders of Irish opinion see the folly of expecting that England would ever peaceably consent to the independence of Ireland, that they do not themselves desire it, and that they would be content with a thorough reform of the land laws and a certain amount of local self-government. Both of these measures are suggested in the Speech from the Throne. . . . The Cabinet, I am safe in saying, are earnestly desirous of doing justice to Ireland, and not only that, but of so shaping reform as to make the cure as lasting as such a cure can be. . . . Their greatest obstacle will be the overweening expectations and inconsiderate temper of the Irish themselves, both of them the result of artificial rather than natural causes."

Three weeks later, he had occasion to write again of Irish affairs, and to note the final passage of the so-called Coercion Bill. At the close of his dispatch he wrote :

" The wild and whirling words of some Irishmen and others from America have done harm to something more than the cause of Irish peasantry by becoming associated in the public mind with the country whose citizenship they put off or put on as may be most convenient.

" . . . In connexion with this, I beg leave to call your attention to an extraordinary passage in the letter of Mr. Parnell to the Irish National Land League, dated Paris, February 13, 1881, in which he makes a distinction between ' the American people ' and ' the Irish nation in America.' This double nationality is likely to be of great practical inconvenience whenever the Coercion Bill becomes law. The same actor takes alternately the characters of a pair of twins who are never on the stage simultaneously."

This utterance would not of course commend the American Minister to the Fenian rank and file in America. In the meantime, there had come a Presidential Election and General Garfield had been elected. In due course a new Secretary of State, Mr. Blaine, entered upon his duties ; but there would be no change, it appeared, in the English mission, despite the murmurs which were already being heard against Lowell's " sickening sycophancy to English influence."

Amongst the matters Secretary Blaine was eager to discuss with the British Government was the Clayton-Bulwer Treaty.

" There has never been the slightest doubt on the part of this Government [he wrote Lowell] as to the purposes or extent of the obligation thus assumed, by which the United States became surety alike for the free transit of the world's commerce over whatever landway or waterway might be opened from sea to sea and for the protection of the territorial rights of Colombia from aggression or interference of any kind. . . .

" If the foreshadowed action of the European Powers should assume tangible shape, it would be well for you to bring to the notice of Lord Granville the provisions of the Treaty of 1846, and especially of the 35th article, and to intimate to him that any movement with the view of supplementing the guarantee contained therein would necessarily be regarded by that Government as an uncalled-for intrusion into a field where the local and general interests of the U.S.A. must be considered before the interests of any other Power save those of the United States of Colombia alone."

America, he pointed out, did not complain of European ownership of the canal or of the railway. But the political control of these was another matter. " If we are at war, no hostile nation should be permitted to pass."

But Blaine was only ten months in office. Not long before he retired, he wrote (November 19, 1881) suggesting modifications in the Clayton-Bulwer Treaty. The clauses forbidding fortification of the canal should be cancelled.

" This is an American question [he insisted], to be dealt with and decided by American powers."

To which Lord Granville rejoined that—

" the position of the United States to Great Britain as regarded the Canal had been regulated by the Clayton-Bulwer Treaty of 1850, and H.M. Government rely with confidence upon the observance of all the engagements of that Treaty."

To return to Ireland : Lowell regarded the Coercion Act as an " exceptional and arbitrary measure . . . contrary to the spirit and foundation principles of both English and American jurisprudence," yet being the law of the land " it is manifestly futile to claim that naturalized citizens of the United States should be excepted from its operation." He recognized that it was his business to uphold the real dignity of the American citizen, and at the same time to avoid entangling his country and Great Britain by an unwary protection of someone who had no title to protection. The cases which now began to succeed each other with confusing rapidity involved not only a mass of correspondence and the sifting of evidence, but the application constantly of personal judgment, and the exercise of much ingenuity in the reading of character.

In a dispatch of June 4, 1881, he wrote :

" Among the most violent are often the Irishmen who have been naturalized in America, and then gone back to Ireland with the hope, and sometimes, I am justified in saying, with the deliberate intention, of disturbing the friendly relations between the U.S. and England."

He went on to describe a visit paid him by a typical agitator of this sort, who in the course of his conversation repeatedly declared that—

" the best thing would be a war between England and the United States. After hearing this man's talk, my belief was that he had purposely exposed himself to the chances of arrest in the hope of adding to the difficulties of the Government. I asked him if he had considered the enormous interests at stake, quite apart from any moral consideration, and that England was our greatest customer for cattle, corn, and cotton ?   He merely repeated what he had said before as to the desirability of war."

Lowell submitted that it was " of some importance that the Department should be informed as to the kind of persons who may ask its intervention and as to the doctrines they preach."

The American Consul at Dublin, for example, had on his hands a case especially troublesome, because the claim of the arrested man to American protection rested on statements of citizenship which were contradictory, and affected the validity of his claim.   Lowell wrote to the Consul :

" It is my duty to protect, so far as I can, all citizens of the United States, whether native or naturalized, who are shown to be innocent of designs to subvert civil order, and I should not perhaps require in such cases evidence of innocence so full and conclusive as that which might be required in a court of law.   At the same time I shall by no means try to screen any persons who are evidently guilty of offending against the criminal laws of Great Britain."

Of Lowell's action in this case, the Secretary of State wrote that it received " the entire commendation of the Department as discreet and proper."

On July 2, 1881, there came to the Legation the startling intelligence that President Garfield had been shot by a desperate assassin.   Of the reception given in Great Britain to this news, Lowell wrote :

" Warm expressions of sympathy with the President, with Mrs. Garfield and with the people of the United States, and of abhorrence of the atrocious attempt on the President's life have reached this Legation from all parts of England and Scotland.   From the Queen to the artisan, the feeling has been universal and very striking in its manifestation.   The first question in the morning and the last at night for the first ten days after the news came was always : ' How is the President ? '   Had the President's life not been spared, the demonstration of feeling would have been comparable with that which followed the assassination of Mr. Lincoln.

" The interest of the Queen was shown in an unusually marked way, and was unmistakable in its sincerity and warmth.   By her special request all our telegrams were at once forwarded to her at Windsor. At Marlborough House on the 14th she sent for me, in order to express in person her very great satisfaction that the condition of the President was so encouraging."

But the President's state worsened and his long illness during the whole summer terminated by his death in September. The Vice-President, Chester A. Arthur, succeeded, and F. T. Frelinghuysen became Secretary of State. Lowell's position in London was unaffected, except in so far as the Irish agitation in Ireland and America grew acute and the Minister's action with respect to naturalized Irishmen was vehemently attacked.

In February 1882 a resolution of the House of Representatives called upon the President for detailed information respecting the arrest of American citizens in Ireland. Accordingly, the American Minister in London was requested to supply this information, and in a lengthy dispatch (March 14, 1882) Lowell describes the ten cases which had come under his notice, accompanied by the correspondence, concluding by the remark:

" Naturalized Irishmen seem entirely to misconceive the process through which they have passed in assuming American citizenship, looking upon themselves as Irishmen who have acquired a right to American protection, rather than as Americans who have renounced a claim to Irish nationality."

Such language as this could hardly fail to provoke fury amongst Irish sympathizers both in Congress and throughout the country. At a great mass-meeting held in New York Lowell was denounced unsparingly, and from this time forth he was the object of attack and sneers for what was called his " apostasy from American principles." However, he did not lack defenders and one great newspaper, the *Tribune*, thus stated the case:

" Mr. Lowell, who has been denounced by Mr. Randall for his ' sickening sycophancy to English influence,' has treated the matter not as an English, Irish or American question, but purely as a point of international law. He has no sympathy with the coercion legislation, and has even taken pains to characterize it as exceptional and arbitrary. . . . That law (the ' protection ' law) legalized the arrest of the suspects in districts where the writ of *habeas corpus* had been suspended, and where the natives were not allowed the privilege of a jury trial. To have demanded their unconditional release, when no discrimination had been made between them and the natives, would have been an open affront to a friendly Power. What Mr. Lowell did was to follow the best precedents of criminal jurisdiction in international cases, several of which had been established during the American civil war, when British subjects were arbitrarily arrested and denied the privilege of trial. At the same time, he has conducted the negotiations with the Foreign Office with so much tact and decision that we are inclined to expect a speedy clearance of the Irish jails from suspects whose citizenship in the United States is authenticated."

Meanwhile, Lowell's course had not lessened the esteem and even affection with which he was regarded by Englishmen, and this affection came to be returned with interest. Lowell, indeed, succumbed, perhaps to a greater degree than any of his predecessors, to the spell of London. From the house in Lowndes Square, where he had established his Legation, he wrote to a friend (February 2, 1883):

" London I like beyond measure. The wonderful movement of life here acts as a constant stimulus—and I am beginning to need one. *The climate also suits me better than any I ever lived in.* I have only to walk a hundred yards from my door to see green grass and hear the thrushes sing all winter long. These are a constant delight, and I sometimes shudder to think of the poor dead weeds and grasses I have seen shivering in the cast-iron earth at home. But I shall come back to them to comfort them out of my own store of warmth with as hearty a sympathy as ever."

Again, three months later to Professor Charles Eliot Norton :

" I like London, and have learned to see as I never saw before the advantage of a great capital. It establishes one set of weights and measures, moral and intellectual, for the whole country. It is, I think, a great drawback for us that we have as many as we have States. The flow of life in the streets, too—sublimer, it seems to me often, than the tides of the sea—gives me a kind of stimulus that I find agreeable even if it prompt to nothing."

One sees the essential modesty of the man in the following extract from another private letter :

" Nothing in my life has ever puzzled me so much as my popularity here in England—which I have done nothing and been nothing to deserve. I was telling my wife a day or two ago that I couldn't understand it. It must be my luck, and ought to terrify me like the ring of Polycrates."

Yet he still could keep up his old critical attitude towards scenes, episodes and institutions which for him fell short of good. He watched the Lord Mayor's Show, as indeed millions have watched it, without entering into the spirit of its antiquity and homely symbolism, which is, after all, that of Bottom the Weaver, and so came away aggrieved. The passage in which he told this to a friend is highly characteristic :

" No, the Lord Mayor's Show was pure circus and poor circus at that. It was cheap, and the other adjective that begins with *n*. 'Twas an attempt to make poetry out of commonplace by contract. 'Twas antiquity as conceived by Mr. Sanger. Why, I saw the bottoms of a Norman knight's trousers where they had been hitched up into a tell-tale welt round the ankle by his chain armour ! There was no pretence at illusion ; nay, every elephant, every camel, every chariot was laden with disillusion. It was worth seeing for once, to learn how dreary prose can contrive to be when it has full swing."

Two portraits of the American Minister were exhibited in the Royal Academy of 1882.

" I am off for the private view [he confides to a friend]. Two portraits of myself there. They are very unlike each other and my duty to the artist requires me to try and look as much like each as I can. What am I to do ? They will be in different rooms doubtless, and so I can manage it, perhaps."

The foregoing whimsically illustrates Lowell's innate desire for complete fairness and impartiality, and he had, as it were, to be occasionally reminding himself to show a little

JAMES RUSSELL LOWELL.

prejudicial aloofness. But it was hard and grew harder. No one could help being touched by a man who was so bravely trying to keep hold of little American traits and legends in order to demonstrate his Americanism *au fond*. Once, when he was in a splendid and august company and was on the point of avowing his emotion, he whispered to a friend, " I think, on the whole, I find no society so good as what I have been accustomed to at home."

Again, there was a Christmas Day feast at the Legation —all very cosy, and appetizing and English. There were some American guests—the Lowells feared it might be too English. Something American was lacking : so they sent out to an American shop in Piccadilly and bought cranberries. Cranberries—that would soothe the New England consciousness that they were enjoying themselves too exotically.

" But the servants, who had mostly come with the Lowells from Spain, could not be made to understand what was wanted, and it was only when, two or three courses after the turkey, Mrs. Lowell hit upon calling for the ' compote rouge ' that we obtained our cranberry sauce as a separate course. . . ." [1]

When Lowell spoke in public he could not always make up his mind whether to be English or American. His literary addresses, especially his admirable address on Henry Fielding, certainly illustrated his ability to act as " spokesman for the common Englishry of two countries. His point of view was at once that of an onlooker and of one indigenous." And yet Lowell was perturbed.

" I am constantly bothered [he wrote] by the disenchanting effect of my sense of humour (of which I speak in the Fielding address), which makes me too fair to both sides. This often makes me distrustful of myself. I am sometimes inclined to call genius not ' an infinite capacity for taking pains ' (though that is much), but an infinite capacity for being *one-sided*."

In the autumn of 1883 Lowell was considered so much a British institution that the student body of St. Andrews

[1] Quoted by Scudder.

proposed him as Lord Rector of that University, in succession to Sir Theodore Martin. The proposal was greeted with enthusiasm, although opposition developed on the ground that Lowell was an alien, and a lively discussion was opened in the Press. *Punch* thus rendered its decision :

> " An ' alien ' ? Go to ! If fresh, genial wit
> In sound Saxon speech be not genuine grit,
> If the wisdom and worth he has put into verse for us
> Don't make him a ' native,' why, so much the worse for us.
> Whig, Tory and Rad should club votes, did he need 'em,
> To honour the writer who gave *Bird o' Freedom*
> To all English readers.   A few miles of sea
> Make Lowell an alien ?   Fiddle-de-dee !
> 'Tis crass party spirit, Bœotian, dense ;
> *That* is alien indeed—to good taste and good sense."

Nevertheless, although Lowell was elected over his opponent, the point of the objectors proved to be well taken, and Lowell wrote to Professor Child :

" My official extra-territoriality will, perhaps, prevent my being Rector at St. Andrews, because it puts me beyond the reach of the Scottish Courts in case of malversation of office. How to rob a Scottish University suggests a serious problem ! "

Accordingly, he resigned, but was triumphantly elected some years later when his diplomatic privilege was a thing of the past.

The American elections of 1884 brought the Democrat Grover Cleveland to the Presidency, and Lowell realized that his London mission would have to be surrendered.

" I should not regret it [he wrote] but for two reasons—certain friendships I have formed here and the climate, which is more kindly to me than any I have ever lived in. It is a singularly manly climate, full of composure and without womanish passion and extravagance."

To Oliver Wendell Holmes he confided (December 28, 1884):

" It was very good of you to take all that trouble about me and my poor affairs with Mr. Cleveland and Boyle O'Reilly. As for the former, I shall be satisfied with whatever he thinks fit to do in my case, for I have a high respect for his character, and should certainly have voted for him had I been at home. As Minister I have always refused to have any politics, considering myself to represent the country and no special party in it. As for Mr. O'Reilly, it is *he* that misunderstands the rights of naturalized citizens, not I ; and he wouldn't have misunderstood them had they been those of naturalized Germans, nor would Bismarck have been as patient as Granville. I made no distinction between naturalized and native, and should have treated you as I did the ' suspects '—had there been as good ground. . . . Some of my Irishmen had been living in their old homes seventeen years, engaged in trade or editing Nationalist papers or members of the poor-law guardians (like Mac-Sweeny), and neither paying taxes in America nor doing any other duty as Americans. I was guided by two things—the recognized principles of international law, and the conduct of Lord Lyons when Seward was arresting and imprisoning British subjects. We kept one man in jail seven months without trial or legal process of any kind, and, but for the considerateness and moderation of Lyons, might have had war with England. I think I saved a misunderstanding. . . When I had at last procured the conditional (really unconditional) release of all the suspects, they refused to be liberated. When I spoke of this to Justin McCarthy (then the head of the Irish Parliamentary party, Parnell being in Kilmainham), he answered cheerfully, ' *Certainly : they are there to make trouble!* '

" But enough of these personal matters. I shall come home with the satisfaction of having done my duty and of having been useful to the true interests of both countries—of the three, if you count Ireland. The fun of the thing is that here I was considered a radical in my opinions about Ireland. I have always advised them to make Davitt or Parnell Irish Secretary." [1]

While he was thus in doubt about his fate, and before Cleveland's inauguration, an event happened in Lowell's life which, though long foreshadowed, rendered him indifferent. On February 19, 1885, Mrs. Lowell died. At the close of the following month he wrote :

" I am on the whole glad to be rid of my official trammels and trappings. I do not know yet when my successor will arrive, but hardly look for him before July. I shall then go home, but whether to stay or not will be decided after I have

[1] What would he have said to making Timothy Healy Governor-General forty years later ?

looked about me there. If I decide to stay I shall certainly visit the Old World pretty regularly."

The new Minister, however, arrived sooner than was expected and Lowell presented his letter of recall May 19. In June he was back again in America and writing playfully to R. W. Gilder :

" I was to have gone to Washington last week (carrying my head, as Bertrand de Born did, like a lantern) to take a look at my decapitators, but the illness of Mr. Bayard prevented me."

President Cleveland selected as his Minister to England an elderly New Englander who held the post of Professor of Law at Yale University, and was utterly unknown in national politics.

There were questions pending between the two countries which, the President thought, demanded a legal mind and expert treatment, and purely social and sentimental considerations might be relegated to the background. Moreover, being a Democrat, he was pledged to a policy of plain living and strict efficiency abroad as well as at home, and deference to the aristocratic and literary circles of London did not enter into his views.

Edmund John Phelps looked and was the earnest, astute lawyer. He had the legal type of face, gaunt, with strongly marked features, and was careless in his dress.

So keen was he in his profession and interested in English administration of the law that he had been scarce three days in the country and had not presented his letter of credence than the news ran that the new American Minister was actually assisting at a murder trial at the Old Bailey. The case was, however, peculiar. The accused were two dynamiters, Burton and Cunningham. They claimed to be American citizens and it had been represented by their friends in America that, owing to the intense feeling in England, they were not likely to receive a fair trial.

" To inform myself [reported Phelps to the Secretary of State, May 18, 1885] as far as possible on the question whether the evidence in the case justified a conviction, I resolved to attend."

Such a proceeding seemed a little shocking to ex-Minister Lowell, who would no more have thought of openly questioning the fairness of British justice than of questioning the piety of an English bishop. But then, he was not a lawyer nor interested in judicial processes. Phelps drove straight to the Court, where he was courteously received by Mr. Justice Hawkins and given a seat on the bench. The trial, however, was nearly over—there only remained a four hours' charge to the jury, which the American followed with the closest attention. He decided that it was eminently just and fair and that the whole trial had been fair and humane. The men were found guilty and sentenced to penal servitude for life. This sentence Phelps avowed to be fully justified. The crime, if not planned in the United States, had been executed by men travelling to and fro between the two countries. Burton and Cunningham were guilty, but they had been the tools of others.

Having thus satisfied himself that justice had been done by the Queen's Bench, Phelps presented himself on the following day (May 19) to the Queen herself at Windsor and entered upon his diplomatic duties.

There was little of prime importance to engage Minister Phelps's attention during the first year or two of his mission. In 1885 the American Government had given notice that the Treaty of Washington, which gave to Americans the liberty of fishing off the Eastern Canadian coast in return for reciprocal rights and a compensation amounting to about £90,000 a year, would not be renewed. With its lapse all reciprocity came to an end and Canadian fish imported into the United States had to pay duty. A new treaty was contemplated, but it was difficult to see how it could be made acceptable to the Senate. Meanwhile, there was a good deal of friction on the fishing-grounds. American vessels were detained in Canadian ports and expostulations were made to the British Foreign Office.

If American money was no longer forthcoming for British fishing rights, there were still other British assets which continued to excite the cupidity of a large class in America. The Secretary of Legation in London, Henry White, had already in Lowell's time made a report on American claims to English estates,[1] and what he called the " useless pursuit of imaginary fortunes in Great Britain. They might as well seek to recover possession of a castle in Spain through the intervention of our Minister to that country." When Secretary Bayard came into office, he found the Dalton family in America much exercised about the enormous and valuable Dalton estate in England which awaited the arrival of an American heir. Minister Phelps was instructed to make inquiries and reported promptly that there was no such estate nor any such title in the peerage as " Lord Dalton."

" The case is one of those constantly recurring delusions among the less intelligent class of the American people which occasion many hundreds of applications to this Legation. Most of that class are possessed of the idea that the respective families to which they belong are entitled to vast estates in England, now in the hands of the British Government, awaiting distribution among American heirs, under titles that occurred several centuries ago. The entire property in Great Britain would not be sufficient to satisfy these claims, if they were all established. . . . This belief is fostered by designing persons who issue advertisements inquiring for heirs of almost all known surnames, and it is given out that these advertisements emanate from the British Government. The Government hold no such property, do no such business and issue no such advertisements."

Then came an ironic touch :

" All the real and personal estate in England, as in America, is in the hands of proprietors who claim it, who are unwilling to relinquish it, and cannot be divested of it except by actions at law based upon sufficient grounds and supported by competent evidence ; and such actions, if instituted in England, would stand the same chance of success as they would in the American courts if the claimants sought to possess themselves there of the lands or money of their neighbours under titles derived from ancestors supposed to have existed two or three hundred years ago."

The Government made Phelps's opinion widely known, but the fallacy was not wholly destroyed.

On the occasion of Queen Victoria's Jubilee in 1887,

[1] November 15, 1884.

E. J. PHELPS.

President Cleveland sent over a letter of congratulation, to be personally delivered by the Minister.

" The Queen [wrote Phelps] received me in private audience at Buckingham Palace on June 20 and expressed the high gratification with which she received the letter of the President and her appreciation of the great kindness of feeling always shown her by my countrymen."

The letter itself ran :

" Great and good Friend, In the name and on behalf of the people of the United States, I present their sincere felicitations upon the arrival of the fiftieth anniversary of your Majesty's accession to the Crown of Great Britain. . . . It is justice and not adulation to acknowledge the debt of gratitude and respect due to your personal virtues, for their important influence on producing and conserving the prosperous and well-ordered condition of affairs now generally prevailing throughout your Dominions. May your life be prolonged and peace, honour and prosperity bless the people over whom you have been called to rule."

Towards the close of 1887 a Joint Commission was convened at Washington to consider a new treaty as regards the Fisheries. Feeling in Canada was running rather high at this time, as Canadians believed that Great Britain was not championing their interests with sufficient force. In January two American fishing-vessels put into Halifax harbour for repairs, with cargoes of fresh fish on board. The Canadian authorities promptly forbade the sale of the fish as a violation of treaty and British statutes. The fishermen, whose only alternative now was to throw the fish overboard, appealed to Secretary Bayard, who cabled to Minister Phelps.

The Minister sat down and drafted the following note to Lord Salisbury :

" AMERICAN LEGATION,
" February 1, 1888.

" MY LORD,—
" I have to acquaint you that I have just received a cable dispatch from my Government informing me that the Consul-General of the United States at Halifax has reported that two American vessels laden with fresh fish have

been compelled to put into that port for repairs and that
their cargoes will rot unless allowed to be landed : which the
Canadian authorities have forbidden as being a violation of
the treaty and of British statutes.   The Consul-General adds
that if this refusal be persisted in, the fish must be thrown
overboard, serious loss being thereby inflicted upon the owners
of the vessels.

"I am instructed to bring your lordship's attention to this
transaction, which is regarded by my Government as a fresh
violation of the provisions of the existing treaty between
Great Britain and the United States, as well as of the ordinary
comity that should subsist between two friendly nations.
It is made more pointed by having occurred while the
representatives of the two countries are actually engaged at
Washington in an effort to adjust the questions in dispute
touching the fisheries.   And it is felt by my Government
to be an attempt on the part of the Canadian authorities
to bring to bear upon the negotiations a pressure similar to
that which they have previously employed to obtain from the
United States an alteration of its revenue laws.

"I venture to add, my lord, the expression of my opinion
that this transaction, if persisted in, will have very grave
consequences in its probable effect on the negotiations now
pending at Washington."

Salisbury immediately cabled Ottawa on February 3 the
permission to land the fish in order to operate *bona-fide*
repairs, but without prejudice to the question of right.

As it did not arrive until the 7th, the cargo of fish had
already been thrown overboard.

Such an episode, added to others, could only create bitter
feeling.   The project for a new Reciprocity Treaty was
rejected by the Senate, and although a satisfactory *modus
vivendi* was arranged no new treaty was feasible for twenty
years.

A far graver difficulty, while it lasted, was the Alaskan
Seal dispute.   The seal fisheries off that coast were in the
hands of Americans, who killed about 100,000 seals annually.
But about the year 1880 certain Canadian vessels took to
intercepting the seal-herd on its way to Alaskan waters and
five years later these vessels entered Bering Sea on their
quest.   The American authorities promptly seized them and

condemned them on the ground that all the waters of Bering
Sea were within American jurisdiction. A convention was
arranged between the United States, Great Britain and
Russia, to put an end to pelagic fishing (i.e. hunting with
spear or shot-gun at sea), which was, the Americans alleged,
ruining the industry.

On August 13, 1888, Phelps had an interview with Lord
Salisbury, in which he again pressed for the completion of
the convention, as the extermination of the seals by Canadian
vessels was going on rapidly. Salisbury " did not," reported
Phelps, " question the propriety or the importance of taking
measures to prevent the wanton destruction of so valuable
an industry in which England had a large interest of its
own," but said that until Canada's consent could be obtained
he and his colleagues must hold aloof.

" It is very apparent to me [commented the Minister] that
the British Government will not execute the desired convention without the concurrence of Canada and it is equally
apparent that the concurrence of Canada in any such arrangement is not to be reasonably expected. Certain Canadian
vessels are making a profit out of the destruction of the seal
in the breeding season in the waters in question, inhuman
and wasteful as it is. That it leads to the speedy extermination of the animal is no loss to Canada, because no part of
these seal fisheries belong to that country ; and the profit
open to it in connexion with them is by destroying the seal
in the open sea during the breeding time, although many
of the animals killed in that way are lost, and those saved are
worth much less than when killed at the proper time.

" Under these circumstances the Government of the
United States must, in my opinion, either submit to have
these valuable fisheries destroyed or must take measures to
prevent their destruction by capturing the vessels employed
in it. Between these alternatives it does not appear to me
there should be the slightest hesitation.

" Much learning has been expended upon the discussion
of the abstract question of the right of *mare clausum*. I do
not conceive it to be applicable to the present case."

That " the colony of a foreign nation, in defiance of the
joint remonstrance of all the countries interested, should
persist in this indiscriminate slaughter " was to the American

Minister intolerable. Could piracy and the slave trade also be prosecuted in the open sea with impunity ? The right of self-defence as to person and property prevails everywhere. What, if the Canadian fish were to be destroyed by scattering poison in the open sea, would Canada say ?

" I earnestly recommend, therefore, that the vessels that have been already seized while engaged in this business be firmly held and that measures be taken to capture and hold every one hereafter found concerned in it. . . . There need be no fear but that a resolute stand on this subject will at once put an end to the mischief complained of. It is not to be reasonably expected that Great Britain will either encourage or sustain her colonies in conduct which she herself concedes to be wrong and which is detrimental to her own interests as well as ours. More than 10,000 people are engaged in London alone in the preparation of seal skins."

But all this display of vigour did not prove that the Americans owned Bering Sea or that Canadian vessels, captured by Americans there, were not entitled to legal damages.

The dispute was not settled until the Bering Sea Tribunal met in Paris in 1893, when it was decided that the United States had not " any right of protection or property in the fur seals frequenting the islands of the United States in Bering Sea when such seals are found outside the ordinary three-mile limit." The award was, as Professor Mowat remarks, " good for everyone except the seals."[1] Later, as compensation, nearly half a million dollars was awarded to the owners of the captured Canadian vessels.

Other important issues came in the last year of Phelps's mission. In 1887 Venezuela had broken off diplomatic relations with Great Britain over the long-standing boundary question, and Phelps was instructed to tender the good offices of the United States as mediator. But he was informed by Lord Salisbury that her Majesty's Government, owing to President Guzman Blanco's attitude, was " precluded from submitting those questions at the present moment to the arbitration of any third Power."

[1] Mowat : *Diplomatic Relations.* " The one failure of President Harrison's Administration," wrote Theodore Roosevelt in 1895, " was in the Bering Sea case."

Later in the year came a bold assertion by Secretary Bayard of the Monroe Doctrine, à propos of a report that Great Britain had taken some official action on the Mosquito Coast.

" The United States [wrote Bayard to Phelps, Nov. 23, 1888, in a dispatch intended to be shown to Lord Salisbury] can never see with indifference the re-establishment of such a Protectorate. Not only would the extension of European influence upon this continent be contrary to the traditional and frequently expressed policy of the United States, but the course of Great Britain in assuming or exercising any dominion over the Mosquito Coast . . . would be in violation of the express stipulations of the Clayton-Bulwer Treaty, whose binding force Great Britain has up to the present time so emphatically asserted. . . .

" Whether the interference of the British Government be regarded as a breach of existing treaty engagements or whether it be looked upon simply as an effort, not prohibited by express agreement, to extend her influence in this Continent—in either case the Government of the United States cannot look upon such acts without concern." [1]

As a matter of fact, Great Britain wanted to have nothing to do with the Mosquito Coast or its inhabitants, who, disgusted at their treatment by Nicaragua, had appealed to the British for protection, an appeal which was received without enthusiasm.

But the most exciting and most dramatic episode of the year, the last also of the Cleveland Administration, was the famous Sackville affair. It can only briefly be summarized here, for it belongs more properly to the history of the British Embassy in Washington. Sir Lionel Sackville-West, or Lord Sackville as he became during the progress of the affair, was the British Minister. The Presidential campaign being in full blast, it occurred to a certain shrewd individual in California to stir up anti-English prejudice amongst the electors by drawing out an opinion in favour of Cleveland from the British Minister. This he did by means of a ruse, writing a private pseudonymous letter, stating that

[1] Minister Phelps had his own opinion of the Monroe Doctrine, which he took occasion to express with some vigour in 1896. It differed *in toto* from that of President Cleveland.

he was a naturalized Englishman and asking for advice. Sackville fell into the trap and abundantly gratified his correspondent.

" You are probably aware [he wrote] that any political party which openly favoured the Mother Country at the present moment would lose popularity, and that the party in power is fully aware of this fact. The [Democratic] party, however, is, I believe, still desirous of maintaining friendly relations with Great Britain."

This was enough : the letter was promptly published ; and the storm broke on Sackville's head. President Cleveland, the candidate for a second term, was furious : the Republicans were jubilant. The newspapers fanned the flame. " The British lion's paw thrust into American politics to help Cleveland " was the headline of a leading New York journal, which, with others, demanded that the offending Minister should instantly be dismissed. The election was to occur on November 4. When on October 27 the news reached London, the American Minister was actually the guest of Lord Salisbury. The latter took the incident calmly : he thought it only fair to hear Lord Sackville's side of the story, but Cleveland refused to wait, and on October 31, 1888, the British Minister received his passports. Of course, such an action aroused indignation in England. The *Standard* said :

" He [Mr. Cleveland] has done to the Minister of Great Britain what British statesmanship would hesitate, save for grave cause, to do to the representative of the smallest State in the world. . . . He degrades our Ambassador before ordering him to leave the country. If war had been declared between the two nations, the State Department could have done nothing more obtrusively unfriendly. We may even say that in such a case the same care would have been taken to mitigate the personal unpleasantness as, thanks to Mr. Bayard's trenchant style, has now been taken to emphasize it. Considered as a mere matter of etiquette, the course pursued at Washington will not redound to the credit of American manners. But that, of course, concerns the Americans : for Englishmen it is quite enough to feel that their Ambassador is being hustled out of the United States in the most contumelious fashion."

It meant the end of Sackville's very creditable diplomatic career. On December 4, a month after Cleveland's defeat, Phelps wrote at length to Lord Salisbury detailing the whole incident, which he described as " constituting a very grave and unprovoked affront by Lord Sackville to the President and the Senate." How this could be so interpreted is even now difficult to understand. But Phelps was a lawyer and was expounding from his brief. In the conclusion Phelps spoke for himself :

" I need hardly assure your lordship that it is from no feeling of unkindness to Lord Sackville, whose previous intercourse with the Government of the United States had been acceptable, that I am instructed to bring these facts to the attention of her Majesty's Government. The Government of the United States deeply regrets the occurrence that, in its judgment, rendered necessary the termination of Lord Sackville's official residence at Washington, as it must always regret any incident that might impair in the slightest degree the most friendly relations that exist between the two Governments."

To the suggestion that another British Minister be sent in Sackville's place, Lord Salisbury returned no reply, and it was not until President Cleveland himself relinquished office in March 1889 that any appointment to Washington was made. Minister Phelps himself had gone regretfully home at the end of the previous January, leaving the capable and well-informed Henry White behind as Chargé d'affaires.

BIOGRAPHICAL NOTES

Lowell returned to England as a private citizen in 1886 and in the immediately following years (" I am as fond of London," he wrote, " as Charles Lamb "). He died at his home in Cambridge, Massachusetts, in the summer of 1891.

Phelps returned to his chair at Yale University, where he was Kent Professor of Law, until his death in 1900.

CHAPTER XX

LINCOLN, BAYARD AND HAY (1889–1898)

HARDLY was President Harrison in office than he was waited on by a deputation of Irish-Americans, who told him that they had not been satisfied with either Ministers Lowell or Phelps and urged the President " to select somebody thoroughly in sympathy with American institutions and not likely to be moved from his Americanism by British flattery."

" The President replied that he proposed to select just such a man, adding that, notwithstanding their Irish sympathies, any of them would probably, if brought within the influence of English social life, be less acceptable to his sturdy fellow-patriots at home at the end of his term than at the beginning." [1]

The difficulty was to find such a man. The post was offered to Mr. Chauncey Depew, who would have made an admirable envoy ; but he, with others, may have shrunk from the obligations involved. At last the President had an inspiration.

The curtain had fallen for months and not until the last week in May did it rise upon a new cast at the London Legation. The leading figure makes his appearance discreetly, almost shyly, on the stage. Yet never has an American Minister—and he is destined to be the last of the Ministerial line—evoked greater curiosity. There is a kind of hush as he makes his bow—even Queen Victoria scrutinizes him long and keenly through her spectacles—for the Lincoln legend has at last reached England and through the mists of detraction and misunderstanding America's war-time President has taken his place on the pedestal of immortality. And this simple, stoutish, well-groomed, bearded gentleman is his son—the son of Abraham Lincoln. No wonder necks

[1] *The Times*, March 22, 1889.

ROBERT T. LINCOLN.

crane forward and there is a hum of incredulity. One thought of that sad-eyed, uncouth giant, of lofty faith and purpose, whose assassination on the very anniversary of Christ's martyrdom sent a shudder of mingled horror and sympathy through the civilized world, and wondered—the contrast to this plump, retiring, matter-of-fact gentleman was so great. Heredity is a fickle, uncertain quality ; in Robert Todd Lincoln there was scarce a lineament or a gesture resembling his illustrious father. He took after his mother, it was said, and his mother was a Todd. Yet, even in youth, he had shown laudable traits of his own. He was steady, endowed with common sense, and he had received his education at Harvard University. Born in 1843, Robert Lincoln was in his twenty-second year when his father was assassinated. He had, only a year before, been taken on the staff of General Grant and given the rank of Captain. Afterwards, he had studied law and practised at the Illinois Bar. His name was a great asset and he could never lack influential friends even in a country where heredity is, at least in theory, disparaged. He was chosen a delegate to the Republican Convention in 1880 which nominated General Garfield, who loved the father only " this side idolatry," and gave the son an office—the Secretaryship of War. President Arthur changed all the Cabinet, but left Lincoln undisturbed.

General Harrison, the grandson of a former President, may or may nor have believed in transmitted genius, but he recognized the value of transmitted prestige. So the son of Abraham Lincoln was sent to represent the United States at the Court of St. James.

Compared with some of his predecessors, the new Minister was at a disadvantage, in point of talent, eloquence, personality. But it was soon manifest that there was much virtue in his appointment. The Sackville incident rankled. There had been far too much aggressiveness—not to say pugnacity— emanating from Washington. These American qualities, admirable in small doses, had been exhibited a little too freely and forcibly on the English scene and a period of quiescence was all to the good. Peace and goodwill are often the product of quiet, and Minister Lincoln was quietness personified. His manner and his methods were particularly congenial to the

British Foreign Secretary, Lord Salisbury, who was, however, aware that in the American Secretary of State, Mr. Blaine, he had to deal with a statesman of a more active, ardent type. The Alaskan Seal negotiations had been transferred to Washington, where they revealed wide differences of national opinion, which arbitration eventually settled. Blaine was now working diligently to establish good relations with the South American republics and in 1890 the Pan-American Congress first met. He particularly wished to compose the Anglo-Venezuelan difficulty. On May 1, 1890, he cabled to Minister Lincoln, instructing him to—

" use his good offices with Lord Salisbury to bring about a resumption of diplomatic intercourse between Great Britain and Venezuela as a preliminary step towards the settlement of the boundary disputes by arbitration. . . . He is requested to propose to Lord Salisbury with a view to an accommodation that an informal conference be held in Washington or in London of representatives of the three Powers. In such conference the position of the United States is one solely of impartial friendship toward both litigants."

Four days later Lincoln had an interview with the Foreign Secretary.

" Lord Salisbury [he reported] listened with attention to my statement, in making which I was careful to keep within the lines of your instruction, and after remarking that the interruption of diplomatic relations was Venezuela's own act, he said that her Majesty's Government had not for some time been very keen about attempting a settlement of the dispute in view of their feeling of uncertainty as to the stability of the present Venezuelan Government and the frequency of revolutions in that quarter, but he would take pleasure in considering the suggestion after consulting the Colonial Office.

" While Lord Salisbury did not intimate what would probably be the nature of his reply, there was nothing unfavourable in his manner of receiving the suggestion ; on the contrary, in the course of the conversation he spoke of arbitration in a general way, saying that he thought there was more chance of a satisfactory result and more freedom from complication in the submission of an international question to a jurisconsult than to a sovereign power, adding that he had found it so in questions with Germany."

Lincoln thought that—

" if the matter had been entirely new and dissociated from its previous history, I should have felt from his tone that the idea of arbitration in some form to put an end to the boundary dispute was quite agreeable to him."

A fortnight or so later Salisbury wrote :

" Her Majesty's Government are very sensible of the very friendly feelings which have prompted this offer on the part of the United States Government. They are, however, at the present moment in communication with the Venezuelan Minister in Paris, who has been authorized to express the desire of his Government for a renewal of diplomatic relations."

Salisbury mentioned that—

" in so far as regards the frontier between British Guiana and Venezuela, I have informed Señor Urbaneja of her Majesty's Government's intention to abandon certain portions of its claims and to submit other portions to arbitration. If Venezuela met this offer in the right spirit, all would be well, but unfortunately public opinion is much excited on the subject and the facts of the case are strangely misunderstood."

Some weeks later Señor Pulido, a special envoy from Venezuela, arrived in London and requested Lincoln to present him to Lord Salisbury, which was done. Afterwards he pursued his negotiations with the Foreign Office. But it all proved futile—Venezuela remained irreconcilable, and it remained for President Harrison's successor, Grover Cleveland, to make the dispute a bone of contention between the United States and Great Britain, as will presently be noted.

Minister Lincoln was spared all this diplomatic excitement. " It is not unlikely that he felt towards this new application of the Monroe Doctrine much as other conservative Americans —including his own predecessor—and was relieved that it had not come in his time."

On May 4, 1893, the son of the great martyred President presented his letter of recall to the Queen, and bade farewell to the Legation and his English friends.

When he arrived in London, ex-Secretary of State Thomas Francis Bayard of Delaware, who had drafted the cavalier note dismissing the British Ambassador, Lord Sackville, from Washington, entered, not a Legation, but an Embassy.

The higher diplomatic status, delayed so long, had been agreed to, and on June 22, 1893, the first American Ambassador to the Court of St. James presented his credentials to the Queen.

Bayard himself was a man of distinguished American political lineage—even if his pretensions to descent from the famous Chevalier " *sans peur et sans reproche* "—would hardly have satisfied a precise genealogist. His grandfather had been an eminent statesman and had once been appointed —though he had not served—as American Minister to France, and his father was a Senator of the United States. In 1869, when he was only forty, he also had been elected to the Senate —so that there was observed the unparalleled spectacle of father and son sitting simultaneously in that assembly.

Bayard was a tall and spare man with a large frame, square broad shoulders, with massive joints and long limbs. His clean-shaven face looked younger than his iron-grey hair, and his grey eyes had the mobility of youth. It was rather an Irish face, with its heavy flexible eyebrows, and this impression was increased while listening to Bayard's rapid, nervous talk.

Of him a friend wrote in 1880 :

" Tom Bayard is not only the soul of hospitality, but one of the most fluent talkers you ever saw. When he gets very much interested he is apt to walk up and down the room with his hands in his pockets and indulge in a monologue. His words flow like water from the mouth of a pitcher, and if taken down in shorthand they will be found to make perfect sentences and notable for the display of a rich vocabulary."

Bayard was apparently all his life much influenced by the legend of his ancestor—" the great original of our name." He once said in a public speech :

" The spirit of true chivalry in all its gentleness and unselfishness, showing tenderness to the feeble and resistance to the overbearing, mercy to whom mercy is due and honour to whom honour, can and does exist in America to-day, as truly as it ever did in the olden time. The American people can justly demand from these who are delegated to represent those abroad or at home a punctilious observance of honour and delicate pride in their private and public conduct, and the moral influence to be obtained by dignified self-respect, intelligence and high personal integrity will far outweigh any attempted competition with the show and glitter of the representatives of other Governments, not based upon the principle of voluntary and orderly self-control."

Bayard had not been many months at the Embassy when suddenly Anglo-American friendship and its happy presage for the future became threatened with disturbance. The Venezuelan question, on which Lord Salisbury had refused arbitration, was taken up by President Cleveland.

On December 1, 1894, Secretary Gresham instructed Bayard to open the question by pointing out to the British Government that " England and America are fully committed to the principles of arbitration and this Government will gladly do what it can do to further a determination in that sense."

Bayard took up the matter with the Foreign Office. In a confidential dispatch of April 5, 1895, he reported that Lord Kimberley had shown him a map of the disputed territory—

" on which were delineated, in different colours, the three lines of delimitation. The line coloured in pink was the Schomburgk line, one of the terminal points of which was a short distance inside the mouth of the Orinoco, and which his lordship stated was conclusively proven and established as a British possession, and would not be submitted to arbitration, but that the ownership of the territory inter-sected by the other two lines they would be willing to submit to arbitration."

When Secretary Gresham received this dispatch, he began the preparation of a report for the guidance of his Government during the proposed negotiations. Before the work was

27

complete, the Secretary was taken ill and died. His loss was a severe blow to Cleveland, both personally and officially.

Ten days later, Attorney-General Richard Olney was made Secretary of State. He spent the remainder of the month in Washington, studying the Venezuelan documents left by his predecessor. Early in July 1895 he left with the President the draft of a dispatch to Ambassador Bayard in London. It was a statement of startling boldness. Cleveland read it carefully and then wrote Olney the following letter :

" I read your deliverance on Venezuelan affairs the day you left it with me. It's the best thing of the kind I have ever read and it leads to a conclusion that one cannot escape if he tries—that is, if there is anything in the Monroe Doctrine at all. You show there is a great deal in that and place it, I think, on better and more defensible ground than any of your predecessors *or mine.*"

The Olney statement, duly delivered by Ambassador Bayard, was carefully considered by Lord Salisbury, who wrote two dispatches on the subject. In the first, while declaring that the Monroe Doctrine had " received the entire sympathy of the English Government," his lordship frankly declined to accept Mr. Olney's interpretation of that doctrine as applicable to the boundary disputed between Great Britain and Venezuela, " a controversy with which the United States have no apparent practical concern."

He emphatically denied the American Government's right to demand " that when a European Power has a frontier difference with a South American community, the European Power shall consent to refer that controversy to arbitration," and insisted that Secretary Olney had misapprehended the meaning of America's historic policy.

Further, Lord Salisbury observed that his Government had—

" repeatedly expressed their readiness to submit to arbitration the conflicting claims of Great Britain and Venezuela to large tracts of territory which from their auriferous nature are known to be of almost untold value. But they cannot consent to entertain or to submit to the arbitration of another Power or of foreign jurists, however eminent, claims based

T. F. BAYARD.

on the extravagant pretensions of Spanish officials in the last century and involving the transfer of large numbers of British subjects, who have for many years enjoyed the settled rule of a British colony, to a nation of different race and language, whose political system is subject to frequent disturbance, and whose institutions as yet too often afford very inadequate protection to life and property."

Bayard wrote to the President on December 4 :

" The replies of Lord Salisbury to your Venezuela instructions are in good temper and moderate in tone.   Our difficulty lies in the wholly unreliable character of the Venezuelan rulers and people, and results in an almost undefinable, and therefore dangerous, responsibility for the conduct by them of their own affairs.   I believe, however, that your interpretation of this boundary dispute will check efficiently the tendency to ' land-grabbing ' in South America, which is rather an Anglo-Saxon disposition everywhere."

Cleveland and his Secretary of State had this letter in their hands when the finishing touches were being given to a document which took the world by surprise.   It was the Message to Congress of December 17, 1895, virtually throwing down the gage of battle to Great Britain.   What one of the President's friends, ex-Minister Phelps, thought of it, may be given in his own words :

" Twenty-four hours before the announcement not a man in either country, outside of the American executive chamber, could have dreamt of such a rupture on any score existing or capable of being anticipated.   But by the message of the President to Congress a controversy of small importance, between Great Britain and Venezuela, which had been dragging along . . . for the best part of the present century, had been taken in hand by the United States Government ; that its proposal to the British Government that an arbitration should take place between that country and Venezuela to determine the question had been assented to in part, but in part declined for special reasons, courteously stated ; and that thereupon, without further discussion, the President had decided to ascertain the line by an *ex parte* commission of his own appointment and to compel Great Britain to accept the result.   It was not pointed out, nor was it true, that the

United States had the slightest interest, present or future, in the settlement of the question or any special alliance or connexions with Venezuela. Nor was it claimed (if that could have made any difference) that Great Britain had taken a step or uttered a word which showed a disposition to encroach upon the rights of Venezuela or to bring any force to bear in the adjustment of the dispute. It was simply assumed, because the boundary dispute was on this hemisphere, that America had the right to dictate arbitration and if that was refused to define the line for herself and to enforce its adoption. . . .

" This extraordinary conclusion was asserted for the first time against a friendly nation, not as a proposition open to discussion, but as an ultimatum. The explanation given to an astonished world is that it is the necessary result of the Monroe Doctrine."

Phelps then exposed the Monroe Doctrine :

" The claim . . . will find no favour among just or thoughtful men. *We have no protectorate over South American nations and do not assume any responsibility in their behalf.* Our own rights there, as elsewhere, it is to be hoped, we shall never fail to maintain. . . . But when we assert that we care nothing for the opinion of the world ; that we are Americans and monarchs of all we survey, because we think we are strong enough, we adopt the language and the conduct of the bully, and shall certainly encounter, if that is persisted in, the bully's retribution."

The Cleveland Message itself was brief. Its essence is contained in the following :

" The answer of the British Government . . . claims that a new and strange extension and development of this [the Monroe] Doctrine is insisted on by the United States . . . that the reasons justifying an appeal to the doctrine are inapplicable. . . .

" The dispute has reached such a stage as to make it now incumbent on the United States to take measures to determine the true division line between the Republic of Venezuela and British Guiana. . . . When such report is made it will be the duty of the United States to resist by every means in its power the appropriation

by Great Britain of any lands which after investigation
we have determined of right to belong to Venezuela." [1]

Although the President seemed at first to have the approval
of the members of both Houses of Congress, the best international lawyers were against him, and his Ambassador in
London was deeply perturbed.[2] He wrote (December 18,
1895):

" With this note I send you *The Times* of this morning—
in order that you may perceive the tone of *average British
comment* on your Message to Congress and position in relation
to the Venezuelan-Guiana boundary dispute and claim of
right and duty under American policy as laid down by
President Monroe to insist upon a submission of questions,
touching the territorial jurisdiction of South American States,
to international arbitration.

" I send to the Secretary of State fuller—or rather more
numerous—public expressions on the subject—which, while
varying in phrase and tone, are entirely at one on the main
point, i.e. of opposition to the propositions laid down in your
Message, and the instructions of the State Department
conveyed to this Embassy.

" In my correspondence while I was Secretary of State—
also with Judge Gresham since I came here—and personally
with you—my opinions have been genuinely stated—and, as
the Venezuelan transactions and history are unfolded, I am
not able to shake off a grave sense of apprehension in allowing
the interests and welfare of our country to be imperilled or
complicated by such a Government and people as those of
Venezuela.

" It is not needful that I should repeat these views—and
I now wish to study carefully and deliberately the situation
as it exhibits itself under the light suddenly cast upon this
profoundly important question—which includes in its prin-

---

[1] E. J. Phelps : *The Monroe Doctrine*. Address delivered March 30, 1896.
[2] John Bassett Moore protested at length against the President's position.
" We have arbitrated boundary disputes, and so has Great Britain, but never,
so far as I am informed, where a line had not been previously agreed upon by
direct negotiations. Governments are not in the habit of resigning their
functions so completely into the hands of arbitrators as to say, ' We have no
boundaries ; make some for us. . . .' It would be at least unusual to leave
it to arbitrators to make a boundary. . . . Boundaries in South America
have almost universally been settled on the basis of the *beati possidentes*,
as the only practicable basis of peaceful adjustment."

ciples the treatment of every European claim of ownership and control of soil in the Western hemisphere."

Bayard's letter showed that he was "mystified and uncertain " regarding the exact position of the President, whose views he was to interpret to the British Government and to the British people. Cleveland replied :

" I am very sorry indeed that I cannot fully understand your very apparent thought and feeling on the Venezuelan question ; and you must believe me to be entirely sincere when I say that I think my want of understanding on the subject is somehow my own fault.

". . . I am entirely clear that the Doctrine is not obsolete, and it should be defended and maintained for its value and importance *to our government and welfare,* and that its defence and maintenance involve its application when a state of facts arises requiring it.

" Great Britain says she has a flawless case. Our interest in the question led us to ask her to exhibit that case in a tribunal above all others recognized as a proper one for that purpose ; and this was done to avoid a wrong procedure on our part in a matter we could not pass by.

" Great Britain has refused our request. What is to be done ? We certainly ought not, we certainly cannot abandon the case because she says she is right nor because she refuses arbitration. We do not threaten nor invite war because she refuses—far from it. We do not propose to proceed to extremities, leaving open any chance that can be guarded against, of a mistake on our part as to the facts. So, instead of threatening war for not arbitrating, we simply say, inasmuch as Great Britain will not aid us in fixing the facts, we will not go to war, but do the best we can to discover the true state of facts for ourselves, with all the facilities at our command. When, with all this, we become as certain as we can be, in default of Great Britain's co-operation, that she has seized the territory and superseded the jurisdiction of Venezuela—that is a different matter."

The President's message " fell like a crash of thunder upon English ears, attuned to the precision of diplomatic language." The *Annual Register* thus refers to the event :

" The President's extraordinary proposal was believed to have been made in view of the approaching Presidential election, in which the American-Irish vote would be an important factor ; and this belief was strengthened by the eagerness of Republicans and Democrats alike to associate themselves with a policy which affected to appeal to a sentiment of patriotism. For several days politicians in the United States, with a few exceptions, gave themselves up to a delirium of jingoism, and had that feeling continued and been reciprocated by the English Press and the English people, the two countries might really have drifted into war."

Congress, having authorized the appointment of a Commission " to determine the true division line between the Republic of Venezuela and British Guiana," the President appointed a number of distinguished citizens to act forthwith.

Their appointment may have prompted Great Britain to see the need of a less dangerous method of settlement. A few days later (January 13, 1896) Ambassador Bayard sent the following cipher telegram to Secretary Olney, containing the plan for an adjustment by which neither Great Britain nor Venezuela would be called upon to abandon long-established settlements.

" Lord Playfair, lately Liberal Cabinet Minister, came confidentially yesterday to my residence, at the request of Lord Salisbury and Secretary of State for Colonies, expressing earnest desire of both political parties here Venezuela dispute should not be allowed to drift, but be promptly settled by friendly co-operation. Suggests as solution, United States should propose conference with United States of European countries now having colonies in American hemisphere— Great Britain, France, Spain, Holland—to proclaim the Monroe Doctrine, that European Powers having interests in America should not seek to extend their influence in that hemisphere. If the United States would propose this, Great Britain would accept Monroe Doctrine, and it would become international law between countries named.

" Assuming, from the President's Message, that any settlement of boundary satisfactory to Venezuela would be unobjectionable to United States, friendly arbitration is suggested. There being no Venezuelan settlement inside Schomburgk line, and no British settlements beyond that line ; therefore, irrespective of that line, mutual condition be accepted that all British and all Venezuelan settlements be excluded from arbitration, but all country between the settlements be settled by a Court of Arbitration drawing a boundary line, which should be accepted by both countries. Such Court of Arbitration to consist of two or three commissioners from England, two or three from Venezuela and two or three from present United States Commission, to represent knowledge they have acquired. Under this principle, districts already settled by Venezuela or British Government or people would not be referred to arbitration, and there would be no difficulty in settling line by friendly arbitration. I will write you fully next Wednesday mail. But desire to express positive judgment, that proclaimed recognition of Monroe Doctrine as international law between Powers named would make it binding, not only on them, but practically on all other European Powers, and would end all contemplated plans of future conquest, or intermeddling alliances in the Western Hemisphere, by European Powers, under any pretext."

After carefully considering these suggestions, President Cleveland decided against calling a conference of European Powers to pass judgment on the Monroe Doctrine, declaring that he preferred to deal with Great Britain alone. To this Lord Salisbury readily consented, and both countries began the preparation of plans. On May 22 Lord Salisbury sent a definite proposal for the substance and form of a treaty for the creation of the joint arbitration committee. Seven weeks later Olney, acting in accordance with England's own suggestion to that effect, as expressed in Bayard's dispatch of January 13, asked whether Great Britain would consent to unrestricted arbitration of the whole matter, " provided it were made the rule of the arbitration that territory which had been in the exclusive, notorious and actual use and occupation of either party for sixty years should be held to belong to such party."

This suggestion, differing from that of the British proposal only in that it specified the period of sixty years as the term of occupancy, was accepted by Lord Salisbury.

And so, in his fourth annual Message of December 1896, President Cleveland was able to announce :

" The Venezuelan boundary question has ceased to be a

matter of difference between Great Britain and the United
States, their respective Governments having agreed upon the
substantial provisions of a treaty between Great Britain
and Venezuela submitting the whole controversy to arbitration. The provisions of the treaty are so eminently just and
fair that the assent of Venezuela thereto may confidently
be anticipated."

That an adjustment, honourable alike to both England
and America, was reached is to the credit of both ; but it
was Lord Salisbury's liberal and statesmanlike proposal,
transmitted by Ambassador Bayard, which enabled America
to abandon her independent study of the Venezuela boundary
and made a peaceful settlement possible.

To Ambassador Bayard it had been a far more trying time
than to any of the others concerned, owing to the clash between
his private convictions and his loyalty to the President.

With the defeat of the Democratic party in the elections of
1896 Bayard resigned his post, and in the following spring the
new President, William McKinley, had chosen his successor.

John Hay, though a Westerner, had little about him of the
West. He was one of those quiet, sensitive spirits, blessed
with an abundant humour, who, while owing nothing to
birth or wealth, gravitate naturally to the drawing-room and
the library.

In his early twenties he attracted the attention of President
Lincoln, who made him his assistant private secretary. Hay
was a born diplomat ; he was patient, courteous and delight-
fully satirical. He proved to be an invaluable adjunct to
Lincoln's household, and after the President's tragic death
was sent as an assistant secretary to the Paris Legation.
After further diplomatic experiences at Vienna and Madrid,
he returned in 1868 to follow journalism under the auspices
of his friend Whitelaw Reid, of the New York *Tribune*.
Came his marriage to a wealthy woman, and thenceforward
Hay appears as a sort of literary dilettante, writing verse
and prose as the mood took him, even publishing anonymously a novel, *The Bread Winners*, which had a surprising
success. His one solid work was the *Life of Lincoln*, in which

he collaborated with his former fellow-secretary, J. G. Nicolay.

Hay had always been interested in politics and, upon the absorbing questions of the day, penned articles for the *Tribune* which were widely quoted and earned him the respect and friendship of the more intellectual elements in the Republican party. Consequently, no one was surprised when President Hayes offered Hay the post of Assistant Secretary of State. But he did not hold it long. When his friend Whitelaw Reid married and went abroad, Hay edited the *Tribune* during his absence. Later, this same newspaper exerted its most powerful influence in the election of William McKinley in 1896. Reid had long coveted the English Embassy, but there were reasons which made him now stand aside in favour of his friend and junior, Hay, who soon after McKinley's inauguration was appointed to London.

Hay had become well known in England ; he had many political and literary friends there, and he was certain of a cordial welcome. But although Whitelaw Reid's occupancy of the Embassy was postponed a few years, the editor of the *Tribune* came to fulfil a special function in London that very summer. For it was the Diamond Jubilee of Queen Victoria ; celebrations had been planned on a scale of great splendour and most of the European monarchies were sending extraordinary embassies in the aged sovereign's honour. It was suggested that America should do the same. Hay's biographer says : " Contrary to his [Hay's] wish, Whitelaw Reid had persuaded President McKinley to send a special embassy to greet the Queen, with himself, naturally, at the head of it." But Reid had not the slightest intention of taking the wind out of Hay's sails. The resident Ambassador arrived in May, presented his letter of credence to the Queen, and was hardly established at the Embassy when early in June the Special Ambassador appeared on the scene. Of course there were diplomatic precedents, even in American history, for this diplomatic duality, and Hay, who could not hope to conduct such matters with zest and on such a scale of magnificence as his friend, looked on good-humouredly and perhaps a little satirically. Reid's rôle, he said, was to administer to the pomps and vanities of this world : he him-

JOHN HAY.

self was no brilliant courtier, but at least he could stand about and emit an occasional cheer. To a correspondent he made the reflection :

" What a curious thing it is that there has been no King in England since Elizabeth of special distinction—most of them far worse than mediocre—only the foreigner, William III, of any merit—and yet the monarchical religion has grown day by day till the Queen is worshipped as more than mortal, and the Prince will be more popular still when he accedes."

Hay, in his letters to his friends, often indulged in amusing raillery, as in the following allusion to his co-Ambassador, who was still (July 25) revelling in the Jubilee gaieties of London :

" The sight of a worthy human being happy is comforting to the soul, and I have seen my friend Whitelaw sitting between two princesses at supper every night, a week running, and I now may intone my *nunc dimittis*. His rapture had the *aliquid amari* that the end must come, but the memory of it will soothe many an hour of *ennui* at Ophir Farm."

Hay himself could not get away from the Embassy in Carlton House Terrace.

" It is no less than a bloomin' shyme [he wrote to Henry Adams, in France] that I cannot accept your kind invitation to your royal pleasure dome. But the flight of my household goddesses does not free me, as you seem to think, from all obligations, human and divine.

" I cannot leave this blessed Isle even at the summons of my betters in the Forest of St. Germain. ' Come again next week ! ' says my Lord Salisbury, or, by preference, ' Wait till I send for thee, when I have a more convenient season.' "

Naturally, in spite of Bayard's oratory and Whitelaw Reid's magnificence, there was still a certain resentment against America in the air, as Hay found when he came to deal with Downing Street. The Venezuela Message and the brusque Cleveland-Olney accentuation of the Monroe Doctrine could not fail to leave a mark, as well as to affect the official attitude toward other outstanding questions. The Anglo-American Treaty of Arbitration had just been killed, for no discoverable reason, by the Senate. Besides the Venezuelan boundary, now in process of regulation by an International Tribunal, there was the Bering Sea Fisheries dispute, the Alaskan boundary and the Dingley tariff. This latter measure of high protection gave particular offence to Canada, and that Dominion was just now playing a particularly important part in Anglo-American diplomacy. The Laurier Administration wanted to renew the Reciprocity Treaty of 1854, which permitted the free entry of certain natural products of either country. But they baulked at Blaine's proposal of a Customs Union, and they were not ready to sacrifice their interests in other directions. The American Government found that the recent Bering Sea award had not prevented the wholesale destruction of the baby seals, and suggested a Joint Conference between the United States, Russia, Japan and Great Britain at Washington. Ambassador Hay ascertained that Downing Street would agree; but he had reckoned without Canada.

"I was never so surprised in my life," he wrote to Washington (October 18, 1897), "as when they objected, at the end of September, to Russia and Japan."

The British Government, in Hay's opinion, "deferred too much to Canada. . . . They frankly avow their slavery to Canada, and chafe under it." "Slavery" was a hard word: but, at least, Sir Wilfrid Laurier, aware of the Dominion's rights, exerted his full influence, and Joseph Chamberlain, the Colonial Secretary, supported him. He was ready for a British-American-Canadian conference, and one was accordingly held at Washington; but it separated without a decision. Another was held in Quebec in the summer of 1898 to settle all outstanding points of difference, the Alaskan boundary, the Fisheries, the fur seals, tariffs and the rest. It also came to nothing. Hay believed that the Alaskan boundary was the most urgent of all, and was anxious to get this settled separately.

In 1898 came the Spanish-American rupture, and there arose other and more important work for the American Ambassador to do in London. The tension between America and Spain had long been increasing, and in March came word that the *Maine* had been blown up in Havana harbour. The fire-eaters from one end of the country to the other demanded a war with Spain. From the first, European opinion showed a tendency to side with the Spanish, which increased when war broke out. Even in England Spain had many sympathizers, and Hay recognized that it was vital to counteract this feeling and to encourage British good-will.

" I do not know [he wrote to Senator Lodge, April 5] whether you especially value the friendship and sympathy of this country [England]. I think it important and desirable in the present state of things, as it is the only European country whose sympathies are not openly against us. We will not waste time in discussing whether the origin of this feeling is wholly selfish or not. Its existence is beyond question. I find it wherever I go—not only in the Press, but in private conversation. For the first time in my life I find the ' drawing-room ' sentiment altogether with us. If we wanted it—which, of course, we do not—we could have the practical assistance of the British navy—on the *do ut des* principle, naturally.

" I think, in the near future, this sentiment, even if it amounts to nothing more, is valuable to us. . . ."

He described how, at a royal levée—

" All the royalties stopped me, shook hands and made some civil remark. The Spanish Ambassador coming next to me, was received merely with a bow. . . . You may think ' it is none of my Lula business,' but I think the Senate Committee's allusion to England in the Hawaii Report was not of sufficient use at home to compensate for the jar it gave over here."

With the inveterate Anglophobe attitude of the Senate Hay was to make a more intimate and vexatious acquaintance later on.

Towards the end of April hostilities began, and the British Government proclaimed its neutrality.

" The position of a foreign Ambassador in a neutral State [says Professor Mowat] when his country is at war is usually delicate, difficult and unpleasant. He has to justify his country, he has to meet honest and dishonest criticism, he has to combat enemy propaganda, and, owing to the absorption of his Government in the war, he has usually not much more information at his disposal than the public among whom he is living."

Hay's friend, Henry Adams, could vividly recall such times at the American Legation in London. But English public opinion had changed, and was now definitely on the side of America. To Lodge, Hay wrote :

" You have had an anxious and exciting week. You may imagine what it is to me, absolutely without light or instruction, compelled to act from day to day on my own judgment, and at no moment sure of the wishes of the Department. What I should have done if the feelings here had been unfriendly, instead of cordially sympathetic, it is hard to say. The commonest phrase here is : ' I wish you would take Cuba at once. *We* wouldn't have stood it this long.' " [1]

The war was waged swiftly. On May Day Admiral Dewey utterly destroyed the Spanish squadron in Manila Bay and began a strict blockade of the town, the British and German fleets looking on, each animated by widely different feelings. Everyone in Europe knew of a German plan for joint intervention, which lacked a favourable opportunity to be promulgated.

" It is hardly too much to say [wrote Hay, May 25] that the interests of civilization are bound up in the direction relations of England and America are to take in the next few months.

" The state of feeling here is the best I have ever known. From every quarter the evidences of it come to me. The Royal family, by habit and tradition, are most careful not to break the rules of strict neutrality ; but even among them I find nothing but hearty kindness, and—so far as is consistent with propriety—sympathy. Among the political leaders on both sides I find not only sympathy, but a somewhat eager desire that ' the other fellows ' shall not seem the more friendly. Chamberlain's startling speech was partly due to a conversation I had with him, in which I hoped he would not let the Opposition have a monopoly of expressions of goodwill to America.

[1] Thayer : *Life and Letters of John Hay.*

" He is greatly pleased with the reception his speech met with on our side, and says he " don't care a hang what they say about it on the Continent.' "

Chamberlain's " startling speech " had been delivered on May 13, when he proposed an Anglo-American alliance.

How different, indeed, was Hay's position from that of his predecessor, C. F. Adams, when Great Britain was " neutral " !

" I spent the great part of my time declining invitations to dine and speak. But on the rare occasions when I do go to big public dinners the warmth of the welcome leaves nothing to be desired. But the overwhelming weight of opinion is on our side. A smashing blow in the Caribbean would help wonderfully."

The " smashing blow " came on July 3, at Santiago-de-Cuba, and three weeks later Spain was suing for peace. In the following month, when the Peace Commission, of which W. R. Day, the Secretary of State, was a member, had been appointed to meet in Paris, Ambassador Hay received the following unexpected message from President McKinley (August 13, 1898) :

" It gives me exceptional pleasure to tender to you the office of Secretary of State, *vice* Day, who will resign to take service on the Paris Commission, to negotiate peace. It is important that you should assume duties here not later than the first of September."

Hay was happy in England as Ambassador, and would have preferred to remain there. He had some doubts as to his capacity to fill the more important, and certainly more onerous, post at home. Physically, too, he was far from robust. But the opportunity for distinction and for rendering a high national service could not be resisted.

" I grieve to go away from England [he wrote to an English friend]. In a year or two I think I should have been ready, but the charms of this blessed island are inexhaustible, and perhaps I should never have had enough of them.

" I have received much kindness here from all sorts and conditions of men. Dearest and most enduring of all my recollections are those happy hours spent at Tillypronie with the earliest and best of our English friends. The chains of office will not fetter me for ever, I hope, and the first use I shall make of my liberty will be to cross the great water and to renew an acquaintance which will be precious to me as long as I live."

According to Henry Adams, the diplomacy of Hay was not merely the coping-stone of a permanent Anglo-American friendship, but rather the key-stone which finally perfected the arch. " In the long list of famous American Ministers in London, none could have given the work quite the completeness, the harmony, the perfect ease of Hay."[1]

BIOGRAPHICAL NOTES

Robert Lincoln returned to the law, became counsel for and eventually President of the Pullman Car Company, and acquired considerable wealth. He spent his final years in Washington, dying in 1926 at eighty-three.

Bayard died in 1898, when Hay was taking up his post as Secretary of State.

[1] *The Education of Henry Adams.*

CHAPTER XXI

CHOATE AND REID (1901–1912)

So completely cordial seemed now the relations between the two countries that whoever followed John Hay could not fail of tranquillity. There is reason to believe that if Hay could have had his way, he would formally have established Henry White as his successor, for in this trained and competent public servant he had the fullest confidence. White had been First Secretary in London for many years, and was on terms of intimacy with all the leading individuals in English public and social life. He was, moreover, an assiduous personal correspondent of Roosevelt, Lodge, Reid, Hay and others, and able to inform them more fully of current affairs than any other American in London. But the London Embassy was too highly esteemed as a political prize for the Administration to hand it over to a mere professional diplomat.

Whatever distinguished man was sent, Secretary Hay had someone in London who thoroughly understood and sympathized with his policy.

" As long as I stay here [he wrote to White in the following year from the State Department] no action shall be taken contrary to my conviction that the one indispensable feature of our foreign policy should be a friendly understanding with England. But an alliance must remain, in the present state of things, an unattainable dream."

Had it rested with him, he would undoubtedly have proposed and supported such an alliance, but " the weak point is the Senate." As he had previously written to Lodge :

" I have told you many times that I did not believe another important treaty would ever pass the Senate. What is to

28   419

be thought of a body which will not take Hawaii as a gift, and is clamouring to hold the Philippines ? "

In December 1898 Hay wrote to Henry White that there had been a great deal of discussion as to whether the Clayton-Bulwer Treaty actually stood in the way of any practical action by the United States in the construction and control of the projected Isthmian Canal, the Nicaraguan route being then favoured. White at once saw Lord Salisbury with a view to modifying or repealing the treaty so as to enable the canal to be built. The result was a convention signed at Washington in February 1900. The clause forbidding fortification was not struck out of the treaty ; nor were the provisions for neutrality.

Unhappily, in the interval, had come the Boer War in 1899, and, in consequence, " a mad-dog hatred of England·" arose in America and also in certain European countries. Hay wrote :

" Whatever we do, Bryan will attack us as the slaves of England. All their [Democratic] State conventions put the anti-English plank in the platform to curry favour with the Irish (whom they want to keep) and the Germans (whom they want to seduce).

" It is too disgusting to have to deal with such sordid liars." [1]

It is clear that Hay was whole-heartedly with England in the South African War. " Sooner or later," he declared, " her influence will be dominant there, and the sooner the better." It was, therefore, fortunate that when an Ambassador was appointed to London at this juncture, it was one who was incapable of any petty jealousy and who was prepared to give Hay the most earnest support in this matter of the Canal Treaty, no matter how loudly the Irish and other foreign elements railed.

A highly successful New York lawyer who had migrated in early manhood from Massachusetts, Joseph Hodges Choate was in his sixty-seventh year when he accepted the London Embassy. He had achieved an almost unrivalled success at the Bar, as had his eminent kinsman, Rufus Choate, long before

---

[1] Hay to White, September, 1899.

JOSEPH H. CHOATE.

him. His good nature was proverbial; he was a witty speaker, and he was wealthy.

Few citizens of New York—unless it was Chauncey Depew —were more widely popular. Yet to his popularity there was an exception—he loved the race of Irish agitators in America even less than Hay or Lowell. Nor had he failed to express his sentiments publicly, as in a speech on St. Patrick's Day, which especially infuriated the Irish-American fanatics.

" In appointing Joseph Choate to be Ambassador to England [amiably observed one leading Irish-American journal] Mr. McKinley has virtually spat into the face of every man and woman of Irish birth or blood in the United States, and he has done so deliberately, knowing well that Mr. Choate is the incarnation of hate to the Irish race, and that the selection of such a man would be a cruel insult to a large and powerful element in the Republican party that has made him President."

Another newspaper greeted his appointment with an editorial entitled " A Compliment to England," in which Choate was described as—

" a virulent enemy of the Irish race ; [as] hating the Irish as the devil hates holy water ; his malevolence not confined to any class or section of Irish, abhorring them all, and whenever occasion offered to spit his venom at the Irish he has done it, and when no occasion offered he made it."

This was pretty strong language—so intemperate that both the President and Choate himself could afford to treat it with good-humoured contempt.

The new Ambassador came perhaps at an awkward moment in English history, for the war was subjecting the British Army to certain humiliations in the field which gave unalloyed pleasure to many foreign countries.

His first public appearance and speech in London was at a dinner of the Association of the Chambers of Commerce, in which he referred to President Cleveland's Venezuela message :

" You know that on our side of the water we love, occasionally, to twist the lion's tail for the mere sport of hearing him roar. Well, that time he disappointed us ; he would not roar at all, but sat silent as a sphinx, and by mutual for-bearance—our sober second thought aiding your sober first thought—we averted everything but a mere war of words."

It is no wonder he was well received by the English Bar, for his fame as a lawyer had preceded him, nor that later he should have been unanimously elected a Bencher of the Middle Temple—a rare honour to be accorded to an American. But everywhere his welcome was hearty and his public appearance the signal for enthusiastic good-will.

The Canal Treaty, which had been negotiated by Secretary Hay and Lord Pauncefote, the British Ambassador in Washington, permitted the American Government to construct a canal with the exclusive right of regulating and managing it. The Senate rejected it in 1900 on the ground that it would prevent the United States from fortifying the canal. Consequently, a new treaty had to be formulated which would prove more acceptable.

Lord Pauncefote, whose understanding with Secretary Hay in Washington was perfect, came to London during 1901, and he, Ambassador Choate and the Foreign Secretary, Lord Lansdowne, met frequently.

Hay wrote to Choate (September 2, 1901):

" You know the line to take better than I can tell you. The necessity of the canal ; the interest England has in it ; the advantage to her of our building and managing it ; the desire of the President to get rid of the Clayton-Bulwer Treaty not only without impairment of our good relations with England, but, if possible, in such a way as to make them more intimately friendly. Press the considerations you have already brought forward as reported in your letters to me. I do not think they can fail to impress Lord Lansdowne ; he is too intelligent not to see that the briefer and simpler the Treaty can be made the better."

But as Choate went on with his negotiations with the Foreign Office, suddenly, in September, the discovery was made that the Treaty under consideration only applied to the Nicaragua route and that, if another route were chosen, it would put the British Government in a " ridiculous position." Lord Pauncefote, then in London, was much disturbed at hearing that the United States were contemplating Panama.

Hay wired (September 29, 1901): "I think that Nicaragua will be chosen." Three days later he cabled: "Our intention is that the Treaty shall cover *all* Isthmian routes." By that time Choate had seen Senator Lodge in London and ascertained that the Panama route was probable, and that Lodge would support the new Canal Treaty in the Senate.

"Before seeing Mr. Lodge, I communicated to Lord Pauncefote your conviction as to the extreme improbability of any Panama route and how strong both Senate and House were for Nicaragua. He still clung to the necessity of adding a few words to make the meaning unmistakable. Hence the insertion of ' by whatever route may be considered expedient ' in the preamble. He spoke of some utterance of Mr. Blaine to the effect that the Clayton-Bulwer Treaty had no reference whatever to a canal by the Panama route, as an additional reason for being very precise this time."

The important clause in the Treaty now read:

"The Canal shall never be blockaded, nor shall any right of war be exercised nor any act of hostility be committed within it. *The United States, however, shall be at liberty to maintain such military police along the Canal as may be necessary to protect it against lawlessness and disorder.*"

As the Senate was to meet on the first Monday in December, no time was to be lost in getting the treaty ready.

"I told Lansdowne [wrote Choate, October 2] that it would be necessary to have it in the President's hands a good while before that date. . . . He promised to do the best he could—he would send it at once to Lord Salisbury and the Lord Chancellor, whom I consider the most important men in the matter. . . . He said Lord Salisbury did not like to be troubled much at Beaulieu, but under the circumstances he would send it to him at once and would hunt up the Lord Chancellor [Halsbury], who has been spending his vacation on the Continent."

Choate could not withhold his tribute from Lord Lansdowne, who " in this whole matter has been most considerate and more than generous.

" In substance, he abrogates the Clayton-Bulwer Treaty, gives us an American canal—ours to build as and where we

like, to control and govern—on the sole condition of its always
being neutral and free for the passage of the ships of all
nations on equal terms, except that if we get into war with
any nation we can shut its ships out and take care of ourselves.

" I shall [added Choate] be disappointed—in fact mortified
—if, after Great Britain has met us so manfully, we fail to
come to an agreement."

But they did not fail, and in its new form the Hay-Pauncefote Treaty passed the Senate and was proclaimed by the
President on December 26, 1901.

By this time there was a new Chief Executive at the
White House.   Three months before, President McKinley
had been assassinated, an event which evoked a burst of
regret and sympathy throughout Great Britain.   The foreign
policy of President Roosevelt was awaited not without a
certain trepidation.

The question of the Alaskan Boundary had taken on a
fresh importance since the discovery of gold in the Klondike
region and the great gold-rush of 1897-8.   All this made the
delimitation of the boundary imperative.   Canada laid
claim to the inlets, harbours and channels which had been
undisputedly American since 1867, when purchased from
Russia.   The Joint High Commission of 1898–9 had been
unable to reach a decision which would settle the controversy, and not until January 1903 were negotiations re-
opened, and a limited Commission appointed, to consist of six
members, three to be nominated by America and three by Great
Britain.   It was taken for granted that the Americans and
the Canadians would each uphold the claims of their respective Governments, and the decision really depended upon
Lord Alverstone, Lord Chief Justice of England, the chief of
the British Commission.   Secretary Hay hoped that Choate
would undertake to present the argument of the American
case to the Commission, because, as he expressed it, " a
mere legal argument is not what is required in this unprecedented case.   A sharp, aggressive lawyer will run a
great risk of getting Lord Alverstone's ' back up.' "   Choate
would have made an argument " faultless in tone, temper,
skill and knowledge of human nature."   Choate, however,

believed it would " not be proper for him, who, as American Ambassador, had negotiated the appointment of the Commission with the British Ministers, to appear before the Commission as lawyer to support by argument the American case. He felt it might be thought he had not been quite candid, and that it would be likely to affect his personal and official relations with the British Government." [1] There is no doubt that in this case he was wise. The result was a victory for the United States, whose claim was upheld by Lord Alverstone as against the Canadian commissioners, who dissented.

" It is difficult to see why the British Government ever consented to go to a tribunal of six without neutral members or provision for a casting vote. It looks as if the British Government had no great confidence in its ' case ' and chose the Commission merely as a means of possibly affording itself a dignified method of surrender." [2]

Canada, of course, could not be expected to look at it in that way, but in the last resort it was Britain and not Canada which had to deal with the United States.

It has since transpired that Roosevelt had written a private letter to be " indiscreetly " shown to Chamberlain and Balfour, making known his determination that in case of a disagreement there would be no further arbitration. He should simply request Congress " to give me the authority to run the line as we claim it, by our own people, without any further regard to the attitude of England and Canada." This was the language of a bully, but then, Roosevelt could be a bully upon occasion. The alternative was war, and no British Government would go to war over the Alaskan boundary. Both Hay and Choate regretted this tone, but both were helpless.

All through the years of Choate's Embassy he was occupied, to a far greater extent than any of his predecessors, even of Lowell, in making speeches and addresses, generally of a popular and humorous character and nearly always striking

[1] *Life of J. H. Choate.*
[2] Mowat : *Diplomatic Relations.*

the same note—the friendship between the two peoples. His biographer hardly exaggerates when he says :

" Chambers of Commerce swooped down upon him and bore him off in triumph as their guest. The Omar Khayyàm Club, the Dante Society, the Wordsworth Society and the Browning Society pressed their claims. The Birmingham and Midland Institute elected him as its annual President and exacted, by way of tribute, an address on Benjamin Franklin. The Philosophical Institution bestowed the same honour and claimed, as a reward, his fine address on Abraham Lincoln. The public schools, playing upon his interests in education, lured him into distributing their prizes, and political leagues expected him to tell them about the United States Supreme Court. The historic City Guilds fastened upon him, and he was a standing feature at their banquets. Charitable and philanthropic societies pursued him. Workmen's Institutes claimed him on account of his democratic sympathies. Libraries refused to be opened except by him. He was the obvious man to unveil a bust or a portrait. Sporting and fox-hunting clubs could not get along without him. His presence was expected at dinners in honour of famous individuals, and his nation's birthday and day of Thanksgiving expected him to add something fresh and new on threadbare subjects. He was turned into a sort of ambassadorial lecturer to the English nation who demanded from him, at every turn, eloquence, versatility, and yet more versatility. He was launched on an oratorical tour from Land's End to John o' Groat's."

In this occupation Choate learned to know all classes and almost all corners of England, and he spent his time, ungrudgingly, in forwarding public and philanthropic movements.

One of Choate's entertaining discoveries was that Downing Street had been named from a native American, Sir George Downing, and he delivered an address on the subject before a distinguished audience which included the Prime Minister, Lord Salisbury.

" It is [he told them] the smallest, and at the same time the greatest, street in the world, because it lies at the hub of the gigantic wheel which encircles the globe under the name of the British Empire. It is all American. I have shown you why it is called Downing Street. But why, Lord Salisbury, is it called a street? I have always thought that a street was a way through from one place to some other place. This does not come within that definition. I have heard it called a *cul de sac*—that has no outlet, except at one end—a place where you can get in but cannot get out. Now, however other nations may find it, we Americans, by reason of our prescriptive rights in the premises, find it to be a thoroughfare. We feel entirely at home in it. Our feet are on our native heath. We can go in and go out, and give and take on equal terms."

A further example of Choate's bright oratorical style may be given.

" When I came into the room and saw the Union Jack and the Stars and Stripes hanging together opposite to the platform I knew that I was all right. Those two flags have not always hung together in so friendly a way, but they have been drawing closer and closer together for many years, and I hope they will never be separated. [Cheers.] I have been introduced to you by the Chairman as the Ambassador from the United States. [I believe that my legal title is ' Ambassador of the United States at the Court of St. James,' but I take a greater pride in being Ambassador from the people of the United States to the people of Great Britain."

Choate remained at the London Embassy until after Roosevelt had entered upon his second Presidential term. Although his successor had been appointed, Choate received an extension of time, in order that he might personally dedicate his memorial window to John Harvard in St. Saviour's Church. On May 23, 1905, he presented his letter of recall to King Edward.

When he was back home again in June, Choate told his New York friends, who gave him a fervent welcome :

" Now, as to what I have done abroad. I have enjoyed myself a great deal. Some of you may have experienced the generosity and freedom of English hospitality. You know what it is. But I am not sure you know what a steadfast purpose there is in our brethren on the other side to maintain that friendship which so happily exists. I may not discuss any of the relations between the two countries, but I believe that I know that all future differences between them may be amicably and honourably adjusted."

Even before his previous appointment, as Ambassador to France, as far back as 1889, Whitelaw Reid had been marked out for the English mission. This tall, slender, bearded figure with something less than Hay's humorous *insouciance* and with more patience than Lowell, yet recalling both, occupied a commanding place in American journalism. His success was not due to the method which had made Thurlow Weed, Horace Greeley, Charles Dana and James Gordon Bennett more feared than loved : it was his suavity, his personal and literary charm and his close political friendships. He had, thanks to an ample fortune, cultivated the grand manner and a taste for the best in life. He was never hurried, never harassed, never ill-tempered.

A native of Ohio, where he was born in 1837, Reid early found himself on the staff of the New York *Tribune*, where his ability won him quick promotion, and, on Greeley's death, the editorship. At well over forty his marriage to the daughter of a famous millionaire, Ogden Mills, enabled him to acquire control of the paper, which was then, and continued to be during his lifetime, the chief organ of the Republican party. Both he and his journal were recognized as standing for the best conservative elements in American life, and his counsel and support were sought by successive Presidents, from Hayes onward. Rich in friendships, he was especially intimate with Garfield, Blaine, John Hay, Theodore Roosevelt and Henry Adams, an intimacy enshrined in hundreds of delightful letters.

" I cannot help telling you with what long-looked-for delight [wrote Secretary Hay, January 6, 1905, six months before his death] I shall countersign your commission as Ambassador to England. When that is done I shall feel like intoning my *nunc dimittis*. It will be the crowning act of a friendship and close association of forty years. This for the personal side of it, without referring just now to the great and lasting advantage to our interests and to our honour and prestige abroad which will come from your Embassy."

Four days after President Roosevelt entered upon his

second term in March, Reid's commission was signed. Ambassador Choate had already written to his successor :

" So far as I have learned no other man has even been thought of for the place, and that seems to be well understood here, so that the English people will take to you at once, and in earnest. With your large and varied experience in public questions, your diplomatic record, and the important part you took in making the last great treaty that changed the map of the world,[1] your complete success may be foretold."

The new Ambassador formally retired from the editorship and management of his paper, the *Tribune*, while retaining the ownership.

" I have long looked upon my ownership of the *Tribune* [he wrote to Roosevelt] as a sort of trust, and should not feel at liberty to divest myself of it without trying to ensure its continuing to stand for good morals, good citizenship and the public policies with which the country has learned to identify it."

When Reid and his family reached London early in June 1905 a house had been secured for them which perhaps for the first time adequately represented the wealth and dignity of his great country in London. Dorchester House in Park Lane, belonging to Sir George Holford, was one of the largest and most imposing mansions in Mayfair. It was perhaps too large and too imposing to please all the exponents of " Republican simplicity," and Reid naturally came in for a deal of petty criticism. As Reid was a wealthy man, accustomed to be well-housed, and as the cost of the Embassy building did not fall upon the American tax-payer, it is difficult to see why anyone should have objected. The President and Hay were all in favour of Dorchester House.

" I think [wrote Roosevelt, characteristically] a man should live in such a position as he has been accustomed to live. If I found just the right man for a given Cabinet position, and he happened to be a poor man, I should not in the least object to his living in the hall-bedroom of a boarding-house. On the contrary, I should be pleased at it. On the other hand, as Root can afford a big house and can afford to enter-

[1] The Spanish-American Treaty of 1899.

tain, I think it would be rather shabby, rather mean, if he lived in a way that would be quite proper for others—that would, for instance, be quite proper for me if I were in the Cabinet. I never feel in the least embarrassed because at Sagamore Hill, at my own house, we have a maid to wait on the table and open the door instead of having a butler. I should feel nothing but scornful amusement for any man who felt that such method of living was improper for a President or Cabinet officer ; but I should have exactly the same feeling for the critic who objected to a rich man who was doing his full duty living as he had the right to live." [1]

Ambassador Reid's arrival coincided with the State visit of King Alfonso of Spain, with whose country America had been at war a few years before and with whom relations were not yet exactly cordial. At this monarch's reception of the Diplomatic Corps, Reid was surprised when Alfonso addressed him cordially in French:

" ' You have served more than once in Paris,' and then inquired as to my liking London. The next thing he said was : ' Your daughter is fond of horses and drives four. I have seen a newspaper picture of her on her coach with you by her side on the box seat. I would like you to have her send me that picture with her autograph and yours on it.'

" A day or two later I met the King again at the dinner given in his honour at Lansdowne House. I was seated nearly opposite him. His greeting across the table, when he glanced over and saw me there, was as frank and cordial as if he had been some college friend of my son's."

Before that, of course, Reid had presented his credentials and been warmly received by King Edward VII at Buckingham Palace. There was at that moment an engrossing theme to discuss, and the King was eager to discuss it. The Russo-Japanese War had reached a crisis, and Hay had cabled the Ambassador : " Togo annihilated Russian fleet in Corea Straits, capturing six and sinking thirteen. Japanese losses trifling." Afterwards the President wrote :

" Togo's smashing of Rojestvensky was so complete that the Russian case is absolutely helpless. I should be sorry to see Russia driven out of East Asia, and driven out she

[1] Royal Cortissoz : *Life of Whitelaw Reid.*

WHITELAW REID.

surely will be if the war goes on. Accordingly, I have urged her to let me propose to both combatants that they meet and negotiate for peace."

King Edward told Reid that the Tsar was disposed for peace, and that the President's plan was the best mode to bring about the result.

" There is no mistaking [reported Reid] the absolute determination of the British Government and the Royal family to embrace every opportunity to show their marked friendship for the United States. I think, however, they regard the whole European situation at the present moment as critical in the extreme, and are exceedingly careful about every new move."

The point was, whether England was disposed to put pressure upon her ally, Japan, especially since Japan had not disclosed her terms. King Edward suggested to Reid that it might be a good idea for Japan to take Vladivostok and restore it to Russia after the war as a gesture of magnanimity. But Roosevelt baulked at this as dangerous. The British Prime Minister, Balfour, was naturally on the side of Japan and favoured a big indemnity, while Roosevelt's policy was to keep the victorious Japanese as far as possible in check. The Portsmouth Conference was held in midsummer, and the Roosevelt intervention had a " colossal success," peace resulting between Russia and Japan.

Ambassador Reid wrote, with pardonable exaggeration, that it was—

" easily the greatest thing in diplomacy over European matters in the memory of this generation or the last, and the thing about it most pleasing was that you did it off your own bat."

By this time the Balfour Administration was tottering ; but it held on until December, when it was succeeded by that of Sir Henry Campbell-Bannerman. Reid was very sorry to part with Lord Lansdowne, but he found one equally congenial in the new Foreign Secretary, Sir Edward Grey. On December 12 the Ambassador reported :

" Sir Edward Grey was, of course, most cordial and he seemed gratified that the first diplomatic visit he received after entering upon his office was that from the American Ambassador. I spoke to him briefly about the only question with Great Britain of the slightest importance which we have on the diplomatic slate at present. . . . I mentioned the satisfaction with which I had heard of his appointment, particularly on account of his recent speech on foreign affairs in which he had dwelt on the necessity of continuing the present policy of the Government in three particulars and had named, first of all among the points on which there ought to be no change, the effort to cultivate constantly the most cordial relations with the United States."

The question to which Ambassador Reid had referred as being the only important one " on the diplomatic slate " was that of Newfoundland. It is to be feared that Reid took a less sympathetic view of that British Dominion's grievance against the American fishermen and the Treaty of 1818 than the exact circumstances warranted. To Reid, Newfoundland was always a little " spit-fire," " cantankerous " colony which was bent upon upsetting Anglo-American good relations ; but, after all, Newfoundland was a self-governing community of the British Empire and had a good case. Her people had suffered much neglect and injustice, first from the French and now from the Americans.

In 1905 Secretary Elihu Root, who had succeeded to the State Department on the lamented death of John Hay, informed the Ambassador that the Newfoundland Government had forbidden American fishing vessels already on the treaty coast—

" to take fish within the treaty limits prescribed in the Treaty of 1818. They consider that their right is perfectly clear, and in accordance with the construction of the treaty always followed and never questioned by the British Government, and they have been so advised by the Department."

The whole business proved very complicated, and, as a divergence in the views of the two Governments made an immediate settlement impossible, Reid negotiated a *modus vivendi,* which further shelved the matter, without pleasing the Newfoundlanders or their champions in England.

" Boiled down [wrote Reid, privately] we have certain fishing rights guaranteed to us by the Treaty of 1818 and absolutely undisputed. They wanted us to give them some privilege in our ports, which I personally (following Hay's lead) would have been glad to see them get, though the Senate thought differently. Because they don't get them, they turn round now and deliberately avow the purpose to avenge themselves by damaging, and as far as they can destroying, our rights under a treaty which has been respected for nearly a century. If they were not so little and so poor, one would be tempted to use strong language about such conduct."

Which recalls the passage in the French school-book : " Cet animal est très méchant. Quand on l'attaque, il se défend." Whatever Great Britain had chosen to give away in 1818, surely it was intolerable that now, nearly a century later, Newfoundland should not be mistress in her own house, now invaded by foreigners who refused to give any- thing in return for the hospitality they enjoyed. However, this question, too, would eventually be settled at the Hague in 1910.

Meanwhile, there was the German menace in Morocco, and a Conference of the Powers at Algeciras to settle the respective claims of France and Germany. This Conference, which had all the " potentialities of a powder magazine," had its rever- berations in Washington and London, as numerous dispatches at the Embassy testify. Roosevelt set great store by his foreign policy, and was constantly seeking to exert his influence to keep the peace in Europe.

" The trouble is [he wrote Reid] that, with Russia out of the way, as she now is, Germany firmly believes that she can whip both France and England. I have excellent reasons for believing that the German naval authorities are as con- fident as the German military authorities. . . . The military men firmly believe that an army of fifty thousand Germans landed in England would with but little difficulty take possession of the entire island."

Prior to the Second Peace Conference at the Hague, Sir Edward Grey assured the Ambassador that the British delegates would be instructed cordially to support the Ameri- can proposal for the reduction or limitation of armaments. At the same time the President wrote (August 7, 1906):

" I do not want this new Liberal Government, with which in many matters I have such hearty sympathy, to go to any maudlin extremes at the Hague Conference. It is eminently wise and proper that we should take real steps in advance toward the policy of minimizing the chances of war amongst civilized peoples, of multiplying the methods and chances of honourably avoiding war in the event of controversy ; but we must not grow sentimental and commit some Jefferson-Bryan-like piece of idiotic folly such as would be entailed if the free people who have free governments put themselves at a hopeless disadvantage compared with military despotisms and military barbarisms. I should like to see the British navy kept at its present size, but only on condition that the continental and Japanese navies are not built up. I do not wish to see it relatively weaker to them than is now the case."

It is curious to note now how this aspiration for European pacification through disarmament persisted through successive American Administrations, those of Wilson, Harding and Coolidge, giving rise to one proposal after another until the end seems now to have been attained in the Kellogg Pact.

All this time the Ambassador and Ambassadress were leading a very full social life at Dorchester House, and Reid was launched into that career of speech-making which has come to be inseparable from his office. It began with his presiding at the Royal Literary Fund and passed from one notable occasion to another. Always Reid impressed his English audiences by the soundness and propriety of his matter and the grace and refinement of his manner. If any criticism were heard it was that his oratory was indistinguishable from that of any cultured Englishman. In this respect it differed *in toto* from the rotund and forceful periods of Mr. William Jennings Bryan, who paid a visit to London in 1906. Reid was inclined to be apprehensive at first, but the " silver-tongued " Nebraskan seems to have made a good impression on the whole, and the Ambassador reported that the net result of his visit was that Bryan had " decidedly risen in the estimation of the English and of the Diplomatic Corps."

As to the work at the Embassy, Whitelaw Reid afforded some details to a prominent Kentuckian publicist, who had been dilating publicly on the uselessness of diplomacy in general and the American diplomatic service in particular.

" If [he wrote] you sat in my office for half an hour and ran your eye over the files showing the questions that suddenly come up and can be dealt with, not by special commissions and not by cabled dispatches, but only by telling your representative to find out how the land lies on certain subjects, and then to move according to his judgment of the local conditions with reference to the end you desire—after looking over even a brief record of this sort of thing you would realize how impracticable is this notion of dispensing with diplomatic representatives to which you have lent the great influence of your name and brilliant work.

" People say the cable has done away with the necessity for them—that mere dispatches between our State Department and the various Foreign Offices can do everything. But a dispatch can't carry any more than a letter used to, in the days when letters were our quickest mode of communication. If, then, the interests of a Government of more than eighty millions of people can be properly and entirely managed from the Home Office by cable dispatches, why couldn't the interests of the three millions in 1776 have been managed just as well by letters ? What was the use of sending Benjamin Franklin over, and Thomas Jefferson, and the rest of our early diplomats ? The cable merely gives us the quickest transmission at the present day ; the letter gave us the quickest transmission at that day, and if need be, that could be sent by a special post-bag as well as by Benjamin Franklin. If the diplomatic service is useless now it was equally useless then, and we have persisted in a costly folly for a century and a third." [1]

As Reid's admirable biographer, Mr. Cortissoz, truly says, official dispatches are only a part of the work. There is also the record of personal contacts, of that interplay of friendly discussion without which the solution of a given problem is impossible. John Bigelow, a former American Minister to France, was inclined to think that the telegraph minimized a diplomat's labours, but he and others forgot that the reduction of time in the transmission of instructions made no difference at all in the responsibility involved in carrying them out. As Reid wrote him—

" I have instructions requiring the use of all arguments and influence I can bring to bear on matters ranging from Canada

[1] To Colonel Henry Watterson. Cortissoz's *Life of Reid*.

29

to China, Russia and Japan, and in fact pretty much over the habitable globe."

Reid, of course, came mostly in touch with Sir Edward Grey during the period of his Embassy, but his personal relations with King Edward VII were unusually cordial, intimate and helpful. To President Roosevelt he wrote :

" The more you know of him the better you will like him, and the more you will come to the prevalent English and in fact European belief that he is the greatest mainstay of peace in Europe."

When one recalls the amount of mid-century diplomacy expended upon the Mosquito Coast, which more than once produced tension between the two countries, it is diverting to read of the pathetic decline of the once famous Mosquito tribe. In 1907 Reid reported that he had " warded off the offer of some brand-new territory and responsibilities " for his country.

" Some years ago Great Britain found her authority on the Mosquito Coast of Nicaragua chiefly a nuisance and contrived to land her control over the Mosquito Indians in the lap of Nicaragua. Since then the Indians think they have been badly treated by the Nicaraguans and have been appealing to Great Britain for protection or intervention, and have, I believe, got a little money out of them, at least for the expense of delegations here. They were definitely turned down, however, a few weeks ago. Whereupon they appeared solemnly at our Embassy offices and sought an interview with me to tender the sovereignty of their country through me to the United States ! "

Reid declined seeing the Mosquito chiefs and referred them to Washington.

At the age of seventy Reid continued to fling himself into the arduous labours of the Embassy, especially the speech-making and the social side, with all the zeal of a much younger man. Fortunately, he had his beautiful country-house at Wrest Park (the seat of Lord Lucas), which saw him as often as Park Lane, and there he lived the life of an English country gentleman. His shooting parties—the first ever given by an American envoy—became famous for the number and quality of the game and for the illustrious guests, frequently, of course, including royalty. It seemed therefore quite in the nature of things that the hand of the Ambassador's daughter should be sought by a scion of the English nobility, and the wedding of Miss Jean Reid to the Honourable John Ward, son of Lord Dudley, took place at the Chapel Royal on June 23, 1908, the King and Queen being present.

Before this event the Ambassador had received the honour of an Oxford degree, which he shared in company with another distinguished American, S. L. Clemens (Mark Twain).   In his letter, Lord Curzon, the Chancellor, had written :

" I should like to be allowed the honour of conferring the degree of D.C.L. upon yourself in recognition of your distinguished career and services and because of the illustrious position that you occupy with so much satisfaction to both countries."

When Roosevelt went out of office and was succeeded by President Taft in 1909, there was a momentary doubt whether Reid would continue in London ; but it was soon dispelled by Taft's Secretary of State, Philander Knox. Secretary Root, with whom he had worked in such harmony for four years, testified to the " admirable tact and good judgment " the Ambassador had shown in all the delicate and important matters they had handled together.

" The country probably never will know how important some of these things have been or how easy it would have been to go wrong or what unfortunate results would have followed if the representative of the United States in London had not been competent and able."

King Edward was especially pleased that there was to be no change.

" I rejoice [he wrote] to learn that your tenure of office as Ambassador of the United States to the Court of St. James is likely to continue. There is no one who could fill such a post with greater distinction than yourself, and I personally rejoice that one whom I have learned to know as a friend will not now leave my country."

In succeeding years there were all sorts of questions, including a vexatious one about Chinese Railway Concessions,

Opium, Liberia, the Congo and Fur Seals; but the one which Reid always said had given him the most trouble was Newfoundland, and this was finally disposed of at the Hague Conference in 1910. America's case was argued by Senator Root, who did not, however, gain all that his countrymen demanded from that sturdy little Dominion.

The death of King Edward was a great shock to Reid. The sovereign had sent for him a few days before to talk about the visit which ex-President Roosevelt was about to pay England.

" Our talk was interrupted by spasms of coughing, and I found that he was suffering from a good many of the symptoms of which I had such painful experience myself during the winters when bronchial asthma banished me to Arizona. Still, he is a man of tremendous vigour of constitution and of extraordinarily energetic habits. The public think him in perfect health [added the Ambassador], but in inner circles much anxiety was manifested."

Within forty-eight hours the King was dead (May 6, 1910). Reid cabled to Washington suggesting that Roosevelt should be appointed Special Ambassador at the funeral and this was done. The Roosevelt visit, in spite of this tragic beginning, proved a great success. True, the ex-President's very frank speech on Egypt at the Guildhall did not escape adverse criticism. Yet Balfour and Cromer approved of it, and Reid reported to the Secretary of State :

" I know confidentially that Sir Edward Grey was equally pleased (although under more necessity to conceal it), and is sure to take the same line in the House of Commons as soon as the subject comes up. Of course he is liable to a little chaff on account of it, since it can be construed as reading him and the Government a lecture on their failure hitherto to do their duty ; but he is too big a man to be annoyed about that."

In the following year came President Taft's proposals for a general Anglo-American Arbitration Treaty. Sir Edward Grey consulted Reid as to " the best means of profiting by the enthusiasm aroused in England by his public response to these proposals. He feared that such popular demonstrations as he had elicited might have a bad effect if they seemed to

outrun the feeling in the United States." It was just as well
not to approve too heartily and so provoke a suspicious
reaction in America. Reid believed that the only serious
obstacle to the proposed treaty in the Senate was the chance
that it might be nullified by the clause in the Anglo-Japanese
Treaty compelling Great Britain to come to Japan's relief
in case of attack. Grey promptly said that that would be
arranged by an article in the new treaty with Japan that—

" should either high contracting party conclude a treaty
of general arbitration with a third Power, it is agreed that
nothing in this agreement should entail upon such contracting
party an obligation to go to war with the Power with whom
such treaty of arbitration is in force."

However, it was all to no purpose, for the Senate rejected
the Taft Treaty.

On September 1, 1911, Reid wrote to Knox :

" Serious business people and serious politicians are equally
frank in speaking of war with Germany as a thing which may
come at any time, and in fact is almost within measurable
distance. They don't want it, but I doubt if they are as much
disturbed by the prospect as they might be. Apparently they
believe that, if war comes, it will be England and France together against Germany, and the German action has been so
wanton and provocative that they will have the moral
support not only of their own people, but to some extent of
other nations."

This significant diagnosis was made nearly three years
before the war, although a few months later Lord Rosebery
publicly dwelt on the early probability of " a war on the
Continent greater than any in the Napoleon era."

One of Ambassador Reid's last speeches was at a dinner
given by the Boz Club to celebrate the centenary of the birth
of Charles Dickens. He then recalled the words he had heard
from the great author's lips in New York forty years before :

" If would be better for this globe to be riven by an
earthquake, fired by a comet, overrun by an iceberg and
abandoned to the Arctic fox and bear, than that it should
present the spectacle of those two great nations, each of
whom has in its own way and hour striven so hard and so

successfully for freedom, ever again being arrayed the one against the other."

Reid's final oratorical effort, from which he was never to rally, so great was the physical strain of its preparation, the journey and the delivery, was one on Thomas Jefferson at the University College at Aberystwyth. For this great figure in American history, Reid, like Roosevelt, never had very much sympathy, although he strove to give him his due. "If," he said to his Welsh audience, "the figure I have been presenting as an honour to Wales has a head of gold, just as clearly will it be seen to have had feet of clay." Which remark was taken amiss by some of his Democratic compatriots.

Reid had passed his seventy-fifth birthday, he had overworked, and his old bronchial trouble supervened. After a brief illness, this able man succumbed on December 15, 1912.

King George himself cabled the news to President Taft:

" It is with the deepest sorrow that I have to inform you of the death of Mr. Whitelaw Reid at noon to-day. As your Ambassador in this country his loss will be sincerely deplored, while personally I shall mourn for an old friend of many years' standing for whom I had the greatest regard and respect."

"We regard him as a kinsman," said Prime Minister Asquith next day in the House of Commons. A memorial service was held in Westminster Abbey. The armoured cruiser *Natal* was assigned the duty of conveying the remains of the dead Ambassador—who was the first of his diplomatic line to die in office—to America for burial.

The President's message to the King might serve as a fitting epitaph for Whitelaw Reid. His death, he said, was—

" a loss to both countries, for his service as Ambassador was exceptional in the closer friendship that he secured between them through his own personality. His intimate knowledge of both countries, his profound respect and love for England, entirely consistent with the highest loyalty on his part to this country, gave him peculiar influence for good in his great station."

CHAPTER XXII

PAGE (1912–1918)

LIKE his predecessor, Walter Hines Page was a successful editor, but his sphere was that of the critical and literary review. He had conducted, in turn, the *Forum*, the *Atlantic Monthly* (of which Lowell had been the first editor) and the *World's Work*, the latter of which had taken a high place as an organ of exposition and opinion. Page had been born in North Carolina in 1855 ; and, after leaving Johns Hopkins University at Baltimore, where he attained distinction in the Classics, he was offered the Chair of Greek in the University of his own State, but preferred a journalistic career. In the early '80s, while in Atlanta, Page had met a fellow-Southerner there, a briefless lawyer named Woodrow Wilson, who was writing a book on *Congressional Government,* and these two young men, whose names will for ever be associated in the diplomatic history of the greatest of modern wars, became friends. Thirty years passed. Page was now widely known as a sane and enterprising editor, a writer of poise and culture and an ardent Democrat ; but when his appointment was announced, shortly after President Wilson's inauguration, his greater qualities were unguessed by the public. In the opinion of the *New York Times* Page was " a capable man, but could not be expected to represent his country in London, in the broad sense, as Choate, Hay, Bayard and Lowell had done." How little they knew the man !

No more sane, just and earnest spirit—responsive to light and shrinking from all meanness—ever dwelt in a human body. He suggested to at least one amongst his friends a compound of Charles Lamb, Oliver Wendell Holmes and Charles Dickens.

Yet never was there an inner personality which revealed

itself less at first sight. Even his eyes told nothing. He was gaunt and flat-chested and his shoulders stooped ; his skin was leathery and corrugated, and dominating his features was a large, shapeless red nose which utterly belied his racial origin, his character and his habits. Page well exemplified the proverb, *Nulla fides fronti*, for all those who came to know him soon yielded to the spell of a gentle, frank, almost boyish nature.

" His spirits [remarks his biographer] were constantly alert for the amusing, the grotesque and the contradictory ; like all men who are really serious and alive to the pathos of existence, he loved a hearty laugh, especially as he found it a relief from the gloom that filled his every waking moment in England."

Elsewhere he speaks of—

" directness and even breeziness of speech and of method, this absence of affectation, this almost openly expressed contempt for finesse and even for tradition, combined with those other traits which we like to think of as American, an upright purpose, a desire to serve not only his own country but mankind—which made the British public look upon Page as one of the most attractive and useful figures in a war-torn Europe." [1]

The new Ambassador reached London May 24, 1913, and his first business with the Foreign Office had relation to Mexico. There, as the result of the murder of President Madero, General Huerta had succeeded as Dictator. Believing that Huerta could assure political stability to the country, the British Minister in Mexico, Sir Lionel Carden, advised his recognition. But the American Government would have nothing to do with Huerta and complained that Carden was plotting against American interests. The situation was rapidly inviting armed intervention. Page soon made up his mind that it was Carden who was to blame and that if he were withdrawn matters could be adjusted. Sir Edward Grey, the Foreign Secretary, was inclined to defend Carden, but he was friendly to Page and yielded to his representations. Carden was recalled. Deprived of British support, the

---

[1] Burton J. Hendrick : *The Life and Letters of W. H. Page.*

WALTER H. PAGE.

Huerta régime fell and all international friction on that score ceased.

There was now another problem in Anglo-American diplomacy to be dealt with. By the terms of the Hay-Pauncefote Treaty of 1901, Great Britain had surrendered her right to participate in the construction and ownership of the Panama Canal, but had stipulated that the canal should be neutral and that the tolls exacted from shipping should be uniform for all users. The United States had in effect, in return for a valuable concession from Great Britain, agreed to restrict their liberty over their own property and had surrendered their right to subsidize American shipping passing through the waterway. This surrender was found so irksome by a considerable party in Congress that they succeeded in getting a measure passed in August 1912 declaring that " no tolls shall be levied upon vessels engaged in the coastwise trade of the United States." This act was promptly promulgated by President Taft. It being contrary to the letter and spirit of the Hay-Pauncefote Treaty, the British Government naturally protested. To this protest Secretary of State Knox made an academic reply :

" It would, of course, be idle to contend that Congress has not the power, or that the President, properly authorized by Congress, may not have the power, to violate the terms of the Hay-Pauncefote Treaty in its aspect as a municipal law."

The matter was in this posture when President Taft went out of office in March 1913.

Although the legal aspects of the dispute seemed clear enough, the position in which the Wilson Administration found itself was difficult, for many of its leading supporters, especially the Irish-American element, defended the Canal Act, characterizing England's protest as " high-handed impertinence." That was not all ; President Wilson himself in the course of his electoral campaign had spoken with approval of " free tolls for American ships."

But Ambassador Page had already made his mind up on the matter even before he arrived in London, and in his first talks with Sir Edward Grey he realized that the Canal Act had touched Great Britain in a most sensitive spot.

High-minded as its foreign policy might pretend to be, his own country was far from " idealistic " in the observance of the treaty it had made concerning the canal. There was—

" a certain embarrassment involved in preaching unselfishness in Mexico and Central America at a time when the United States was practising selfishness and dishonesty in Panama."

In the opinion of the Ambassador and that of most other dispassionate students of the Panama Treaty, the British view concerning the spirit and terms of the Hay-Pauncefote Treaty was absolutely right. America could not charge different tolls to her own subjects from those charged to other nationals. Page's letters to the President for several months continued to press this point of view. He wrote, September 10 :

" Everywhere—in circles the most friendly to us and the best informed—I receive commiseration because of the dishonourable attitude of our Government about the Panama Canal tolls. This, I confess, is hard to meet. We made a bargain—a solemn compact—and we have broken it. Whether it were a good bargain or a bad one, a silly one or a wise one, that's far from the point, isn't it ? I confess that this bothers me. . . .

" And this Canal tolls matter stands in the way of everything. It is in their minds all the time—the minds of all parties and all sections of opinion."

By this time President Wilson had become convinced of the impolicy of the Act, and decided to waive the American claim. Not, however, until March 5, 1914, and when backed by the Republican Senators Lodge and Root, did the President go before Congress and ask the two Houses to repeal the clause in the Panama legislation which granted preferential treatment to American coastwise shipping.

The debate which followed in Congress proved to be one of the stormiest in its history. The " easy victory " that the Administration had evidently expected was not to be. Public meetings in New York and elsewhere denounced an

Administration that disgraced the country by " truckling "
to Great Britain. The President was accused of seeking an
Anglo-American Alliance and of sacrificing American shipping
to the glory of British trade. The history of international
diplomatic relations was ransacked to prove that Great
Britain herself had " broken every treaty she had ever made."

The struggle lasted for three months ; and was Woodrow
Wilson's first serious conflict with the Senate—the body which
was destined five years later to destroy his policies and wreck
his career.

While the Panama debate was thus raging in Congress, the
Ambassador in London, at a dinner of the Chambers of Commerce early in March, delivered an impromptu speech. Half-
serious, half-jocular, he indulged in a few references to the
Panama Canal and British-American relations.

" I would not say [he observed] that we constructed the
Panama Canal even for you—for I am speaking with great
frankness and not with diplomatic indirection—we built
it for reasons of our own. But I will say that it adds to the
pleasure of that great work that you will profit by it. You
will profit most by it, for you have the greatest carrying
trade."

Referring to the Monroe Doctrine, Page said :

" We prefer that European Powers shall acquire no more
territory on this continent."

Instantly the cable carried the speech to America and
there arose a tempest of disapproval. It was pretended
that the Ambassador had used the word " prefer " in its
literal sense, and interpreted the sentence to mean that, while
the United States would " prefer " that Europe should not
overrun North and South America, they would really raise
no serious objection if Europe did so !

Already Page had infuriated the Anglophobes by a speech
he had made the previous summer at Southampton in dedi-
cating a monument to the *Mayflower* Pilgrims.

" Blood [he had said] carries with it that particular
trick of thought which makes us all English in the last
report. . . . And Puritan and Pilgrim and Cavalier, though
different, are yet one in that they are English still. And thus,

despite the fusion of races and of the great contributions of other nations to her hundred millions of people and her incalculable wealth, the United States is yet English-led and English-ruled."

On the previous occasion, Page's meaning had been absurdly mistaken. Now petitions poured in upon the President demanding his recall. To Wilson on March 18, Page was moved to write :

" DEAR MR. PRESIDENT,—

"About this infernal racket in the Senate over my poor speech, I have telegraphed you all there is to say. Of course, it was a harmless courtesy—no bowing low to the British or any such thing—as it was spoken and heard. Of course, too, nothing would have been said about it but for the controversy over the Canal tolls. That was my mistake— in being betrayed by the friendly dinner and the high compliments paid to us into mentioning a subject under controversy.

" I am greatly distressed lest possibly it may embarrass you. I do hope not.

"I think I have now learned *that* lesson pretty thoroughly. These Anglophobiacs—Irish and Panama—hound me wherever I go. I think I told you one of their correspondents, who one night got up and yawned at a public dinner as soon as I had spoken and said to his neighbours, ' Well, I'll go ; the Ambassador didn't say anything that I can get him into trouble about.'

" I shall, hereafter, write out my speeches and have them gone over carefully by my little Cabinet of Secretaries. Yet something (perhaps not much) will be lost. For these people are infinitely kind and friendly and courteous."

He went on to say :

" Of course, what some of the American newspapers have said is true—that I am too free and too untrained to be a great Ambassador. But the conventional type of Ambassador would not be worth his salt to represent the United States here now, when they are eager to work with us for the peace of the world, if they are convinced of our honour and right-mindedness and the genuineness of our friendship.

" I talked this over with Sir Edward Grey the other day, and after telling me that I need fear no trouble at this end of the line, he told me how severely he is now criticized by a

' certain element ' for ' bowing too low to the American.'
We then each bowed low to the other.   The yellow Press
and Senator Chamberlain would give a year's growth for a
photograph of us in that posture !

" I am infinitely obliged to you for your kind understanding
and your toleration of my errors."

In spite of the abuse launched against Page, both Houses
of Congress passed the repealing Bill by large majorities.   The
Ambassador and Mrs. Page were attending a ball at Buckingham Palace when the news reached London, and we are told
that the King and the Prime Minister, Mr. Asquith, as well
as the Foreign Secretary, were deeply affected by this evidence
of fair-dealing at Washington.   Page exulted : he declared
that he was prouder of his country at that moment than ever
before in his life.

" A great nation had committed an outrageous wrong—
that was something that had happened many times before
in all countries.   But the unprecedented thing was that this
same nation had exposed its fault boldly to the world—had
lifted up its hands and cried, ' We have sinned ! ' and then
had publicly undone its error." [1]

As the months rolled on, Page's deep interest in European
and especially British politics, and the life of people of all
classes about him, showed no abatement, but, as his letters
show, increased.   On taking up his official duties, he was
shocked at the shabby provision made by his Government
for the transaction of business at the American Embassy.
For nearly thirty years the Chancellery had been in a commonplace block of buildings in Westminster.

" The moment I entered that dark and dingy hall at 123
Victoria Street, between two cheap stores—the same entrance
that dwellers in the cheap flats above used—I knew that
Uncle Sam had no fit dwelling there.   And the Ambassador's
room greatly depressed me—dingy, with twenty-nine years of
dirt and darkness, and utterly undignified. . . . I did not
understand then, and I do not understand yet, how Lowell,
Bayard, Phelps, Hay, Choate and Reid endured that cheap
hole."

[1] Hendrick : *Life and Letters of W. H. Page.*

He rented a commodious house, No 6 Grosvenor Square, for the Embassy, and in later strenuous times caused the Chancellery to be transferred to No. 4 Grosvenor Gardens, where it still remains. Page's immediate predecessors had been rich men who could defray the cost of the Embassy from their own private means, but Page was obliged to encroach on the savings of a lifetime, and there were limits to such liberality on his part.

" Of course [as he wrote Colonel House] I am open to the criticism of having taken the place at all, but I was uninformed and misinformed about the cost as well as about the frightful handicap of having no Embassy. . . . Without a home or a house or fixed background, every man has to establish his own position for himself, and unless he be unusual, this throws him clean out of the way of giving emphasis to the right things."

In his new home in Grosvenor Square the Pages kept a large staff of servants and entertained generously, although " nothing could induce him " to tell what it cost him.

The people one met at the Embassy were precisely the kind that is most congenial to the educated American. " I didn't know I was getting into an assembly of immortals ! " exclaimed Mr. Hugh Wallace,[1] when he called one afternoon for tea, and found Sir Edward Grey, Henry James, John Sargent and other political, literary and artistic celebrities foregathered in Mrs. Page's drawing-room.

Page himself attributed the social attraction of the Embassy to his wife, and Mrs. Page made a truly admirable Ambassadress of a great Republic.

" I should also like to say [wrote Mr. Lloyd George at the end] how much we shall miss Mrs. Page. She has won a real place in all our hearts. Through her unfailing tact, her genuine kindliness and her unvarying readiness to respond to any call upon her time and energy, she has greatly contributed to the success of your Ambassadorship."

Amongst the Ambassador's earliest American visitors was the President's closest friend and confidential adviser, Edward Mandell House. This gentleman was a Texan, three years younger than Page, of independent means, who had made

[1] Afterwards American Ambassador to France.

politics, and especially international politics, his hobby, as other men become bibliophiles, picture-collectors or horse-breeders. House had never had any connexion with the Army—like John Hay and many others—he was a " Colonel " by courtesy ; but his title will probably persist in history.

House, like Page and, indeed, all other clear-sighted observers on the eve of the Great War, felt the imminence of disaster, unless steps were taken to avert it. Woodrow Wilson believed this could be done by international agreement to abstain from war, and he sent House to Europe to sound European statesmen as to its feasibility. House's first visit was in July 1913, and he came again in the autumn and in the following year.[1] He had just returned when the explosion came and Page was at a country cottage he had taken for the summer. On August 2 numbers of Americans, alarmed at the reports in the newspapers, flocked to the Embassy.

" The Secretary whom I had left in charge on Sunday telephoned me every few hours and laughingly told funny experiences with nervous women who came in and asked absurd questions. Of course, we all knew the grave danger that war might come, but nobody could by the wildest imagination guess at what awaited us. On Monday I was at the Embassy earlier than I think I had ever been there before and every member of the staff was already on duty. Before breakfast time the place was filled—packed like sardines. This was two days before war was declared. There was no chance to talk to individuals, such was the jam. I got on a chair and explained that I had already telegraphed to Washington—on Saturday—suggesting the sending of money and ships, and asking them to be patient. I made a speech to them several times during the day, and kept the secretaries doing so at intervals. More than two thousand Americans crowded into those offices (which are not large) that day.

[1] In the autumn of 1913 Sir William Tyrrell, a high official of the Foreign Office and Private Secretary to Sir Edward Grey, had paid a friendly visit to Washington as the guest of the British Ambassador, Sir Cecil Spring-Rice. He had conversations with Mr. Wilson, Bryan and House chiefly on the Mexican question, but also on the European situation. House appreciated the sincerity of the British Government in its peace policy and he took Sir William Tyrrell's advice on the subject of his coming visit to Europe. Mowat : *Diplomatic Relations.* Sir William Tyrrell is the present British Ambassador to France.

We kept there till two o'clock in the morning. The Embassy has not been closed since."

American bankers and wealthy men in London collected money and called on their English banking friends for help—to relieve all cases of actual pecuniary want that came to them. American committees worked manfully day and night. There was an orderly organization at four places: the Embassy, the Consul-General's Office, the Savoy Hotel, and the American Society in London. As Page describes it:

" Upon those two first days there was, of course, great confusion. Crazy men and weeping women were imploring and cursing and demanding—God knows it was bedlam turned loose. I have been called a man of the greatest genius for an emergency by some, by others a damned fool, by others every epithet between these extremes. Men shook English banknotes in my face and demanded United States money and swore our Government and its agents ought all to be shot. Women expected me to hand them steamship tickets home. When some found out that they could not get tickets on the transports (which they assumed would sail the next day) they accused me of favouritism. These absurd experiences will give you a hint of the panic."

In his letter to the President (August 9) Page reports the dramatic declaration of war:

" Tuesday night, five minutes after the ultimatum had expired, the Admiralty telegraphed to the fleet : ' Go.' In a few minutes the answer came back : ' Off.' Soldiers began to march through the city going to the railway stations. An indescribable crowd blocked the streets about the Admiralty, the War Office and the Foreign Office, so that at one o'clock in the morning I had to drive in my car by other streets to get home.

" The next day the German Embassy was turned over to me. I went to see the German Ambassador at three o'clock in the afternoon. He came down in his pyjamas, a crazy man. I feared he might literally go mad. He is of the anti-war party, and he had done his best and utterly failed. This interview was one of the most pathetic experiences of my life. The poor man had not slept for several nights. Then came the crowds of frightened Germans, afraid that they would be arrested.

" Upon my word, if one could forget the awful tragedy, all this experience would be worth a lifetime of commonplace. One surprise follows another so rapidly that one loses all sense of time. It seems an age since last Sunday. I shall never forget Sir Edward Grey's telling me of the ultimatum—while he wept ; nor the poor German Ambassador who has lost in his high game—almost a demented man ; nor the King, as he declaimed at me for half an hour and threw up his hands and said, ' My God, Mr. Page, what else could we *do* ? ' Nor the Austrian Ambassador's wringing his hands and weeping and crying out, ' My dear colleague !—my dear colleague ! ' "

Sir Edward Grey asked the Ambassador to explain the situation to President Wilson, expressing the hope that the United States would take an attitude of neutrality and that Great Britain might look for " the courtesies of neutrality " from America. Page tried to tell him of the sincere pain that such a war would cause the President and the American people.

" I came away," the Ambassador afterwards said, " with a sort of stunned sense of the impending ruin of half the world."

The taking over by Page of the Austrian and Turkish Embassies as well involved an enormous amount of work.

" We put up a sign ' The American Embassy ' on every one of them. Work ? We're worked to death. Two nights ago I didn't get time to read a letter or even a telegram that had come that day till eleven o'clock at night. For on top of all these Embassies, I've had to become Commissary-General to feed 6,000,000 starving people in Belgium ; and practically all the food must come from the United States."

From the first moment and for nearly three years there was no American in Europe who strove harder to be neutral than Page. His consciousness of his official neutrality became a painful obsession with him. " Neutral ! " he once exclaimed. " There's nothing in the world so neutral as this Embassy. Neutrality takes up all our time."

And again :

" Neutrality [he wrote to his brother] is a quality of

30

Government—an artificial unit. When a war comes, a Government must go in it or stay out of it. It must make a declaration to the world of its attitude. That's all that neutrality is. A *Government* can be neutral, but no *man* can be."

After this, it is amusing to read that when the news of victory at the Marne came in, the whole Embassy Staff noted that, although " neutral," the defeat of the Germans " added liveliness to the Ambassador's step, gave a keener sparkle to his eye, and even brought back some of his old familiar gaiety of spirit."

One day the Ambassador was lunching with Irwin Laughlin, his First Secretary, and a few friends.

" We did pretty well in that Battle of the Marne, didn't we ? " Page broke forth, unguardedly.

" Isn't that remark slightly unneutral, Mr. Ambassador ? " asked Laughlin, which sent the table off into a roar of laughter in which Page joined.

In early December 1914 Colonel House was compelled to transmit a warning to the American Ambassador at London.

" The President wished me to ask you to please be more careful not to express any unneutral feeling, either by word of mouth, or by letter and not even to the State Department. He said that both Mr. Bryan and Mr. Lansing had remarked upon your leaning in that direction and he thought that it would materially lessen your influence. He feels very strongly about this."

Page believed it was his duty—

" to collect information and impressions, to discover what important people thought of the United States and of its policies, and to send forward all such data to Washington. According to Page's theory of the Ambassadorial office, he was a kind of listening post on the front of diplomacy, and he would have grievously failed had he not done his best to keep head-quarters informed. He did not regard it as ' loyalty ' merely to forward only that kind of material which Washington apparently preferred to obtain ; with a frankness which Mr. Wilson's friends regarded as almost ruthless, Page reported what he believed to be the truth." [1]

[1] Hendrick : *Life of Page.*

To Page, as to Sir Edward Grey, there was always present the danger that two courses of American official action might be taken at Washington, which would have a disastrous effect on Britain's war effort.   One was that Congress would place an embargo upon the shipment of munitions from America. The other was that the Government might yield to anti-British pressure and ordain that American cargoes should be convoyed by American warships.   For this reason, in order to propitiate America, Grey insisted to his Cabinet colleagues that cotton should not then be contraband.   This step saved the situation in 1914–15.

It was inevitable that, while Great Britain and the Allies were fighting for their lives, many irregular and intolerable actions should occur on the high seas.   These actions, as well as the general maritime policy behind them, became the subject of many protesting notes of Page to the Foreign Office.   But as for the Declaration of London which Secretary Bryan had pressed on the British Government from the first, they would have none of it.

" In this great argument about shipping [reported Page to the President], I cannot help being alarmed, because we are getting into deep water uselessly.   The Foreign Office has yielded unquestioningly to all our requests and has shown the sincerest wish to meet all our suggestions, so long as it is not called upon to admit war material into Germany.

" Since the last lists of contraband and conditional contraband were published, such materials as rubber and copper and petroleum have developed entirely new uses in war. The British simply will not let Germany import them. Nothing that can be used for war purposes in Germany nor will be used for anything else.

" So far as our neutrality obligations are concerned, I do not believe that they require us to demand that Great Britain should adopt for our benefit the Declaration of London. Great Britain had never ratified it, nor have any other nations except the United States.   In its application to the situation presented by this war it is altogether to the advantage of Germany."

But Wilson was unconvinced, and through the Secretary of State, Lansing, who had succeeded Bryan, he told Page to warn the British Government about its obnoxious Order-in-Council which increased the list of contraband articles. Page commented :

" Lansing's *method* is the trouble. He threatens Great Britain, to start with, as if she were a criminal and an opponent. That's the best way I know to cause trouble to American shipping and to bring back the good old days of mutual hatred and distrust for a generation or two. If that isn't playing into the hands of the Germans, what would be ? And where's the ' neutrality ' of this kind of action ?

" If Lansing again brings up the Declaration of London—after four fair and reasonable rejections—I shall resign. I will not be the instrument of a perfectly gratuitous and ineffective insult to this patient and fair and friendly Government and people, who in my time have done us many kindnesses and who sincerely try now to meet our wishes."

At length, on October 17, Page proposed by cable an arrangement which he hoped would settle the matter. It was that the King should issue the Proclamation accepting the Declaration with modifications, and that a new Order-in-Council should be issued containing a new list of contraband. Sir Edward Grey was not to ask the American Government to accept this Proclamation ; all that he asked was that Washington should offer no objections to it. It was proposed that the United States at the same time should publish a Note withdrawing its suggestion for the adoption of the Declaration, and explaining that it proposed to rest the rights of its citizens upon the existing rules of international law and the treaties of the United States. This solution was accepted and for the present all was plain sailing. Only, sometimes, the State Department at Washington sent over Notes to be shown to the British Government couched in distinctly arrogant and undiplomatic phraseology. Page usually undertook to edit these before submitting them to Sir Edward Grey, but once, being in a hurry, he exhibited such a document in all its crudity. Had it been delivered formally, it would certainly have been indignantly returned. Grey, however, glanced over it and looked up with a smile to the Ambassador.

" This reads," he said, " as though they thought they are still talking to George III ! "

One of Page's happiest inspirations through the whole war related to a German merchantman called the *Dacia*, which had been lying idle at a wharf in Texas since the outbreak of war. Early in 1915 she was purchased by a German-American from Michigan, who announced that he had placed the *Dacia* under American registry, had put in her an American crew, and that he proposed to load her with cotton and sail for Germany.

Cotton was not at that time contraband, but the vessel itself was German and was thus subject to capture as enemy property. The seriousness of this position was that technically the *Dacia* was now an American ship, for an American citizen owned her, she carried an American crew, she bore on her flagstaff the American flag, and she had been admitted to American registry under a law recently passed by Congress.

If Great Britain seized the *Dacia*, she would be embroiled with the American Government—which would serve German purposes admirably.

And this would certainly have happened if Page had not quietly suggested to Sir Edward Grey that, although Britain ruled the waves, she had a naval partner who might carry off some of the odium in neutral eyes. The misdeeds of the British fleet were being advertised somewhat too exclusively. " Why not let the French fleet seize the *Dacia* and get some advertising ? " he asked. The suggestion was at once acted on ; a French cruiser went out into the Channel, seized the offending ship, took it into port, where a French prize court promptly condemned it. When the news reached America there was not even " a ripple of hostility." There was no bitter Francophobe party to protest at Washington. The *Dacia* was sold to Frenchmen, rechristened the *Yser* and put to work in the Mediterranean trade, where it continued until a German submarine torpedoed the vessel and sank it.

Meanwhile, German submarines had perpetrated their greatest crime. When on May 7, 1915, the news came to London that a German submarine had torpedoed the *Lusitania* and that one hundred and twenty-four Americans, some of them his personal friends, had lost their lives, Page, like many others, was so staggered that for a day or two he went about as if under the influence of a drug. Later, he went to Euston station to greet the American survivors, whose " listless and bedraggled " aspect ineffaceably impressed him. Yet he had felt a premonition of such a tragedy—for only a few days before he had written, " If a British liner full of American passengers be blown up, what will Uncle Sam do ? "

Page dreaded to think that the President would not act with prompt and stern decision against the Government which had devised and now applauded this crime. Then Colonel House, who was again in London, came in to say that " while walking in Piccadilly, he caught a glimpse of one of the famous sandwich-men, bearing a poster of an afternoon newspaper. The glaring broadside bore the following legend : " We are too proud to fight—Woodrow Wilson."

The whole of England was soon ringing with those six words, the newspapers were filled with stinging editorials and cartoons, and the music-halls found in the Wilsonian phrase material for ridicule and scorn.

Followed a period of " distress and disillusionment." Three *Lusitania* Notes were sent and were evasively answered, and Washington still seemed to be marking time while " all the world wondered."

Page, nevertheless, continued to pin his faith to President Wilson, and still expressed confidence in his determination to uphold the national honour. His own position was becoming hard. He found himself, for the first time since his arrival in England, a solitary man. He shrank from attending functions where he knew his own countrymen would denounce the President's policy.

To Wilson himself, the Ambassador continued to unburden himself freely, fully, unsparingly, as he did to House, knowing that his letters would be shown to the President. Wilson had always been delighted with Page's brilliant, racy letters and often read them to the Cabinet.

" Some day [he said] I hope that Walter Page's letters will be published. They are the best letters I have ever read

They make you feel the atmosphere in England, understand the people, and see into the motives of the great actors." [1]

But now he read them no more—or if he read them, he hardened his heart against their reproaches and their appeals. That Page would resign was his constant dread. On October 26, 1915, Lansing cabled Page requesting him to deny the rumours that he was contemplating resignation and expressing the President's earnest hope that they were baseless. Page reassured his official superiors, but he could not reassure himself.

In the midst of his foreboding came further difficulties over the British blockade.

" I cannot begin to express my deep anxiety and even uneasiness about the relations of these two great Governments and peoples [Page wrote about this time]. The friendship of the United States and Great Britain is all that now holds the world together. It is the greatest asset of civilization left. All the cargoes of copper and oil in the world are not worth as much to the world. Yet when a shipper's cargo is held up he does not think of civilization and of the future of mankind and of free government ; he thinks only of his cargo and of the indignity that he imagines has been done him ; and what is the American Government for if not to protect his rights ?

" The telegrams that come to me are full of ' protests ' and ' demands '—protest and demand this, protest and demand that. A man from Mars who should read my book of telegrams received during the last two months would find it difficult to explain how the two Governments have kept at peace. It is this serious treatment of trifling grievances which makes us feel here that the exactions and dislocations and necessary disturbances of this war are not understood at home."

The Wilson Note about neutral rights, which London had so much dreaded, reached the Embassy on October 1915. The State Department had taken nearly six months to prepare

[1] Mr. Hendrick speaks of " his unwearied industry with the pen. His official communications and his ordinary correspondence Page dictated ; but his personal letters he wrote with his own hand. He himself deplored the stenographer as a deterrent to good writing ; the habit of dictating, he argued, led to wordiness and general looseness of thought."

it ; it was the American answer to the so-called blockade established by the Order-in-Council of the preceding March. It made the worst possible impression on England and the Allies.

" As nearly as I can make out, the high-water mark of English good-feeling toward us in all our history was after the President's Panama tolls courtesy. The low-water mark, since the Civil War, I am sure, is now. The Cleveland Venezuela message came at a time of no nervous strain and did, I think, produce no long-lasting effect. A part of the present feeling is due to the English conviction that we have been taken in by the Germans in the submarine controversy, but a large part is due to the lack of courtesy in this last Note—the manner in which it was written even more than its matter."

At the President's request, Page went to Washington—for an intimate discussion of the situation. But Wilson appeared to be too busy to grant him the long private interview Page had hoped for, and indeed, the whole visit was utterly futile. He did not " find a man in our State Department or in our Government who has ever met any prominent statesman in any European Government, nor a man who knows the atmosphere of Europe."

His suggestion that one of the Secretaries should go to England for a week's observation was vetoed as not being " neutral."

No wonder Page could cry out :

" It isn't the old question we used to discuss of our having no friend in the world when the war ends. It's gone far further than that. It is now whether the United States Government need be respected by anybody."

Soon after President Wilson's re-election, Page sent his resignation to Washington. He believed that his work in London had been finished, that he had done everything in his power to make Wilson see the situation in its true light and that he had not succeeded. He therefore wished to give up his post and come home.

But by the time an answer came (February 5) the whole situation had changed. Lansing wrote :

" The President hopes you will not press to be relieved

from service ; that he realizes that he is asking you to make a personal sacrifice, but he believes that you will appreciate the importance, in the crisis which has developed, that no change should be made."

Two days before Page received this the United States had broken off diplomatic relations with Germany (February 3, 1917).

At the Embassy one of the secretaries met in the hall the head of the British Naval Intelligence, who was hurrying up to the Ambassador, with the code message which he had just received from Captain Gaunt, the British naval attaché at Washington. They hurried into the Ambassador's room and there read :

" Bernstorff has just been given his passports. I shall probably get drunk to-night ! "

From that moment Page became a changed man. The strain which he had undergone for twenty-nine months had been intense ; it had had the most unfortunate effect upon his health ; and the sudden lifting might have produced that reaction for the worse which is not unusual after critical experiences of this kind.

" Londoners who saw him at that time describe him as acting like a man from whose shoulders a tremendous weight had suddenly been removed. For more than two years Page had been compelled, officially at least, to assume a ' neutrality ' with which he had never had the slightest sympathy, but the necessity for this mask now no longer existed." [1]

In the street an English friend stopped and shook his hand. " Thank God," the Englishman said, " that there is one hypocrite less in London to-day."

" What do you mean ? " asked Page.

" I mean you. Pretending all this time that you were neutral ! That isn't necessary any longer."

" You are right ! " the Ambassador answered as he walked on with a laugh and a wave of the hand.

Not to Page alone was the change confined. All London, the whole of Great Britain, and the Allies became changed

[1] Hendrick.

towards America. A sigh of profound relief went up from millions. Both Houses of Parliament held commemorative sessions in honour of America's participation ; and leaders to welcome their new allies. The Stars and Stripes broke out on private dwellings, shops, hotels and theatres. The Star-spangled Banner acquired a sudden popularity ; and the American and the British flags were unfurled side by side over the Houses of Parliament—for the first time in history.

Page went to Brighton for a few days to recover from the strain. His heart was full to overflowing with thankfulness. To his son he wrote (April 28) :

" I cannot conceal nor can I express my gratification that we are in the war. I shall always wonder, but never find out, what influence I had in driving the President over. All I know is that my letters and telegrams for nearly two years— especially for the last twelve months—have put before him every reason that anybody has expressed why we should come in—in season and out of season. And there is no reason—only more reason of the same old sort—why we should have come in now than there was why we should have come in a year ago."

There was much remaining to do, but Page's greatest work was over. With shattered health and growing visibly weaker, he stayed at his post until the autumn of the following year, long enough to see American troops marching in the London streets, to read bulletins of their successes in France and to be assured of the final triumph of the Allied cause.[1] He would like to have held on to the very end, but he was now so frail that he dared not delay, for he longed passionately to see his native land again.

The news of Page's resignation was the signal for tributes from the British Press and from British public men " such as have been bestowed," says his biographer, " upon few Americans." " A Great Ambassador " was *The Times's* verdict, and its opinion was echoed on both sides of the Atlantic.

[1] " Lively as were his spirits, however, his physical frame was giving way. In fact, Page, though he did not know it at the time, was suffering from a specific disease—nephritis ; and its course, after Christmas of 1917, became rapid."—Hendrick.

" The Ambassador [wrote ex-President Roosevelt] who has represented America in London during these trying years as no other Ambassador in London has ever represented us, with the exception of Charles Francis Adams, during the Civil War."

From the King came a message :

" The information communicated to me yesterday through Mr. Laughlin of your Excellency's resignation of the post of Ambassador and the cause of this step fill me with the keenest regret. During your term of office in days of peace and of war your influence has done much to strengthen the ties of friendship and goodwill which unite the two English-speaking nations of the world. I trust your health will soon be restored and that we may have the pleasure of seeing you and Mrs. Page before your departure."

Custom prescribes that a retiring Ambassador shall present his letter of recall to the sovereign ; but King George, solicitous about Page's health, offered to come himself to London from Windsor for this leave-taking. Page insisted on carrying out the usual programme ; but the visit exhausted him, and he found himself unequal to any further official farewells. But there was a visit from the Mayor and Council of Plymouth, who came to the Embassy in September to present the freedom of that city. The parchment was enshrined in a beautiful silver model of the *Mayflower*. No more appropriate farewell gift could have been devised for Page from the English town whose name is so closely linked with the earliest history of the United States.

It was a pathetic figure that they half-led, half-carried one October day on board the steamer at Southampton. At Waterloo Station a distinguished company, including Lord Balfour, had assembled to bid him farewell.

They all stood with uncovered heads as the train slowly pulled out of the station and caught their final glimpse of Page as he smiled at them and faintly waved his hand.

Perhaps the man most affected by this leave-taking was Lord Balfour, who often in subsequent years told of this parting scene at Waterloo Station and always with emotion.

" I loved that man," he once said to an American friend, recalling this event. " I almost wept when he left England."

Page came home only to die. In fact, at one time on the voyage it seemed improbable that he would live to reach New York.

BIOGRAPHICAL NOTE

Page lingered for a few weeks and died, at eight o'clock in the evening on December 21, 1918, in his sixty-fourth year. He was buried in the Page family plot in the Bethesda Cemetery, near Aberdeen, in North Carolina.

CHAPTER XXIII

DAVIS, HARVEY AND KELLOGG (1918–1925)

It is hardly doing an injustice to Page's successor to say that his was distinctly a war-time appointment and due to circumstances connected with Page's irremediable breakdown in health and the difficulty of finding any suitable man to replace him—whose services were not imperatively demanded by the war.

John William Davis was Solicitor-General in the Wilson Cabinet and was only forty-five. He had been born and bred in a small town in West Virginia, also the birthplace of " Stonewall " Jackson, and here he later practised law. At thirty-eight this pallid, earnest-faced gentleman with the projecting forehead had been sent by his local friends to Congress. His political opinions had been, of course, determined for him by his Virginian frontier ancestry, but there was an additional circumstance in his life which made his Democracy as academic as it was inevitable. He had first seen the light on Thomas Jefferson's birthday, and his family and admirers were always straining to detect points of often esoteric resemblance between himself and the great Democrat.

" I am [Davis once told a public assemblage] a genuine Jeffersonian Democrat. I think Jefferson was the greatest political thinker this country has produced, and I expect to die in that faith. If Jefferson's principles are true—and I think they are—then they remain true, even with changing times. Their application may change, but they do not."

The election of Woodrow Wilson in 1912 naturally brought this capable young Southerner to the front and circumstances brought about his selection for the post of Solicitor-General. It was an ill-paid office, but it gave its holder an opportunity

to distinguish himself at the Bar of the Supreme Court.   But
the war in Europe supervened, and the attention of the public
and of litigants was largely diverted elsewhere.   Nevertheless,
there came to be several cases of national importance, as well
as some bearing directly on America's relations to that conflict, in which Davis's advice was valuable to the President.
With Robert Lansing, the Secretary of State, Davis became
extremely   intimate.   A   year   after   his   country   entered
the war the Government appointed an American High Commission to treat with the Germans for an exchange of war
prisoners, and Davis was invited to be a member.   He duly
set out for London, *en route* to Berne, where the Conference
was to be held in September 1918.   Arrived in London, Davis
heard that Ambassador Page had already resigned.   He
called at the Embassy and there found two cable messages
awaiting him.   One was from his wife and read :

" I insist you accept the President's offer regardless of
personal interests or sacrifice.   You must not decline."

Davis, who was passing quietly through the British capital
as a simple member of an American Prisoners of War Mission
in Switzerland, was greatly puzzled until he opened the
second message.   It was from his friend Secretary Lansing :

" I am directed by the President to ask if you would accept
the Ambassadorship to Great Britain tendered you.   This
is done after consultation with Gregory, who, though feeling
deeply that he cannot fill your place, has given his unqualified
approval to offering it to you.   I need not say how earnestly
I hope you will accept, because I know well that you have
every qualification for the position, and because it would
be most gratifying to me personally.   You cannot render
greater service at this time, and I unhesitatingly urge you to
do so, because your country needs you."

Such an offer was rather startling.   There was, too, one
qualification that Mr. Davis did not possess.   He had left
his law practice too soon in his career for him to amass any
considerable fortune.   Uncertain as he might be as to his
diplomatic merits, as to his pecuniary resources there could
be no doubt whatever.   He was a far poorer man than Page.
He therefore cabled the Secretary of State, expressing his

JOHN W. DAVIS.

doubts on both points, to which Secretary Lansing replied (September 7) in a message marked "Urgent. Strictly confidential":

" Your eminent fitness beyond question. Understand that financial demand is between thirty and thirty-five thousand per annum. I know that it would be a great sacrifice, but unhesitatingly say that I feel it your duty to accept. I have discussed this feature with your wife, who agrees absolutely that you ought to accept in spite of financial sacrifice.

" As I understand it, your obligation need not be for longer than two years, that is, until the end of the present Presidential term. With that in mind I must earnestly beg you to authorize me to say to the President that you will accept. You may discuss the matter with Sharp. I hope you will decide to accept before it is too late."

Davis accordingly crossed to Paris and discussed with Ambassador Sharp, who, though he himself knew what sacrifices were involved, advised acceptance, and a week later public announcement of the appointment was made.

The choice evoked surprise, the *Washington Post* hastening to explain it on the grounds that Mr. Davis was intensely anti-German.

" It is doubtful if there is a man in public life to-day who has a more genuine and a more intense loathing of all things connected with the present German system than Mr. Davis. . . .

" Through some means it has become known to many of the diplomats that Mr. Davis hates Germany worse than almost any other man in public life, and that no one sees clearer through the subterfuge and sham characterizing German diplomacy than Mr. Davis, whose legal mind has been for years trained in distinguishing between right and wrong, no matter in what guise the wrong appears."

This was a healthy war-time sentiment, but undying hatred of the Germans was to prove a bad campaign cry in the reaction following the war.

It soon appeared that the appointment would not interrupt the negotiations at Berne, and so the Ambassador-designate continued to take part in the negotiations relating to an exchange of war prisoners between Germany and the United

States, until hostilities were over and the Armistice was signed. Davis arrived in London on December 16.

" Reaching London but a little more than a month after the signing of the Armistice, he found the overseas war organization at its peak. The Embassy staff . . . had expanded to many times its normal size. There were some two hundred and fifty officials and subordinates directly under the Ambassador. All the European activities of the American Navy were directed from London. Admiral William S. Sims, the stormy petrel of the naval establishment, famed for official indiscretions, was acting in the dual capacity of Naval Attaché and Chief of Operations of the American Naval Forces. J. Butler Wright and Irwin Laughlin, both ' career men ' in the diplomatic service, were assigned to the Embassy as Counsellors. Laughlin, who had served in that capacity during the war, was detailed to new duties shortly after Davis reached London, while Wright remained as Counsellor during his tenure as Ambassador. The official Embassy staff at that time comprised three secretaries, three second secretaries, three third secretaries, a commercial attaché, a trade commissioner, a naval attaché and five assistants, and a military attaché and four assistants." [1]

How astonished old John Adams or even his son or grandson would have been at this aggregation of American diplomatic talent in the British capital—they who had conducted so many intricate and important negotiations with a single secretary and a single clerk !

The new Ambassador sought at the outset to concentrate all the activities of the American Government in Great Britain under one head, " not," as was explained, " for purposes of autocratic administration, but in the interest of greater co-ordination and efficiency." And he did succeed in bringing all the various organizations into closer cohesion, without interfering with their autonomy.

There was a mass of business to attend to, and the old official routine, by which the notice of the Foreign Office was drawn to a given case by letter and a circumlocutory course followed, was replaced by swifter transatlantic methods. We are told that :

" An American actually appealed to the Embassy one day

[1] Theodore A. Huntley : *John W. Davis.*

for assistance in obtaining settlement of a shipping claim of considerable proportions. An attaché took down the receiver.

" 'Hullo, Bill, Mr. So-and-so is here with a shipping claim. How can we handle it ? '

" 'Send him down to see Blank,' was the reply.

" 'I'll call up and tell him he's coming.' The American left, to return next day with his face wreathed in smiles. The British official had taken him out to lunch, a favourable settlement had been agreed upon and he was going home happy."

It is hardly surprising that, such intimate and informal relations having been established between the American Embassy and British Government Departments, an enormous quantity of business was dispatched with ease and expedition.

It was a time, moreover, when American popularity and American influence in London, and indeed in Europe, was highest, when Mr. Lloyd George and the members of the Cabinet vied with one another in showing friendliness for Americans and in acceding to their every wish. The spirit did not—it was impossible that it should—last. A change was at hand, and a few months later, when the diplomatic atmosphere grew less cordial and the struggle began for predominance at Versailles, a reversion came to the old formal methods.

During the Peace negotiations, Ambassador Davis was summoned by President Wilson to Paris and there took part in several conferences. By him was drafted the section in the Treaty of Versailles relating to the Rhineland. But it was soon apparent that the treaty would be opposed by the Senate. The President returned home, discredited abroad and eventually stricken down in health. To Davis in London it fell to carry on the vast official interests of his country while maintaining his personal loyalty to the invalid statesman at Washington up to the close of his term of office.

That he did this, at a time of reaction, and maintained his own prestige unimpaired is sufficient evidence of Davis's qualities. Always he showed a simple, straightforward, modest bearing, which not the most petulant could criticize.

Several of his public addresses while in England, though

31

lacking any special power or originality, yet made a favourable impression. In one, delivered on Independence Day 1919, to a gathering of his countrymen, he thus referred to the instrument which the President had signed and the Senate were about to reject :

" We have just emerged, thank God, from the greatest war effort that America has ever been called upon to make. It has been a united effort, and now the end has come. The Treaty has been signed. Yet it is a significant coincidence that the two most important treaties to which the signature of the United States has ever been appended have been negotiated and signed in the city of Versailles. . . .

" How tremendous is the scope of this treaty ! Alsace and Lorraine renew their bonds with France ; the Danes of Schleswig turn their faces home again ; Poland rises from the ashes of her past, and Bohemia is free once more. Prussian militarism disappears, paying the penalty of its crimes, and in its place there rises a League of Nations to teach the world a saner and a wiser and a better way of life."

One of the best of his addresses was that at Oxford (February 20) on " The Treaty-making Power in the United States," in which, after dwelling on its history, processes, and the functions of the Senate, he summed up :

" An unfriendly critic might denounce it as complicated and cumbersome, ill-adapted to the complex demands of international intercourse, slow in action and uncertain in outcome. The requirements of a two-thirds rather than a majority vote in the Senate he might criticize not unjustly as a dubious excess of caution. He might point his moral and adorn his tale with many instances of sharp and frequently bitter discord between Presidents and Senators. However, I only ask that if you think it, like Rob Roy McGregor, ' ower bad for blessing,' you pronounce it also ' ower good for banning.' For, believe me, the American people are likely for many years to accomplish through this means their compacts with mankind. The checks and balances by which it is surrounded, the free and full debate which it allows, are in their eyes virtues rather than defects. They rejoice in the fact that all engagements which affect their destinies must be spread upon the records and that there is not, and there never can be, a secret treaty binding them either in law or in morals. Looking back upon a diplomatic history which is not without its chapters of success, they feel that on the whole the scheme their fathers builded has served the children well. With a conservatism in matters of government as great perhaps as that of any people in the world, they will suffer much inconvenience and run the risk of occasional misunderstanding before they make a change."

In the autumn of 1920 the Republican party was voted back into power, and soon after President Harding's inauguration Ambassador Davis presented his letter of recall. His two and a half years' occupancy of the post had given him international prestige, and already at home he was spoken of as a Democratic party leader.[1]

There now came, to fill the vacant place, a wholly new type of man, one who, it was remarked, represented a new strain in American politics. Yet George Harvey was, like Whitelaw Reid and Walter Page, a journalist, and a powerful one.

There was, to some observers, a certain humorous appositeness in that this quaint, tall, gaunt figure should hail from a small Vermont town named Peacham. For it evoked images of an old-world gallery of reckless and picturesque human types, the like of which are in this century only known to the world through the medium of the stage. Harvey's predecessors had been, many of them, self-made men, sometimes men from small rural communities, but amongst them all there was no figure quite resembling his. And what worlds apart, in character and bearing, seemed Charles Francis Adams, John Hay, Russell Lowell or Joseph Choate! True, there were certain points of resemblance between him and Page, but Page had been a university graduate and a Greek prizeman, and had a high sense of political and literary decorum.

A "Scotch Yankee" Harvey called himself, his two grandfathers having come to Vermont from Scotland soon after the Waterloo period. He was born in 1864, and had started as a mere boy on the village newspaper, the Peacham *Patriot*, had gone thence to the Springfield *Republican*, and

---

[1] Mr. Davis was nominated by the Democrats in 1924 for the Presidency, but was beaten by Mr. Coolidge.

at twenty-one was a New York reporter. For the next
ten years his colleagues spoke of him as dynamic, inquisitive,
irrepressible—just like all good New York reporters. His
fund of energy and ideas was inexhaustible, so that no one
was surprised when, at thirty, Joseph Pulitzer appointed
him manager of his paper—the *World*. In this position
Harvey acquired powerful friends amongst the Wall Street
capitalists, who pointed the way to a moderate fortune, and
enabled him to withdraw from daily journalism and to
purchase the *North American Review*. About this time, too,
the famous publishing firm of Harper fell into difficulties,
and Mr. Pierpont Morgan, representing the bondholders,
asked Harvey to take charge of the business. One of the new
interests was *Harper's Weekly*, which Harvey undertook to
edit according to his own ideas and methods. With such an
organ he was soon able to make himself an influence in
politics. The Democratic party, disrupted by Mr. Bryan,
sadly wanted a leader, and Harvey, as early as 1906, scented
one in the high-minded and austere scholar who at that
time presided over Princeton University. Harvey played his
cards adroitly—so adroitly that Mr. Woodrow Wilson became
in 1910, almost in spite of himself, Governor of New Jersey.
From this post he stepped into the Democratic candidature for
the Presidency two years later. Between two such men, Wilson
and Harvey, there could be little real or lasting affinity.
The candidate ultimately resented Harvey's journalistic
methods, and Colonel Harvey—(he, too, owed his title to his
appointment to a State Governor's staff)—cooled towards
his former hero. When Wilson was installed at the White
House, Harvey devoted himself to criticizing the Administration. The war came, and Harvey, fiercely disapproving of
the President's policy, launched an outspoken and fiery
War Weekly, bearing the audacious but characteristic motto :
" To hell with the censors and bureaucrats." At the close
of the war Harvey was living in Washington, surrounded by
and inspiring a clique of the President's bitterest enemies.
A venomous opponent of the League of Nations, he, the
former Democrat, played a prominent part in the nomination,
in 1920, of Warren Gamaliel Harding as Republican candidate
for the Presidency. After the election people wondered

GEORGE HARVEY.

what reward would be offered to Harvey, whose journal, *Harvey's Weekly*, continued to explode satire and opprobrium throughout the precincts of the national capital. It brought intense relief to many vulnerable bosoms when it was announced that the terrible little newspaper was to suspend hostilities, as its editor had been appointed to the Court of St. James to represent the power and dignity of triumphant America.

On reaching London the new Ambassador was given a hearty greeting. His fellow-journalist, Lord Northcliffe, devoted to him a leading article in *The Times* of a most flattering character. The initial utterance of the American envoy was looked forward to eagerly. It was delivered before a distinguished assemblage at the dinner given in his honour by the Pilgrims' Society. In a tense silence, Colonel Harvey began :

" ' Fine words butter no parsnips ' it has been said ; but the adage is false. So the words be true, fair words not only, as a famous English essayist shrewdly remarked, ' never hurt the tongue,' but also they clear the way for deeds, which alone in the end can produce enduring results. That is not the work which our more active and self-sacrificing Pilgrims have done ; theirs has been a sustained labour of love and of patriotism, which only now is beginning to fructify in the earnest desire and determination of both our peoples to blow away the mists of misconstruction and misunderstanding which for too long have hidden their true natures one from the other."

It was a curious, almost archaic, oratorical style, and the long rows of well-disposed British hearers sat quiet and wondering. The diplomatic new-comer continued :

" Inferences thus drawn may be right or may be wrong, but, whether right or wrong, their bases obviously are subject to sectional and peculiar influences."

Some pricked up their ears when the speaker went on to describe the new President, Mr. Harding.

" This is not the time, although soon the time will come, for one to adventure a portrayal of our present Chief Magistrate."

The Ambassador did, notwithstanding, "adventure a portrayal," but the result is one which will hardly be recognized by posterity. The President, it appeared, was a very great, although a modest man—one who was, "in his own charming phrase, 'humble, but unafraid.'" (It was afterwards denied that Mr. Harding had ever used such a phrase.) Harvey pursued :

"When I add that, by universal assent, Mr. Harding's outstanding attributes are breadth of vision, greatness of heart and fidelity to his race—no less than to his clan and no more to his family than to his ancestry, drawn from all parts of the United Kingdom, not excluding Wales—I have indicated sufficiently the reasons why he not merely thinks, but feels, in the very fibre of his being, that, at this crucial period, more than at any other in history, 'friendliness and goodwill should exist always between the peoples of the two great English-speaking nations,' and why, through his representative, he now pledges that unfaltering co-operation for which, in the apt words of our Secretary of State, he has 'positive genius,' achieving that noble, and as I, at any rate, believe, absolutely essential aspiration."

It is not surprising if many of those who were present at that welcoming banquet, or who read the speech in *The Times* next morning, rubbed their eyes and wondered if the speaker had not taken this amazing jargon out of some unpublished deliverance of Mr. Pickwick or other character in fiction. There was no dereliction in style as the orator continued :

"I may say then, at the outset, with full assurance, that while charged, naturally, with the agreeable task of striving to maintain the existing cordial relations of our two countries, I shall fail miserably in my mission, to the grievous disappointment of my chief, if I do not so greatly strengthen those bonds of friendship and mutual helpfulness that hereafter our respective Governments will not only prefer durable agreements to tentative compromise, as between themselves, but will instinctively approach all world problems from the same angle as of common and inseparable concern. . . . That, I have no question you will agree, is as it should be. We would not have it otherwise. Nor, of course, would you."

Cloaked in all this verbiage, it soon began to appear that Ambassador Harvey really had a message to deliver, and his auditors strained their faculties to divine what it could be.

" Nothing could be more futile, more delusive or more mischievous than to pretend that, however deep and true may be our affection for the Mother Country, our proffer of a helping hand is attributable primarily to a tender susceptibility. It is not. My country stands ready to work with yours, first because it is to her own interest to do so, and secondly because it is to the advantage of both. We do not resent being called idealists even, as sometimes happens by those whose anticipated reward for extolling our idealism is transparently material. When the man in the fable dove into the well to seize the mirrored moon, he succeeded only in drowning himself, without disturbing in the least the placid progress of the smiling Queen of the Night.

" We deceive ourselves occasionally, of course—pray, who does not ?—but generally to our own amusement, just as other folks delight in calling one another names, but do not encourage the practice on the part of outsiders. Prevalent until recently was the impression—and this was and still is, in a measure, sincere—that we went into the war to rescue humanity from all kinds of menacing perils. That is not the fact. We sent our young soldiers across the sea solely to save the United States of America, and most reluctantly and laggardly at that. We were not too proud to fight—whatever *that* may mean."

One who was present states that the speaker paused and glanced about the assembled company, as if his allusion should provoke applause, laughter, a smile. But the faces of all were blank ; a few amongst the young Americans who had fought in the war were flushed. Why, why, they may have asked themselves, had this been said by the representative of their country in the cradle of their race ?

Elucidation came at last.

" It follows then, inevitably and irresistibly, that our present Government could not act, without betrayal of its creators and masters, and will not, I can assure you, have anything whatsoever to do with the League or with any Commission or Committee appointed by it as responsible to it, directly or indirectly, openly or furtively."

So that was it: America emphatically repudiated the League of Nations, to which a shattered Europe had pinned its faith, relying on the strength and assurances of America's chosen leader and spokesman—who now, alas! lay disowned and dying at Washington. America's young manhood had not championed the cause of Belgium and the Allies from any motives of chivalry, humanity or desire to right a wrong. Cravenly, reluctantly, they had fought merely to save themselves!

In the silence which followed, the Ambassador must have read disapproval. Perhaps he expected disapproval. He had wanted to be original, audacious, extravagant—to be, in short, himself.

" If I have gone too far in my discussion of public affairs, I must ask the company to attribute the overstepping to the self-bestowed prerogatives of a novice. You see, I have never been an Ambassador before. Yet even so, I quite promptly deny any suspicion of unawareness that suitable acknowledgment of this most cordial greeting is all that is expected or probably desired of me upon this occasion."

There was a murmur of voices, a general movement of impatience in the company, and only a few caught the final words and the quotation. Could it be a further reference to his friend Mr. Harding?—

> " God's in His heaven,
> All's right with the world."

The Ambassador sat down, his boyish face smiling behind his huge, grotesque spectacles. There had been, in nearly a century and a half, many speeches of America's envoys to England, many messages of fraternal goodwill, but never a speech, never a message like this.

The speech was a little too much for the American Press— although the anti-Wilsonians chuckled over it. " This Yankee Colonel at King George's Court—who is he to formulate our foreign policy? " asked one New York journal. The American Legion convened and sternly rebuked the Ambassador's " insolent misrepresentation."

But Harvey knew that the Harding Administration would

not protest. He had long played the game of politics according to his own rules, the underlying principle of which was audacity :

" He knows very well that the weak spot in the armour of politicians is their assumption of superiority, a sort of mask of benignant political venerability. They dread satire. They shrink from ridicule. A well-directed critical outburst freezes them. . . . Having reduced his subjects to a state of terror, Harvey flatters them, cajoles them and finally makes terms with them ; but he always remains a more or less unstable and uncertain quantity, potentially explosive.
" His mental habits bewilder the President, shock the proper and somewhat conventional Secretary of State, and throw such repositories of national divinity as Senators Lodge and Knox into utter confusion." [1]

During the summer of 1921 Ambassador Harvey was named the American representative on the Supreme Council, and attended several of its meetings. He also took occasion to make further speeches which, he said, exemplified the policy of the Harding Administration. A Western newspaper remarked of Harvey that, like Wali Dad in Kipling's ballad, he " carries the curse of an unstaunched speech." The New York *Independent* said editorially (November 19, 1921) :

" We recognized a certain trait of irresponsibility that had been displayed in his journalistic career, but we hoped that the manifold responsibilities of his new position would have a sobering effect, and that his long and varied political experience would teach him the value of team work in his relation to the Department whose agent he was. We hoped also that his natural shrewdness and quick wit would be a valuable asset. But we were mistaken. His gifts of quick wit and ready—too ready—speech, displayed now on two important occasions, have become a distinct menace to our international relations."

The British Government could hardly fail to be apprehensive as to the exact intentions of the Harding Administration. At Washington also it was felt that some great constructive

---

[1] *The Independent*, October 20, 1921.

action was necessary to reassure the American people, who were also growing restive. A master-stroke was decided upon —an appeal to the great nations of the world to disarm, the summoning of a new Washington Conference of the leading Powers to consider the abolition of naval armaments. It was an idea worthy of the idealist Woodrow Wilson himself. The cost of maintaining vast navies was crippling the resources of Britain, France, Italy and Japan. America alone could support the expense, and she was ready to forswear further competition in the interests of universal peace and humanity. Would Great Britain attend such a Conference? Secretary Hughes instructed Ambassador Harvey to consult the British Prime Minister at once. The Ambassador thus, in a public speech, described his reception:

" Nor can I, nor would I, forget that peaceful Sunday afternoon in July when I found Mr. Lloyd George seated under the spreading branches of the famous tree at his country place, engaged in animated discussion with the Premiers of the Dominions. He knew that I was coming. By a singular, if not indeed a signifying coincidence, he had asked me to pay him a visit that afternoon. He could not have known what I was bringing; I did not know myself until, on my way, I read a telegram which had been handed to me after I had entered the motor-car. But his intuition, as ever, was quick and true.

" Drawing me aside instantly, he motioned me to a rustic chair and himself took another. We had walked a considerable distance across the lawn and through the mansion to the place which he had selected. Not a word had been said. Not a word in fact was said after our arrival in those familiar few seconds which at some time in everyone's life have seemed of almost infinite duration. When presently he turned that wonderfully mobile countenance towards me, there rested in his eyes, far-famed for glimpsing the gaiety of his nature, that deep gravity approaching solemnity which at critical moments you who are his intimate friends will know, seems to take possession of his very being. Quietly he asked:

" ' What is it? '

" I drew the cablegram from my pocket and held it towards him.

" ' Read it,' he said.

" I did so slowly and carefully. Needless to inform you that it was a message from the Secretary of State announcing the intention of the President to summon a Conference of Nations and asking if such a move would be acceptable to the British Government.

" In a flash the Prime Minister was on his feet.

" ' We accept,' he almost shouted. ' We accept gladly, and we will do all in our power to make the Conference a success.' "

With the Disarmament Conference, which duly took place at Washington, at which Lord Balfour was amongst the British delegates, Ambassador Harvey had nothing to do. But in London he never lost an opportunity to explain to British audiences the unselfishness of America's attitude and aims.

" America [he cried] is unconquerable. We have nothing to fear from the efforts of the combined navies of the world. If you should bombard us, if you levelled our coast cities to the ground, they would rise again even as San Francisco has risen, finer and stronger than before. To be levelled to the ground is a natural process with us. New York is rebuilt afresh every thirty years. . . . Then, as to our armies, do you know that we have twenty-four million men capable of bearing arms ? " [1]

As time went on in England, the American Ambassador came, as other Ambassadors had done, to lose a little of his audacity, his naïve fervour, to adapt himself more to the English social tone, the English social formula. Yet he always had courage, caring no more for his American critics, who taunted him with being a renegade Democrat, than he did for British conventions. Even at the height of his equalitarian exuberance, he donned the laced coat and silken breeches and sported the plumed hat which so many of his diplomatic predecessors had gazed at longingly, but dared not press upon their republican brows. He did more—he was photographed in the proscribed garb, and sent copies across the ocean to his friends and to some who were not so friendly.

In his Independence Day speech of 1921, he made a daring reference to the Anglo-Irish problem at a moment when both parties were at fever heat over a settlement. Once again his

[1] Speech, October 31, 1921.

hearers were dismayed : but the English are a patient race ; it was only one more ember on the blaze they had been trying to quell for centuries, and it was quickly forgotten.

Ambassador Harvey made very many speeches, some of them cheery and topical, his very last utterance being on the value, practical and sentimental, of village sign-posts to the motoring community. It is a subject rich in metaphorical possibilities.

During his term of two and a half years at the Embassy many things happened affecting Anglo-American relations. Besides the Washington Conference, which removed potential naval rivalry, the Anglo-Japanese Alliance had been replaced by the Four-Power Pacific Treaty. By the settlement of the Irish question a long-festering ulcer had at last been removed. Then there was the Funding of its War Debt —a master-stroke of British policy. Finally, the American Government had been persuaded to allow an American expert to take part in a European Conference on German Reparations.

These were all vital matters, and upon some of them, if not all, Ambassador Harvey's opinion was taken. Altogether they contributed to a great change in the Anglo-American outlook.

The Ambassador suffered a great loss when his English friend and stout champion, Lord Northcliffe, died in the autumn of 1922. But a still greater loss was in store for him in America. At the beginning of the ensuing August, President Harding passed away suddenly, and was succeeded by Vice-President Calvin Coolidge.

The event made a great change in Colonel Harvey's fortunes, although some hoped that he would be retained in London for a year or two longer. But the new President was not, it seemed, to be persuaded.

Shortly afterwards Colonel Harvey went home, ostensibly on a visit ; he never returned, and it was left to his successor to present his letter of recall.

The new President would gladly have sent Senator Elihu Root as America's representative in England, but there were

F. B. KELLOGG.

personal reasons which made this distinguished statesman
decline the mission. It was then offered, again in vain, to
ex-Governor Frank Lowden of Illinois. Finally, the choice
was made of a prominent Republican Senator from Minnesota,
who had just been defeated for re-election. Everyone had
long recognized in Mr. Frank Billings Kellogg a capable and
highly successful lawyer. His was a simple, quiet figure, not
in the least flamboyant, not brilliant, but wholly reliable.
Albeit a native of the East, he had grown up and become
identified with what used to be known as the North-West
—farther West than any envoy whom the United States
had yet sent to London.

" I was born [he told an English audience] near that
invisible line which separates the Dominion of Canada from
the United States. I was reared and have lived nearly all
the years of my life in the Middle West, close to our Canadian
neighbours. In a little over half a century I have seen that
country lying between the Great Lakes and the Pacific,
on both sides of the line, redeemed from the wilderness,
peopled with virile progressive races, traversed by lines of
railway, filled with great cities and centres of industry."

Before Mr. Kellogg's election to the Senate, he had practised law in St. Paul for a quarter of a century. Amongst
his more important clients was the United States Steel
Corporation. At the time when President Roosevelt was
organizing his famous war on the Trusts, he sent for Kellogg,
and although his adhesion to the Government as special
counsel meant the loss of £20,000 a year, the lawyer made the
sacrifice. It was he who conducted the prosecution of the
Standard Oil Company, which resulted in the formal dissolution of that gigantic corporation. Afterwards his political
opponents recalled his former connexion with the Trusts, to
which his supporters replied, " If Minnesota can get a hundred-
thousand dollar representative for seven thousand dollars,
then Minnesota has made a great bargain."

The new Ambassador was now well past sixty, a compact
figure rather below the middle height, white-haired, dark-
skinned, his eyes set within dark sockets. A sort of nervous
alertness distinguished him. He had lost the sight of one

eye, but this did not prevent his reading or his playing golf. He was noted for keeping his body fit, and never omitted daily calisthenics. " I can," he once said quietly to a much younger colleague, " reach down and touch the floor with my hands a hundred times running." " Then I take off my hat to you, Mr. Ambassador," was the reply. " You are a physical as well as a mental athlete ! "

Mr. Kellogg arrived in London on the last day but one of December 1923. During the following months he made an excellent impression both on the British Government and the public at large by his quiet, earnest methods and freedom from any kind of self-assertion. To his wealth was added the social experience of Mrs. Kellogg and himself : he was an admirable host. Already he had many friends in London, having crossed the Atlantic nineteen times, and took pains to add to his knowledge of political and economic conditions. In the London Conference of 1924, which brought about an agreement on the application of the Dawes scheme of German Reparations, he took a prominent part. At a similar Conference in Paris he met the leading European statesmen and studied the problems all were seeking to solve.

Ambassador Kellogg's increasing competence was remarked by the President ; it made him a valuable man at that juncture. Wide international policies were being meditated. Mr. Kellogg had only been a few months in London when the resignation of Secretary of State Hughes proved decisive to his own fortunes. He found himself summoned to Washington to fill the chief post in the Cabinet. As Secretary of State his name will always be associated with the International Pact of 1928, whose object is the outlawry of war.

BIOGRAPHICAL NOTE

George Harvey died in August 1928, since this chapter was written.

CHAPTER XXIV

HOUGHTON (1925–   )

For the London Embassy, thus vacated, there was at that time in Europe one American diplomat who had demonstrated his competence under singularly trying conditions. This was Mr. Alanson Bigelow Houghton, the Ambassador at Berlin for the previous three years. Although a wealthy manufacturer, Houghton's early career and in a measure also his later years had been a preparation for diplomacy. He was a native of Cambridge, Massachusetts, born in the shadow of Harvard University and of a family which had produced more than one public man of note. As a youth he had travelled to Europe, receiving a part of his education at Göttingen. His ambition then was to be a professor of Sociology. Industrial, economic problems interested him deeply ; but his father's ill-health diverting his aim, he entered the family business and with his brother created a great industry and a large fortune. The exceptional educational advantages he had enjoyed in youth were not destined to be wasted. When the war came he offered himself as a candidate for Congress, was elected and served as a member of the Foreign Relations Committee. After the war, when Secretary Hughes was seeking an American upon whose judgment, experience and ability he could rely, and who would be willing to go to Berlin at that critical, even desperate juncture, he approached Houghton. The latter knew what was in store for him, but he did not hesitate.

Houghton made good in Germany : he won the confidence, the respect of the people. He had, of course, been called a " pro-German," especially by the French ; but he had dared, at a time when wartime prejudice was still rife, to take his stand as a champion of human rights, of fairplay to a beaten foe. Germany was now on the road to re-

481

habilitation, and few had worked harder for that just end than Ambassador Houghton, whose efforts were well understood and appreciated by the British Government. Consequently, the announcement that he had been transferred to London aroused more than usual interest.

Mr. Houghton arrived in England, April 23, 1925. It was St. George's Day, one of auspicious omen. In his first public utterance he struck the right note, the note that Choate and Hay had sounded so successfully. Anglo-American relations was a theme which must not be stressed too seriously. The new Ambassador quoted Lowell's phrase concerning :

" the difficulty of beguiling a new melody out of the one-stringed instrument upon which we have been thrumming so long.

" If [he went on] I must say something about Anglo-American relations, let me, following the conventions of a wide-open diplomacy, confide to you that, as I take over my duties here, I find after diligent search only one important issue now dividing our peoples, and that concerns the status in your markets of the American potato. There, apparently, certain doubts remain to be resolved. It would obviously be improper in me to speak in greater detail. But I may perhaps say this, that I begin my work in the high hope that justice, substantial justice, British justice, will ultimately be done to that really excellent American tuber and the episode so terminated to the benefit and satisfaction of us all."

It was an admirable beginning—a return to the pleasant and familiar strain to which experienced statesmen resort when they wish to discount and dispel an undue gravity. It was a favourite device of Palmerston's, when he had anything oppressive on his mind. In Ambassador Houghton's case it did not denote any habit of levity nor any illusions. Anglo-American friendship was safe—but the general condition of Europe which might affect that friendship, which might even strain their joint resources, was far from tranquil. No one could read of the actions and utterances of European statesmen in their own Press, of their attitude during the sessions of the League of Nations at Geneva, without being filled with misgivings. Even the political and industrial condition of Great Britain itself was anything but reassuring.

A. B. HOUGHTON.

Throughout 1925 Houghton studied the prevalent state of things closely, anxiously, from the standpoint of an American who was deeply interested in the welfare of humanity at large. He was thus able to give valuable first-hand counsel to the Secretary of State, and through him to the President, both being bent on finding some means to reconcile the jarring interests of Europe, which otherwise might some day again involve their own country.

Accordingly, having made up his mind as to European conditions, the Ambassador resolved to tell the President the exact truth about Europe as he saw it. In the early spring of 1926 he went to Washington and placed in the President's hands a full report on European conditions.

Its only apparent immediate consequence was that Senator Borah submitted a resolution raising the question of claims for compensation for losses caused to neutral American shipping during the first part of the war. But this was withdrawn at the President's request. It was only aimed at England, and England at present was giving no active cause for offence.

On the whole, matters being what they were, in Mr. Houghton's opinion, the American efforts then making towards world disarmament must be postponed, and in this President Coolidge reluctantly acquiesced. When two years later the Kellogg proposals were launched, they found Europe and the world in a better state to receive them.

Indeed, the effect throughout Europe had been that of a timely rebuke and warning, which could not go unheeded as long as America's economic help was indispensable to all national recovery.

At Crewe House, in Curzon Street, Mayfair, which had been rented from the Marquess of Crewe, during his own tenancy of the British Embassy in Paris, the Ambassador and Mrs. Houghton dispensed a wide and agreeable hospitality, until the American Government at last acquired premises of its own close to Prince's Gate, Hyde Park, formerly the residence of Mr. Pierpont Morgan. During this period the Ambassador continued to mingle freely in London social life and to utter those occasional addresses which have come to be expected from one holding his important office.

32

Amongst these, one delivered before the Chamber of Commerce at Manchester, April 22, 1927, was especially notable for its avowal of the speaker's matured view of the relations between Britain and America, and the dangers attending any formal alliance.

" I dislike, frankly [he said], those engaging phrases which seem almost inevitably to offer themselves on occasions like this.

" I believe, as a matter of course, that the future of the world—its peace, its happiness, its general well-being— depends largely upon the existence of a sound and cordial understanding between the British and American peoples. In fact, I may go even further. I believe that, fundamentally, the basis of such an understanding already exists—not because of any marked regard or liking we may feel for one another's excellent qualities, not because of a common language, not because of ties of blood, but because, being what we are, it is inevitable that we should look out on the world and its affairs from much the same point of view.

" Our immediate interests are not always identical. Nations, like individuals, have to earn their livings. Each people has its own special interests to consider and to protect. That could not be otherwise. But I do believe that in that larger realm of affairs which necessarily concern us both, we ought to find a measure of agreement easy. We certainly think in much the same terms. We have much the same scale of values. We want the same kind of world. Consciously or unconsciously, we are seeking the same kind of future. So much, it seems to me, we may accept without hesitation. And it offers us an opportunity which, you will agree with me, is unique in human history. We have no need to discuss the fact. The question for us to consider is, What are we going to do with the opportunity ? For it is in our hands to do with as we will. . . . The answer will depend far more on what we do than what we say. A little more patience, a little more belief in one another's good faith, and, above all, a little more effort to understand the difficult problem each people is facing, will take us a long way.

" We will do well not to seek to develop those wholly natural and helpful relations between the British and American peoples into anything like an alliance. There are moments when it may seem to offer an open and an easy way to obtain results we all desire. Nevertheless, I believe the idea to be wholly false. To bring the English-speaking peoples together into an armed and exclusive group, prepared if need be to enforce its collective will by force, would, if it were possible, tend neither to promote peace nor to assure our mutual security. Its result would be to unite all the rest of the world against us. It would slowly, perhaps, but very definitely, make an end of peaceful progress. It would turn this earth of ours once again into an armed camp. In the end, precisely what we sought to avoid—a war—would result. . . .

" We may have to fight side by side in the future as in the past. But if the need arises, which God forbid, let it be for a cause and for a reason which brings us instinctively together, not by a calculated arrangement which might of itself tend to bring about the catastrophe we dread."

Ambassador Houghton had been privy from the first to the notable act of world statesmanship which was launched by his friend (and diplomatic predecessor) Secretary of State Kellogg in the spring of 1928 and consummated at Paris, August 27, 1928. This Pact for the renunciation of war there received the official adhesion of the leading nations of the world. With all this support it is recognized that the real strength of this instrument resides in the united good-will and action of the English-speaking nations alone, that —to quote again Mr. Houghton's words—" the future of the world—its peace, its happiness, its general well-being—depends largely upon the existence of a sound and cordial understanding between the British and American peoples."

It is only by a study of history, of the temperaments, susceptibilities, speech and actions of the representative men of each branch of our race, that statesmen may learn how to speak and act considerately and with sympathy when national divergences occur and so prevent these from becoming crises.

INDEX

Aberdeen, the Earl of, Foreign Secretary, 230, 232, 241

Adams, Abigail, wife of John Adams, 15, 16, 17–18

Adams, Charles Francis, extracts from his memoir of his grandfather, John Adams, 9 *n.*, 13, 14, 16, 17, 309; appointed American Minister to Britain by President Lincoln through influence of Secretary Seward, 312; his previous career, 312; his interview with President Lincoln, 312–13; his first interview with Lord John Russell, 315–16; startled by a bellicose dispatch from Seward, 316–17; his opinion of London Society, 318; endeavours to negotiate America's participation in Declaration of Paris, 318–19; his embarrassment over the " Trent " affair, 321–2; his heated correspondence with Palmerston over General Butler's order, 323–6; warns Seward of the possibility of Anglo-French intervention in the Civil War, 328; his efforts to frustrate building of *Alabama* and " Laird rams," 329–30, 331–2; forced to endure visits from amateur diplomatists, 332–3; his prestige in London, 333–5; his anti-Fenian views cause some enmity in America, 335; resigns, 335; biographical note on, 335; American arbitrator at Geneva, 365

Adams, C. F. (Jr.), extracts from writings of, 313, 314, 333

Adams, Henry, son of C. F. Adams, extracts from his books and letters, 82, 90, 92, 115, 166, 168, 317, 319–20, 321, 322, 323, 331, 333–4, 353–4

Adams, John, first American Minister Plenipotentiary to the British Court, 4; his character and career, 5–7, 18, 19, 72; relates his arrival in London, 8; his account of his first interview with George III, 9–11; his growing disillusion, 12–14; his life in England, 15, 17; realizes the impossibility of his position and is recalled, 17–18; biographical note on, 19; extracts from his writings, 41 and *note*

Adams, John Quincey, son of John Adams, appointed Minister Plenipotentiary to Britain, 116; opinions on his character, 116; his first interview with Lord Castlereagh, 117–18; is not impressed by his interview with the Prince Regent, 118–19; recounts the negotiations for an Anglo-American treaty of commerce, 120–5; recounts his interview with Lord Liverpool, 126–7; talks with Alexander Baring on the defence of Canada, 127–8; his interview with Castlereagh on similar subject, 128; his speeches at various banquets, 128–30; presented, with Mrs. Adams, at a Drawing-room, 130–1; dines with Lord Castlereagh, 132–3; hears Robert Peel speak in Parliament against the Catholics, 135–6; appointed Secretary of State under President Monroe, 135; his estimate of the Prince Regent, 136–7; has final interview with Castlereagh, 137; biographical note on, 137

Alabama, building of the, for the Confederates, 329–30; claims settled by Joint High Commission, 358, 359, 362–5

Alaskan Boundary question, 424–5

Alaskan seal dispute, 393–4, 400, 414

America, composity of, viii; English basis of, viii; her supposed sympathy with the French Revolution, 36–7; her attitude towards France

486

Printed in Great Britain by
Hazell, Watson & Viney, Ld., London and Aylesbury.